IL DUCE
AND HIS WOMEN

IL DUCE

AND HIS WOMEN

ROBERTO OLLA

TRANSLATED BY STEPHEN PARKIN

ALMA BOOKS

ALMA BOOKS LTD
London House
243–253 Lower Mortlake Road
Richmond
Surrey TW9 2LL
United Kingdom
www.almabooks.com

Il Duce and His Women first published by Alma Books Limited in 2011

Copyright © Roberto Olla, 2011

Printed in Great Britain by CPI Antony Rowe, Chippenham, Wiltshire

ISBN (HARDBACK): 978-1-84688-135-0
ISBN (TRADE PAPERBACK): 978-1-84688-146-6

Contents

IL DUCE
AND HIS WOMEN

Introduction

Sex and politics, sex and power, sex and violence: this book is about sex, and readers should know this before they begin to turn its pages and learn about the private life of Benito Mussolini, the man who invented Fascism and became a model for other twentieth-century dictators. Obviously it is possible to write about sex in many different ways; normally it is best to treat the subject with tact, to find words which mediate the reality and an approach which doesn't weigh the narrative down. In the present case, however, where sources have been cited directly, thus giving a direct contact with the historical truth, tact and elegance have occasionally had to be sacrificed. The sex which is the subject of this book was at the centre of the myth of Mussolini: all the rest turned on this, like a wheel round a hub. His image as a man of power, the supreme man of power, drew directly on the idea of sexual potency as a symbol of eternal youth, physical and political. Many rumours about Mussolini's potency circulated among women – whispered no doubt, accompanied by blushes – during his twenty-year dictatorship, and in the same way anecdotes, tinged with envy, were bandied about among men. In the taverns and bars no doubt such tales, in frank and frequently off-putting detail, abounded. Such material has been deliberately ignored by academic historians. But this is the nub of the issue in this book, since it deals directly with such accounts. The recent publication of new documents relating to the Duce's principal mistresses and lovers has made it possible to focus on the sexual dimension – in all its reality – which lay at the heart of the cult of Mussolini. And although efforts have been made to tone down some of the more vulgar and violent features found in these accounts, in citing the documents directly such aspects inevitably come to the fore. What kind of sex am I referring to? One example – one quotation – can illustrate this better than lengthy explanations. Mussolini's remarks to his last mistress, his favourite, Clarice Petacci, known as Claretta, show – with uneuphemistic directness – the way he displayed his sexual potency: "You should be scared of my lovemaking, it's like a cyclone, it uproots everything in its path. You should tremble. If I could have done, today I'd have entered you on a horse."[1]

What kind of source material has Clarice Petacci provided? She enjoyed keeping her diary, she enjoyed writing in it for the sake of writing, and rereading what she had written to while away the hours of waiting between a telephone call and the next meeting. She wrote quickly, putting down all that she recalled – Mussolini's outbursts of anger, the sensations and emotions she felt, remarks he made: "I'm an animal, I'm made like that, I resist and then I fall. It's like screwing a whore, as if I'd gone with a whore."[2] Clarice-Claretta makes small mistakes in spelling, she gets certain names wrong – Roosevelt's for example – or words which are unfamiliar to her like "pederast". She transcribed all she could as quickly as she could, and the errors she makes in her speed are, in one sense, evidence of her real wish to write down in her diary as faithfully as possible everything she heard and experienced. "Thus she was recounting as accurately as possible – and as much as she was able to – what Mussolini said to her, even when some of the names he mentioned were unknown to her. She was certainly not stupid; leaving aside the question of sex, one might say that in a manner of speaking she was exactly the right person for the job. She was good at listening and remembering what she heard. Sometimes she intervened with a comment of her own."[3]

So Clarice-Claretta was far from being a "silly goose of a girl" like some of the giddy-headed mistresses powerful men tend to seek out. She had had a decent education, had studied music and drawing, and came from a solid and prosperous middle-class background. Her father, Francesco Saverio Petacci, was a leading medical doctor who had held the highly prestigious position of "Archiatra Pontificio", Pope Pius XI's personal physician. Despite the spelling mistakes and occasional omissions of a subject or verb, her style manages to be both restrained and vivid. Despite her efforts to record them faithfully, when she felt she couldn't reproduce the deliberately obscene and excessive aspects of Mussolini's talk, she tried to put matters as delicately as possible, as if the readability of the diary and the pleasure a reader – including herself as a rereader – might take in it mattered to her: "His face is tense, his eyes are burning. I am sitting on the floor; quite suddenly he slides off his armchair onto me, curved over me. I can feel his body strain to unleash itself. I pull him close and kiss him. We make love with a kind of fury; he cries out like a wounded animal. Then he falls exhausted onto the bed; even in repose he looks strong."[4]

There is a story that one day in the 1920s Mussolini decided to drive his sports car himself, putting his usual chauffeur in the passenger seat, and had to stop at a level crossing to wait for a train to pass through. While waiting he opened the door, took off his driving goggles and got out to have a look round. Some women were also waiting to cross and watched him. "He looks like the Duce," one of them said to general amusement. Mussolini saw them and immediately struck a familiar pose, with hands on hips, chin raised and chest pushed out. One of the young women who was bolder than the others stepped forward and said to him: "Do you know you look a lot like the Duce?" "What would you say if I told you I am the Duce?" replied Mussolini. The woman retorted: "Come off it – he's much better looking." This is the kind of story or anecdote which frequently crops up in the following pages, according to the situations described, just as they circulated among Italians who lived during the Fascist regime and were told to later generations. The stories are not in the book as part of an attempt to fictionalize the historical account; they represent an aspect or element of the myth of Mussolini the Duce which needs to be acknowledged and examined. He himself liked to be kept informed of the stories and rumours that circulated about him, even the anti-Fascist ones so long as they centred on him and his personality. They must have been common in the daily life of the Italians living under the regime: uncles or other relatives could feel safe in passing on to their families the latest anecdote they'd heard, or friends chatting in the coffee bar or taking a weekend stroll together could swap stories about their leader's private life. There was always someone who'd heard something from someone else, someone who'd actually set eyes on him, even if only from a distance: Mussolini's closely shaved "Roman" head, which fascinated women; Mussolini's jutting square jaw; Mussolini with his cat, on his horse, playing his violin, fondling his pet lion, driving his Torpedo, in swimming trunks, with his blazing eyes and powerful naked torso, with a look of gritty determination at the wheel of his racing car or an air of daring at the controls of his plane. Whoever had seen the Duce close up – and lots of people had – had a story to tell those who hadn't been so lucky. All these voices, all these people with their stories, created a huge wave of popular consensus, filling in, like some kind of putty, the cracks and gaps in the vast mosaic of the regime's propaganda, helping to lend three-dimensionality to the myth: Mussolini the sportsman, Mussolini the aviator, Mussolini the writer, the musician, the dancer, the warrior and even, if need be, Mussolini the peasant. Anti-Fascism too at a popular level thrived on stories and anecdotes, to be told in secret only to trusted friends, otherwise one risked ending up in forced internment or in prison. A booklet – by a pseudonymous "Calipso" – was published in Rome in the immediate wake of the city's liberation in 1944 with the title *Vita segreta di Mussolini* (*Mussolini's Secret Life*); it is made up entirely of such stories in a kind of anthology designed to dismantle his myth and reveal his narrow-minded pettiness, coarseness, vulgarity and violence. These stories had circulated widely during the years of the regime, cropping up in very different contexts – political news, social gossip, wartime reports – and provided the booklet's author with ample source material.

Mussolini was not handsome, he wasn't slim or tall, his demeanour wasn't elegant – in short, he had none of the physical characteristics which normally attract the attention of the public. And yet, despite this, a vast number of Italians formed a kind of psychological symbiosis with the image of his body: women desired it and men admired it. There's a fascinating insight – all the more fascinating because it's an intuition, jotted down just as it occurred, rather than elaborated in a finished work – in Pier Paolo Pasolini's last book, which he didn't live to complete: *Petrolio*. The book was going to be an exploration of Fascism and the Partisan Resistance, a kind of "novel made up of novels" which would present a panorama of Italy's history up to more recent events. Pasolini's murder in 1975 means we do not know how the project would have developed, but among the drafts of the two thousand pages he was planning, we find this passage: "There are things – even highly abstract or spiritual matters – which are only experienced through the body. When they are experienced through other bodies they are different. What our fathers experienced with their bodies can no longer be lived through ours. We can try to reconstruct their experience, to imagine and interpret it – in other words, we write history. But history is so absorbing a study (more than any other branch of knowledge) precisely because what is most important in it is irremediably lost to us."[5]

Il Duce and His Women concludes with the invasion and conquest of Ethiopia in 1936 and Mussolini's official visit to Germany in 1937 amid acclaiming crowds orchestrated by the Nazi propaganda machine. There are two reasons for ending the volume at this point. The first is that the visit to Germany represents the critical turning point in Mussolini's political development, what Renzo De Felice has described in his biography as the moment of decisive change. Other historians have acknowledged De Felice's thesis, including George L. Mosse who, in a letter to De Felice written on 25th August 1981, said: "Your theory that Mussolini changed course after the war in Ethiopia is highly convincing and well documented. It seems to me that after this change Hitler and Mussolini were closer ideologically speaking, at least as far as certain aspects are concerned."[6] Needing to choose a point at which to conclude the present volume, therefore, the defining rapprochement between Hitler and Mussolini seemed the most appropriate one. The second reason for interrupting the story in 1937 is that not all the sources on the following period in Mussolini's private life have yet been made available to researchers. These are the years which saw the development of his intense relationship with Claretta Petacci up to the day of their deaths when they were both shot in Giulino di Mezzegra, or in the house belonging to the De Maria family, or perhaps somewhere else entirely in the area north of Lake Como, depending on which reconstructed version of the facts one chooses to believe.

Faced with a dictator who is shot with his mistress at the end of the cruellest war humanity has ever experienced, it must be obvious that a detailed historical study of Mussolini's private life and of the influence which it had over his public existence and political career is needed. Proper historical research has been impeded by the inaccessibility of the relevant written sources, leaving the field free for chance compilations of the few documents and first-hand reports which have from time to time come to light and which avid publishers of all kinds have seized on, much to De Felice's scorn: "Nowadays the people who killed Mussolini are everywhere in the papers and magazines and books, offering their bargain-basement wares of absurd eyewitness accounts and revelations."[7] De Felice himself was not allowed access to the Petacci papers held in the national archives in Rome. As a result, this period of history has been for too long the happy hunting ground for non-professional historians – enthusiastic amateurs, journalists, collectors, seekers of memorabilia and dealers.

The recent publication, in 2010, of some of the letters exchanged between Mussolini and his mistress at the time of the Repubblica Sociale Italiana (Italian Social Republic), the so-called Repubblica di Salò (Republic of Salò) (1943–45), only shows how urgently a proper critical edition of all the papers in the Petacci archive is needed. Just from these letters a surprising and hitherto unsuspected portrait begins to emerge of someone who played a significant role in the events of the time: not merely Mussolini's leading mistress, intent on defending her territory against rival claimants, the old flames like Romilda Ruspi, Alice De Fonseca Pallottelli and Angela Curti, but a young woman who gradually takes on the role of political counsellor, the leader of a faction. With shrewd ability she moved behind the scenes in a power struggle between Mussolini and Hitler, between the former's residual authority and the control which was imposed by the latter through his various plenipotentiaries. The sexual relationship between Petacci the favourite mistress and the dictator now in terminal decline remains fundamental, but the letters show us how she gradually advanced to the front of the stage, in the process becoming perhaps the one person in whom Mussolini could confide his real thoughts and intentions. She never stopped writing, using everything which came to hand – diaries, address books, scraps of paper, the back of letters, even toilet paper when she was held in prison between the fall of the regime on 25th July 1943 and the freeing of Mussolini on 12th September. And she was also careful to keep everything, despite Mussolini's advice, repeated in many of his letters, to "tear it all up – I urge you to destroy every scrap. If you don't you're running a risk which could turn out to be fatal for you."[8]

Only a full and close study of all the sources which have hitherto been kept back would enable historians to revise their image of Petacci and the role she played, beyond the gossip column or the historical romance, as a thinking and active political protagonist. Frivolous Claretta is gradually superseded by a determined Clara, the first lady in the regime's final days, intent on steering a defeated Mussolini into a post-war future, one in which, whatever shape it might take, he would be around to use his skills as a public speaker, as a journalist and as a politician. Much of this final period from 1937 onwards will need to be reassessed in the light of the new sources which are gradually becoming available before one can begin to look again at the dictator's private life. One example which stands out is

Petacci's role in the decision to execute Galeazzo Ciano, Mussolini's son-in-law, who finally sided with other leading Fascists against him. She doesn't let up her pressure on Mussolini to go ahead with the execution and thus take her revenge – a violent and tragic one – on his favourite daughter, Edda, Ciano's wife: "She's forfeited her right to plead family ties. It's easy to play the penitent now their attempt to get rid of her father has failed. When you've betrayed your own family once, you'll do it again – it's useless for her to pretend otherwise."[9] This new version of Clara even advises Mussolini on how to handle his political relations with Hitler, telling him to show proper gratitude to the German dictator for rescuing him from captivity but at the same time not to concede an inch for fear of finding himself completely subjugated to the Nazis. When in March 1944 a general strike was declared throughout the factories of northern Italy – not so much as a challenge to the regime, now in its death throes, as to the ferocious Nazi occupation – Clara analyses the situation lucidly in a letter to Mussolini: "Individual cells are working to undermine… it's obvious it's all being coordinated – the whole purpose of the strike is political. But the mass of the workers are striking for more immediate reasons [...] and it's this aspect – which might be called the struggle to live – that the movement's leaders are using as a cover for their own tactics."[10]

Yet it will be extremely difficult to prepare a proper edition of all the autograph papers in the Petacci archive, essential though that is as the basis for a proper account of Mussolini's private life in his final years and an analysis of the political influence of the women who were close to him, in part because various Italian publishers tend to rush to exploit the success of newly published material on the Duce. Only professional historians should be allowed to examine the problem of Mussolini in modern Italy; on the contrary, as De Felice once pointed out, they appear to keep their distance almost as if they refuse to deal with the problem in an attempt to resolve it. If the interest in Mussolini's private life is ever to get beyond the phase of sensationalist publishing, then new and wider research needs to be carried out both in public and private archives. That much documentary material remains to be studied has been demonstrated by scholars such as Mario Cereghino, whose indefatigable research has uncovered important evidence, such as the report sent to the Foreign Office at the end of 1938 by the British ambassador in Paris, Sir Eric

Phipps: "Bonnet has informed me that for the last six months or so Mussolini has been infatuated with a young Italian woman... the daughter of a medical doctor in the Vatican and the wife of a naval officer."[11]

Petacci's diaries have only recently become available in their entirety. Much of the autograph source material relating to Margherita Sarfatti (there are 1,272 letters alone) still has to be made available to researchers. Mussolini's grandchildren own material which is important for an understanding of his private life, but the periodic waves of prurient curiosity in what they hold can only discourage them from releasing it. Furthermore, certain issues are in themselves extremely sensitive and difficult to handle – most notably, the question of Mussolini's anti-Semitism. De Felice has tackled this question and, after examining Mussolini's attitudes to Jews on the basis of much documentary evidence, posed a blunt question: "Can you imagine Hitler having a relationship with a Jewish woman?"[12] Two of Mussolini's mistresses were Jewish, both prominent intellectuals: Angelica Balabanoff and Margherita Sarfatti. He made use of them for what advantages they could bring to him and exploited them so long as he thought they were needed for his political career. The same cynicism can be seen in his relations to the Jews in general. His attitudes vacillated until the increasing rapprochement with Hitler enforced a change, at which point Mussolini found it expedient to introduce the *Manifesto degli scienziati razzisti* (*Manifesto of Racial Scientists*), a set of laws which discriminated against Italian Jews while waiting to see what future developments would mean for them. The persecution of Italian Jews carried out under Fascism can by no means be considered a minor phenomenon; it was no less cruel than the Nazi policy. In the years before the surrender to the Allied forces on 8th September 1943, Italian Jews were stripped of all their civil rights: the right to work, to move about freely, to human dignity. After the watershed of the Armistice, they began to be rounded up, frequently with the help of Fascists, and then were held in transit camps in Italy before being deported to the Nazi concentration camps. Yet, as De Felice shows, there are significant differences between Mussolini and Hitler, between Nazism and Fascism, which histories of the period, including popular histories, must take into account. For the last fifty years, on the other hand, German Nazism and Italian Fascism have been taught to new generations of schoolchildren and university students as a single phenomenon, so preventing a proper understanding of Fascism as part of the Italians' national history. So-called "Nazi-Fascism" has become something of an unquestioned and unassailable truism especially among those who have grown up since the end of the Second World War. De Felice points out: "'Nazi-Fascism' might be meaningful as a political concept in the context of the Italian Social Republic from 1943 to 1945, but as a historical concept it is completely unfounded."[13]

De Felice's monumental biography of Mussolini can itself almost be regarded as a primary source, so wide-ranging and so detailed is the supporting documentary evidence the author incorporates into the work. The first volume was going to be entitled *Mussolini il socialista* (*Mussolini the Socialist*), but was published instead as *Mussolini il rivoluzionario* (*Mussolini the Revolutionary*). It is a detailed and closely argued analysis of Mussolini's early socialism, the first of its kind, and it came out under the auspices of Italy's leading left-wing publisher, Einaudi, in 1965. Two years earlier, on 17th December 1963, a new government headed by Aldo Moro, which for the first time included the Socialists, had won a parliamentary vote of confidence: the centre-left was born in Italy. On 28th December 1964 a Social-ist, Giuseppe Saragat, was elected president of the Republic – the first head of the Italian state who had been an anti-Fascist and had fought in the Resistance (he also spent time in prison with Sandro Pertini, a fellow Socialist who was later among the first to collaborate politically with Democrazia Cristiana, the Christian Democrats). A new political chapter appeared to have been opened in the country's history, with the left no longer in perennial opposition but a party of government; the winds of change were also felt within the Partito Comunista Italiano, the largest communist party outside the Soviet Union. Shortly after Saragat's election, the first signs appeared of what were to become worldwide student disturbances, which in Italy soon took on a politically radical character. At such a time and in such a context a book on Mussolini as a socialist and revolutionary seemed like a wilful provocation. No one then could foresee how De Felice's work would continue or the vast scale it would assume; here instead was a new history book which, counter-culturally, dared to examine an almost taboo period and subject: the years in which Mussolini rose to become in effect the unofficial leader of the Partito Socialista Italiano (Italian Socialist Party). Moreover, the book's author treated his subject objectively and dispassionately, as if it were a historical phase like any other to be reconstructed on the basis of the available documentary evidence. The worldwide student uprisings in 1968 lasted far longer in Italy than elsewhere. They gave rise to a kind of ideological straitjacket, in which one of the fixed beliefs was that Fascism remained an imminent danger because it was rooted in bourgeois capitalism, indeed emerged as a direct consequence of it, with the result that all politicians and all political programmes seen as opposed to the student radicals were automatically branded as "Fascist". In the 1970s, left-wing groups waged an "anti-Fascist" campaign against De Felice and his books in complete disregard of the principles of intellectual freedom: he needed police protection at some of the lectures he gave, and even as late as 1996 his home was attacked with incendiary devices. Every now and then the newspapers and weekly current-affairs magazines would dedicate some pages to a debate which always focused on the same question: has De Felice made Fascism respectable again? "In a certain sense I think he has," replied the British historian of Italian Fascism Denis Mack Smith, "but I don't think he set out to do it intentionally, and I don't believe it matters."[14] De Felice was at pains to point out that Mussolini the man was different from the images both Fascists and anti-Fascists had constructed of him. In his opinion the only reliable way to arrive at a critical understanding of the regime over the twenty years it held power and to bring some kind of resolution to the national psycho-drama of the Mussolini myth was to study the available documentary evidence objectively: "Mussolini was less coarse and more cultivated than he appeared to be. He had psychological problems. He was present among the people, but by no stretch of the imagination was he a man of the people. If writing this makes me appear to be a sympathizer, a supporter, then the belief is wrong. My study is a kind of radiography, designed to penetrate as deeply as it possibly can."[15]

De Felice wanted historians of Fascism to leave their ideological preconceptions behind, to write history with no sense of *parti pris* or hidden political agenda; he defended his approach which was based on ascertaining the facts, on patiently finding and gathering the documentary evidence, on what, in short, he called scientific method. But authoritative voices contested this view, among them Norberto Bobbio's:

Does scientific method exist in historical research? What kind of a science is history? If we adopt De Felice's radical distinction between scientific method in historical research and standard approaches to the subject, history almost seems to become one of the exact sciences [...] because it's based exclusively on known facts and excludes all value judgements. [...] Naturally historians must base their work on the ascertained facts. But not all the facts are equally relevant, and the criterion we apply in selecting those which are and ignoring those which are not is not itself a fact. It derives from the historian's purpose or goal in carrying out the research, and that purpose, whether the historian is conscious of it or not, in turn derives from a value judgement.[16]

The subsequent volumes of De Felice's biography continued to appear over the next twenty years; when it was finished, the entire work consisted of nearly seven thousand pages, but it has never got free of the shadow cast by the furore that greeted the first volume in 1965, almost as if De Felice had committed an unpardonable sin in deciding to examine objectively – as a historian – a subject which is essentially a political and moral one. It didn't count that one of the most prominent – and, by the time he spoke, most overlooked – figures in the Italian Communist Party, Giorgio Amendola, spoke in his defence: "You can't accuse De Felice of being an apologist for Fascism simply because he describes certain methods adopted by the Fascist police or by Mussolini in person. [...] The Fascist police had a whole repertoire of methods and were skilful in choosing which ones to use. [...] It was a particular kind of regime and it needs to be studied for what it was. [...] If thirty years on we're not yet capable of understanding the tangled complexities of the phenomenon then we'll never succeed in understanding the disease of Fascism and how deep its roots go."[17]

De Felice's work has been more criticized than it has been read; it is generally thought to be extremely difficult to read, requiring an enormous expenditure of time on the part of its readers. Lucio Colletti is one of the author's defenders, but even he admits that "De Felice's style is on occasion muddled and hard to follow, at least partly as a result of the exhaustive mass of source material he has deemed it necessary to digest before writing".[18] Nevertheless, as the historian Giovanni Sabbatucci has pointed out,[19] De Felice's work has become an indispensable point of reference for anyone working on Mussolini and Fascism;

moreover, all serious readers of his great biography will acknowledge that in its pages De Felice subjects the figure of Mussolini to penetrating criticism, while the myth of the Duce is gradually dismantled precisely because it is analysed in the light of all the available documentary evidence.

On 27th May 2010, during a meeting of the Organization for Economic Cooperation and Development in Paris, the Italian prime minister Silvio Berlusconi remarked:

> I'm not powerful – perhaps I was powerful when I was an entrepreneur, but now I'm a politician I haven't got any power. Heads of government have practically no power. Allow me to quote from someone who was regarded as a great dictator – Benito Mussolini. I read his diaries recently and came across this remark: "People say I have power but it isn't true. Perhaps some of the party officials are powerful – I wouldn't know. All I can manage to do is to order my horse to turn right or left and I'm happy with that." That shows you'll never find a head of government anywhere who has power – perhaps it doesn't exist.[20]

Italy is a curious country, dissimilar to other nations; its past remains always present, because that suits the politicians. Even the partial renewal of the country's political system in the wake of the corruption scandals in the "Clean Hands" investigations in the early 1990s hasn't altered the situation much. Italy's anomalous condition doesn't seem to excite much attention any more, even from its fellow members in the European Union: a prime minister who quotes a dictator to explain his position as head of government doesn't get more than a brief mention in the daily newspapers. But the quotation is in fact the most interesting thing about Berlusconi's remarks, for the diaries he says he's recently been reading are false. Many historians, including De Felice, have declared they are a forgery – with the exception, as we shall shortly see, of two, and then only in part. And yet in November 2010 a volume of selections from the diaries was published by one of the country's most important and prestigious publishing houses, Bompiani, directed by a well-known historian (and former student of De Felice), Paolo Mieli. Even he agrees that the diaries are patently false.

The title of the volume, which relates to the year 1939, involves a linguistic sleight of hand: *I diari di Mussolini. Veri o presunti*, in

English *Mussolini's Diaries, Authentic or Presumed so*. The diaries are false, but nowhere on the cover or title page can this word be found, presumably on the grounds that potential buyers of the book might find it off-putting. The publication represents a reckless commercial gamble, merely the most recent development in the long history of the hunt for Mussolini's diaries, an untiring pursuit which no doubt has yet more surprises in store for us. Historians have found firm evidence that Mussolini kept a diary; he used leather-bound ones produced by the Red Cross. According to Duilio Susmel (known for his scrupulously accurate knowledge of Mussolini's papers), the dictator did not keep a diary for the years 1933, 1934, 1939, 1941 or 1942. He gave the volumes for the years when he did write a diary to his sister Edvige as he finished them year by year, for safekeeping. Leaving aside its potential as a remarkable publishing coup, the discovery of the diaries would undoubtedly be of great significance – but, as De Felice has cautioned, the process of authenticating them would almost certainly not be straightforward after so many false discoveries and the resulting creation of distrust and scepticism among professional historians. Edvige kept the diaries with her until 1944, when, with the help of the Japanese ambassador in Rome, Shinrokuro Hidaka, they were transferred to the Japanese legation in Bern in Switzerland for greater security. Hidaka was later tried as a war criminal, but he was acquitted and went on to hold several important diplomatic postings in the United States. On the surrender of Japan, all the papers in the Bern legation were burnt, in accordance with Japanese diplomatic protocol, and with them Mussolini's diaries. There exists a possibility, as De Felice has suggested, that Hidaka had copies made of the diaries and used them as a trade-off to save his political skin after the war. But if he did, then all traces of these genuine diaries have been lost, despite the host of interested people who have hunted for them over the years. One of these is Marcello Dell'Utri, a close collaborator of Silvio Berlusconi, sentenced for his connections to the Mafia, but also a passionate bibliophile. Dell'Utri obtained from a Swiss lawyer the late "diaries" kept by Mussolini, which had come onto the market in London in 1994; they had previously been offered to various Italian publishers, who had all turned them down.

Readers of the present book need to be told that it does not take these diaries into account, for the simple reason that they are forgeries. Nevertheless it is worth knowing the story of how they came to be published in Italy. One of the only two professional opinions which differ from the otherwise unanimous belief they are counterfeit comes from Brian R. Sullivan:

> My personal opinion, arrived at after much investigation, is that these are indeed Mussolini's diaries, but in a fake version which he himself created. They were certainly written between 1935 and 1939, when Mussolini is said to have written them, but there are too many details in them which would be beyond the capacity of any forger to know or even invent, details confirmed by other research. [...] The text of them is very strange: there are details which only Mussolini could have known about, but also quite extraordinary blunders which even a forger would never have made.[21]

Thus Sullivan creates a third category: the diaries are neither authentic nor false; instead they were forged by their own author. According to this version, Mussolini would have refashioned the diaries as documentary evidence he could offer up to mitigate his guilt, changing his view of the war (he didn't want one), of the invasion of Ethiopia (he tried to avoid it), of the racial laws (they were imposed on him). "I am not Hitler," we read on page 239 of the false diary for the year 1939, "I don't get obsessed with hatred of Jews. On the contrary I admit that I have had worthwhile colleagues and true friends who have come from the tribes of Israel. In my youth I was in love with a Jewish woman – no one could hold a candle to her intelligence, her grace, her immense good nature."

But the whole thing doesn't add up: it isn't clear why Mussolini would send his real diaries to Switzerland while at the same time settle down to the laborious job of falsifying new ones.

> It might not have been an interminable task, but this image of Mussolini busy rewriting just doesn't convince me. There's absolutely nothing in any of the papers which come out of his office to suggest that he could possibly have undertaken a job of this kind. [...] As for the time in Salò, Mussolini couldn't even think without the Germans knowing about it. There's nothing from him – no remark or comment, not a single document which, even straining interpretation, could give rise to the idea that Mussolini was deeply absorbed in rewriting his diaries.[22]

When these so-called diaries first surfaced in public, the leading historian of Italian Fascism Denis Mack Smith was consulted for his opinion. He told *Corriere della Sera* in 1994:

> In Zurich we were met by a car and driven for a long time through places I wouldn't recognize now. [...] We reached a small town which I guessed was very near the border with Italy. The gentleman known as Mr X was waiting for me at a small table in a café. [...] He had the diaries with him and showed them to me. I told him I would need to examine them properly, that I would like to take them back with me to my hotel to study them overnight. But he refused, so I read them there with him for a long time. [...] I'm no expert on the authenticity of paper or ink. As far as the contents were concerned, it seemed to me that they couldn't have been forged – there were too many details, too many precise descriptions.

The lengthy (and unsigned) introduction to the recently published edition of the diaries in Italy surveys all the expert opinions on their authenticity; the exceptions to the belief they are fakes are Sullivan and Mack Smith. It mentions that in subsequent interviews Mack Smith has somewhat "softened" his opinion; in fact Mack Smith has merely stressed that he wasn't given the opportunity to study the diaries properly. The introduction slides over the fact that Mack Smith said right at the outset he had only been able to examine the diaries for a few hours seated at a café table. The question of the diaries' authenticity could be solved by expert examination. The technical analysis of handwriting is accepted as evidence in the courts as well as testified to and included in the documentation relating to a trial: a defendant's fate can depend on accurate graphological identification. No such test has been carried out on the presumed diaries before they were published. An expert in handwriting, Nicolas Barker, carried out an analysis back in 1995, which was by his own admission an incomplete one: for comparison he only had photocopies and very few originals to work from. He omits to mention whether the originals were compatible as terms of comparison – in other words, dating from the same year as the diary and written in similar psychological circumstances. He drew the following conclusion, however: "I find it impossible to believe that so detailed an account could have been produced as a forgery", which is tantamount to saying that the diaries must be genuine because they cannot be false. An academic criminologist from the University of Lausanne, Beatrice Züger Antognoli, has also carried out an analysis of the handwriting by comparing photocopies; she states that in the absence of original documents of the same type for comparison she cannot pronounce on their authenticity with any certainty. She adds, however, a statement which the publishers have used as a justification for issuing the diaries as "presumed to be authentic": "Nevertheless, from the comparisons carried out, the present writer believes that it is certainly possible that the diaries in question were written by a single individual and by the same individual – i.e. Benito Mussolini – who wrote the other examples of handwriting which have been used for the comparison."[23]

The introduction also includes the interesting view expressed by Roberto Travaglino, the president of the Professional Graphologists' Association in Italy, who suggests that while the diaries may have been written by a single individual, that individual could have been an exceptionally inventive fantasist: "The possibility cannot be ruled out that the two diaries were written by an individual who in terms of character closely resembled Mussolini, came from a similar cultural, social and ideological background, and had the same kind of psychosomatic make-up, to the point of imitating in many ways Mussolini's actual behaviour and coming to identify with him..."

It has been necessary to spend a large part of this introduction explaining why the book concludes in 1937 and to point to the need for more research before the question of the connections between Mussolini's public and private life in the years which followed can be properly tackled. Publishing "coups" like bringing out the false diaries make the prospects of such research more problematic, but in certain ways more fascinating. The volume of the diaries sells for a retail price of 21.50 euros, not exactly "bargain-basement wares" in De Felice's scornful expression, then, but sufficiently economical to ensure a wide readership. The publisher claims that purchasers of the book will have all the information they need to form their own judgement of the diaries' authenticity, as if such a thing were possible without having the necessary historical knowledge as background. It is probable therefore that some of those who read the book will persuade themselves they are reading the genuine diaries kept by Mussolini – if, that is, the dullness of the experience doesn't convince them otherwise. For there is nothing of striking interest in them in terms of either his public or private lives. The Mussolini who is supposed to have written these diaries describes how happy he is to return to the family home at the end of the day and also has a fondness for cloyingly sentimental expressions: "I shall probably die poor – though only in terms of money, because whenever I can gaze at the sea, smell the fragrance of my native region, watch the sun come up and set, the anxieties which afflict me all gone – then I shall be the richest man on earth, desiring nothing else – except the undying greatness of the Italian nation."[24]

The publication of the false diaries is only the latest in a series of such publishing ventures in the years since the end of the Second World War, all intended to present Mussolini in a positive light, as "a good sort", who didn't hate Jews, "only" punished his opponents with internment, made the trains run on time and kept the country in working order, who certainly had his faults but shared them with his fellow Italians. The only real interest in the diaries for historians would be to find out who really wrote them and when, as well as what political motives and publishing interests lay behind the operation. For the rest, all those concerned with researching and writing serious history must take up the challenge, go back to the sources and reconstruct the story on that basis.

One final note for the reader of this book. The Appendix, entitled 'Mussolini and the Crowd', explores Mussolini's skills as a public speaker, but the analysis can be used as a key for a broader understanding of his political activity in general. In this way, the Appendix may also serve as a kind of preface to the book, a preliminary approach to the subject; or, if the reader prefers, left to the end of the book, containing some concluding reflections.

Chapter 1

The Blacksmith's Strength

He wasn't just one of the voices shouting in a meeting, one of the hands raising a banner aloft, one of the heads kicked in when fighting broke out in the streets – he wasn't just anyone. He was an agitator, an extremist, a leader, a socialist. This was – and remains – the problem.

When Benito Mussolini came into the world, at a quarter-past two on a sunny Sunday afternoon at the end of July 1883, his blacksmith father was banging away with his hammer at an anvil, producing showers of fiery sparks with every blow of the bellows, and shifting crates of old iron around in the sultry summer heat. In the morning the church bells had rung out long and loud to welcome in the local patron saint's feast day. To his ears the infernal noises of his work were like the first notes of the approaching revolution. He was nearly twenty-nine; he thought his youthful vigour inexhaustible. A son had just been born to him, and all his companions, supporters of the socialism of the International, in the old village of Varano dei Costa, above Dovia, a locality of Predappio, were hurrying to greet him. Among the clouds of smoke and gusts of air from the bellows, against the sizzling of the iron in the water and the deafening hammer blows, they recalled the names they had suggested for the boy: Giuseppe, after Mazzini, or Garibaldi, who had died on the island of Caprera a few months previously. Guglielmo, after the nationalist Guglielmo Oberdan, who had been executed by hanging in Trieste on 20th December of the previous year. Carlo, like Karl Marx or the anarchist Carlo Cafiero, Michele like Mikhail Bakunin, Filippo, after the great Buonarroti, or Augusto after the theorist of revolution Louis Auguste Blanqui.

Alessandro Mussolini waited while the names were bandied back and forth in the afternoon heat and went on hammering and blowing until he could start to bend the bits of iron into the hinges he was making for the gate the local school needed urgently. Suddenly he stopped. Their banner was hidden away in a secret hiding place, so secret that only three of the local leaders of the Partito Socialista Rivoluzionario di Romagna (Revolutionary Socialist Party of Romagna) knew where it was kept. Alessandro was one of them. He went over to get it, and his companions started to go with him across the smithy, but suddenly stopped dead without a word. A look from the blacksmith was enough. None of them were allowed to see where it was hidden. His Majesty's police had never been able to discover the hiding place, and nor would they. He came back holding a soiled, rusty metal box, so tarnished and battered that even the hardest-up old-iron merchant wouldn't have dared to try to sell it. Out of it emerged a red flag, silkily gleaming. They all stood round in a group as if they were still trying to conceal it. They commented in low voices on its miraculous state of preservation; it was specially protected in all their demonstrations, raised aloft during strikes, kept safe during police raids and round-ups, venerated like a relic. One of them asked the blacksmith to speak, and the rest readily agreed since he was regarded as a skilful orator. He started off in unusually restrained tones. He explained what he had already decided long before: his son would be a socialist, no doubt about it. And in order that he would never stray from this path he would be called Andrea, after Andrea Costa, their leader, the first socialist to win a seat in the Italian parliament. They themselves had helped to elect Costa just a year ago – weren't their votes among the thousand or so which Alessandro Mussolini had secured for the founder of the Revolutionary Socialist Party of Romagna? It might be just coincidence but his son had been conceived in 1882, the very year Andrea Costa had spoken out on behalf of the proletariat in the national Chamber of Deputies. So the boy's name would be Andrea, like the socialist member of parliament who was now getting ready to form the Fascio della Democrazia (League of Democracy). It was only a matter of days now, the declaration would be made before August was out.

But, Alessandro continued, his son would have another name: Amilcare. Of course! Amilcare after Cipriani, the "prophet of revolution", the hero of the Paris Commune, the friend of Marx and Engels, of Garibaldi and Mazzini, no man was more feared by the police, the bosses, the bourgeoisie. He had been condemned to death in France, had managed to escape to New Caledonia, was under threat of arrest if he ever came to Italy. Raise a cheer then! Andrea and Amilcare!

But his son's first name – the one everyone would use when they talked to him and when they talked about him – would be another. It was a name which signified the victory of socialism, that it wasn't just a utopia, a cherished hope, a vision of the future. His first name was to be Benito – after Benito Juárez, the man who had defeated France, England and Spain, with all their capitalist wealth and with all their armies, the revolutionary who had brought down the puppet emperor Maximilian of Habsburg, who had abolished the clergy's privileges and who had begun to apply socialist principles in Mexico. Benito Juárez was a lawyer and legislator, but he also belonged to the proletariat, having taken a job in a cigar factory to keep faith with his ideals.

Benito Andrea Amilcare. Rosa, the boy's mother, exhausted from the pain of giving birth, heard and obeyed, like the pious, docile wife she was. The red flag was put back in its hiding place, someone looked outside to check the road was clear, and the small meeting disbanded.

The names of Georges Sorel, Vilfredo Pareto, Friedrich Nietzsche and Gustave Le Bon are usually cited in the biographies of Mussolini as the authors the future Duce imbibed while young, by himself, with no proper academic guidance. Out of the disordered heap of their theories emerged the path which took him all the way from revolutionary socialism – the socialism of the barricades – to the authoritarian and reactionary ideas of Fascism. Yet his sister Edvige Mussolini maintained it was impossible to understand him only by referring to these writers. She knew her memoirs would be seen as a fundamental source of information, but at the same time a partisan one, and she sought to pre-empt the severe judgements professional historians would pass on her work by defending herself in advance. They might talk ironically of her way of simplifying matters, but nevertheless she asserted that those writers are not the key to understanding Mussolini's appearance on the political stage: that was to be found instead "in his father's smithy and in the family home". Edvige believed there was some kind of hidden force in her brother which "enabled him to appropriate and impersonate the most vital and significant trends of modern life while at the same time remaining independent of them, unaffected by them, even cancelling them out in the authentically tragic experience of his own career".[1] And this hidden force originated in the father's smithy. No doubt her publisher had warned her in advance of the disdain and scorn such an idea would arouse.

And yet implicit support for her theory can be found in the historian Renzo De Felice's views. De Felice's monumental biography of Mussolini offers a detailed analysis of national and international politics through the magnifying lens of the dictator's life and career; his work has been hugely influential on a whole generation of contemporary historians. De Felice thought that it was important to find out more about Alessandro Mussolini, the socialist blacksmith. A thousand votes might not seem very many to those unfamiliar with the practices of tribal politics, yet even today that number of votes could decide who gets elected to the city council in Rome or is put in charge of a municipal department. The campaign office of any aspiring member of parliament would put out the flags for anyone who could guarantee them a thousand votes: even in modern-day politics they're a good start-up for a political career. In January 1882 the Italian parliament had passed a law reforming the electoral system: so long as all those newly entitled to vote had completed the first two years of primary schooling, the voting age was lowered from twenty-five to twenty-one, and the level of income tax which was one of the conditions of the franchise under the old electoral law was halved. The result was an electorate of two million (male) voters, compared to the six hundred thousand under the previous system. Yet this was still only 6.9 per cent of the country's population. Of these two million men entitled to vote, a mere sixty per cent went to the polling stations on 22nd October 1882, in other words little more than one million ballot papers. One hundred and thirty years ago, a thousand guaranteed votes – the number of votes Alessandro Mussolini secured for Andrea Costa's election – represented significant political capital.

In an interview he gave to the journalist Emil Ludwig, whose career spanned the first half of the twentieth century, Benito Mussolini called hunger "a good teacher". He probably liked the sound, the stage effect, of the phrase; perhaps he was remembering some of the bleak days he spent in Switzerland, for in his childhood he never went hungry. "My mother earned fifty lire a month as a primary-school teacher" – Ludwig transcribes Mussolini's words – "while my father earned what any blacksmith earned. We had just two rooms. We almost never ate meat. But there were passionate discussions, a sense of struggling and hoping for something better. My father went to prison for spreading socialism. When he died, a thousand of his companions accompanied the hearse."[2] There they are again: like Garibaldi, Alessandro the blacksmith had his loyal companions, the "Thousand" who followed him. But take a closer look at them: under the new electoral law they all paid enough income tax to have acquired the right to vote, in other words their income put them among the 6.9 per cent of the population who were allowed to decide the political direction the country should take. They weren't in rags then, and nor was Alessandro Mussolini, who "earned just what any blacksmith earned" in the still predominantly rural economy of nineteenth-century Italy, where everything depended on the metal implements and parts he and his like made and repaired: scythes and hoes, hinges for gates and shoes for horses. His income must have been quite substantial to gain the confidence of the austere bank officials – even more severely disposed towards revolutionary social-ists – since he often signed as the guarantor for cheques presented by his socialist companions: his signature reassured the banks. And if someone defaulted on a payment he stepped in, even if it meant a bit of belt-tightening for him and his family: proletarian solidarity was paramount. He himself never defaulted on any of the financial commitments he took on. Mussolini once described his father for the benefit of English readers: "My father was a blacksmith, a heavy man with strong, large, fleshy hands. Alessandro, the neighbours called him. Heart and mind were always filled and pulsing with so-cialist theories. His intense sympathies mingled with doctrines and causes. He discussed them in the evening with his friends, and his eyes brightened up."[3]

Alessandro Mussolini was born in 1854 in Villa Montemaggiore, near Forlì, on an estate belonging to his family. His father Luigi, the grandfather of the future dictator, was somewhat misanthropic, with anarchist inclinations, an unrepentant womanizer, who liked a glass or two of Sangiovese or any other good wine. He certainly didn't have socialist sympathies and nor was he hard up. His rebelliousness, if we can call it that, consisted in neglecting his family and other social connections and having scant regard for the rules of common moral-ity and social life. His granddaughter Edvige describes him as the owner of a small property who nonetheless left nothing to his son: he sold off his land, including his house, bit by bit, to pay for a life of pleasure-seeking in the company of his beloved brother Tancredi. When he learnt that his son Alessandro had become a socialist, he merely remarked ironically: "Private property is theft, right? Then I've done him the favour of not turning him into a receiver of stolen goods."[4]

Alessandro was sent off, still little more than a boy, to serve as an apprentice to a blacksmith. He learnt the craft – and a good deal else. In his workshop in Dovia, books and magazines started to accumulate. He read a lot; he learnt to write well and also to speak persuasively. He was just eighteen when there was an uprising in the country between Imola and Bologna: revolutionaries were going round destroying the symbols of the modern era – telegraph poles, railway tracks – and attacking police. Among the leaders of the revolt there was Bakunin but above all Andrea Costa, the first star of Italian socialism. Costa had much support in Romagna, which had seen the first popular socialist uprisings, but he also had good connections among the socialist intellectual elite, close to the world of industry, such as the Milanese circle of Anna Mikhailovna Kuliscioff, with whom Costa had a child. According to Renzo De Felice, knowing who Alessandro Mussolini was is important for understanding his son: "There was very little Marxism in Alessandro Mussolini's socialism – though we know he read the first volume of *Das Kapital*, probably in Cafiero's abridgement; there was instead a marked strain in it of populist anarchism."[5]

In 1876, when he was only just twenty, Alessandro Mussolini was elected as a delegate to represent Predappio and Meldola at the socialist congress in Bologna, so becoming one of Costa's leading supporters in the region. Socialists, like Catholics for that matter, still had no parliamentary representation. In October 1876 the third congress of the Federazione Italiana dell'Internazionale (Italian Federation of the International) was held in Florence. The guiding principles of the movement were drawn up: collective ownership of the products of labour, with all other private property regarded as theft. Organizing insurrections had its problems, however: Alessandro was immediately put under special surveillance and found himself in prison for several months. But he continued to support Costa's progress, which culminated in the latter's election to parliament in 1882 as the first socialist deputy: the world of socialist rebellion now entered the country's parliamentary chambers. Political action started to become more defined.

Alessandro Mussolini organized the first labourers' cooperative in his neighbourhood. "Workers of the world, unite!" – so the call had gone out in 1864 in London; Alessandro set aside his early anarchism and dedicated himself actively to the ideal. He started to write for many of the periodicals which were then starting to be published, whose titles alone spell out their combative spirit: *La rivendicazione* (*The Vindication*), *Il sole dell'avvenire* (*The Sun of Tomorrow*), *Il risveglio* (*The Awakening*). On 29th March 1884, Andrea Costa, working in collaboration with the Partito Repubblicano Italiano (Italian Republican Party), organized in Forlì the Congresso Operaio Romagnolo (Congress of Workers in Romagna): one of the leading delegates was the blacksmith from Predappio. Meanwhile the political scene, dominated by reform and uprisings, was changing rapidly. In December 1888, during a demonstration in memory of Oberdan, fights broke out with the police which led to Andrea Costa receiving a three-year prison sentence. In the same month, a new electoral law extended the franchise even further: the annual income tax threshold for voters was lowered to five lire, while they were required to have basic literacy.

The new political climate offered an opening for Alessandro Mussolini. He formed an alliance with left-wing liberals and in 1889 won the local council elections in Predappio, becoming a councillor and subsequently deputy mayor for its population of four thousand. It was a slap in the face for the clerical factions which had up until then governed the place. Italy's conservatives were beginning to emerge from the cloud of Church incense which had always accompanied them: on 9th June of the same year the unveiling of Giordano Bruno's statue in Rome took place in the midst of a tumultuous anticlerical demonstration. Newspapers carried reports that engine drivers often stopped their trains if they realized a priest was among the passengers and wouldn't set off again until he'd got off.

Benito Mussolini was six years old at this time, when socialism both in Italy and in his home was rapidly evolving. His father began to take him along to committee meetings and political assemblies.

But manual labour in my father's blacksmith shop was not the only interest we shared. It was inevitable that I should find a clearer understanding of those political and social questions which in the midst of discussions with the neighbours had appeared to me as unfathomable, and hence a stupid world of words. I could not follow as a child the arguments of lengthy debates around the table, nor did

I grasp the reason for the watchfulness and measures taken by the police. But now in an obscure way it all appeared as connected with the lives of strong men who not only dominate their own lives but also the lives of their fellow creatures. Slowly but fatally [*sic*] I was turning my spirit and my mind to new political ideals destined to flower for a time.[6]

If an orator is someone who teaches others how to speak, how to develop effective techniques of persuasion, then Benito Mussolini's father was the orator who taught him these skills. He absorbed the lessons on the field of action, in the midst of turbulent political assemblies when securing the attention of the public was merely the first step. You also had to learn how to lead this riotous and violent crowd to fight in the squares or vote in the polling stations. Unlike others, Benito Mussolini had the advantage of being able to follow the debates and further discussions which took place within the four "stone walls" – as he romantically characterized it in his English autobiography – of home.

In the twilight days of the regime, in 1943, Hitler sent one of the best doctors in Germany, Georg Zachariae, to ensure that Mussolini was in good enough physical shape to lead the new Fascist state, the Italian Social Republic. The dictator spent much time chatting with Zachariae. His memory wandered back to his childhood, while the doctor, thinking perhaps that he was making a contribution to the grand narrative of history, transcribed what was said: "I came into life a socialist and I'll leave it a socialist. My father was a committed socialist; I drank those ideas in with my mother's milk. Later on, as I was growing up, I continued to be interested in them, to pursue them and develop my own thoughts on them. I owe a lot to my father. I found the road of socialism chalked out for me: all I had to do was follow it, which I did with real conviction."[7]

Even at that moment of darkness and bloodshed, when the war arrived in the homes of ordinary Italians, bombing their walls and roofs, the blacksmith's son still thought of himself as a socialist, he still harked back to his parents' two-roomed house with its walls of stone. There were in fact three rooms but the third was used as a classroom where Rosa, his mother, taught him to read and to do sums. When Benito was eighteen months old, in 1885, his brother was born. He too was given a name – Arnaldo – with revolutionary antecedents: Arnaldo of Brescia was a priest who preached a return to the poverty of the Gospels, only to be excommunicated, hanged and burnt by the Church authorities.

It was only with her third child, a baby girl, that Rosa succeeded in choosing a name that she wanted: Edvige, after the Polish saint who had built hospitals for the poor and sick among her countrymen.

One day, when they were playing around unseen in some corner of the house, among piles of books and magazines and newspapers, Benito and his brother came across their father's love letters to his wife before they were married. Rosa was spellbound by Alessandro, the way he held himself, the committee meetings he organized, the assemblies he could excite and the crowds he could dominate – and the letters he wrote to her. He was the right age for her – four years older – he was good-looking and he also owned his own smithy, so his financial standing was solid. Rosa had acquired a diploma as a primary-school teacher when she was just seventeen, spent a couple of years teaching in a village near Forlì, after which she was transferred to Predappio – where the two young people fell in love. She was the daughter of her father's second marriage; her parents were elderly and found the idea of a socialist son-in-law deeply shocking. Rosa Maltoni might have had the air of a timid primary-school mistress, but she was determined: on 5th March 1882 she married Alessandro Mussolini. She was a devout Catholic, who went to church every Sunday, but she had no difficulty in reconciling her beliefs with her husband's fiery anticlericalism. According to Edvige, her mother thought there was a continuous line linking the Gospels, St Paul, Marx and Bakunin; and then there was her conviction that a wife's obedience to her husband was one of her religious duties.

Rosa's background, like Alessandro's, was not impoverished. At a certain point she received an inheritance of ten thousand lire. As a primary-school teacher her monthly salary was fifty lire, so the inheritance was the equivalent of sixteen years' pay – not bad for a young woman who had married against the will of her parents. Now she was the wife of the deputy mayor of Predappio with her own capital – not a word much liked by followers of the socialist International. Rosa and Alessandro's small house served as a refuge for all those revolutionaries who found themselves in deep trouble in the various police crackdowns; they were always sure of finding a meal and a bed to sleep in. For Alessandro it was a way of showing socialist comradeship, for Rosa an act of Christian charity. With their ten thousand lire – their "capital" – the couple had acquired a small estate. One day one of the local labourers had knocked at the door and, as is normal when one pays a visit to respectable folk, wiped his boots and took off his hat before entering. He looked round, abashed and hesitant, and asked to speak with the master of the house. If he'd thrown a bomb he couldn't have caused more damage. Alessandro the blacksmith – the revolutionary who was fighting for a society in which there were no masters or servants, the socialist who was waging a war on private property, the sworn enemy of capitalism – had been addressed as a master by one of the labourers who worked in his vineyard... The local Revolutionary Socialist section – the one he himself had founded – expelled Alessandro for six months. He came back home in silence from the meeting where the decision had been taken and it remained difficult to get a word out of him for the duration of the six months. Despite the insulting setback, he returned to politics.

Following on from Andrea Costa, at each parliamentary election more and more socialists became deputies. In 1892 Costa's Revolutionary Socialist Party merged with the Partito Operaio Italiano (Italian Labour Party) to form the Italian Socialist Party. In 1902, when Benito Mussolini was nineteen years old and had obtained his diploma as an primary-school teacher, his father was still the leading figure among the local socialists. On 6th July local elections were held. The situation was tense: there was only a handful of votes between the right-wing clerical faction and the revolutionaries. But there were many in the small town who now knew a political trick or two. A trap was set to catch the leader of the local socialists; though Alessandro was forty-six, an experienced politician, he fell straight into it. The leaders of the opposing faction in the village waited for him to come along the road, then, as if it were an entirely chance encounter, greeted him with much bowing and doffing of hats. They knew without doubt – they said – that they were speaking to the representative of their political opponents who had "true moral authority", to a person with a high sense of responsibility, but, nevertheless, they were extremely concerned about the threats to public order posed by the revolutionary excitement of the local socialists. Alessandro Mussolini declared in the hearing of all that there was no reason for concern; the election would pass off without disturbance, he himself would guarantee the security of the polling stations.

Election day came and the polling stations were overrun with violent clashes. Alessandro returned home exhausted and went to bed without the faintest idea that he was being sought out as the instigator of the disturbances. His wife literally dragged him out of bed when she realized "they" were coming, "they" being the police and *carabinieri*. Alessandro escaped in haste across the fields, while Rosa told them her husband had had to go to Forlì. As a practising Catholic, she thought telling a lie was a sin, but in the circumstances it was a venial one. At dawn on the following day Alessandro emerged from his hiding place, but "they" were waiting for him – they hadn't believed Rosa – and caught him on the road. This time he ended up in prison, enduring a long hard spell inside which broke his spirit and his health. Benito learnt about what had happened from a brief newspaper report, which mentioned the arrest of various socialist leaders, including his father. After this event, Alessandro Mussolini started to take on an air of legend for socialists in the region. His adventures were told in the local taverns, the legend got passed around, no doubt getting more colourful with each version – a small detail here, another circulated there – so that the fights started to resemble pitched battles and Alessandro finished up as a solitary Samson, pulling down the columns of the polling stations and overturning all the ballot boxes.

A proof of how well known the blacksmith from Predappio became can be found in Angelica Balabanoff's story of the welcome given to his son Benito when the young man first became a newspaper editor. Before letting him speak to the assembled staff in his new role as editor-in-chief of the periodical *La lotta di classe* (*The Class Struggle*), the chairman introduced him: "I have the pleasure of presenting to you the young son and comrade of Alessandro Mussolini, a tried and tested revolutionary, whose name alone – like a banner, a sure guarantee – is sufficient for us to welcome his son."[8]

It would be useful to have a look inside the Mussolini family home in Dovia. Family and political life may have been intense, but the living space was narrow, especially when Rosa's mother went to live with them. A presence in those two rooms – and the third used as a schoolroom – "tall, skinny, always on the move" as Mussolini later described her, Marianna Ghetti exerted a certain influence over her grandson. As a child, Benito was – naturally – the leader of a gang of local boys who patrolled large areas of the neighbourhood. It was to be expected that he looked up to his grandmother with admiration; he would meet her frequently walking along the exposed river bed gathering up pieces of driftwood brought on the currents, some of which he and his companions would carve into fantastically shaped weapons for use in their encounters. Marianna was careful not to disturb the household more than was necessary: she occupied little space and used up minimal resources.

> She had another habit of never wanting to sit with us at table when we ate our frugal meals, which during the week consisted in a bowl of vegetable soup at midday and in the evening one plate for all of us of radishes from the fields. On Sunday there was a small piece of mutton to make broth, which needed to be continually skimmed. My grandmother was very devout; her only expression of annoyance, in dialect, was "begone with the Devil". She loved us very much; we in turn often drove her to distraction.[9]

In the image of the Duce created by Fascist propaganda, the family diet was always seen as a sign of their poverty; even what he ate as a child had to suggest that Mussolini was a self-made man who rose from nothing. From today's perspective, in a time of outlandish diets, the family meals look rather different to us. Healthy vegetable soups were then – as is no longer the case today – widely prepared and eaten: it was a perfectly normal dish in rural working households, for ordinary not impoverished families – real poverty at the end of the nineteenth century was much starker. But the normality of Mussolini's family was not very useful in the construction of his myth; the story had to be made more dramatic by picking out and highlighting certain details. Over the years Mussolini selected from his family memories whatever was most useful to him at that particular moment: when he wanted to play the revolutionary, his atheist socialist father was invoked; when he needed to negotiate with the Vatican, it was the turn of his pious mother instead, who made him get down on his knees and say his prayers every night by his bed.

Chapter 2

Three Knives

The first time he used a knife on someone, it happened out of the blue, just after he'd left the classroom. At first it seemed like the normal set-to of young lads hurling insults at each other for no real reason. Then it turned into a grimly silent scuffle – punching, kicking, scratching, all in a heap on the ground, trying to tear hair and jackets, to dig with their elbows and knees, with not a groan to be heard – they didn't want to attract the attention of their teachers, the strict fathers of the Salesian order. One of their schoolmasters, a priest with large hard hands, would have come and broken up the fight with a few harsh-sounding blows of his fist. None of the others intervened; they looked on, watching what was for them a genuine fight or duel. Such fights didn't often occur, but when they did you had to let them play out to the bitter end. In the fast-moving scrum of boys, led by some kind of instinct, he took the knife from his pocket and stabbed it through the hand of his schoolfellow, who started to scream, at first with pain and then at the sight of the blood squirting out everywhere.

The second time he stabbed someone with a knife was in the maths room in a fit of cold rage at a classmate who had scribbled on his exercise book. His first reaction was to hurl abuse at the boy. He was always good with words and it was effective; the other lad was nonplussed and struck out with his fist. Mussolini took hold of the blade with which he was trying to scratch away the ink from the sheet of paper and stuck it into the other's buttock.

And the third time: this came to light in retrospect when the twenty-eight-year-old was locked up in the prison in Forlì, cell thirty-nine. He'd asked his guard for a small notebook, and in it wrote what was to be his first autobiographical account of his life: *La mia vita dal 29 luglio 1883 al 23 novembre 1911 (My Life from 29th July 1883 to 23rd November 1911)*. His thoughts took him back to his time in

Switzerland when, on his arrival, he found himself this time really impoverished and without resources. "On the afternoon of 10th July I got off the train at the station of Yverdon. I had two lire and ten cents in my pocket. I managed to sell a good knife which I'd bought in Parma and had once used to stab Giulia in the arm during one of our frequent rows. I got five lire for it – enough to live on for a week."[1]

It would be hard to find teachers who had not in their time confiscated knives and blades from among the desks of their worst pupils, those singled out for black marks from their first day at school. These were not unusual incidents in Italian schools. More than fifty per cent of the population was illiterate. The school-leaving age was fixed by law at nine years, in other words, the end of the second year of primary school, one of the lowest in Europe, but even so it was difficult to enforce it. Textile, paper-making and tobacco factories continued to employ children aged eight or even younger, paying them less than half what an adult worker earned. In the countryside the *carabinieri* had to go round to families to try to persuade them to send their children to school, and so in the process deprive themselves of a valuable extra source of labour. Each year saw a slight increase in the number of children who arrived in makeshift classrooms, like the one run by Mussolini's mother. In a language – Italian – with which few of them were familiar, these boys and girls started to learn about a culture which didn't always fit with the habits and traditions they knew at home, where they would return at the end of the school day.

It was therefore normal that lads from families of smallholders or farmers, even very young ones, knew how to handle a knife. But it wasn't normal at all that a lad like this would use one to wound a classmate. The very harsh reaction of the institution merely mirrored the violence endemic among children. On the day – 24th June 1893 – Mussolini first used a knife to stab his classmate's hand a schoolmaster had appeared as soon as he heard the shouting. Discipline in the institution – the College of San Francesco di Sales in Faenza – was normally severe, but on this occasion they devised an extraordinary punishment with the aim of instilling fear into the guilty boy and leaving a permanent mark. The priest dragged him away and shut him in a small room: "Tonight you'll sleep with the guard dogs. A boy who tries to kill his classmates isn't fit to associate with them."[2] When he was left out in the yard at night, he found the ferocious dogs were kept untied; he managed to climb over a gate just in time to shake off – as he tells the story – a dog who had bitten him in the seat of his trousers.

The second episode involving a knife – on 14th January 1894 – also produced shouts which attracted attention and brought the principal of the boarding school in Forlimpopoli running up. He found one boy writhing in pain with a blade stuck in his bottom while the other was standing stock still. The college – this time a non-religious one – decided it would be better not to have a boy among its students who was so quick to attack a fellow pupil with a knife, and their decision was final. They may have tried to soften the impact of the verdict by phrasing it differently, but for Mussolini it meant only one thing: expulsion.

Little is known about the circumstances of the third incident when Mussolini wielded a knife: what he casually calls in his first autobiography "rows" must really have been fights in which the couple came to blows. He picked up a knife, used it against a woman, and on this occasion no one was around to punish him. He even recalls with satisfaction selling the knife for enough money to live on in Switzerland. Mussolini himself gives us a glimpse of what his relationships with women were like when he recounts, without misgiving or regret, an episode which took place in the period he was looking for work as a primary-school teacher. He had his eye on a woman: he wrote her first name in his prison notebook, but just put the initial of her surname: Virginia B. (as if she would be difficult to identify in the small town of Varano where the incident happened).

> She was a generous girl. One fine day, when everyone else in Varano had gone to San Cassiano to listen to some pompous sermon from a friar, I led her up some stairs, pushed her into a corner behind a door and had her on the spot. When she got up she was distressed and crying and started to insult me. I had "stained her honour" she said – I'd like to know what kind of honour that was. In any case Virginia didn't sulk for long. Our affair lasted three months – let's just say it was more a meeting of bodies than of souls. She came from a poor family, but her skin was wonderfully white and delicate.[3]

What occurred was rape by any standards, today's or indeed those of the time (1901). How many men then indulged in sexual violence of this kind is hard to say, but it was not at all unusual to hear men boasting of such behaviour, as if it was only to be expected of any self-respecting male.

When we look at his early years, Mussolini does not stand out as different from the common run of men at the time. In his childhood and youth there's no dramatic family situation involving strange sexual practices or incestuous leanings. We find nothing like Hitler's perverse attachment to his niece Geli Raubal. In the Führer's case it's possible to talk of dysfunctional family relations; his birth is surrounded by mysteries, his authoritarian grandfather kept his grandmother in a state of sexual servitude, there's a bigamous half-brother, a black-mailing nephew, a mistress – Eva Braun – forced to perform abnormal sexual practices and kept half-concealed between the mountain hideaway of Berchtesgaden and a villa in Munich. Several witnesses testify to the uncontrollable fits of rage which affected Hitler from his youth onwards, the series of failures which led him "to abandon his school full of implacable loathing".[4] What we know instead of Mussolini's childhood shows him to have been like any other boy growing up in that part of the country, with a violent streak which was "normal" in that society and at that time. He didn't speak until he was three, which caused his family considerable concern. However, they could afford to pay for him to be examined several times by specialists in Forlì. One of these visits to the doctor contributed a useful piece towards the subsequent myth of Mussolini. He had been accompanied by his grandmother Marianna, who recalled "the doctor, perhaps impressed by the energy of the truculent boy, saying to her, 'Don't worry, he'll speak all right – in fact, I think he might end up speaking too much.' The grandmother reported the doctor's words to the family, who remembered them shortly afterwards when, at the age of three, Benito started to talk in an improvised language made up of Italian and dialect words, full of grammatical oddities and nonce words."[5]

Pitched battles in the fields with stones being thrown, hunting after lizards and other small creatures, clambering nimbly up trees to steal some fruit, stealing cages with hunting birds, hazardous escapes from authority, grazed knees: the daily escapades in Mussolini's early childhood were like those of all his companions. His sister Edvige too liked this kind of life in the open, racing along the riverbanks or trapping small birds. It's true Mussolini quickly became the leader of a gang, but there were lots of gangs and each had its own leader.

Another person who had an important influence on Mussolini – in addition to his father, mother and grandmother – was his brother Arnaldo. The pattern of their relations established itself while they were still boys and endured during their lifetimes, forming, in adulthood, a kind of political and human symbiosis. Arnaldo's calm and reflective character, inclined to mediate, was a useful counterbalance to Benito's frenetic political activity, first as a socialist and then later when he became a Fascist. "Arnaldo's temperament was clear right from the start. He was infinitely more patient and good-natured than I was. When I played with the other boys we always ended up fighting, but Arnaldo, as far as I recall, never did. He was gentle and thoughtful. He would restrain me, give me advice and help, and then make sure I was all right by taking me to see Father so I avoided a scolding."[6]

Benito's school years left lasting marks on him. There's nothing remarkable to record before he's nine years old: he was educated first by his mother and then by a primary-school teacher in Predappio. In September 1892, however, he was sent away to the boarding school run by the Salesian brothers. This represented a small victory for his mother: she had grown increasingly worried by his running wild through the fields. Perhaps under the influence of a notoriously bigoted friend of hers, Palmira Zoli, she was confident that the quality of the education provided by the Church would be better. So the reluctant little boy was sent off to Faenza, accompanied by his father: the image became one of the family's shared memories.

An education at the San Francesco di Sales institution was not free. His mother Rosa asked for financial support, a grant to help the family pay the fees, but she was turned down. Her son was enrolled in the third or lowest-paying category of students, at a monthly rate of thirty lire, a lot out of the Mussolini family budget and indeed that of most families, yet for the Salesians this category was reserved only for boys from the poorest backgrounds. "In recognition of the equality preached in the Gospels, the Salesians divided the pupils in the college into three groups who sat at different tables in the school refectory: for the nobility, for the middle ranks and for the common people. The first group paid sixty lire a month, the second forty-five, and the bottom class thirty. So I sat at the commoners' table, which was also the most crowded."[7]

The food the boys ate was different according to the tables they sat at. At the commoners' table the bread was often stale and the meals were always meagre and often uneatable. They had to be eaten in strict silence while they listened to one of the older students reading from the *Bollettino salesiano*, the official journal of the Salesian order. The division of the boys into three categories permeated their daily lives: "I always ate at the bottom of the table among the poorest classmates. I could have learnt to put up with having to eat mouldy bread, full of weevils; what I found – and still find – intolerable was the same division in the classrooms."[8]

The so-called commoners were allowed to take baths, but only in summer – in this way less hot water was used and costs were reduced. Heating was non-existent in 1893: once the last warm days of autumn had gone the boys had to face severe winters. One of the effects of the biting cold on them was chilblains, an unfamiliar affliction nowadays with the changes in lifestyle and nutrition. When they appeared on the hands they were unsightly and painful. Some couldn't draw because their split skin stained the pages with pus. Some had chilblains on their ears, which swelled up and seemed to grow in size every day. The sufferers were mocked by the other children, who would run after them braying like donkeys. But chilblains on the feet were even a greater problem: the skin would break, and the fact these pupils were not allowed to take a bath only exacerbated their condition. The wounds became infected and the feet, full of blood and pus, started to fester. Some of the boys had heard of an old remedy which consisted in urinating on the wounds; those who were brave enough to try it only demonstrated its inefficacy.

Despite the severity of the winter, Alessandro Mussolini decided to go to Faenza to check how his son was progressing in that school run by all those priests. He saw him approaching with a limp. He listened to Benito's faltering explanations and then told him to take off his shoes. A disaster: a kind of mush covered the swollen feet. Denied once again the permission to take a hot bath, Benito had tried to get round the prohibition by washing his feet in cold water – ice-cold water, since that's what came out of the tap. As a result his chilblains got even worse and he could hardly walk. Alessandro had enough money to pay for his son to see a doctor urgently. He complained vigorously to the Salesian fathers before returning to Predappio, insisting furiously that the advice the doctor had given was followed: the feet were to be washed in hot water and a medicinal powder applied to dry the skin. The priests saw him off and then, in agitated whispers, discussed the situation. They had allowed into their school the son of someone who was a rabble-rouser, a revolutionary: this was the real problem. Chilblains weren't the problem, they came and went, along with the seasons, the prescribed powder was useless, everyone knew that, only the return of the spring would dry out chilblains, and then a bit of pain never did anyone any harm – and none of the other parents had ever complained. Not a word of protest from any of them except for this socialist ruffian, a man who was plotting to overthrow the King, his country, even God. No, there was only one way to tackle the problem: they had to stay watchful.

So the priests started to keep the blacksmith's son under observation, just like the police had done with his father. Once, during a school walk, the nine-year-old Benito wandered off from the group. He was capable of doing it deliberately just to escape the suffocating discipline, but on this occasion it was just by chance he strayed off, not even realizing he'd done so until he was caught and beaten. And that wasn't the end of it, because his teacher immediately filed a report on the boy's "attempted escape". "I was given the punishment of three months in the corner, in other words I had to stand still and silent in a corner of the playground while I watched the other boys at their games."[9] Every day for three months, from 11.30 to midday, immobile and silent in a corner, watching the others play.

Education among the Salesians followed a set sequence which over the years had proved efficacious. One of the highlights was the preparation for the boys' first Communion. The prescribed spiritual exercises included prayer, reflection, meditation and lots of sermons, not always very subtle: on one occasion the pupils were taken to hear a brother who explained, with his finger pointing to heaven, how a boy from Turin had been struck dead on the altar because he had dared to approach the Eucharist in a state of mortal sin. All the boys were shocked: the authority of the priest preaching in front of the altar was bolstered by his insertion of numerous circumstantial details. On a much later occasion, when he was an adult and a fiercely committed socialist living in Switzerland, Mussolini remembered that menacingly raised finger when he publicly challenged another priest, as if he was trying to get his own back on the memory. But at the time he too was frightened. He took to observing draconian fasts and was tormented by doubts as to what he should do in case

– a terrible eventuality according to the priest – the host stuck to his palate, since it was a mortal sin to push it down your throat with your finger.

Rosa Maltoni came from Predappio, full of pride, to see her son's first Communion in the Salesian school chapel. Before Communion Benito went to confession: "I told the priest everything: the sins I'd committed, the sins I hadn't committed but had thought about, and the sins I had neither committed nor thought about. *Melius erat abundare quam deficere* – better to have too much than too little."[10]

The course of school life offered the teachers many opportunities to influence their pupils' development. Once, in the spring term, a terrible event happened: a boy by the name of Achille Paganelli, one of Benito's classmates, suddenly died. The news was announced briefly in the morning assembly; the astonished pupils were left to reflect by themselves on the mystery of death. There was a large crowd of mourners at the funeral, the whole school, in the different classes each with their teacher, gathered outside the church. When Paganelli's parents arrived, the crowd opened up, like a sudden rift, to let them through; as they walked through, the couple kept looking for the faces of their son's classmates and when they recognized one of them they stopped as if they couldn't move on. The young Benito was struck by the father's terrible groans: "They seemed hardly human, more like inarticulate moaning, as if his grief had suffocated his ability to weep."[11]

Mussolini's religious education came to an abrupt end with the stabbing incident in June 1893. By the autumn he'd been transferred to the Regia Scuola Normale in Forlimpopoli, where the headmaster was Valfredo Carducci, the brother of the famous poet Giosuè Carducci; it was under the protection of powerful Masonic lodges in the region and took boys from the increasing number of local families who supported the socialist cause. Now that he was free from the Salesians' discipline, their constant checks and punishments, Benito Andrea Amilcare started to turn himself into the young revolutionary, the experienced socialist his father had dreamt he would become. Now he could try out some of the phrases he had heard in his father's forge on his new classmates: "the international proletariat", "social revolt", "the fight against capitalism". One of the teachers decided to alert the *carabinieri* as a precaution. There's a story – half-chronicle, half-legend – of the time Mussolini persuaded a group of his classmates to go along to a political meeting held by Salvatore Barzilai, a professor of criminology from Trieste, a member of parliament who would go on to have a successful political career, ending up as a cabinet minister and then a senator in 1920. But for Mussolini and his school companions when they went along to hear him, the austere-looking gentleman was a revolutionary republican. Barzilai stopped speaking when he saw them enter the room, and then announced to the audience how pleased he was by the sight; just by daring to enter the room where the meeting was being held they'd shown how courageous they were. They would become, he declared, the young men who would fight to make Trieste part of Italy and so complete the nation's unification. The audience's applause made his companions group themselves round Mussolini who, as the story – or legend – goes, calmly proceeded to take notes in a small exercise book. As soon as Barzilai had finished his speech, a hand shot up and someone asked to speak: it was Mussolini. One of his classmates, Rino Alessi, recalled how the local mayor, who was seated next to Barzilai on the platform, tried to prevent the youngster from speaking. "No one can deny me my freedom of speech!" shouted Benito, with the ferocious determination he had seen in some of his father's socialist friends. He had to defend what was his right. Barzilai held out his hand, inviting him to step up, and Mussolini approached, shook hands with him and began to speak. While he'd been taking notes, he'd rapidly sketched out in his mind what he would say. The heroes and revolutionaries of the Risorgimento had been betrayed, he began. Italy's middle class thought only about themselves, not about the good of their country and the nation as a whole. But, he went on to say, also the left had lost the faith of the Italian people. It seems improbable that the young Mussolini would have criticized in these terms and at that time the revolutionary left of which his father was one of the leaders; Alessi's account, like so many others, must have been influenced by hindsight, by later events, subsequent sympathies and rivalries. Mussolini continued to hold forth: party politics were useless, barricades, violence, even assassination was necessary to bring down the monarchy and establish the republic. His words enflamed the audience from Romagna and they roared their approval. Mussolini and his schoolmates left the hall in triumph, almost disdaining to notice Barzilai and the mayor. But the school was worried: even though it was a lay institution and the headmaster was the brother of the poet Carducci, it found such revolutionary fervour from the son of the blacksmith from Predappio disturbing. The young extremist refused to heed his father's calm advice to show – at least – some moderation in his attitudes.

The second stabbing incident led to his expulsion. Mussolini decided to prepare for the school-leaving certificate privately by studying on his own. On 27th January 1901 Giuseppe Verdi died: his funeral in Milan was a great public occasion and drew people from all over the country, with Arturo Toscanini memorably conducting a vast choir during the service. The newspapers were full of the event and every city and town in Italy organized meetings and ceremonies to commemorate the passing of the great composer, among which, as a brief paragraph in the Socialist Party daily *Avanti!* on 1st February informs us, a speech in memory of Verdi from the party comrade and student Benito Mussolini had been given the previous day. So a young revolutionary came to public attention.

The future dictator's childhood then was no different from that of his contemporaries in that part of Italy. What happened to him in the Salesian boarding school happened to others in similar institutions all over the country: in Piedmont, in Sardinia, in Veneto there are innumerable accounts left by generations of students of the inflexible and brutal methods used to educate the boys in their charge and stifle their growing sexuality. Many recall experiences which school discipline failed to suppress, as in Mussolini's comments on the abdication of Edward VIII, transcribed by his mistress Clara Petacci in 1938: "He's well known for his addiction to alcohol. His other vice hardly matters in England, almost all Englishmen are like that. In English schools the teachers even get paid to allow it… You find it in Italy, too, though certainly not to the same extent as in England… I remember a fair-haired boy in my boarding school, his name was Dall'Olio, he was pale and thin. All the boys had him, he went from one to another. He tried to come on to me until he realized his mistake. Every night I used to see him going from one boy's bed to another."[12]

The single most remarkable feature of Mussolini's school years is the gradual emergence in him of the revolutionary socialist ideas he had learnt from his father. There's no sense of his being an outsider, a misfit, nothing like this to explain how he later became a dictator. In Angelica Balabanoff's book entitled *Il traditore Mussolini* (*Mussolini the Traitor*) there's an essay by Maria Giudice, a prominent woman in the Italian Socialist Party. Giudice was the daughter of one of Garibaldi's followers and had been imprisoned on various occasions for her political views and opposition to Fascism. She was born in 1880 and was therefore only slightly older than Mussolini himself. In her essay Giudice mentions her activities as a lecturer all over Europe at the end of the Second World War, with her insistent message that no country, no people was immune from Fascism. She reminded her audiences of the years when Fascism reigned supreme in Italy: "At the time there were many in other countries who deceived themselves – whether because they were naive, or ignorant, or over-confident, or because they just didn't want to be bothered – that it could never happen in their countries, they would never have a Mussolini. They didn't understand that once the conditions are right a Mussolini will emerge."[13] As the nineteenth century drew to a close, Italy too had no Mussolini, but he would emerge – from among the revolutionaries, the Internationalists, the socialists.

Chapter 3

Youth and Dances

On 26th July 1943 the police called at the Roman villa – La Camil-luccia – of Mussolini's best-known, most powerful mistress, Claretta Petacci: she was not at home. The officer in charge, Lieutenant Colonel Giovanni Frignani ordered his men to search the house and later drew up a detailed report. Twenty-four hours earlier, Frignani had arrested Mussolini as he left Villa Savoia after a brief audience with the King, during which the former had been stripped of his role as head of the government – the inevitable outcome of the *coup d'état* launched the previous night at a meeting of the Gran Consiglio del Fascismo (Grand Council of Fascism) which had voted their leader down. It was also Frignani who some months earlier had discovered hints of Hitler's secret plans to invade Italy and had gone to Mussolini to warn him, to no avail. Frignani later paid with his life: he was arrested by the Nazis, tortured in front of his wife in the prison cells of the Gestapo headquarters in Via Tasso, and finally, on 24th March 1944, killed in the massacre at the Fosse Ardeatine.

In those terrible days at the end of July 1943 Frignani had been given an extremely sensitive and dangerous mission. He knew all about the important role Claretta Petacci had played in the events which marked the end of the regime. Cesare Rossi knew Mussolini well and had been one of his leading collaborators until he was re-moved in the murky aftermath of the murder of the socialist deputy Matteotti. His considered view was that the sixty-year-old dictator was in terrible physical condition. Mussolini had turned sixty in prison, four days after his fall from power and his arrest. He was ageing rapidly. As a politician he had encouraged the cult of youth, had turned the song called 'Giovinezza' ('Youth') into the anthem of the Fascist movement; now, in the regime's final crisis, youth seemed more than ever fleeting and remote.

Mussolini's power over others was absolute; over himself he had only one option: he had to find some substance which would enable him to exploit his declining physical forces as best he could. Cesare Rossi's attention was caught by a detail in the report drawn up by Frignani's officers when they searched the Camilluccia villa: "Together with bundles of love letters from 'Ben' – in which Clara's lover expressed unexpected heights of pathos and which are interesting also from a literary point of view – many tubes of Hormovir pills were found. Claretta's father – a renowned and enterprising doctor – had taken it upon himself to find a way of increasing the virility of his daughter's exceptional lover. This discovery reveals one unsuspected cause of Mussolini's – and Italy's – tragedy."[1] When Rossi was jotting this down he was being held in the Regina Coeli prison in Rome, waiting to find out what the Allies and the parties forming the new Italian government would decide to do with him: the fact that he had fallen out of favour with Mussolini twenty years earlier was seen as no guarantee of his reliability. "Hormovir" is probably a spelling mistake for an aphrodisiac pill called Hormovin, a German product manufactured in a laboratory in the Ruhr, which must have met the dictator's requirements, as Rossi describes them, perfectly.[2] It was a cocktail of substances: *muira puama*, yohimbine hydrochloride and pure lecithin – almost as powerful and efficacious as its modern successor Viagra. *Muira puama* (*Ptychopetalum olacoides*) came from the Amazon forests, extracted from the bark and, especially, the roots of a shrub which could grow to a height of five metres and which the natives of the region called "strong wood" (*muira*). The peoples of the Amazon forest used its properties to regain or reinforce their virility, sometimes with an infusion they then applied directly to their genitals. It was a nerve tonic, therefore, a natural aphrodisiac which could help with maintaining an erection and problems generally with one's sexual performance. The German laboratory cleverly combined the *muira puama* with yohimbine hydrochloride, which could produce an erection within an hour of taking the substance. A side effect was that it was antidiuretic and could lead to raised blood pressure. The mixture was reinforced by the addition of lecithin, still popular today in supermarkets and health-food shops: active in combating free radicals and cell oxidation, it can also reduce cholesterol and some of the effects of ageing, and helps to increase mental alertness and memory retention. The German laboratory made pills from the three ingredients; the full effect was reached after you took them for three weeks. A sixty-year-old man in the 1940s was very different from a sixty-year-old today: then, in most cases, you were considered elderly. On the verge of sixty, Mussolini needed to exploit what was left of his physical potential to the full, and the aphrodisiac tablets found in his mistress's villa enabled him to do this. A network of power, of string-pulling and business deals, had grown up round Claretta Petacci and her family: "The Duce had created a secret account for Claretta, officially to enable her to carry out 'charitable activities', but the money in it circulated without any form of control or auditing. Buffarini Guidi acted as the middle man for the supply of funds; he shrewdly realized how powerful the Petacci clan had become. Claretta and her close friends intervened actively in Mussolini's political affairs: they proposed names, favoured their own chosen candidates, obtained protection and favours."[3]

But this entire system depended on one thing and one thing only: Mussolini's continuing relationship with his favourite mistress was reliant on his ability to achieve a sufficient number of erections. The Duce began to have problems: Claretta saw this and turned to a doctor who could solve them, who happened to be her father; he was a renowned medical specialist, whose career had been advanced because of his daughter's relationship. He immediately understood what was at stake and obtained the best treatment available at the time. In Cesare Rossi's view, if it hadn't been for the pills Dr Petacci prescribed, Mussolini would have ended up a different man. With Hormovin, like Viagra today, it was possible to regain, effortlessly, as if by magic, one's sexual potency – and not only sexual, since this enhanced Mussolini's power – or rather the feeling of being powerful – in all his relationships, with his colleagues and collaborators, with his ministers, party officials and army generals. Any other man might have welcomed Hormovin as a "find", taken it as a kind of game, in the pursuit of pleasure which, for a while at least, would keep inexorable age at bay. But for the man who invented Fascism, taking those tablets was a political act: they helped to prolong the myth of the Duce beyond its natural limits and as such they are part of the tragedy which befell the country. The myth of Mussolini had many facets: there was the accomplished violinist, the pilot, the journalist, the horseman and the swordsman; he could ski, play tennis, swim and race cars, and excelled in all kinds of sport; he danced

well, wrote novels and plays, designed buildings; naked to the waist
he helped with the threshing in the fields, played with children, was
photographed with flowers and animals. As Gaetano Salvemini has
noted, the regime's control of propaganda was ingenious, even more
so than the system created by Hitler and Goebbels in Nazi Germany;
every form of communication was exploited, and images and films
poured out to reinforce every aspect of the myth. But all these things
revolved round or sprang from the idea of Mussolini's sexuality, the
image of him as a great lover. The regime's system of communication was skilful enough to avoid the problems which might arise
with this approach, preserving the tacit rules of agreement with the
Vatican and with them the image of the "man of destiny", as Pius XI
had described Mussolini, and the political solution to the so-called
"Roman Question", which the Duce had achieved with the concordat
between the Italian state and the Holy See. Thanks to the meticulous
organization of his public and private life, Mussolini was able to
conduct hundreds of relationships with women, some lasting just a
few weeks or months, others more enduring and stable. The women
who lived under Fascism – the young, the not-so-young, and even
those past middle age – saw in Mussolini a model of male sexuality;
they realized that other officials in the party hierarchy merely tried
to imitate him but fell far short of the original. Many women tried
to approach the leader, sending him letters expressing, not so implic-
itly, the nature of their interest. There was even a special office in the
Palazzo Venezia to deal with this correspondence: the letters would be
sorted and sifted, with a selection of women who could go through
to the second round and be brought to the attention of Mussolini.

Since his sexuality was at the centre of his myth, the element that
reinforced and held it all together, the entire edifice was a fragile one,
liable to collapse as soon as real difficulties arose, when war was
declared. Up till then the problems had been avoided with a series
of political decisions or glossed over by propaganda; the myth of
Mussolini, his ability to connect personally with the Italian people,
became the defining feature of the regime. It became a political
necessity for Mussolini to eliminate all possible rivals or potential
successors in the Fascist movement and to free himself from the
constricting duopoly of having to share prestige with the King. As
Renzo De Felice puts it: "It is vital to appreciate the general characteristics of the myth of Mussolini and how indispensable it was to

the regime as a whole and its principal elements by means of a vast diffusion of propaganda (exploiting for the first time – it shouldn't be overlooked – all the techniques of modern mass communication, from radio to cinema). Once this is understood, the rational purpose behind the myth can be seen, its significance shared with the other political decisions Mussolini made in this period."[4] De Felice is referring to the years between 1925 and 1929, when the myth was created and started to grow rapidly, and the period when Mussolini took increasing control over all sources of power and all decision-making. Mussolini's sexuality, with its mixture of truth and legend, survived longer than other components of the myth, sustained for a long time after his death with the production of biographical articles and memoirs.

The subject of Mussolini's relationships with women has proved a profitable business for publishers and authors from the end of the Second World War until today. Every piece of evidence and every witness, however uncertain or unreliable, could be put to use. So there's a story of how little Benito, taken to church in San Cassiano for Mass by his mother, would pinch girls' legs under the pews, and how, away from the church, he found other opportunities to touch them too. Such episodes can't be verified, of course, but even admitting that they did occur it's not unusual behaviour in a boy. His years as a boarder in the harsh college run by the Salesian fathers have inevitably been embroidered with tales of his escapades outside the school in search of girls, but boys' boarding schools, especially religious ones, all over the world and in every generation have always been full of such secret adventures undertaken in breathless pursuit of the female sex. A wall is never going to stop a young male with raging hormones reaching a girl on the other side of it who is equally enthusiastic. It's not improbable that the young Mussolini managed to play truant overnight for such a reason, even though, as we've seen, such disobedience was especially risky. While unlikely it's not impossible that on occasion he escaped from the school to go dancing after making a secret assignation with a girl; in Romagna it was easy to find a public dance or an open-air party where men and women cavorted. In the darker corners of the makeshift dance floors the young boy could have found the time and the space to make out with some girl or other unseen by others. There's a widespread local tradition that he was a passionately enthusiastic dancer.

The so-called "red balls" organized by the socialists as well as the public dances held by working men's associations began to emerge, in a belated recognition that the enthusiasm for dancing was a way of involving the working classes in social occasions which could also be used for political ends. Organizing dances was acceptable because they were seen as a pretext for fundraising for the political cause. [...] As the working men and women took their places on the dance floor, they were always accompanied by the speech of some local or national leader, making the point that the social festivity was also an opportunity for political involvement.[5]

Such public dances and evenings spent in dance halls were not without political overtones; indeed, they became a political issue in themselves. The socialists organized endless dances for working men and women, while the Catholics saw such dances as seedbeds of vice: in their view such occasions were a concealed way of encouraging the "free love" favoured by the socialist Internationalists. "The moralists of the time were horrified by the thought of bodily contact while dancing. They saw it as inevitably encouraging sexual desire. In opposition to such 'transgressive yearnings' a mass movement was started in order to protect the conventional moral standards of the day. Dancing was a fever, a contagion affecting young men and women who, languishing in its grip, started to taste passion and lust."[6] In waltzes and polkas, tangos and mazurkas, it was not only hands that touched; physical contact grew bolder, more impetuous, on the verge of a full embrace, the moving and turning together in time to the music led to a state of stupefaction. Dancing grew to be an irresistible attraction which contributed rapidly to the popularity of socialist meetings; the importance of public dances in the development of Italian political life from the late nineteenth century onwards should not be underestimated. Rémi Hess's analysis of the phenomenon uses a quotation from the surrealist poet Ramón Gómez de la Serna:

When couples embrace while dancing, the woman's breasts feel more than ever alive, grow warm once again with their first yearnings, the friction of bodies once more has the innocence and grace which many, alas, have lost in their intimate contacts. The breasts point the way to the public dance, although it is her legs which carry her there in a hurry... The emotion felt in dancing is the sweetest emotion felt by the breasts; only then are they fully aware of their own desire and the desire of others, they swell with subtle tremors.[7]

Dancing, with all the power of sexuality enclosed in its winding movements, ready to explode, became the site of social and political conflict. An Italian priest, Father Berardi, realized how pointless it was to try to fight the phenomenon head-on on this terrain: there was an irresistible fascination with public dancing, and the socialists exploited it to the full. Berardi sought instead a way of containing and controlling it, by emphasizing the development of technique. It was technique, and the formal requirements of technique, which would help to curb the expression of passion. The priest had heard many accounts in the confessional of the sexual longings caused by dancing and thought he'd found a way to prevent them. He summed up his approach in Latin in 1897 thus: "*Qui saltat attendere debet ad bene saltat*", or, "who wants to dance should learn to dance well". According to Berardi, a concentration on technique would bring the sexual passions aroused in dancing under control: "*Fatigatio, tripudium, saltatio, agitatio, distractio, defatigatio, etc., malitiæ et libidini auditum præcludunt, aut illam cito evanescere faciunt* – in other words, the wish for enjoyment, the energy of the dance itself and the subsequent tiredness obstruct the passions and help to calm them. The technical skill involved in dancing too could diminish them, since if the technique of dancing was not perfectly mastered you had to be especially attentive."[8] The Church realized there was nothing it could do to stop public dancing, and one piece of advice handed out in the confessionals to young girls who wanted to go dancing was to wear a white rose at the waist, which they were to make sure remained intact and undamaged at the end of the evening. But they were fighting a lost battle: dancing became a mass entertainment. The passion for it must have affected Mussolini in his youth, like all the rest; when the band struck up, it was as if a door opened on a magically accessible realm of sexual enchantment. His sexual prowess lay concealed like an iceberg under his virile bluster and display; people would whisper about it with amazement; his sexuality was at the centre of his myth and therefore at the centre of his politics. In this sense the expression "political animal" is peculiarly appropriate for him. Just as his sexuality was the last aspect of his myth to disappear, so it was the first to emerge, encouraged by Mussolini himself, who talked quite openly about it, even boasting of his virility and stamina.

At first there were only his innocuous love letters to his first love, one Elena Giunchi, the cousin of one of his classmates, who had spoken about her; she was evidently pretty enough to gain the attention of these two schoolboys. In the college at Forlimpopoli, a lay institution where the boys were older and had more freedom, whoever had sisters or cousins easily made friends. "In this period I fell in love with a beautiful young girl called Vittorina F., who was the sister of one of my schoolmates. I declared my feelings for her and she replied, putting me off. So I decided to stop her in the street."[9] The expulsion from the school in Forlimpopoli was also in part due to Mussolini's nocturnal truancies. The headmaster Valfredo Carducci, who ran the institution on enlightened lay principles, nevertheless couldn't overlook such disobedience. When as a consequence of his expulsion he became an external student, the nature of his escapades changed: a dalliance with a girl called Caterina might have started off with billets-doux and gifts of roses, but it moved on to kissing. As an external student Mussolini prepared for his exams with his friend Eugenio Nanni; the school had allowed him to follow classes even though he was no longer allowed to board. He realized that getting a diploma was necessary if he wanted to earn his own living and make his own way, so he concentrated hard on his studies. But both he and Eugenio were disturbed by impulses which were too insistent to ignore:

One Sunday we both went over to Forlì to visit one of those places. As soon as I entered, I could feel myself blushing. I hadn't a clue what to say or do but one of the whores took me on her knee and started to excite me by kissing and stroking me. She was well on in years and fat. I lost my virginity with her, for just fifty cents. [...] The sudden revelation of what sexual pleasure meant disturbed me. Naked women started to haunt my daily thoughts and dreams and desires, I would undress the young girls I passed in the street with my eyes, and lust after them. During the carnival season, I used to go to public dances. The music, the rhythm of the movements, the physical contact with girls, their perfumed hair and the tang of their sweaty skin excited my desires, which I would relieve every Sunday in one of the brothels in Forlì.[10]

Once he'd obtained his school diploma, Mussolini went back to live with his family in Dovia. He turned eighteen that summer, still below the legal age of majority at that time; his diploma allowed him to work as a trainee primary-school teacher but, even with this qualification, he couldn't find a job.

That summer saw many strikes and clashes in the factories and in the countryside. On 27th June, in the countryside round Ferrara, the forces of order had fired on a group of agricultural labourers, killing three and wounding twenty-three. A month earlier the anarchist Gaetano Bresci, who had come to epitomize the disturbances affecting the whole country, died in prison. Just eleven months before, on 29th July 1900, the King of Italy Umberto I had been assassinated. The newly established official body set up to examine the question of emigration could do nothing to prevent the constant flow of Italians in search of a better life in a new country, a flow which now came increasingly from the south rather than the north of the country. A determining factor in this reversal of the pattern had been the defeat and brutal suppression at the hands of the police and army of the so-called "Fasci Siciliani dei Lavoratori" or Sicilian Workers' Leagues, in 1894, when Mussolini was just ten years old. The defeat spelt the end to the hopes and ideals of social reform on the island and the creation of a new economic system to replace the large landowners and the Mafia. Many labourers and peasants lost their lives in the shootings, while the movement's socialist leaders were sent to prison. The ships filled with a flood of famished and despairing emigrants. The defeat thus suffered had serious repercussions on the Italian Socialist Party. In the years that followed the party's leaders began to be criticized for failing to pay heed to the needs of workers in the south, while the working-class movement in the north of Italy was accused of turning a blind eye to the fate of the agricultural labourers, from the establishment of the Fasci onwards. In the Po Valley, in Emilia and Romagna, the political climate was different: the disturbances there had led to an improvement in wages and the setting up in 1901 of a Federazione Nazionale dei Lavoratori della Terra (National Federation of Agricultural Workers). Yet the political and social tension meant that it was hard for a young primary-school teacher, just qualified and already known as a revolutionary-socialist firebrand, to find a post. Mussolini went in for several jobs, including posts as a supply teacher, to no avail. But his personal life went on its now accustomed way; as we've seen, to all intents and purposes he raped the girl he calls Virginia B. and for three months in the summer of 1901 they were together "though more in body than in soul". His father Alessandro stepped in to help with the problem of finding a job. As an acknowledged

Socialist Party leader and a skilful manipulator of votes, he used
the classic method of pulling strings. The small town of Gualtieri
– just beyond Bologna in the province of Reggio Emilia and quite
a long way from Dovia, especially at that time when transport was
so limited – had become the first Socialist Party-controlled local
council in the region. Alessandro Mussolini's political influence
extended even as far as Gualtieri, and the Socialist mayor owed him
a favour. So the eighteen-year-old Mussolini obtained his first job, as
a supply teacher. The local Socialists organized an official welcome
for him at the station, perhaps slightly taken aback when they saw
him get off the train dressed from top to toe in black, a habit he
had acquired while at school in Forlimpopoli and had maintained,
either because he thought it distinguished him from his Socialist
Party contemporaries, who frequently wore a red tie, or for simple
convenience. The mayor presented him at a party meeting: this was
the son of Alessandro Mussolini, his arrival in the town would be
very important for the local Socialists. But Benito attended their
meetings very infrequently; his fellow Socialists were more likely
to come across him sprawled drunk on the pavement outside the
shop of a local cobbler with whom he'd become friends. His job
consisted in keeping forty young boys in class for the entire morning; for this he was paid fifty-six lire a month, of which forty went
towards his rent, so he didn't have much left to squander on having
a good time. But there were dances every Sunday, in the open air or
inside depending on the season – those dances which opened the
way to sex and free love. And, apart from staying at home or going
for a walk in the fields, there wasn't much else for young men to
do in their spare time in Romagna. At one of the dances Mussolini
came across Giulia, a strikingly beautiful woman of twenty, married
with a young husband, away on military service, and a little boy. In
Socialist free-thinking Gualtieri her going to a public dance on her
own wasn't seen as scandalous. Each Sunday Mussolini observed
her; it took some time, but eventually the goal was reached:

On the evening of 20th March, at No. 9 in Vicolo di Massa, second floor. I
remember. Giulia F. was waiting for me in the doorway, she was wearing a pink
blouse which stood out in the darkness. We went up the stairs and once inside
she gave herself to me for two hours. [...] Our relationship lasted for a few weeks
until we were found out. Her husband heard about it and ordered his wife to be

driven away from the house. She took her little boy with her and joined me in the room where we'd first come together. We felt more free. [...] Our love affair was violent and full of jealousy, with quarrels and short-lived outbursts of anger.[11]

The Socialist Party in Gualtieri didn't know what to make of Alessandro Mussolini's son and his behaviour. He almost never came to their meetings, but never missed a dance. And now he was involved with a married woman, giving the town's conservatives fuel for scandal and criticism. They had found out about his secret relationship with the soldier's wife after they had invited him to speak at the dinner to celebrate May Day in 1902, in front of an audience of four hundred guests. Mussolini did give the speech, and as they listened to it they saw the son of the far-famed blacksmith from Dovia: when he finished he was wildly applauded and acclaimed. A month later on 2nd June the local council organized a commemoration of the twentieth anniversary of Garibaldi's death. The man who was supposed to give the address had fallen ill, so the crowd went off to fetch Mussolini. They found him in his shirtsleeves and, just as he was, he was carried off to the platform and asked to give a speech, which he improvised on the spot. When the ceremony was over and the clapping had died down, they were certain that a new leader had emerged. But Mussolini had other ideas: his monthly pay was too low and he had come to realize that primary-school teaching was not for him. He had become fixed on the thought of emigrating to Switzerland and trying his luck there. It was also true that his affair with Giulia, her husband's violent reaction at her betrayal and the bitterness of the family who had turned her out were causing problems for the local council. Each day that passed made it clearer that his contract as a supply teacher in the local school would not be renewed; with all the esteem due to his father, they felt they could not offer his son the post. Yet in the end this merely confirmed his desire to look elsewhere; he was content to let things develop as they had. As soon as the school year had finished, he quickly arranged his departure for Switzerland. "I spent my last days in the town almost entirely in Giulia's house. I remember very well our last night together, Giulia was crying and kissed me. I too was moved."[12] Many years later, in the Roman prison cell where he jotted his autobiographical notes down in an exercise book, he seems once again to have been moved by what he calls "my heart's sweetest memory"; he hopes that Giulia remembers him and his love for her and will continue to do so "until she is very old". He never changed his judgement on Giulia Fontanesi, not even in the comments made to Claretta Petacci and transcribed by her: "Yes, Giulia was the woman for me – she was a beauty, poetical, romantic, all flowers, stars, moon and sunset – she was even too romantic. Our lovemaking too – not so much afterwards. Poetry above all: 'You haven't brought me violets or a poem.' I sometimes gazed at her in amazement: she was so fine, so delicate and beautiful. I loved her, our relationship lasted four months. She was supposed to come with me to Switzerland, but in the end she didn't."[13] As it turned out, the beautiful twenty-year-old Giulia did not remain on her own: her husband forgave her and took her back when he returned from military service. Meanwhile Benito Mussolini's attention had turned to the new opportunities which Switzerland offered him.

Chapter 4

Exiles in Switzerland

Small, deformed, obsessive, a fetishist, spinsterly, self-flagellatory, irrational, prone to bouts of hysterical mysticism, unbalanced and fanatical, insidious like some infectious disease and, to cap it all, with a wretched little greyish face, watery eyes and a squeaky rasping voice – Margherita Sarfatti's portrait of her hated rival Angelica Balabanoff seems almost literally to tear her to pieces. Yet the two women had much in common. They were both committed socialists, both elegant, cultivated and refined; both were widely read and both were rich, extremely rich: Angelica Balabanoff had inherited wealth from her Ukrainian family while Sarfatti's Venetian family had been successful in trade. Both were Jewish and both, in succession, dedicated more than ten years of their lives to Benito Mussolini. Balabanoff first met him in Switzerland and, with her superior knowledge, took the young man – rough-edged and much the worse for wear – in hand and transformed him into a socialist leader. Sarfatti met him when he was already a socialist and applied herself to building his new image as the leader or "*duce*" of the Fascist movement. In the course of his life Mussolini had relations with hundreds of women, perhaps as many as four hundred – Renzo De Felice thought this a plausible estimate – but Margherita Sarfatti was not much troubled by his womanizing. Nor for that matter was the only woman he ever married, Rachele, though her investigations were not as far-reaching as those of her rival: "He didn't care for thin women. It didn't matter if they were blonde or brunette, short or tall. Too much perfume was bad. Obviously I'm referring to my husband's successes with women. [...] Looking back now I can say that he had a long list of conquests, but not much more so than any other Italian man who liked women and who in turn was attractive to them."[1] Rachele Mussolini admitted her husband was no saint; she believed she knew all about his extramarital adventures. But how

57

many or how few she was really aware of is immaterial: it is obvious that none of them had any importance for her, they were nearly all based "merely" on physical attraction: these women ran after her husband because he was attractive to them. The relationships were more troubling when there were indications that the other woman had developed a strong influence over him. Unlike Sarfatti, Rachele Mussolini wasn't interested in politics and was not bothered about Balabanoff: "Yet it's true to say that his relations with three women caused me much suffering, and I fought hard against them, to save my marriage and my love for him: Ida Dalser, Margherita Sarfatti and Clara Petacci."[2] But Margherita Sarfatti knew without a shadow of a doubt that Angelica Balabanoff was no mere infatuation: the talents and resources and means at her disposal made her a dangerous rival. And even though she was no longer present on the scene and hadn't been for some time (Balabanoff returned to Russia after the Revolution), the woman had still initiated a relationship with Mussolini during his period in Switzerland and therefore had to be eliminated:

> In Italy women – even the revolutionaries – are usually shy or retiring, but Comrade Balabanoff's boldness was positively flirtatious. As ugly as she was, thanks to her electrifying oratory, or her famous name, or simply the engagingly direct way she propositioned men who were too polite to turn her down – the fact is that the spinsterly Angelica used to boast she was never without a companion as she spread the socialist gospel through the length and breadth of Italy. Let's hope – at least for the sake of the aesthetic judgements of young socialist males – she was exaggerating. [...] She had no sense of humour, and no sense of beauty – just as well, really, since if she had, she would have drowned herself in the nearest well – or perhaps not, she was never very fond of personal hygiene.[3]

Sarfatti's pen is dipped in poison: it had to be if she was to humiliate Balabanoff both as a woman – painting a picture of someone who used political meetings to pick up men – and as a socialist – a dreary fanatic who when she took a walk in the country and came to a crossroads would say in all seriousness, "We must turn to the left – the road to take is always on the left."

Moving between Geneva, Bern and Zurich, the young man who had hitherto been known as the son of the famous blacksmith of Dovia began to gain positions for himself as an emerging socialist.

The image he presented to the world started to change, his political personality started to mature – behind both changes lay the influence of Angelica Balabanoff: hence Sarfatti's malicious attack on her.

While Benito Mussolini was on his way to Switzerland, on 9th July 1902, his father was arrested for the episode of the wrecked polling stations. His son read the news in *Il secolo* and wondered whether he should break his journey and return, but in the end decided to continue. On the train there were many Italians; one of them, a kind of itinerant salesman from Pontremoli, seemed to want to strike up a friendship with him. He spoke confidentially of a relative he had in Switzerland who would be able to find work for them both, but the relative turned out to be an emigrant who was in no position to find jobs for the pair of them. However, he invited them back to eat at his home; after the meal, before leaving, Mussolini sold him his knife, the one he had used on his mistress Giulia during one of their rows. The money he got for it enabled him to survive until he found a job as a building labourer in Orbe, for a chocolate factory which the Bertoglio company was constructing. His work was back-breaking, at night he slept under a bridge, he lived in abysmal poverty: all these things he would recall later in various interviews, while isolating and framing them as elements in the development of his myth; he tried to cast a bohemian light on his existence in Switzerland, with himself at centre stage, a famished vagabond and anarchist. As a labourer on the building site he earned twice as much as he had as a teacher, but he worked eleven hours a day continually climbing up and down carrying a hod with building materials. He lasted a week, with a total pay of twenty lire and a few cents.

On the night of 27th July, barely two weeks after his arrival in the country, the local policemen found him sleeping in a cardboard box under the Grand Pont in Lausanne. They were kind: they gave him a meal and a bed to sleep on – but in a cell in the local station where they'd taken him on a charge of vagrancy. After three days they released him. This was the first of eleven arrests he underwent during his lifetime. In Lausanne there was the Swiss headquarters of the Federazione Socialista Italiana (Italian Socialist Federation) as well as of the Sindacato Italiano Muratori e Manovali (Union of Italian Building Labourers and Bricklayers). He introduced himself there; once more his father's well-known name proved useful. The secretary of the Socialist Federation, Gaetano Zannini, welcomed him with open arms, and introduced him to Emilio Marzetto, the editor of the newspaper *Avvenire del lavoratore*. On 1st August 1902 his first article appeared in it. It was striking for its brilliant style and its unexpected subject: it was an attack on the public indifference to the first of the massacres of Armenians that after the First World War would become known as "Metz Yeghern" or the "Great Calamity". It was the first genocide of the twentieth century, the one which Hitler referred to in his frosty reply to a woman who asked him if he was bothered by public reaction to the persecution of the Jews: "Why should I be? After all, who remembers the Armenians?"

Various socialists helped Mussolini out financially as far as they could while he was in Switzerland. He was able to supplement his small earnings from his journalism by giving Italian and French lessons, by working a few days as a shop assistant or a bricklayer; his mother sent him whatever she managed to save. Even though he had worked on a building site for no more than a handful of days, he thought it was his right to belong to the Union of Building Labourers and Bricklayers; by the end of the summer, in September 1902, he'd become their general secretary, with a monthly salary of five lire, to add to the rest of his income.

His other newspaper articles in this period are notable for their extreme revolutionary views and their contempt for reformist measures, but he maintained the support of the Socialist Federation. He started to speak at meetings all over Switzerland, with his expenses paid. By now the police were keeping a file on him and watching his movements. Gaetano Zannini also recommended him to Giacinto Menotti Serrati as the Swiss correspondent for the Italian-emigrant newspaper in New York *Il proletario*, and also to Arturo Labriola for *Avanguardia socialista* in Milan. Mussolini moved to Bern, where his activities as a political agitator among the Italian immigrant population increased, ending in his arrest by the Swiss police on 18th June 1903. He was given the number 1751, and his photograph was circulated to all the Swiss cantons so that his movements could be tracked more easily. After holding him for ten days in a cell they sent him back to Italy via Chiasso; nobody, however, stopped him buying another train ticket as soon as he arrived and returning to Switzerland the same day. There was another reason he wanted to return to the country: "Over the course of that summer I'd made various acquaintances among the community of Russians living in

Switzerland. With some of the women I'd struck up warm friendships. I remember Miss Alness from St Petersburg and Eleonora H.
with whom a friendship quickly turned into a love affair."[4]

Eleonora H. was a fascinating medical student whom Mussolini was
interested in for a long time; however, she wasn't the only woman in
his life at the time, since he himself mentions taking frequent walks
in the public park in Bern in order to "meet as often as possible a
German blonde who'd caught my attention". He and his friend Salvatore Donatini planned a double sexual conquest while they were
working on an abortive project to start a new journal, *I tempi nuovi*
(*The New Times*). Donatini had become enamoured of a woman
from Paris, Rosa Dauvergne, while Mussolini's eye had fallen on her
neighbour Emilia C. She was older than he was, but that didn't matter; as he wrote, "love conquers all", although it's clear from what
he goes on to say that in this case the woman in question's extensive
sexual experience brought their relationship to a head: "That love
affair was one of the strangest episodes in my youth. She was over
thirty and had five children, yet her behaviour was completely reckless in the period I knew her."

In the town of Annemasse he wasn't around long enough to cultivate
his relationship with the "charming, pale-complexioned" Giulietta
F.; during the few days at his disposal they didn't get further than "a
sentimental, platonic interlude", but the episode shows us how he
was always ready to seize every opportunity, every possibility in the
hope that such initial contacts might lead on to his real goal.

Towards the end of 1903 he returned to Dovia, where his mother
Rosa had fallen seriously ill. By Christmas she had recovered and
on 27th December Benito left again for Switzerland, this time with
his brother Arnaldo, whom he left in Bern, while he continued on
to Geneva, where Eleonora H., the beautiful medical student whose
wealthy Russian family was paying for her studies, was waiting for
him. By now Mussolini was a well-known figure among the expatriate communities in Switzerland; his arrests had also contributed to
his fame.

In the early months of 1904 an Italian evangelical pastor, Alfredo
Tagliatela, was travelling on a mission among the Italian emigrants.
When he was told by some of them how good a speaker Mussolini was
as a socialist, Tagliatela decided to invite him to take part in a public
debate. For a while – it was one of the most confused and troubled

periods of his stay in Switzerland – Mussolini didn't respond, but eventually on 25th March he decided to take up Tagliatela's challenge. Five hundred people crowded into the hall to hear them; the debate became one of the most exploited episodes in the subsequent construction of the myth of Mussolini in his youth. In reality it's a banal and even foolish story; the most charitable interpretation is that Mussolini was taking his revenge for all the sufferings inflicted on him in the Salesian fathers' boarding school. When the chairman of the discussion asked him to speak, Mussolini got to his feet, asked someone to lend him a watch, and then issued an ultimatum: if at the end of five minutes he had not been struck down by the hand of God, this was a proof the deity didn't exist. No one seems to have remarked on the idiocy of the challenge; on the contrary Mussolini was warmly applauded. The contents of Mussolini and Tagliatela's debate were published in a pamphlet in Lugano in 1904: De Felice describes the former's arguments as printed there as "far from original, they merely piece together rationalist and anti-religious 'texts' which were modish at the time. It should also be pointed out, however, that the pamphlet is marginally more worthwhile than most literature of this kind. It shows Mussolini's wildly disorganized learning, typical of an autodidact but – at least in the socialist context of the time (think of Serrati and others like him) – fairly wide-ranging, and on occasion not entirely superficial."[5]

The most significant conference held in Switzerland while Mussolini was living in the country was the commemoration to mark the thirty-third anniversary of the Paris Commune on 18th March 1904, with the participation of many of the exiles in Switzerland, including the Russians. It was on this occasion that Angelica Balabanoff first met Mussolini: she was struck by how unhappy he seemed. She describes him as restless and very shabbily dressed, so much so that, even among a crowd of impoverished emigrants, he stood out. She added as a final touch to her picture of him that he also seemed very dirty. But before accepting her account at face value we should remember that Balabanoff was writing in 1945, with the encouragement of Maria Giudice, in order to provide a detailed and convincing explanation for a wide international socialist and communist readership as to why she had been connected to Mussolini for so long. Among her readers there would have been many who fought on the winning side in the Second World War, who had defeated Nazism and Fascism with a huge cost in human lives. There were false rumours, tactically circulated, that Balabanoff was the real mother of Mussolini's first daughter, Edda, whom Rachele subsequently adopted as her own, showing an admirable willingness to accept the consequences of the revolutionary credo of free love. Another version in an anti-Fascist pamphlet published in Rome just after the liberation in 1944 declared that Edda was the daughter of Anna Kuliscioff, the muse of the socialist movement in Milan, in whose drawing room a socially ill-at-ease and awkward Mussolini had been among the guests.[6]

Shabby, dirty, touchy and morose, obsessed with himself and his own problems, telling people he had syphilis as though it were some kind of visiting card: Balabanoff's picture of Mussolini shows someone who resembles a street vagrant rather than an esteemed orator called on to represent his fellow Italians. He was probably not well dressed, possibly even shabby, but he can't have been dirty or smelly, since if he were it would be hard to understand his success with women, especially someone like the wealthy and attractive Eleonora H.

Lenin was also at the conference, and it's probable that he and Mussolini met. In the interview held with Ludwig, the latter insists that Lenin certainly knew him, since he criticized an Italian socialist delegation for not keeping hold of Mussolini, the man whom Lenin judged capable of bringing the revolution to Italy. In reply Mussolini admitted that he knew about Lenin's remark but went on to say: "I'm not sure if I met him with the others in Zurich. They were always changing their names."[7] His sister Edvige also maintained that Lenin had said that Mussolini was the only Italian socialist who was intellectually and temperamentally suitable to lead the revolution. Vittorio, Mussolini's second son, also wrote that his father might have met the Russian: he was probably introduced to him by the Bulgarian exile Boris Tomoff, who, however, didn't know Lenin's real identity. Changes of names and identities were normal for these people at this time, in order for them to remain safe. In the interminable monologues transcribed by the German doctor Georg Zachariae, a now isolated and weary Mussolini admits he knew Lenin:

When I was living in Switzerland as a political exile I spent some time with the circle of people around Lenin. He was undoubtedly a man of quite extraordinary intelligence, but I immediately saw that all the others were merely brainless chatterboxes – indeed some of them should have been locked up in asylums. I tried to find a way out of having to mix with these people; I wanted my usual freedom of manoeuvre back. After I'd left them, I heard that Lenin had said to them: "How could you have let that man go?" [...] But I was glad to escape from Lenin's tyrannical control of the group.[8]

When we read this, it's worth remembering that in this final phase of his life and career Mussolini was trying to find ways of reorienting himself to the left: a memory of his meeting with Lenin could come in useful.

At occasions like this conference for the anniversary of the Paris Commune, it was normal for militant socialists, especially if they were called upon to speak, to pay special attention to all the other speakers and to try to control the various balances and shifts of power which occurred in the course of the meeting. It is hard to believe that Mussolini would not have taken note of Lenin's address to the assembly. He also mixed regularly with the expatriate community in Switzerland, one of its attractions being the women, among whom he made several friendships, including the Miss Alness from St Petersburg and the woman who became his main mistress at the time, Eleonora H. Others who have tried to compile a list of Mussolini's relationships with women, such as Giorgio Melli, indicate another Russian exile, Hélène M., who took to calling him "Benitusha" and following him round his various political engagements in the country.

Yet even if he never met Lenin, and he was certainly never involved with him politically, there was an important link between the two men: Angelica Balabanoff. Since as a woman in the Ukraine she was not allowed to pursue university studies, her wealthy family had sent her first to Brussels and then to Rome, where she had been taught by Antonio Labriola. She had joined the Italian Socialist Party and was familiar with its social ambience. She was also a member of the Soviet Communist Party; Lenin gave her several jobs to do, including a spell as secretary to the Comintern in 1919. She wrote two books on the two political leaders she'd known: *Lenin visto da vicino* (*Impressions of Lenin*) and *Il traditore Mussolini* (*Mussolini the Traitor*). But the book on Mussolini is steeped in self-justification, which on certain pages can hardly be ignored, and historians using the book as a source would do well to be aware of this. If we take Balabanoff's account at face value, it becomes impossible to understand her long relationship with Mussolini, the fact she stayed with him until 1914, or why he asked her to collaborate in the editorial work on the Socialist Party newspaper *Avanti!*.

A typical instance of her untrustworthiness is the anecdote of the stolen food, which was taken up by much of the polemical literature intent on demolishing the myth of the Duce. It was a fine day and Mussolini was walking in the park when he saw two refined ladies preparing a picnic for themselves; out of their elegant hamper came buttered rolls, meat, mandarin oranges and various cakes. Mussolini was unemployed; he usually ate at the home of a former workmate, a bricklayer, but that day his friend was away and he had gone without a meal. As he saw the rich foods being taken out of the hamper, the pangs of hunger increased; he wanted to attack the women and strangle them. He was overcome with fury, rushed up to them, snatched the bread and the meat from their hands and ran off. Mussolini afterwards said he had run off not to escape, but because he was scared that in his anger against the two women he might kill them. He told the story to an astonished Balabanoff, with a lot of local dialect swear words (according to her he always swore a lot in dialect), who reproved him: "What would have been the point of such a crime? You don't solve social injustice by getting rid of people; you need to change the system so everyone's rights are respected..."[9]

Maria Giudice also inveighed against the wilder instincts of the young Mussolini. In her opinion, Balabanoff's entire relationship with the young Italian after their first meeting in Switzerland would appear to have consisted in her attempts to bring a rough, uncouth, ignorant and undisciplined personality under some form of control. Such an account may have served its purpose in the years immediately following the fall of the Fascist regime, but it means that her memoir is written in such a way that it is hard to get at the real facts, above all at the reasons the two stayed together for so long. Mussolini seems like some alien who has landed by chance on the planet of the revolutionary left; as Balabanoff describes him he is an anomaly, an out-of-control fanatic, whereas in reality he became one of the most popular and successful protagonists in the Italian socialist movement. Furthermore, Balabanoff's account carefully avoids any reference to their sexual relations. We've already seen that the fact that this intellectual from the Ukraine was no beauty and was five years older than him was not important for Mussolini; beauty was not an essential criterion in his choice of sexual partners. His wife Rachele writes:

"He never denied that he was attracted to women, with one misgiving which one day he revealed to me: 'You will always be the only beautiful woman in my life, because beauty is untrustworthy – it can make even the wisest man lose his head'"[10] – only an apparently kind remark, it shows considerable cynicism to have made it to the wife he betrayed so frequently. Yet while it's true that beautiful women were ready to go to bed with him – or on occasion get down on the carpet in his office in Palazzo Venezia – throughout his life, it is also the case that he did not put much store on female beauty when he chose a woman. In Switzerland he was shabbily dressed, and Balabanoff got him to wear good clothes; his reading was disorganized, so she told him which books and journals to look at; he was without a guide, so she became the muse or mentor who inspired him. In her hands, this fiery political agitator, known for his revolutionary drive, started to learn the art of politics. Yet Balabanoff doesn't make clear why, out of all the socialists she knew, she chose to follow and support Mussolini and why for over ten years she spent so much energy and time concentrating on a man she describes as shallow:

> Mussolini has never had a personality of his own, just as he's never had an original idea. He was extremely skilful at adopting the ideas of others and showing them off as if he'd thought of them first. He found it easy to do this, because he didn't have any deep-rooted convictions, he never studied anything properly but only superficially in order to acquire a smattering, plagiarizing others; he was capable of changing principles from one side to the opposed one, at the drop of a hat, completely unbothered. When he associated with our group he always needed encouragement, control, some kind of brake if he was going to stick to the point.[11]

Thus Balabanoff's account, her historical testimony, is permeated with her scorn for the man, tantamount to a refusal to make the important contribution she could have provided to our critical understanding of Mussolini as a socialist. Edvige's description of the numerous letters she received from her brother while he was in Switzerland reveal his accounts of the women he met while he was there – women full of political commitment, exiled and in flight from their native countries, all of whom his sister back in Dovia liked to imagine were beautiful, bold and intelligent. One phrase on Balabanoff stands out in this voluminous correspondence; it was probably written after one of the couple's heated discussions, and contains a crude sexual reference as well as a severe judgement on his partner's intellectual stature: "She knows and understands a lot of things; she's read all the Marxist texts. But while her body is full of juice, her mind is full of dried-up ideas."[12]

One of Mussolini's projects was to enrol at the University of Geneva, perhaps in order to be nearer to Eleonora or because his new relationship with Angelica Balabanoff had encouraged him in this direction; it's also possible he had nursed the ambition for a long while. But his passport had expired in 1903, and without a current one he wasn't allowed to register; the Italian Embassy wouldn't renew his passport because he had been called up to do his compulsory military service back in Italy. He decided to take a risk by falsifying his passport, overwriting the date 1903 with 1905, but the device was too crude to deceive the Swiss police. He was arrested for the third time on 9th April 1904 and sent first to prison in Geneva and then to Lucerne, followed by a new order for his expulsion from the country. This time if he had been taken back to the Italian border under police escort he wouldn't have found it so easy to turn round and come back in, since a military tribunal in Bologna had condemned him to a year's imprisonment as a deserter for not responding to the call-up; he would go straight from a Swiss prison to an Italian one. But the fact he was now a well-known figure started to impede the Swiss bureaucratic process. The Swiss socialists rallied to his cause; the press started to follow his case; a radical member of parliament presented a petition in his favour to the cantonal council in Ticino. Some ingenious lawyer found the right loophole: technically Mussolini's expulsion was from the canton of Geneva. The decree just had to be followed to the letter and the case would be solved. After holding him twelve days in prison, guards accompanied him to the station of Bellinzona in Ticino and left him there, a free man. Despite being banned from the city, he managed to get back to Geneva on a secret visit to see Eleonora H., who was preparing to return to Russia: "She left at the beginning of August, accompanied by her faithful servant Sirotonina. She stopped one night in Lausanne and we left Lausanne together. We said goodbye to each other in Zurich. I never saw her again."[13]

But, under Balabanoff's guidance, Mussolini's life and political career had taken off in such a way that Eleonora's departure meant little to him. His arrest, far from leading to a crisis, had been personally advantageous for him. Once freed from prison, he enrolled at the faculty of social sciences on 9th May. He followed the course given by Vilfredo Pareto, the professor of political economy; it was Pareto who introduced him to the works of Georges Sorel. Together with Balabanoff he translated a book by Karl Kautsky for the *Avanguardia socialista*, for which he wrote from time to time. Much later, when he was Duce, in his interview with Ludwig, he said that his period in Switzerland had coincided with that time of life when, despite the ups and downs of enthusiasm and discouragement, a man remains a rebel at heart. However, when Ludwig sent him the proofs of the interview to correct, the last phrase – about being a rebel – was deleted; Ludwig only managed to publish the full text of his interview in a critical edition that appeared after the war. "My years in the Salesian boarding school had depressed me; I'd grown up feeling disinherited, longing for revolution. What else could I have become if not a radical socialist, a disciple of Blanqui, almost a communist? I carried a portrait medallion of Marx around with me like some kind of talisman." "What would your reaction be today on seeing such a portrait?" Ludwig asked. "Marx was a great spirit of enlightenment, even in part a prophet," came the reply. "But in Switzerland I didn't have much opportunity to talk about these things. Among my fellow labourers I was the most educated, but I had to work the whole day, carrying hods of bricks from one storey to another a hundred times a day in building the chocolate factory in Orbe."[14]

In the autobiography he published for an English-speaking readership – which was written in reality by his brother Arnaldo – Mussolini tries to present himself as a kind of student worker for whom the intellectual exercise of Pareto's lessons was "refreshment after manual labour". According to this version of his life – serialized in instalments in the Philadelphia *Saturday Evening Post* – the pleasure he took in this "refreshment" soon transformed itself into a passion for the social sciences. And it is true that although he started off life in Switzerland as a manual labourer working on building sites, he ended up spending much time in the university library, working on his not inconsiderable intellectual contributions as a writer for various journals and newspapers, but above all engaged in intense and at times almost chaotic political activity with his participation in many conferences and meetings. There are also obscure periods which elude us: one of these is worth mentioning, a hypothetical clandestine visit to Paris, undertaken when he was living in Anne-masse. No documentary evidence exists for such a trip; De Felice believes it was just one of the many projects Mussolini had in mind and never carried out. Yet that very curious personality Maria Rygier fiercely accused Mussolini more than once of having become a spy for the French police during his secret visit to Paris. Rygier was the daughter of a devoutly Catholic Polish sculptor. She'd been born in Cracow but after the death of her mother moved to Rome, where she was educated in a convent school. She broke off relations with her father and started to frequent socialist circles; when in Switzerland she had come to know both Angelica Balabanoff and Mussolini. Fiery in temperament, a brilliant speaker and indefatigable organizer, she spoke several languages fluently, contributed to various journals and newspapers, and, naturally enough, was recorded in police dossiers all over Europe. Her personal career is hard to trace; however, it's known that she managed to join the Freemasons and helped to establish a lodge – the Gran Loggia Mista d'Italia – of which the Grand Master was one Enrico Cesarò of Caserta. The admission of a woman to a Freemasons' lodge in Italy at that time can't have led to many opportunities for her: she moved to France and became a member of the Epopis Lodge in Paris. An essay in French by her was published with an introduction by Lucien Le Foyer, the Honor-ary Grand Master of the Grand Lodge of France. "She was given documents by a fellow Freemason Maurice Monier from the Sûreté Générale, which are supposed to have shown that the young Mussolini worked as a spy in 1903–4 in the pay of the French police, report-ing back to them on several of his socialist comrades."[15] Unlikely as it seems that a Freemason – and a Grand Master to boot – would speak of secret police files with a woman who had only just joined the lodge and had a background of revolutionary militancy in the socialist cause, one cannot exclude the possibility that Rygier had got caught up in some complex network of espionage. The various circles of political exiles at the beginning of the twentieth century lived surrounded by informers, infiltrators and traitors; it was an atmosphere which can even today still make the news. In February 2009 several press agencies carried the news of the publication of a book by a former officer in Soviet intelligence, Colonel Igor Ata-manenko, called *What the Lubyanka Never Revealed*. Atamanenko's books provide no documentary evidence and are controversial, but it is worth noting that, in an interview with the author in the Russian newspaper *Komsomolskaya Pravda*, he asserts that Mussolini worked as a secret agent for the Tsar. An agent working for the Tsarist secret services – the homosexual Ivan Manasevich-Manuilov – was said to be working undercover as a journalist in Paris in 1902; he later moved to Rome as the ostensible head of Russian religious affairs in the Vatican. Behind this new identity and spending freely the funds the Tsarist police provided him with, Manasevich-Manuilov became friends with many Italian socialists, including Mussolini, who is said to have written reports for the Tsarist intelligence services – reports which later fell into the hands of the Communists. As it stands, there are far too many "ifs" in Atamanenko's story; without documentary evidence it is worthless. But it is interesting to see how, even a hundred years after the purported events, such story can still make the news (and earn money for opportunistic publishers). There is on the other hand much official evidence of the surveillance carried out by the police in several European countries: the Swiss kept dossiers on all the leading personalities among the expatriate communities, the French recorded every movement or period of residence on their territories, while the Italians too checked up on not only their own political agitators but also foreigners, as the official reports on the journeys in Italy of Lenin, Trotsky and other revolutionaries show.

Mussolini tells us that, with his inner restlessness, he was planning a new departure. He had in fact decided to leave Switzerland for the United States, when an event occurred which made him change his plans and go in the opposite direction, back to Italy rather than across the Atlantic. On 15th September 1904 a son – his first – was born to Victor Emanuel III at Racconigi: Umberto Nicola Tommaso Giovanni Maria di Savoia. The birth of an heir to the Italian throne was celebrated all over the country. As was the custom, an amnesty was declared to mark the event, which also included those who had been found guilty of desertion. Mussolini's sentence had been annulled: all he had to do was complete his military service. He decided to go back to Italy.

Chapter 5

Teacher, Soldier and Journalist

The blow was completely unexpected, out of the blue, while she was daydreaming at her desk in the classroom of the primary school in Dovia. The ruler hit her hand, the fingers; she gave a start and felt an intolerable stinging. The teacher was staring at her intensely, as if he wanted to turn her to dust, and he still had the ruler raised menacingly. Rachele couldn't think why she had been punished – or indeed even what she'd been thinking of just a moment before. In her childish daydreaming she'd not been aware she was scratching the wooden desk with an old nail she'd found on the pavement. Her angelic appearance – golden curls and blue eyes – was misleading: she loved running through the fields and climbing trees – she was always on the move or wanting to be, wanting to do something, anything except sit and attend to the lesson. She led a little gang of girls; she was more beautiful than her sisters, even Augusta and Pina. She lifted her hand to her mouth without looking at the teacher; she knew that if she raised her face to look at him it would have seemed like a challenge. Actually he was not her real teacher and not even a real supply teacher. Their usual teacher – Mrs Rosa – was ill, and since it didn't look as if she'd be able to come back soon, her son, Benito, just qualified, had been appointed to replace her. All the children feared him, particularly his furious eyes, which seemed to make the blows of his ruler even more painful. This was how Rachele met her future husband, the man who was to become the Duce: "Eighty years on, I don't feel the pain, but I remember how painful it was. I was crying and was angry and brought my hand to my mouth, and at that moment was struck dumb by his eyes, large, black, penetrating, so that I suddenly calmed down without even hearing what the teacher was saying to me. [...] Later I thought that only one word could describe those eyes of his: phosphorescent."[1]

Mussolini hadn't especially noticed the little fair-haired girl and he didn't remember smacking her with the ruler. She was just one of his pupils, and he often handed out blows. Once the unexpected period of supply-teaching was over. Rachele too lost sight of him, even though she admitted she heard the name Mussolini mentioned frequently, and always as if there were something special about it – but this was Alessandro, renowned in the region for his political battles as a socialist.

On his journey back from Switzerland, on 14th November 1904, Mussolini met his brother Arnaldo in Bern. On the 15th and 16th he stopped in Lugano, where he made contact with Angelica Balabanoff and Maria Giudice. During his stay in Switzerland he also worked on some translations, including Pyotr Kropotkin's *Words of a Rebel* and *On the Day after the Social Revolution* by Karl Kautsky. He finally reached Dovia where he found his parents considerably aged and oppressed. His mother's health was once again failing. His father was no longer the sturdy oak of revolutionary Internationalism: his spell in prison had broken him, and the pardon when it eventually came after months in the cells hadn't restored his former energy. Mussolini tried to help him out in the smithy, as well as doing the things his mother used to do, but his military service was about to begin. The officers of the regiment to which he had been drafted were alerted: a militant socialist was about to arrive, for the next two years among their ranks they would have the son of a notorious and dangerous rabble-rouser. Their instructions were to keep a close eye on this potential subversive, whom the King of Italy in his goodness had seen fit to pardon, even though he was guilty of desertion.

The political situation in the country remained tense, with troops sent by the government to put down demonstrations and strikes. The soldiers didn't hesitate to use gunfire. At Buggerru, in Sardinia, three striking miners had been killed and twenty wounded on 4th September 1904, while in Castelluzzo, near Trapani in Sicily, there were two dead and ten wounded on 14th September. In this kind of civil war, no officer wanted a subversive among his men who might seize the opportunity to support the strikers.

Revolutionary syndicalists, followers of Georges Sorel and his theories, were in a majority in the Italian Socialist Party. They believed in action. On 16th September the Chamber of Labour in Milan had announced the first great general strike in Italian history, which in less than a week had spread from Turin to Parma, and then down to Rome and the remote countryside of Apulia. The success of the strike – with its mass support from agricultural labourers and factory workers all over the country – was still vivid when Benito Mussolini reported to the military district of Forlì on 31st December 1904 as a conscript (class 1). "Postponed call-up of conscripts born 1883" was the category invented in the amnesty to get round the condemnation for desertion. On 8th January 1905 Mussolini joined the 10th Regiment of Bersaglieri in Verona, to which he had been assigned. Thus he found himself on the other side of the barricades, serving the powers he had been opposing every day, among those soldiers who were sent out more often to fight labourers in the countryside than foreign enemies on the border. The officers kept a close eye on the revolutionaries among the conscripts, wishing to prevent any attempt on their part to preach to their fellows and recruit them to their cause. Mussolini was just one among many revolutionaries being forced to do their military service. He was known to be anti-military, like all the other local socialist leaders in his district. The physical energy he had displayed in his political battles didn't distinguish him in the army, where such energy was to be found in many of his companions. The officers of the 10th Regiment noted with surprise that the new arrival turned out to be calm, thoughtful and self-disciplined; there was no sign that he intended to pursue his subversive politics in the midst of the Bersaglieri. Mussolini discovered he enjoyed military life, as he himself tells us in his letters and other writings:

...and then I joined the regiment – a Bersaglieri regiment at the historic city of Verona. The Bersaglieri wear green cock feathers in their hats; they are famous for their fast pace, a kind of monotonous and ground-covering dog trot, and for their discipline and spirit. I liked the life of a soldier. The sense of willing subordination suited my temperament. I was preceded by a reputation of being restless, a fire-eater, a radical, a revolutionist. Consider then the astonishment of the captain, the major and my colonels who were compelled to speak of me with praise![2]

Here is the first image to contrast with that of the fiery and wholly committed revolutionary which Mussolini had constructed for himself before. But when we analyse his period of military service, we must remember that it opened with a family bereavement just a month after he had started it. "Mother extremely ill. Come immediately." When he received this telegram from his brother, Mussolini asked for permission to take leave. His mother had been seriously ill the year before but she had recovered, apparently cured. The return of the illness was rapid: she died within a week, at the age of forty-six, on 19th February 1905. The event cast a shadow over the entire year, as Mussolini records in *Vita di Arnaldo*: "I was a soldier in Verona: I returned just in time to see her, but perhaps she did not recognize me."[3]

His mourning for his mother did not stop his womanizing; his return home for the event even presented him with a new opportunity. A young primary-school teacher from Forlì, a friend of Edvige, came over to share the family's mourning; her name was Paolina Danti. "We gradually became friends and then our friendship turned into love. Our intense love affair continued when I returned to Verona to continue my military service."[4]

Edvige in her memoirs conceals the surname of another woman who became involved with her brother: a certain Giovanna P., the daughter of wealthy landowners who lived near Predappio. She wrote that both Paolina and Giovanna "were charming and intelligent. They confided in me, sometimes they cried, sometimes they complained about my brother and the hand fate had dealt them. Contrasts of social class and ideas embittered Benito Mussolini's early love affairs, but this also shows how politics even then was shaping his character."[5]

On occasion the parents of the young women he had seduced stepped in, with brisk determination; they would carry their daughter back home, putting a firm stop to any hopes of marriage with an unruly and notorious young man. But even as they departed, Mussolini's attention would be attracted elsewhere. Many times Edvige had to break the family piggy bank to fund her brother so he could buy soft drinks for the girlfriend of the moment; he had a passionate need, she wrote, "to have some young woman – or several – next to him, to look in their eyes, to see those eyes fill with tenderness for him, to hold them in his arms at country barn dances, to show off, when carnival time with its parties came round, with the most beautiful girls who'd come eagerly to enjoy the dancing and in the hope of finding a lover".[6]

Edvige believed her brother was ready to marry the girls he desired; he seemed to want it so convincingly that all of them, more or less, fell for it. Then he'd immediately be attracted to another, leaving the first to cry and complain in an atmosphere of tragedy. But his period of military service was a lot less romantic than Edvige paints it; she didn't know his remarks to Claretta Petacci on 4th March 1938: "I have a vague memory of falling in love when I was about twenty – like a poet, with pure longing. It was when I started my military service that my instincts were aroused. I used to go to a brothel where the women were experienced and rather dirty; they initiated me into the mysteries and vices of sex. From then on I've always regarded the women I've had like those in the brothel: there just for my carnal pleasure."[7]

While he was on leave because of the bereavement, Mussolini received a letter from a friend urging him to try and recruit his fellow soldiers to the revolutionary cause. He wrote a measured reply in return explaining why he wouldn't do this: he was going through a difficult period, with many moral and material worries, and needed tranquillity and silence. But he also showed his adroitness – he knew the friend would show his letter to his fellow socialists – by justifying his attitude politically: he agreed entirely with the fundamental principles and ideas in his friend's letter, but the plan of action seemed to him too vague; besides, radicalism was still weak among soldiers and officers. In any case, just so that all should know, he was ready to use his rifle whenever the Italian people rose up in rebellion. A letter to his commanding officer is completely different. In the letter to his socialist friend, while refusing his request to proselytize among the soldiers, he still leaves his options open for future political activity. In the other he reveals an unexpected nationalism in order to ingratiate himself with the officer. He writes that the heroes who had built Italy and the blood they had shed for the dignity of the nation must be commemorated; their blood held the nation together and in the name of their sacrifice Italians must stand firm, their bodies in massed ranks, against the barbarians of the north. Italians must show no cowardice in defending their heritage against those who wished once more to reduce their country to a mere "geographical expression". Such words coming from him would have astonished any militant Internationalist, first and foremost his own father Alessandro. Mussolini's opportunism and self-contradiction begin to emerge, as well as his capacity for rapid tactical U-turns. Yet it is probably also true that his mother's death had indeed instilled in him a need for tranquillity and reflection during which he began to see military life in a different light. In his autobiography in English, he described what he'd got out of his period of military service:

> It was my opportunity to show serenity of spirit and strength of character. [...] I found an affectionate regard for the mass, for the whole, made up of individuals, for its manoeuvres and the tactics, the practice of defence and attack. [...] I learnt in that way how important it is for an officer to have a deep knowledge of military matters and to develop a fine sensitiveness to the ranks, and to appreciate in the masses of our men our stern Latin sense of discipline and to be susceptible to its enchantments. I can say that in every regard I was an excellent soldier.[8]

There is certainly cynical opportunism in the way Mussolini ingratiates himself with his commanding officer, yet it is true that his military service brought out a new aspect of him, different from the socialist agitator. It is an important period in his life which should not be dismissed as irrelevant. In the autobiography in English, published when he had already become Duce, Mussolini attributed to himself in hindsight a new sensibility towards the ferment taking place as masses of young men from all over Italy served their time in the army. According to this account written over twenty years later, military service showed him those masses organized according to military discipline – which was to become a fundamental feature of the stage-setting of the Fascist regime. As the nineteenth century gave way to the twentieth, the Italian army was changing. Mass conscription, officers who came from all over the country, men from a wide variety of backgrounds and professions in civilian life, different languages and dialects heard in the dormitories: the old Piedmontese army was disappearing, the kingdom of Italy was building modern armed forces to undertake new types of war. Shepherds from Sardinia and the Abruzzi, agricultural labourers from Apulia and Romagna, factory workers from Genoa and Milan – all were beginning to learn to see themselves as members of one nation. Wearing the same uniform, they found a way of living together during their military service and discovered appreciatively that they could communicate with each other; they returned to their homes with this new experience of life. It was an attempt to "make Italians", that sense of belonging to a single nation which the Risorgimento had not been able to create. One manifestation of the transformation that was taking place was the reaction to the earthquake in Messina and Reggio Calabria which occurred two years after Mussolini's military service, in 1908, the greatest natural disaster to befall Italy in the twentieth century. The new Italian army was called in to help: the soldiers were sent to dig people out from the ruins, to ward off jackals and wolves, to assist the survivors. With the eyes of the world's press on them, Italians had to show they existed as a nation, as a single people. The newspapers wrote of "a nation in mourning" and those who had died in the earthquake were commemorated as Italians. All over the country there were queues to leave money for the survivors in urns wrapped in the Italian flag. A collective wave of grief ran through the entire nation for the first time, as John Dickie has written, and the army and the navy played a central role in the events. The writer Edoardo Scarfoglio was sent by *Il Mattino* newspaper of Naples to report; he wrote on 9th January 1909: "We should see the catastrophe as the episode of a war which could have broken out yesterday or could break out tomorrow – and we should allow ourselves to be perturbed by this thought." When that war did arrive, in the development of his political career Mussolini would be able to call on this experience of military service to understand the unextinguished force of nationalism as well as the social and political potential of those militarized masses, of all the men who had entered the army.

"Has distinguished himself for ability, enthusiasm and good conduct": this was the report on Mussolini – unexpected for a revolutionary and anti-militarist – when he finished his military service on 4th September 1906. On returning home, he sent off, with new self-confidence, numerous applications for supply-teaching posts all over the country. The local council of Tolmezzo, in the province of Udine, replied; it was run by the Italian Socialist Party, and his father's name still had a cachet. The soldier commended for his conduct slipped back into the role of an undisciplined, anarchic subversive. The suddenness of the transformation is striking: enthusiasm and self-discipline vanish, to be replaced by disordered revelry with regular bouts of drunkenness in the company of his friend the local cobbler. He often spent the night stretched out senseless on the ground. The biographers Duilio Susmel and Giorgio Pini write that he fell ill at this time with gonorrhoea or – in barracks slang – "*scolo*" ("the clap"). Together with the syphilis which Angelica Balabanoff claims he told her he had contracted, he was clearly paying a price for his exploration of the mysteries of sex, in fetid brothels or more fragrant ambiences as the case may have been. But it doesn't appear his illness was serious enough to stop his sexual activity for long. In her book Balabanoff takes her revenge – or attempts to – for the years she spent in her tormented relationship with Mussolini when he continually ran after women in the name of free love. She recounts an episode from his time in Bellinzona:

> One day, at a loose end – the early trains had all gone and there wasn't another one I could catch till later – I was alone in the office. I felt tired and was leafing through newspapers. Suddenly Mussolini burst in. He was distraught, almost wild, with his eyes bursting out of his head. "Tell me," he declared, "tell me why women don't fall in love with me." I looked at him in amazement, but also somewhat amused as well as puzzled. It was a bit awkward to know how to reply to him. But in any case he didn't wait for an answer; with his eyes staring even more madly, he went on: "Am I so ugly?" I could easily think of an evasive reply to that and did: "Well, as far as being ugly is concerned, there's Turati who's much, much uglier than you, and yet lots of women have always fallen for him." [...] "So how come I never find anyone, like all the others find someone?" There was in his eyes a kind of hunger, very different and much more desperate than the hunger which drove him to the Lugano-Paradiso restaurant. "How should I know?" I didn't have the courage nor, I confess, the wish and the heartlessness to tell him the truth. For it was true, no girl fell in love with Mussolini. He was that rare sort of man – at least when he was young and penniless – who was just incapable of being attractive to women – indeed he almost repelled them."[9]

The local branch of the Socialist Party in Tolmezzo had been certain the candidate they had chosen to be the village schoolmaster was the respectable son of a prominent leader; instead they found themselves having to deal with someone who seemed as devoid of good qualities as he was dedicated to vice, who was embarrassing, unkempt and almost never came to their meetings. Among the rare occasions on which he took part in events organized by the Socialist Party in Tolmezzo, the anniversary to mark the three-hundredth anniversary of the death of Giordano Bruno stands out: Mussolini's speech so excited the anticlerical passions of the audience that they trooped out of the hall to go and protest in front of the local priest's house.

It was while he was in Tolmezzo that he realized he was not cut out to be a schoolteacher; his period there merely served as an outlet for the energies he had had to repress while doing his military service.

Under the name "Vero Eretico" ("A True Heretic") he wrote an entire issue of the local anticlerical newspaper *Lo staffile* (*The Whip*), much to the consternation of many families whose children he taught every day in school. He was also immediately on the lookout for women who might fall into his net. "I discovered that Virginia Salvolini was living in Osoppo and Paolina Danti was in Resia, so I got in touch with them again. We exchanged many letters."[10] If his drunkenness and general indiscipline had shocked the local community when he first arrived, it was one of his relationships which really disconcerted them and caused embarrassment for the Socialist Party-controlled council: "During the carnival holiday I had a fling with one Graziosa Bocca, whom I then left for the woman who ran the local inn, Luigia P., a woman in her thirties and still attractive despite many adventures in the past. We saw each other frequently from April through to August. Her husband didn't like it, of course, but the poor wretch didn't know what to do about it."[11] At first her husband demanded an explanation from this intrusive schoolteacher – who also happened to be a lodger in his inn. Mussolini's replies were evasive and he also caught his wife on many occasions going into or coming out of the lodger's room: rows ensued and rumours started to circulate in Tolmezzo. Luigia's cuckolded husband grew more and more unhappy with her increasingly brazen relationship and began to attack Mussolini physically, resulting in a fight between them in which the younger and stronger of the two – Mussolini – won. He and Luigia continued to have sex together. Accounts of her from those who knew her describe her as good-looking, blonde, with a strong sensual physique. Her full name was Luigia Pajetta Nigris, but she was usually called Gigia. A son was born in 1907 from her affair with Mussolini: Candido Nigris. Mussolini denied the boy was his and refused to acknowledge his existence; he carried on his dissolute way of life, drinking and blaspheming. Thirty years later, when he was beginning to feel old, tired and much less confident in his ability to perform sexually, but also wanted to put his relationship with the young Claretta Petacci on a firm footing, he told her, no doubt hoping to impress her:

I must admit I now regret wasting my energies on all the women I slept with. How many of them there were! Too many. I wasted time and energy on women who were probably not worth the trouble. I should just have had a single woman I loved and dedicated all that side of my life to her. Perhaps in that case I'd never have known you, but now that I do, the idea of all those other women just disgusts me. They were all like prostitutes – they gave themselves to me like prostitutes and I had them. I don't really remember a single one of them, or only trivial things. [...] In Tolmezzo all the women went crazy for me. I had one who was called Graziosa [Bocca] and another whose name I can't remember but who was really jealous...[12]

Mussolini had the clarity of mind to try to take stock of his situation and his behaviour. He guessed that it would be pointless to apply for a renewal of his teaching post; the council in Tolmezzo would never have agreed. When Margherita Sarfatti started work on her biography of Mussolini – *Dux* – she realized it would be difficult to write about this period in his life: his behaviour had been so way-ward and scandalous that a truthful account would have opened up a large black hole in the radiant image of the man she was trying to fabricate. So she set to work to transform the facts, turning his time in Tolmezzo into a positive interlude, showing Mussolini's genius and unconventionality. The anarchic, undisciplined schoolteacher was turned into a figure "the locals would not forget in a hurry"; his nightly bouts of drinking and all the disturbances they caused became "practical jokes, like dressing up in sheets as ghosts in the old castle to frighten those who were still about late in the evening or wandering round the local graveyard crying out in a sepulchral voice 'At last, O my tomb, I embrace you!' and then sinking down to sleep the night away there."[13]

His pupils in the school remembered him as "the Tyrant" but in Sarfatti's account his whole class adored him despite his glaring looks, his shouts and the way he would thump his desk in anger. Their parents had protested and formally accused him of blasphemy, but Sarfatti dismisses them as "prudes" and says the headmaster paid no attention to them, because he had ascertained that it did not involve real blasphemy: "While it may be true that the school-teacher Signor Benito Mussolini's language is somewhat excessive on occasion, he never takes God's name in vain but only Buddha's or Muhammad's."[14]

Sarfatti swiftly glosses over Mussolini's sexual excesses and the scandal they caused: "The young girls of the region came to appreciate him; they are known for their beauty and kindness; towards Mussolini they were especially kind."[15] And if their kindness led them to become rather more involved with the young thrusting schoolteacher than they should have done, then, never mind, they could boast in later years that they'd had the country's Fascist leader in their bed and perhaps provided sons for the new Italian race. There's a maliciously veiled phrase which refers clearly to the son – Candido – Luigia Nigris gave birth to during her affair with Mussolini: "In those regions of Friuli today, there is a young man, coming up to his twentieth birthday, who doesn't look like a typical native of those parts."[16] Sarfatti had a long-lasting relationship with Mussolini and must have heard directly from him all the details of that period of his life: "In the midst of all his wild joking and revelry, the scholar and politician in him found the time to study and to work with seriousness, without giving himself airs. He took lessons in Latin and Greek from a local clergyman, the erudite Monsignor Condotti; he gave lectures and organized political meetings."[17] As far as his public speaking abilities are concerned, we know that Mussolini had learnt his skills from his earliest years at the knee of one of the acknowledged orators of the time: his own father, who had taught him how to use words, pauses and gestures to arouse the public, win over the hecklers, wound one's opponents. Having been brought up in such a school, public speaking came easily and successfully to him. Balabanoff, however, is dismissive of his abilities – but she is intent on preventing any close analysis of their relationship, on concealing its underlying aspect, as well as on destroying any idea that Mussolini's political origins lay in the world of socialism; she writes:

At that time – it was one of the fruits of the freedom of speech which had been achieved – there were agricultural and factory workers who were capable of speaking well and forcefully in public. [...] Mussolini was one of them: whenever he spoke to a crowd about their poverty and their rights to justice, he was always warmly applauded, like many others. But because he lacked confidence and also liked to show off, he used to imitate – as he also does in his writing – non-Italians, using short detached phrases. His listeners didn't realize he was imitating or paraphrasing others; they thought him genuinely original.[18]

Dismissed by the school in Tolmezzo, his departure accompanied by hearty sighs of relief from the local Socialist Party, Mussolini returned to Dovia, where he found his father no longer the people's leader of Romagna legend. The stories of his former deeds still circulated, but the man himself had lost his vigour after a spell in prison and the death of his wife. Perhaps he was already pondering a change of life, of giving up the blacksmith's trade and opening an inn, but the decision to change course must have seemed daunting for a man who was tired and disappointed. His son decided to try other possibilities of employment and started taking French lessons from a Miss Mercuri in Forlì. She must have been a good teacher and Mussolini must have applied himself, because in November 1907 he passed the exam to become a secondary-school teacher of French. He sent off a flood of applications and waited several months before getting a reply. While waiting he didn't lose any time in his private life: "Between September and October I got to know and had an affair (not a very deep one) with Signorina Giovannina P. from Fiumana."[19] But the fling can't have satisfied him, since as soon as the opportunity arose he returned to Tolmezzo and the scene of his passionate affair with the innkeeper (and the fights with her husband): "I arrived about ten in the evening, wrapped up in a heavy cloak and with a fur hat pulled down over my eyes, and knocked at the door of the trattoria 'della Scala'. Luigia came to open: she looked me in the eyes and recognized me. She seemed quite overcome with surprise. We went up the familiar stairs and into the small room where I used to take my meals [...] and her husband? He was asleep. I took my fill of her. We spent some delicious hours together."[20]

After all the letters he'd sent off applying for positions, a reply finally arrived in March 1908 from the Socialist Party-controlled council of Oneglia, in Liguria. The Catholic college Ulisse Calvi offered him the post of French teacher in the private technical school which was attached to the institution. On his arrival in the town, he turned once more to Giacinto Menotti Serrati for help: Serrati had two brothers in Oneglia, Manlio and Lucio, who were both prominent socialists and he introduced Mussolini to them. Thanks to his name and the people who backed him, he started to write for the local Socialist Party weekly newspaper *La lima* (*The File*). Articles brimming with a fierce anticlericalism started to appear, once more signed "Vero Eretico" ("A True Heretic"). Everyone knew who the real author was; the local Church authorities put pressure on the college to have Mussolini removed from the staff, but their request was always refused. He was an excellent teacher, and to dismiss him without notice was out of the question. Apart from anything else, it wouldn't be easy to find a replacement so near to the end of the school year. Mussolini started to feel at home: "I took a liking to the people of Oneglia. A young girl, Giovannina A., had also fallen in love with me."[21]

His period in Oneglia was his last as a teacher and it closed a chapter in his life. Cesare Rossi, who was a friend of Mussolini's and his aide-de-camp until the assassination of Matteotti, sums up his time there in these words: "A small-time socialist primary-school teacher from Romagna who came not so much to impart crumbs of knowledge to the little working-class children in a rural school as to devote his time to the pursuits of drinking and dancing in the local inns and dance halls. [...] Mussolini the teacher, Mussolini the part-time journalist, Mussolini the orator in his shirtsleeves, and from time to time, as necessity dictated, Mussolini the proletarian."[22]

In the summer of 1908, a time of greater than usual social unrest in the country, Mussolini returned to Dovia. That year had begun badly for the Italian Socialist Party. One of their deputies in parliament had presented a motion for the abolition of catechism classes in state schools, provoking a large wave of opposition, so large that the motion was defeated by 347 votes to sixty. But this crushing parliamentary defeat had other serious repercussions. Those members of parliament who were Freemasons had been instructed by the organization, whatever lodge they belonged to, to vote in favour of Leonida Bissolati's motion, but many of them angrily refused to toe the line, arguing that precisely because they were Freemasons they were free to vote as they decided. The Grand Master was furious and demanded an internal disciplinary hearing before which the rebels should appear. The deputies who had disobeyed the instruction were however for the most part very high-ranking in the organization and could be judged only by their peers. They were absolved – or rather their peers decided not to proceed against them. This led to a split in Italian Freemasonry into two schools or so-called "obediences" – a rift which, far from healing over the course of the last century, has deepened.

1908 should also have been a significant year for Italian women, who had kept up with the international suffragette movement (almost all

Italian newspapers had adopted the English term as a mark of their scorn for the idea). A Women's Congress had been called with delegates attending from all over the country. The Queen herself, Elena, had agreed to be present. Socialist women were warier, however, and Anna Kuliscioff refused to attend – a prudent decision as it turned out since the congress was doomed: from the discussion on teaching religion in schools, it was clear that it was deeply divided. At the end of the conference the Catholic women leaders chose to set up their own independent organization. The presence of the Queen was significant: Elena wanted to encourage the emergence of new roles for Italian women and later in the year played an important part in the aftermath of the Messina earthquake. She went straight to the earthquake zone, worked as a nurse, providing a model of how women could make a contribution in disasters to the care of the wounded.

On the same day that the congress ended, revolutionary syndicalists in Parma organized a strike of agricultural labourers which rapidly spread. The government sent the army in to restore order, but the landowners decided to respond independently by recruiting teams of thugs, arming them and unleashing them on the strikers. When Mussolini arrived back home on 2nd July 1908, clashes were still taking place in the countryside round Predappio. The labourers had resisted and the strike continued, even though the strikers, under attack from the landowners' vigilante troops and the army, were gradually giving way. After weeks of violence, the landowners' victory was complete; the squads they had organized to defeat the strike went on to become the nuclei of the first Fascist squads. At this time Mussolini still supported the strikers in their cause. "That summer the whole of Romagna was in turmoil largely due to the fierce conflict between the share-croppers and the labourers. Naturally my brother sided immediately and with his usual vehemence with the workers; he attacked the whole system of land ownership in Romagna as feudal..."[23]

Mussolini took part in the clashes on the side of the labourers and wrote reports which also got published in the Socialist Party daily *Avanti!*. This is from an article in the issue for 14th July: "Once they were on the road your correspondent managed to gather together the crowd with a few words. The government representative declared he was contravening the law and threatened to arrest him. While the labourers prepared to return to their homes, the cavalry violently charged and routed them." He described a similar incident which took place on 16th July, once again from the stance of a journalist-cum-agitator who doesn't want to observe the facts from the outside but live the experience alongside the striking labourers, frequently becoming their leader. The clash centred on the new threshing machines, loathed by the vast majority of the labourers. On 18th July there was a further incident: Mussolini threatened the owner of some of the new machines, a certain Emilio Rolli, by waving a stick in the air and shouting "I'll whack your head off", and Rolli denounced Mussolini to the police. There was an immediate trial with a severe sentence of three months' imprisonment, which was later reduced to twelve days. The whole episode worked to Mussolini's advantage, since his name was bandied about among socialist groups everywhere, although this didn't advance his political career. "Once out of prison, I took up again with Giovannina P. from Fiumana. After a few weeks I ended our relationship."[24]

In the summer of that year Alessandro Mussolini decided to open a restaurant in Forlì, in an outlying part of the town. He entered into a kind of business partnership with a widow called Annina Lombardi, who happened to be the mother of Rachele, the Duce's future wife. She was now an attractive young woman. Accounts at this time often describe her as a servant in Alessandro Mussolini's restaurant: "His father, tired of being a blacksmith, had opened a squalid tavern. Serving among the tables in this smoky eating hole out in the country was an attractive wench, coarse-mannered but inviting: Rachele. Skimming the pages of a book by Stirner, Marx or Max Nordau – the authors popular at the time – Mussolini threw lustful glances at the skivvy working for his father, and the night came when, among the stale kitchen smells, he had his domineering way with her and satisfied his insatiable lust."[25] This is the description found in a pamphlet entitled *Mussolini's Secret Life* and no doubt intended to start demolishing the myth of the dictator, especially among his working-class supporters, which circulated in Rome in the days immediately after the city's liberation, with half the country occupied by Nazis and the war still raging. It is true that Rachele had to do the lowliest and most exhausting jobs in the establishment, but while her role may have been to work as a servant her social status was somewhat different:

Business in the first weeks after the restaurant opened was good, so good that one of the daughters of Annina Lombardi – Rachele – left the family where she was employed as a domestic to come and live with us. She was no longer the little girl I had taught so many times when my mother couldn't take the class. She was a young woman in the first flush of youth and from the first moment I set eyes on her I liked her and decided to make her my wife, which I proceeded to do.[26]

Rachele's father had died leaving the family in poverty. In order to earn a living, the mother and her daughters looked for work as domestic servants or cleaners in Forlì. Rachele was taken on by a couple who ran a greengrocery. It turned out to be a terrible situation – they treated her harshly, there was little to eat, and she had to sleep on a lumpy straw mattress whose previous occupant had been a girl suffering from tuberculosis. Her circumstances improved slightly when she changed her job and moved to the family of a fencing teacher; she was able to play games – pretend duelling with wooden swords, trying to imitate the lessons she had observed – with the daughter when she wasn't working. Her final move was to work for a prosperous family in the city, the Chiadinis, where the wife treated her kindly. As a result the sixteen-year-old girl began to see the future rather more optimistically. She attracted the attention of a local youth, who followed her one day when she had to go to her employers' estate. He was on horseback, and speaking from this position – perhaps he thought it was the appropriate one in the circumstances – he declared that if the girl agreed to marry him, he would certainly be capable of making her happy. Rachele looked at him dumbfounded as he continued to speak, astride the saddle. She didn't reply but always remembered that one of the arguments the young man used with her was that she was too beautiful to remain a domestic servant. One morning in 1908 she once more met the supply teacher with the penetrating eyes: "It was a Sunday morning – I was coming out of church together with my employers' daughter when I heard someone calling my name. It was Benito Mussolini, sporting a moustache and goatee, wearing a worn black suit and a bow tie and a hat – also black – set square on his head. His pockets were bulging with rolled-up newspapers. But it was his eyes which struck me above all – they seemed even larger and more ablaze than the last time I'd seen them…"[27]

In the meantime her mother was helping to run the Bersagliere inn, where she'd become to all effects and purposes Alessandro

Mussolini's second wife. She was tall, thin and bony, with huge eyes – from Rachele's description of her it's clear who her granddaughter Edda took after in looks. Benito asked Rachele to come and visit them, in the hope he could meet her again. Rachele was still under the age of majority and needed permission from her employer's wife to go out, but Signora Chiadini had expressly forbidden her to go near the inn, which she regarded as a den of radicals (Rachele had also overheard her mention Benito Mussolini's various arrests with satisfaction). But she insisted and eventually, on Sunday, was given leave to go out on her own. She ran immediately to the tavern. "I spent the whole morning there and ate with them. I helped my mother serve the customers. In the afternoon Benito and I went dancing – like everyone from Romagna we loved dancing. To my surprise he turned out to be a very experienced dancer: he clasped me round the waist and spun me round in waltzes, mazurkas, polkas!"[28]

Mussolini's version of his meeting with Rachele is very different. He was at first more interested in one of her sisters, Augusta, who turned him down because she wanted a respectable husband with a fixed job. Only then did his attentions turn to her younger sibling, Rachele. Many years later he spoke contemptuously of her to Claretta Petacci, though perhaps it was a way of introducing Petacci to his sexual ways:

> When I finished my military service I went back to stay with my father, who was living with the woman who would be my future mother-in-law. It was four years since my poor mother had died, there'd been a lot of gossip and rumours about my father's living arrangements, but it was all very simple. The daughter Rachele was also living with them: she was blooming, buxom, with nice breasts, attractive. I followed her around, paid court to her, she pleased me. One day I got her down on an armchair and, in my usual way, roughly took her virginity.[29]

His father Alessandro had definitively retired from politics to manage the tavern, but his son and his revolutionary companions were still suffering the effects of the defeat of the labourers' strike in Parma. On the other hand, the metalworkers' strike in Turin which started on 30th May was victorious. The Congresso Nazionale Socialista (National Socialist Congress) which opened in Florence assessed the two contrasting outcomes. The reformist wing of the party, led by Filippo Turati, regained control. They also successfully ignored

Gaetano Salvemini's plea that the party should take an interest in the situation in the south of the country. Shortly before the end of the year the earthquake hit Messina, and the south's centuries-old problems re-emerged in all their force. Salvemini himself, a native of Messina, lost his entire family in the disaster and only survived because he managed to stand under a doorway arch which didn't collapse. But the strange contradictions of the South came once again to the fore some months later, during the country's general election in 1909, when the sitting government, led by Giolitti, who was not interested in the south and had never bothered to visit the earthquake zone, won an overwhelming majority in, of all places, Messina.

In December 1908, Mussolini obtained his first significant political job, in Trento, which – although part of the Tyrol, on the borders of the Austro-Hungarian Empire, and therefore outside Italy – was the focus of the Italian irredentist movement led by figures such as the socialist Cesare Battisti. Angelica Balabanoff and Giacinto Menotti Serrati used their considerable influence with the Socialist Party in the regional capital of Innsbruck, which was responsible for the appointments, to get him appointed to the secretaryship of the local Camera del Lavoro (Workers' Association) as well as the editorship of the socialist weekly *L'avvenire del lavoratore* (*The Worker's Future*). Shortly before he left, Mussolini called Rachele and told her the news: "'Listen, my little Rachele, I'm leaving for Trento in a week's time, I'm going to work for Cesare Battisti's newspaper. I'd like you to take a permanent position in the tavern before I go.' 'I'll see,' I replied. I was hurt by the news of his imminent departure."[30]

Business in the Bersagliere tavern was going well with lots of customers; extra help was needed, and instead of looking elsewhere Alessandro Mussolini decided to take Rachele and one of her sisters on – they were, after all, given his relationship with their mother, practically "family". Rachele wrote of her role in what became the family management of the tavern: "Soon all the customers wanted to be served by 'little blondie'." Alessandro was convinced his son's prestigious new job in Trento was the first step in a brilliant career in the Socialist Party which would see him become a revolutionary leader; they opened a bottle of sparkling Albano wine to celebrate and Benito played the violin, an instrument he had learnt to play passably well. He took Rachele aside towards the end of the evening and told her brusquely, not even expecting a reply, that when he came back from Trento he would marry her.

"Benito Mussolini is a committed socialist and revolutionary. I respectfully enclose a copy of the biographical details from his dossier and request that you would let me know how long he has been resident in Trento, how he comports himself and earns his living, and, if possible, his current address." On 16th February 1909 the Italian police sent the Austrian authorities the information they had on Mussolini, the better to enable the latter to keep him under observation. Just ten days before, in the middle of a heavy snowstorm, Mussolini had crossed the Italian frontier for Trento. The authorities sent back an immediate response: "Please be informed that the said Benito Mussolini is resident in Trento in Via Ravina 20, as the secretary of the Workers' Association. As for his comportment, apart from his being an active campaigner, nothing can be notified hitherto in the brief time he has been here." But, as the new arrival took to stirring up the tranquil political life of the city, the imperial authorities found they very soon did have things to notify. Mussolini targeted in particular the Catholics, especially Alcide De Gasperi, with whom he formed an enduring enmity: when he became dictator, and after the signing of the concordat with the Vatican, he made sure De Gasperi was kept under observation. He also wanted to manoeuvre himself into the circle close to Cesare Battisti, the leading socialist irredentist. He started to frequent Battisti's friends, but it was far from easy to establish relations: many of the men round Battisti were Freemasons who were distrustful of outsiders and wanted to find out more about them before they were allowed to meet the charismatic figure of the leader himself. And Mussolini filled his leisure time with his usual pursuits: "I spent some unforgettable evenings, but I won't talk about the women I knew. I had various relationships but I won't name my partners because it's all too recent."[31] He was already beginning to realize that he needed to protect himself. His excuse for not giving the women's names is feeble, since in recounting his life he had up to this period always written their names; and while he had often omitted their surnames, this wouldn't have prevented local people identifying soon enough from Mussolini's descriptions who the women were.

The identity of one woman he was seeing in Trento and passed some of those unforgettable evenings with is known: this was Fernanda Oss Facchinelli, extremely beautiful but consumptive. She was very young, separated from her husband and a fiercely committed Marxist, heavily involved in propagandizing her socialist beliefs. But Mussolini didn't meet her in some local party office or at a political meeting or demonstration; she served behind the bar of the café he usually patronized. A son was born from this relationship too, but, as before, Mussolini stuck to his principles of free love and completely ignored the existence of the child, who in any case died of consumption after only a few months. Very little is known about him but it appears he was called Benito Ribelle ("rebel"), which seems not improbable given his mother's revolutionary inclinations. Fernanda eventually died too of consumption at the age of thirty-eight, disappearing from Mussolini's life; she had never asked him for anything.

Mussolini found it easy to remain in control of his relationships with women like this, but in Trento his insatiable appetites led him to meet someone who was very different, a woman who was not prepared to be submissive but was tenacious and stubborn, and caused him many problems: Ida Irene Dalser, who gave birth to the only child of Mussolini's born out of wedlock to obtain legal recognition, an unhappy and unfortunate son called Benito Albino. Mussolini was careful to avoid any sentimental attachment which threatened to become complicated; he preferred one-night or at most one-week stands. He could, exceptionally, remain attached to some women for several months, but always and only on the basis of "free love", meaning that he was able to come and go as he pleased, without commitment. Ida Dalser refused to be reduced to such a status. She understood Mussolini's sexual tastes and was able to find ways and times to hook him in again. Their stormy, passion-driven relationship was to go far beyond the limits Mussolini had established to become at first an embarrassment and later a tragedy. But for the time being it was a question of "unforgettable evenings" and bouts of heavy drinking which served as the counterweight to his increasingly frenetic political activity.

A local priest, a committed Catholic activist, published a newspaper article in which he accused Mussolini of having a police record, in effect of being a criminal. Mussolini retorted by writing a piece for his own newspaper in which he publicly vowed to crack the priest's tonsured head while he was still around in Trento to do it. Events then moved swiftly: Don Chelodi denounced him to the police, a trial took place, but to everyone's surprise Mussolini was acquitted by the Austrian judges. Leaving the courtroom he quoted a Russian proverb to the socialist companions who were celebrating his victory: "a man can only call himself a man when he's done six years of high school, four years at university and two in prison". He'd done various spells inside – and would face prison on other occasions in the future – but for the moment he himself was still far off the requisite of two years stipulated by the Russians.

Under his editorship *L'avvenire del lavoratore* was closed down eleven times, receiving a formal condemnation and the imposition of a fine on six occasions. He was increasingly the object of denunciation. At the end of May 1909 he spent six days in prison as a result of two combined court sentences against him; he passed this unexpected spell of tranquil leisure reading Sorel's *Reflections on Violence*.

Mixing in the city's intellectual circles helped him to lose much of his awkwardness. As he turned twenty-six, the prize for which he had been waiting and hoping arrived: Cesare Battisti saw that the polemical energy of Mussolini's journalism might be useful to him and on 29th July – Mussolini's birthday – he offered him the job of editor-in-chief of his newspaper, *Il popolo*. According to Rachele Mussolini, Battisti proposed a monthly salary of seventy-five lire which, again in her version, Mussolini turned down, declaring that fifty lire would be enough for him. Whatever the pay he received, he earned it, because sales of the paper immediately began to increase. Battisti wanted to exploit and if possible increase its growing circulation: so the idea arose of getting the new editor-in-chief to write a story for serialization. Perhaps Mussolini had mentioned the idea casually, perhaps Battisti himself suggested it; whichever of the two first thought it up, they both agreed on the subject of the novel: the relationship between a seventeenth-century Prince Bishop of Trento, Carlo Emanuele Madruzzo and his mistress Claudia Particella. The story was a tortuous and passionate one, dating from 1631 and still at the time the stuff of local legend. Apart from the serial story and the numerous articles he wrote, the only significant political text to arise from Mussolini's experience in Trento, according to De Felice, was written in 1911, a year after he had left the city:

> In my opinion there can be no doubt that Mussolini's contact with the realities of
> political life in Trento, wholly shaped as it was by the pressure of pan-Germanism
> and with men like Battisti who made the struggle for autonomy the focus of their

political activity, led him to perceive and appreciate certain values which often eluded the majority of Italian socialists, and in particular those, like Mussolini himself, on the revolutionary wing of the party. The importance of language as a factor in the situation was not lost on him: he wrote at length about the issue in his 1911 book *Il Trentino veduto da un socialista* [*The Trento Region as Seen by a Socialist*] but the first references to the subject can be found earlier in articles he published in 1909...[32]

The increase in circulation of Battisti's newspaper was a source of concern for the Habsburg Empire's police. They decided they must stop this socialist fanatic newly arrived from Italy who was stirring up the region's sleepy politics and who, as the editor, was behind this alarming increase in the influence of a vehicle of socialist propaganda. With the unsubtle methods occasionally adopted by the police – and the police of the Austro-Hungarian Empire had special powers – they planned to set Mussolini up. A month after Mussolini started to work for Battisti's newspaper, the Emperor Franz Josef visited the city of Innsbruck. In Trento someone stuck a life-size puppet dressed in Tyrolean costume round the town's statue of Dante. During the night a considerable sum of money was stolen from the vaults of the Catholic Cooperative bank. The same day twenty-five kilos of dynamite disappeared from a quarry in Val di Non. The man responsible for carrying out the theft was Cesare Berti, a socialist carpenter who supported Mussolini's extremist views. At this point the police claimed they had received a tip-off that Mussolini and Battisti were plotting an attack on the printing firm run by De Gasperi. Mussolini was arrested, but once again, to everyone's surprise, the judge who tried the case in nearby Rovereto saw through the police's machinations and freed him. He had only just left the court building when the police arrested him again for non-payment of a fine relating to a previous conviction.

Once more in prison, Mussolini began a hunger strike as a form of propaganda, but the imperial authorities in Trento decided to prevent public support building up for him by secretly sending him to Ala on the frontier with Italy and expelling him from the territory. Some of his socialist companions managed to get wind of the move and accompanied him – there are photographs of Mussolini with the group taken at the border crossing. He is wearing a broad-brimmed hat, looks grumpy, but is elegantly dressed, with a gold watch chain visible on his waistcoat. Other socialists in Trento were pleased to see the back of this difficult character and felt the Austrian police had done them a favour by expelling him. Battisti too had begun to see his new editor-in-chief as potentially troublesome, but at the same time wanted to maintain his newspaper's increased circulation, so he urged Mussolini, even though he was no longer in the city, to continue writing the novel for serialization which they had planned.

While Mussolini was away in Trento, Rachele in the meantime had received other marriage proposals, which she turned down, to the concern of her mother and also of Alessandro: "He was upset because he knew what Benito was like and thought that our married life would not be easy for me."[33] On his return from Trento, Mussolini threatened to beat up her most recent suitor – a quietly behaved accountant from the province of Forlì – and, such was his reputation, rapidly saw him off. News of his activities in Trento had preceded his return; the solid backing he had always received from his fellow Socialists in the party managed to secure his nomination as secretary to Forlì's local socialist federation, which was affiliated with the Italian Socialist Party. His father was pleased, but his son's behaviour towards Rachele still worried him. He told Rachele to ignore him and Benito to stop bothering her, but to no avail. Mussolini had seen how the tavern's customers looked at Rachele and ordered her not to wait at the tables. To keep her under observation he himself worked as a waiter for several days and even did the washing-up in the kitchen, much to the chagrin of his father, who according to Rachele complained: "'Just think! A qualified schoolteacher who decides to become a waiter.' But he didn't care. He was so jealous he would have done anything to keep me away from the men who came to the tavern."[34]

Mussolini had also forbidden Rachele to go to socialist meetings which often ended up with dances, when men and women could get together. Alessandro didn't know about the prohibition and one evening took her along with him to hear his son speak and to share his pride in his developing political career. At first Mussolini didn't notice Rachele in the audience; it was only at the dance which followed when a young man invited her to join him for a waltz that he spotted her. He marched up to her with a furious expression and snatched her from the arms of the young man, who knew nothing about the attractive blonde who'd accepted his invitation. This was what "free love" meant after all. Mussolini spun her round wildly for the rest of the waltz and then dragged her home, still glaring fiercely at her. Meanwhile his father, deep in discussion with friends, hadn't noticed what was happening. Mussolini started to threaten Rachele: either she agreed to live together with him or her refusal would drive him to commit some violent act.

> One evening my mother couldn't take any more and decided to intervene. I re-member all three of us were sitting in the kitchen, my mother and I next to each other, Benito facing us. My mother told him: "I'm warning you – Rachele is still just a girl. If you go on tormenting her in this way I'll report you to the police and have you put away." "Fine," replied Benito, and left the room. We were left puzzled, but not for long. He came back immediately, brandishing a revolver which belonged to his father under my mother's nose and said with cold and dramatic deliberation: "If that's what you want, it's my turn to give you a warning. You see this revolver, Mrs Guidi? It's got six bullets in it. If Rachele rejects me again, one bullet will be for her and the rest for me. The choice is yours."[35]

Rachele accepted him on the spot in front of her astonished mother; now she was officially engaged to Benito Mussolini. As his fiancée she had to submit immediately to his jealous demands: he ordered her to go and live with her sister Pina in Carpena, a village seven kilometres outside Forlì, until he could find a suitable place for them to set up house together. He went to see her every evening, walking the seven kilometres there and back. At the beginning of January 1910 he told her sister that he had found an apartment where they could live together: "He told Pina: 'I want Rachele to come and live with me and be the mother of my children. [...] Go and tell her to get ready to come with me, and be quick about it, I've got lots to do...'"[36]

In her memoirs Rachele gives a romantically tinged description of her wedding trousseau: a pair of three-year-old shoes, a blouse, a pair of handkerchiefs and an another to cover her head, an apron, a handful of coins. The couple walked for seven kilometres under the pouring rain to the inn where they would spend their "first" night together. The following morning Mussolini took her to the flat he'd rented in Via Merenda in a large but run-down palazzo built for local nobility: a couple of rooms containing a few sticks of furniture on the top floor where the domestic servants had had their living quarters. In the early autobiography he penned in prison, Mussolini describes the events simply: "On 17th January 1910 Rachele Guidi and I were joined together without any official ceremony, civil or religious."[37] They would get married in a civil ceremony on 16th December 1915 as a result of pressure from the presence of Ida Irene Dalser, who was going around claiming she was "Mussolini's wife"; much later, when Mussolini was in secret contact with the Vatican in efforts to resolve the issue of its territorial status, reasons of political convenience led him to marry Rachele in church, on 28th December 1925. Back in the flat in Via Merenda, Rachele immediately became pregnant with their first daughter, Edda. Following the old proverb which advises a man to choose his wife and his cattle from his native place, and making an abrupt decision, based on instinct and temperament, Mussolini set up home with a woman from his local village, someone who would keep the house tidy, make the bed, cook and look after their children. A son, Vittorio, was born five years later in 1916, followed by Bruno in 1918, Romano in 1927 and Anna Maria in 1929.

> Mussolini's idea of fatherhood was patriarchal, and while respectful towards his wife he kept himself completely detached from her: with the sons increasingly ruling the roost and the wife's role limited to that of the loving mother, it might be called a very Italian family set-up. One of Mussolini's lovers once revealed to me that he'd told her "my wife is an attractive blonde and the mother of my children. She doesn't try to wear the trousers, and that suits me fine. I'm fond of her because she lets me do whatever I want to do."[38]

While he was determinedly pursuing Rachele, Mussolini was also working on the novel to be serialized in Battisti's newspaper; by January 1910 he had written two chapters of what was to be called *L'amante del Cardinale* (*The Cardinal's Mistress*). He was earning a hundred and twenty lire a month, he had started up a weekly paper called *La lotta di classe* (*The Class Struggle*), he was always in debt and now that he'd set up house with Rachele, he needed to supplement his earnings. Battisti had succeeded in persuading him, and when Mussolini sent him the text he immediately began to advertise the forthcoming attraction. On 10th January 1910 his newspaper carried the following announcement: "*Claudia Particella – L'amante del Cardinal Madruzzo*. Benito Mussolini, our editor, expelled by the Austrians and now back in Italy, has not forgotten the newspaper for which he fought so many noble battles. He promised us he would write a historical novel for the paper and, after much painstaking research in libraries and archives, he has now completed one."

In their new flat in Via Merenda, on the outskirts of Forlì, a heavily pregnant Rachele climbed painfully up the narrow stairs. The only table to write on was the kitchen table next to the stove. In his interview with Ludwig, Mussolini declared the novel about the cardinal to be "a dreadful piece of trash. [...] I wrote it for a political purpose, for serialization in a newspaper. *In those days the clergy was full of corruption*. It's a book of political propaganda."[39] When he corrected the proofs of the interview Mussolini struck out the phrase in italics, as well as censoring numerous other remarks; the interview with Ludwig took place after the signing of the Lateran Pacts, when he had become, in Pius XI's phrase, Italy's "man of destiny" and from his solitary eminence governed the country in the name of God, the Fatherland and the Family. The phrase was only reinserted in the critical edition of the interview published in 1950.

But is *L'amante del Cardinale* really "a dreadful piece of trash"?

Chapter 6

The Two Racheles and Prison

He had the courtiers arrive in the small forest clearing at dusk. He got their servants to lay carpets out on the grass so that they could stretch out at their ease. And then he waited, while the smells of good food tempted the company to start picking at the contents of the hampers they had brought with them. He set the guards to stand at attention around them and paid no heed to the fact they were joking and laughing distractedly. Right in the middle of the travellers he placed Claudia Particella, smilingly turning now to one of the knights, now to one of the ladies. Close by her side was her faithful maidservant Rachele, who looked on in silence while she distributed the food – game, cheese, fruit.

As he was seated at the table opposite the stove in the top-floor apartment in Via Merenda, the pen in his hand felt as cold and heavy as the dagger of the killer who was just about to enter the scene set in the forest glade. He'd had enough of this novel, of its heroine Claudia, of its featureless noblemen. Every evening, coming in tired from the endless political discussions and the turbulent meetings and checking the proofs of the newspaper, he had to sit down and start writing. There was one way to end it: to kill off Claudia Particella. The ambush was prepared. He'd make sure none of the guards was aware of the danger. He stopped with his pen poised to write as Rachele turned to him. She was pregnant – her stomach had just started to swell. They looked at each other: she had learnt how to meet his steely gaze without flinching. All right, they were in need of the income, a baby girl was on the way, but enough was enough! There must be some other way of earning money than churning out new chapters of this nauseating story for Trento.

Mussolini prompted his killer to get out of the boat which had brought him across the lake from the other side of the island. This way was longer but safer. Wrapped in a black cloak, the man had to slide silently under the trees in the dark like a snake, so he could arrive near the group of travellers without being noticed. Now he could end it, once and for all. On a sudden the assassin rose up and, gripping the dagger high in the air, threw himself on Claudia Particella. One of the guards cried out, but it was too late. The man seemed to fly as he leapt on her; the others didn't have time to stand. It was the matter of a moment.

Suddenly Rachele left the stove and came to lean over the table, forcing him to stop writing and listen to what she was saying. Claudia Particella couldn't be killed off, she said, not now, not yet. They couldn't pay the bills, the baby was on its way, they had bought nothing for it, they didn't even have anything set aside for the birth. They started to argue and shout, but Rachele held firm, with the determination of a mother-to-be. She seemed to have interposed her whole body between the sheet of paper and Mussolini's hand holding the pen. He snorted with anger and told her to get out of the way, but in the end he did what she said and started to write again, to go on writing as she wanted him to.

The assassin's blow fell on Claudia Particella: it seemed her end had come. The others watched frozen with terror. Only Rachele, her maidservant, reacted. She threw her body between her mistress and the dagger so that the killer stabbed her and Claudia's life was saved.

He must be patient, he must hold on, he must go on writing – they really needed the money.

He brought horsemen and guards running up to throw themselves in a scrum on the assassin. They tied him up and took him to the castle. Rachele's bodice was dripping with blood; speaking faintly she was trying to reassure her mistress she would be all right, she would survive, but her face grew more and more pale. Claudia made her lie down on the rich carpets spread out on the floor of the boat.

The other Rachele was quiet again and began to talk gently to him, all the time keeping her eye on the stove. He only needed to write a few more chapters, just enough to pay for an outfit and a cot for the baby. Now supper was ready: he could take a break and go on writing later. She would sit by his side and help him.

Cesare Battisti was unaware he had an ally in the Mussolini household. For weeks he'd been pleading with his former editor-in-chief to continue the serial which had increased the sales of the newspaper to such an extent that they had been obliged to print this announcement on 22nd January 1910: "In order to satisfy the many readers who have tried in vain to buy from newsagents copies of back issues containing the first two episodes of Benito Mussolini's new novel, we are pleased to announce that we are reprinting them together with two new parts."[1] When his author decided to go "on strike", Battisti was forced to divide some episodes in half in order to eke out the publication and gain time. He tried to keep Mussolini on his side and persuade him to continue – the same battle which Rachele was waging back at home. When Mussolini stopped sending new instalments, Battisti wrote to him: "The serial is being read avidly. It's true you may not get paid much for writing it, but there's a chance they'll put up a statue to you in the main square. Doesn't that impress you?"[2]

For Mussolini, not much. Praise and acclamation meant little to him: his only reason for continuing to write was money. He replied to Battisti:

> As you'll see from the newspaper cutting I enclose, my father has been taken to hospital paralysed by a stroke. We had to sell everything we've got to put him there. We had to pay in advance the money for a month's stay at three lire a day. The crisis is made more acute by my *faux ménage*, since January, with Rachele. Don't think I've written *Claudia Particella* for the entertainment of your young lady readers in Trento, or to squeeze money out of the *Popolo*. In short, I'm asking you for a loan of 200 lire.[3]

It is true that Mussolini's finances were fairly precarious, yet he was not unduly concerned. For example, his father gave him the money to return to Forlì. Claudia Particella was in danger on several occasions of being killed off, but money from Battisti or Rachele's pleas saved her. In writing what he later described to the journalist Ludwig as a "dreadful piece of trash", Mussolini drew on all the notes he had made while researching the novel. He recycled the stories about the two lovers which could still be heard in Trento. His visceral hatred of the clergy found expression in the episodes he rapidly set down on paper. With one exception, all of the characters – whether they are fictional creations or based on historical originals – are evil: Carlo Emanuele Madruzzo, the cardinal and prince bishop of Trento, Claudia's lover, who is determined on marrying her although prevented from doing so by the Pope's veto; Claudia Particella herself, a negative, shadowy figure; her hateful brother Vincenzo and Father

Ludovico, who is also the cardinal's leading counsellor; and the grim, black-hearted assassin Paolo Martelli. Among these leading characters Mussolini introduced two inventions of his own. The first was the evil Don Benizio, the cardinal's private secretary, driven by an obsession with Claudia – as his name might indicate, the character is a sort of negative alter ego of his creator, a puppet he could bring on stage as fantasy or the plot demanded. He also made up the figure of the faithful maidservant – the only positive and sincere character in the book – whom he named Rachele after his own wife, pregnant with their first daughter Edda, busy doing the household chores round him while he wrote.

After their quarrel over his wish to finish the novel followed by Rachele's soothing words, the virtuous maidservant in the novel, her namesake, starts to be described in cloyingly sentimental terms. Perhaps he was trying to make up for the fact that in a fit of temper he had had her stabbed instead of Claudia. He wrote rapidly, not lifting his eyes from the page: the killer was sentenced to death

and Claudia was not inclined to pardon him. But Rachele, now recovered and resuming her normal activities, grew increasingly insistent. [...] "Now that it's all over and what happened is only a memory, pardon the poor wretch who is facing his last day on earth... be generous towards him and I will continue to serve you humbly and lovingly, as I would serve the Madonna..." These words, which came from a pure and still unspotted heart, moved Claudia. Her debt of gratitude towards her faithful servant was great and in the end she yielded to her wish.[4]

By the end of the book's fifty-six published instalments, after a series of miraculous rescues, Claudia Particella manages to survive. After the Pope had dubbed him "a man of destiny" it is only to be expected that Mussolini would have been quick to dismiss his novel as "trash", but *L'amante del Cardinale* is no worse than other stories serialized in the newspapers of the time with the principal aim of making money both for the paper and for the author. It could probably still earn a profit today if adapted for the television screen as a short drama series, especially if flashbacks and flash-forwards from the author's own life were added – his various experiences at the time, his lovers, his wife Rachele – as a background to the tale of Claudia Particella's passions three centuries earlier. The figure of Don Benizio, Mussolini's alter ego, gives us an inside glimpse of the centre of what was to become the myth of Mussolini the man, its sexual dimension which gave rise to so many stories and on which the whole structure rested.

It was commonly thought – and confirmed by his private valet – that the Duce slept with a woman a day – an impossible number; even if we halve it, it's still highly improbable. If we say that on average he slept with a different woman once a week, the total would be in the order of several hundred, which begins to look more plausible as a realistic estimate. Many of these, as we shall see, were extremely brief encounters, lasting no more than half an hour or so, and that included, in addition to the act of penetration itself, entering and leaving the room they were using, any social preliminaries, getting undressed and dressed, or at least partly disrobing and then adjusting their clothes afterwards. There was a continual stream of women: as mentioned before, a special office was set up in Palazzo Venezia in Rome when the leader himself no longer had time to spare for their pursuit and seduction. It is important to understand the sexual energy which enabled Mussolini to deal with this continuous relay or supply of women, the approach towards sex which he developed while still a young man and which led him in later years to create this kind of bureaucratic organization for his sexual activities. The bureaucracy worked efficiently: it screened out his "insatiable female pursuers" and shielded him from the world's – especially foreign journalists' – curiosity while at the same time it allowed the public a glimpse of the activities which would nurture the myth of the Duce as "the great lover", "the alpha male" who was potent in every sense of the term.

Don Benizio in the novel helps us to trace Mussolini's attitude to sex:

Don Benizio accompanied his colleagues to the door. On returning to his room he could not restrain a gesture of triumph. As he undressed to get ready for bed, his mind reeled with thoughts of revenge, of conquest, of enjoyment. [...] Ah Claudia!... Tomorrow you will be mine... as I want... And the woman – in a vision of nudity such as only the lusts of those vowed to celibacy can imagine – tomorrow the beautiful, shameless woman would throw her arms round his neck, looking at him with her eyes black as the Devil's, with her round fragrant shoulders, her heavenly mouth, her soft white skin. Claudia the courtesan tormented Don Benizio's sleep with the nightmare of unsatisfied desire, with the yearning for caresses he had never experienced and for sensations of indescribable pleasure to the point of exhaustion and of satiety. His priestly flesh trembled like some sylvan god who espies a naked nymph reflected in the clear water of a quietly flowing stream. Claudia had rejected him, had pushed him away as one would an importunate beggar. [...] Yet the priest had not given up his dream. He had made it the purpose of his existence. In order to possess Claudia he would have sold his soul to the Devil and preferred eternal hellfire to the bliss of heaven. The grip of passion, in which hatred and love alternately assailed him, had hardened his soul: he was petrified, fossilized in his desire, and now that the energies of his manhood were in decline, the flames of lust obsessively tortured his flesh. He was like the bow drawn to shoot its arrow, stretched to the point when it breaks and shatters.[5]

Don Benizio's vision of sex then is typical of those who are obliged to remain celibate – one that has no time for sweet words of love but explodes in carnal desire, which seeks relief from its burning obsessive lust, which shoots an arrow from the tensed – over-tensed – bow. There's a violence in Mussolini's description which evokes a rapacious sexuality, like a hunter stalking his prey, like a faun provoked by brazen nymphs, by the image of women playing on men's sexual urges and provoking them to the point of exasperation, and so justifying their being taken by force.

Compare this page from *L'amante del Cardinale* with what Mussolini wrote in the autobiographical account he worked on when he was in prison two years later: "The sudden revelation of sexual pleasure disturbed me. The vision of naked women entered my life, my dreams, my lusts. I used to undress in my imagination the girls I met and lust after them in my thoughts."[6]

Another remark which helps us to understand how the sexual dimension was at the centre of Mussolini's myth and was the primary force which drove it forward is the already quoted comment he made on Angelica Balabanoff when he was in Switzerland, after she had become his mentor and occasional lover. As we have seen, the remark comes in a letter written to his sister Edvige, but Mussolini shows no awareness of the violence of his words or of the vision of sexual relations they reveal, which betrays a profound contempt for women: "While her body is full of juice, her mind is full of dried-up ideas."[7]

Margherita Sarfatti saw that it was not possible to dismiss, in a scornful aside, *L'amante del Cardinale* as "trash". She realized that it contained the central element of the myth she was helping to construct.

> The historical novel in the style of Dumas *père*, *Claudia Particella ossia l'amante del Cardinale* [*Claudia Particella or the Cardinal's Mistress*] is a formless and overlong potboiler, resembling a film melodrama in its overblown style, but nevertheless there's something vital in its coarseness and brutality. Just as in one of his speeches or newspaper articles or political acts, the author knows instinctively which word or phrase or event will be most effective. [...] Since the heroine had to be spared, the killing instinct is deflected onto the secondary characters. In Trento, that charming town at the foot of the mountains, all the seamstresses, the artisans, the young working men would run to buy their copies of the newspaper, eager to read the latest tragic turn of the plot, tears streaming from their eyes as they scanned the densely printed columns. Then they would lift their eyes to the towers of Buonconsiglio castle, and thoughts of the feudal Prince-Bishop and his mistress would fill their drab working day with delicious frissons.[8]

Mussolini finally got what he wanted when he sent Battisti the final instalment on 11th May 1910 and so brought the serial to a close. Perhaps Rachele, now in her fifth month of pregnancy, was too tired to oppose his decision.

"My God, your heart's beating fast. Sit down, have a rest. Feeling a bit better now?" Mussolini's words to his mistress Claretta, many years later, in 1938: "Now just see what I've got planned for you, while you sit and listen – while I read from the manuscript of a book I wrote when I was twenty-five. It's been found by a publisher who didn't know whether to destroy it or send it to me. It makes me laugh now when I reread it. I was certainly a bit strange in those days."[9] When his mistress is sitting comfortably in the armchair, he starts to read from the manuscript he wrote while still living in Trento, *La tragedia di Mayerling* (*The Tragedy of Mayerling*). It's a small arithmetic exercise book consisting of about forty numbered pages: over the years it had disappeared and then re-emerged by chance a number of times. The first time Mussolini lost it was during the police search of his apartment when he was expelled from Trento. Sixteen years later, in 1926 – by then Mussolini was the dictator of Italy – a publisher came across it and sent it to him. Perhaps he was hoping to reap the benefits of a publishing coup: an unpublished story from the pen of the Duce no less. But the time was wrong:

engaged in secret negotiations with the Vatican, Mussolini had no intention of publicizing his earlier opposition to the Church as this emerged in his writings at the time. In its radical anticlericalism, *Mayerling* is very similar to other pieces he wrote while in Trento, such as *Claudia Particella* or *Giovanni Huss il veridico* (*John Huss the Truth-Teller*). So the unfortunate publisher who'd found the piece probably received nothing more than a curt letter of acknowledgement and thanks. The little exercise book then disappeared among Mussolini's papers. He probably came across it by chance in 1938 and decided he could read it – at no risk to his reputation with the Vatican – to his mistress. After the war the manuscript once more disappeared. Since then, most of Mussolini's writings during his period in Trento have been "rescued", so to speak, from oblivion and republished, largely with the critical intention of showing the extent of their author's self-contradictions and tendency to change with the circumstances, revealing him to be, in De Felice's words, the political turncoat he actually was.

Only *Mayerling* didn't come to light until one day in 1972 when, in an episode itself like something out of a novel, a lawyer, Giorgio Assumma, who in recent times was president of Società Italiana degli Autori ed Editori (the Italian Society of Authors and Publishers), was asked to provide expert advice on a mass of letters and other documents which had been found inside a trunk.[10] They included the manuscript of *Mayerling*. It was duly valued and fetched a high price, going to a private collector before ending up where it is today, in the library of Stanford University in the US. It was published for the first time in the periodical *Il Borghese* in 1973. In 2005 the popular weekly magazine *Gente* republished it. There is probably more than one reason Mussolini wrote this historical account intended for a popular readership: without doubt he wanted to paint a negative picture of the religious establishment, but he also intended to discredit the Habsburg rulers. The text is brief, as we have seen, no more than forty manuscript pages, but it represents only the first chapter of a longer book which Mussolini wasn't able to finish after he was expelled from Trento. He lists the titles of the projected chapters: 'La tragedia di Mayerling' ('The Tragedy of Mayerling'); 'Il fucilato di Querétaro' ('The Querétaro Shooting'); 'L'Imperatrice Elisabetta' ('The Empress Elisabeth'); 'Franz Joseph intimo' ('The Private Life of Franz Josef'). Mussolini divided the *Mayerling* part into two sections: 'Rodolfo d'Austria' ('Rudolph of Austria') and 'La notte di sangue' ('The Night of Blood'). In 1938, when he read some pages aloud to Claretta Petacci, it was with a critical and ironical air, but her account of the evening also shows that he was amused by the way the recently discovered story mirrored the amorous complications of his own private life. *Mayerling* too is peopled by a cast of women – including one who is Jewish – from various social classes:

> Rudolph used the services of a cabman called Bratfisch to ferry him to his various secret love assignations in his humble carriage. Princess Stefania knew from the spies she had employed to follow him that one day Rudolph had visited a Jewish lady. She ordered her carriage to take her to her rival's house, whereupon she left it waiting outside the gate while she returned home in a hired vehicle. When Rudolph finally emerged, he found himself surrounded by a crowd of well-wishers who had recognized the imperial coach and wanted to greet its occupant. This cruel practical joke started to undermine the tyrannical rule of the Habsburgs. Stefania and Rudolph now loathed each other openly. He started to pursue all kinds of love affairs without the slightest consideration for his wife.[11]

Every now and then, while reading to Petacci, Mussolini asked her if she was enjoying it; he wanted to see her reaction, to win her approval. He asked her to sit with him in his chair while he read the next passage to her, the climactic scene of castration – but, he hastened to assure her, he'd made it all up, it was just the product of his imagination.

> Towards midnight Rudolph let out a high-pitched, terrifying cry of pain. Mary had carried out her threat and performed the abominable act: she had castrated the man who was trustingly asleep beside her, tired after their sweet lovemaking. The blood spread across the white sheets while Mary, half-undressed, tried to move towards the door to escape. After his first cries, assailed by intolerable pain, Rudolph no longer uttered a sound. He'd fallen back across the bed as if he was dead; Mary dressed and made to leave the room. At that point Rudolph suddenly reached her and fired his revolver into her. She collapsed to the ground: Rudolph had killed her. He laid her on the bed, covered her and stretched out beside her. A few minutes later another muffled shot was heard… Rudolph had killed himself.[12]

At the same time as the exercise book with *Mayerling* mysteriously went missing and *Claudia Particella* was helping to increase the sales of Battisti's newspaper, Mussolini's publishing activities were taking a different direction. On 9th January a new socialist weekly started to come out in Forlì: *La lotta di classe*. Under Mussolini's editorship it became the leading journal of the movement in the province. The local Socialists found themselves in difficulties; they hoped their new leader would inspire them with the determination and energy to move forward from a period of inertia during which they had lost a lot of ground to the other main "opposition" party, the Republicans. Mussolini's career as a Socialist leader now began to take off. He succeeded in reorganizing the Federation of Forlì under his leadership and increased its membership by several hundred new subscriptions, almost all of them from the younger generation, he developed his skills in political meetings, showed no restraint in criticizing the central organization of the Italian Socialist Party, which was in the hands of the reformist wing, and harshly denounced the presence of Freemasons within the party.

At the eleventh National Socialist Congress, held in Milan from 21st to 25th October 1910, the reformist line as represented by Turati was victorious, but Mussolini didn't give up and maintained his ties to the revolutionary wing among the delegates who held intransigently to their positions. Shortly after the congress, on 19th November, his father Alessandro died; tired and ill, he had observed his son's involvement in that turbulent summer of strikes. The year had been full of social disturbance in the countryside with the conflict over the mechanical threshers: the labourers' cooperatives had purchased new machines and thus came into direct competition and conflict with the share-croppers. An early agreement had been reached, but this broke down when actual threshing began on 7th July. The army intervened against the demonstrators. In August the Federazione Repubblicana (Federation of Republican Parties), led by their new secretary Pietro Nenni, persuaded the labourers who supported them to form their own independent cooperatives. Mussolini immediately turned on them with the accusation that they had broken ranks with their fellow workers. Relations between the Republicans and the Socialists deteriorated rapidly: on occasion the war of words led to fisticuffs. At the same time the Socialist Federation of Forlì started to differentiate and distance itself from the line being followed by the national party: "The requirements of the political struggle on a daily basis, the initial reorganization of the socialist group in Forlì,

the increasingly bitter conflicts with the Republicans, the preparation of the Forlì delegates to take part in the Milan congress, and
finally, after the congress, the breaking away of the Forlì Federation
from the national Socialist Party – all these matters took up most of
Mussolini's energies and time over the course of eighteen months."[13]

Mussolini's political dexterity can be seen in the way he reacted to
what was known as the "Bissolati case", when in March 1911 for the
very first time, Bissolati, a leading Socialist member of the Italian
parliament, was formally involved in the consultations, summoned
by the King, to form a new government. Mussolini set a choice before
the national Socialist Party leadership: either they withdrew their support of Bissolati's involvement or the Forlì Federation would secede
from the party. He knew very well that the reformist wing in the party
(still the predominant one, although they would be expelled from it
the following year) would never accept such a demand. Mussolini
prepared the ground for the local federation's congress very carefully. He contacted all the local sections one by one, even individual
members, and as a result carried the motion at the local congress
that the Forlì Federation should break away from the national party,
with twenty-seven sections out of thirty-eight voting in favour (five
abstained and six accepted the proposal but wanted the move to be
delayed). Mussolini's strategy had led to the Forlì Socialists isolating themselves from the national party, but at the same time he had
increased their membership.

How this newly acquired isolation would play out politically did
not become clear, since the country was overtaken by another crisis:
the military campaign in Libya and the war with Turkey. The left
wing in Italy was divided on the issue, but the majority, represented
by the Republicans and the Socialists, came out against the war. In
Forlì the two parties at first held separate demonstrations and meetings, but joined forces when the Confederazione Generale del Lavoro
(General Confederation of Labour) declared a general strike. On the
morning of 26th September there were clashes with the police, but
in the afternoon a huge demonstration passed off without incident:
Mussolini spoke on behalf of the Socialists, and Nenni for the Republicans. On the 27th, when the general strike began, there were only a
few outbreaks of vandalism across the country, but most took place
in Forlì, where telegraph poles were brought down and demonstrators occupied the railway station, with women lying down on the

tracks to prevent the military convoy trains from passing through. Mussolini used the situation to declare in an article that the general strike marked the defeat of reformism among the workers.

On 29th September Italy declared war on Turkey, and the political situation took a new turn. As in all wars, the country had to prepare itself for the possibility of military setbacks and launch a campaign to attract new recruits to the armed forces. The provincial prefecture in Forlì was worried about possible disorder; the police started to examine Mussolini's and Nenni's declarations, with the result that both – together with Aurelio Lolli, the caretaker at the local workers' association – were arrested, under eight separate charges, including the incitement of violence. The socialist weekly *La lotta di classe* organized a financial appeal to pay the men's legal costs; leading Socialist and Republican lawyers were hired to defend them. The trial only enhanced the two men's political stature. Mussolini made a speech in the courtroom which was addressed more to his fellow Socialists than to the presiding judges. He began by declaring: "I categorically deny that the general strike broke out in Forlì because I supported it. This conjecture is absurd. The decision to go on strike lay with the workers of Forlì and not with me. [...] The masses have acquired their own voice, they can reason and will; they won't allow themselves to be towed along by their so-called leaders; on the contrary, the leaders have to follow them in their wake." Mussolini's statement – it was more like a harangue – to the court continued amid the encouragement and applause of the public. Unable to reintroduce calm to the courtroom so that the trial could proceed, the judge ordered proceedings to be adjourned to the following day, just as Mussolini reached his summing-up by turning to the bench and declaring: "Let me say this, honourable sirs: if you acquit me, I will be content, because you will have allowed me to continue my work for society. If you condemn me, I will be honoured, because I am no wrongdoer or common criminal standing here before you: no, I affirm my ideas, I stir up men's consciences, I fight for a faith which demands your respect because it is strong in truth and will shape the future!"[14]

A few months earlier Mussolini had become a father. On 1st September 1910 his daughter Edda was born; she would always remain his favourite child, even in the later tragic developments of her life, in the last year of the war, when he ordered her husband, his son-in-law

Galeazzo Ciano, to be shot at dawn. But for now his father's warning to Rachele before she and Mussolini started living together seemed to be coming true: one good reason for not setting up home with him was that she would have to look after the children and the house on her own while he spent time in prison. On this occasion the judges were determined it wouldn't be a short stay: he was sentenced to a year's imprisonment, while Nenni received a year and fifteen days, and Lolli six months. When the case came to appeal, the punishment was reduced to seven and a half months for Nenni, five and a half for Mussolini, and four and a half for Lolli.

In his cell in the ancient fortress of Ravaldino, which had been converted into a prison, Mussolini asked for an exercise book and a pen and started to write *La mia vita dal 29 luglio 1883 al 23 novembre 1911*. Nenni's own account of their period in jail includes a description of his socialist friend as cheerful, even boisterous, a model prisoner, kindly with their fellow inmates, patient in putting up with the daily difficulties of life inside, ready to explain everything as the result of social injustice; the lack of space got on his nerves, and he missed playing his violin and especially seeing his baby daughter, now just one year old. Mussolini and Nenni became firm friends during their spell in prison, as did their wives, Rachele and Carmen, who met for the first time as they visited their husbands and from then on began to help each other out. One of Nenni's memories is of holding Edda while her mother and Mussolini talked and the little girl weeing down his trousers, which happened to be the only pair he possessed in prison. While they were both still inside, the two men celebrated the birth of Nenni's first daughter Giuliana, while Rachele took Carmen a bottle of Marsala, which was thought to be fortifying for women who had just given birth. Nenni would go on to have two more girls, Eva and Vittoria. Vittoria died in Auschwitz on 15th July 1943. But as Mussolini and Nenni shared their prison rations like two brothers during the Christmas of 1911 and the first few months of 1912, Auschwitz, the racial laws and the persecutions were still far in the future.

His spell in prison increased Mussolini's political renown. His name began to circulate beyond the Socialist circles in Forlì. He was no longer the delegate of a small and rebellious local federation; he began to be seen as a leader of the revolutionary wing of the national party. When he was released from prison on 12th March 1912, his comrades celebrated with a banquet in his honour. Years later, when they had become lovers, Margherita Sarfatti managed to get hold of the autobiographical account Mussolini had written while in prison – it was no doubt buried among his papers – and used it when writing her own biography of him. Afterwards Mussolini made sure it disappeared again, but the fact that Sarfatti had been able to refer to it as a source was one reason why her biography *Dux* was so successful, with editions in nineteen languages selling millions of copies. She and Mussolini had agreed to share royalties, and for several years they earned the then impressive sum of a thousand dollars a week – until he reneged on the agreement, using the racial laws against the Jews as the crushing justification.

Chapter 7

Banquets and Drawing Rooms

The Sangiovese wine – deep red, with a vague fragrance of violets, dry with a sharp aftertaste – had gushed out from dozens of demijohns, but it didn't stay untouched for long on the banqueting tables. The guests waved the empty bottles in the air and the waiters would snatch them up and refill them. As soon as news of Mussolini's release had reached them, all the women among the Forlì Socialists had taken to making yards of pasta, smoothing it out with a rolling pin, unwinding it in sheets, and cutting the sheets into long strips – the local pasta known as *strozzapreti* or "priest-strangler" (an appropriate dish for this occasion...) – which they then dressed with a rich meat sauce. There were also large helpings of tortelli *al raviggiolo* and lasagne with slowly cooked chicken livers and hearts and the fleshy parts of the stomach which remained slightly crunchy. There were dishes of the local pasta with baked sausages, diced bacon, tomato sauce and sprinklings of parmesan cheese and black pepper. Such a spectacular feast had not been seen in those parts for a long time, the kind which could make up for an entire year of living on vegetable broth with, on Sundays, a plate of stew made from a few almost bare bones from the butchers, but you needed an iron stomach to get it all down. Every now and then, amid the cigarette smoke and the steaming fragrant dishes and the animated talk, someone would stand up and salute the hero of the hour, Mussolini, so proud yet friendly too, Benito their dear comrade. It must have seemed as if every political subversive in the country had turned up to celebrate Mussolini's new-found freedom. After all the courses had been served, while the guests were finishing off the slices of ham and stuffed roast chicken and soft white cheese spread out along the tables, the toasts began to shouts of approval and applause. The room quietened down only when Olindo Vernocchi rose, holding a glass in his hand. He was one of the oldest and most respected of the local party leaders, and when he cleared his throat to start speaking all fell silent and turned towards him. He raised his glass towards Mussolini: "Today, Benito, you are no longer merely the champion of the socialists in Romagna, you are the leader – the '*duce*' – of all the revolutionary socialists in Italy."

Cesare Rossi, who at the time of the banquet was a Socialist in charge of the Workers' Association in Parma and editor-in-chief of the paper the *Internazionale*, later wrote this account of the evening: "It was on this occasion, amid the revelry of the guests and the reminiscent speeches, that an old word, once familiar to Dante and to the medieval *condottieri*, re-emerged, which would later become part of our common political vocabulary – more than that, would come to sum up the history of Italy over the last twenty years."[1]

Mussolini didn't like the toasts after public dinners, a problem at Socialist Party gatherings, where there was always an abundant supply of Sangiovese. He was overcome by embarrassment and could hardly lift his glass. But he shortly managed to solve the difficulty by letting his circle of supporters know how much he disliked the habit, as is shown by an article which appeared in *La lotta di classe* on 14th December 1912 on a dinner at which a lawyer, Giommi, had stood up among the other guests round the horseshoe-shaped table to pay tribute to Mussolini:

> When the fruit had been served, Giommi, Valmaggi and others were invited to make a speech. Giommi stood up and said, "Comrades! Benito Mussolini doesn't want us to toast him or to make any speeches. Let us respect his wish. Yet, in order to show our affection for the man who has been our upstanding *duce* now for three years, let us demonstrate our gratitude by making a contribution towards *Avanti!*" All the guests rose to their feet and clapped and cheered in a display of affection which left Mussolini visibly moved.[2]

So the title of "*duce*" was first bestowed on Mussolini by his fellow Socialist Party members. It was not a random choice, inspired by the quantities of Sangiovese wine they consumed. The word "*duce*" emerged spontaneously from their daily political activity; their dinners and feasts served to mark the beginning of the cult of Mussolini. As the courses went on being served, Mussolini merely tasted them; only the guests sitting near him could see how small a quantity of food he actually consumed. According to Rachele, he always ate very little, and very fast. As secretary to the Socialist Federation of

Forlì he earned one hundred and twenty lire a month, and that was what they had to live on, but he gave twenty to the party and paid out fifteen in rent for his office, so there was little left for carefree living. Coffee, bread, soup, long periods at the news-stand browsing the papers he couldn't afford to buy, and on occasion a plate of tagliatelle for supper with salad or cooked vegetables.

But it's also true that the political meetings he attended in the various sections were usually followed by a certain degree of social conviviality. One night Rachele opened the door to find him being carried up the stairs by two strangers. It was almost dawn: the men told her not to worry, it was nothing serious, he had just talked rather a lot and drunk a bit too much. What had he been drinking? Well, some coffee, and then... some brandy, perhaps rather too much brandy. Once inside, Mussolini started to smash up everything – plates, glasses, even the furniture. A neighbour came in and she and Rachele called a doctor. They managed to get him into bed. When the morning came, Mussolini woke with his head completely befuddled; he couldn't remember a thing, even though Rachele showed him the wrecked apartment and despairingly asked him where they would find the money to buy new things. From then he steered clear of drinking alcohol, although he didn't advertise his abstinence.

At dinners he made it look as if he had drunk from the glass by bringing it to his lips; nobody would notice the glass was still full when he placed it down on the table. After that night of complete drunkenness he almost never drank again, although such abstinence was almost inconceivable in someone who led a political federation – and in Forlì, moreover, which was proud of producing the best wines in Romagna, people wouldn't have understood his choice. It was important to respect appearances. The Socialist Party members who wanted to subvert the system had found a new leader; the men in charge of the local sections thought that Mussolini was the best candidate. The cult of the strong leader was growing among the party members in the province: someone who would take charge of their movement's destiny, would guide it to power. Once the man who could lead them had been found, all they needed to do was follow him down the road to revolution.

A National Socialist Congress had been called in Reggio Emilia, at which the party's various factions could finally air their differences. On 4th March, before Mussolini had been released from prison, the weekly paper *La soffitta* (*The Garret*) announced his imminent return to political life: "When they gather at Reggio Emilia, both the right- and left-wing factions in the party will realize how much the votes from the Forlì section will count, especially now they have a '*duce*' whom they love and look up to, forceful in character and incorruptible: Benito Mussolini."

After the Second World War, the banquet to celebrate Mussolini's release from prison at which the guests had acclaimed him as their "*duce*" would have been entirely forgotten had it not been for Cesare Rossi – who had survived Fascism and anti-Fascism, had been both a fervent supporter of Mussolini and a radical opponent of his cult – who thought he could spend his remaining years peacefully writing his memoirs. The political left in Italy has always made sure that words like "*duce*" and "*fascio*" are firmly excluded from its own version of its history. The movement of the Fasci in Sicily was seen as belonging to the remote nineteenth century; on the rare occasions they were mentioned it was always with the qualification that they had nothing to do with Fascism. The defeat of the "Fasci Siciliani", who were brutally repressed by the army, took place in 1894, when Mussolini was just eleven years old and was beginning to accompany his father to political meetings and assemblies. The newspapers reported what was happening in Sicily, members of the Socialist Party would discuss the plight of those labourers in the deep south who were demanding social justice and the abolition of the parasitic and Mafia-like landowning system with their cries of "Give the land to those who work the land".

Alessandro Mussolini also followed the course of those faraway uprisings which brought together peasants, sharecroppers, artisans, miners and even small landowners, all fighting courageously for progress under the leadership of socialist-leaning men like Nicola Barbato and Giuseppe De Felice-Giuffrida. But in the eyes of Italian socialists in general this vast protest movement of agricultural labourers had one shortcoming: these men were not "workers" in the socialists' accepted sense of the term. Their revolt did not belong to the political plan. They were dreamers, pursuing confused ideas, making demands which were contaminated by "bourgeois" interests. "When we examine their demands, we find some which genuinely spring from the people, which chime with socialism. But you can also see the influence of the interests of the relatively well-off sections of the peasantry..."[3]

Only the great mass of industrial factory workers – the working class in the classic sense of the term – were fit to pursue the aims of revolution and create socialism on earth. It mattered little that the Fasci in Sicily were the largest popular uprising in Europe since the Paris Commune: the movement didn't have a political programme which could form part of the socialist approach; they were abandoned to their defeat at the hands of the army, sent in to suppress the revolts, in a series of massacres which provoked no mass demonstrations of protest and solidarity among the working class in northern Italy. With their uncomfortable name, their struggle was erased from the collective political memory. Yet, however confused their aspirations might have been, however much the organization was influenced by outside interests, the Sicilian Fasci were an authentic popular upris- ing, an important episode in the history of the people's movement, and the word *"fascio"* (meaning literally "bundle" or "sheaf"), at least until the advent of Mussolini's party, did not have negative con- notations in socialist eyes. Andrea Costa himself – the first Socialist parliamentary deputy in Italy, Alessandro Mussolini's mentor and guiding light – spoke of building a *"fascio"* for democracy, a group- ing of democratic forces.

Acclaimed as their *"duce"* on release from prison, Mussolini threw himself with renewed energy into an attack on the reformist wing of the Socialist Party, the deputies, the parliamentarians, the proponents of mediation who in his view had infected the party. With a dramatic flourish he declared in one article that for the next ten years the party should pay no attention to social legislation or the trade-union move- ment, but commit itself to bringing about the revolution – only to realize he risked antagonizing the trade-unionists in the party, and so he changed tack.

The young Mussolini is often described as a "teacher in Predap- pio". As we've seen, he did teach in schools, but it was during his time as a journalist that his political career really began and started to develop. He learnt to apply the fundamental rules of journalism to political activity: one piece of news can be swiftly cancelled out by a subsequent more colourful story, a clever attacking style can mask a lack of truth and confer authority. The fact that his policies had led to the Forlì Federation becoming isolated from the national party was forgotten in the enthusiasm his release from prison had generated.

On 14th March 1912, a bricklayer and anarchist by the name of
Antonio D'Alba made an assassination attempt on the King, Victor
Emanuel III. He fired a revolver but missed. Mussolini had just come
out of jail. Nenni was released on 29th May, but was almost immediately rearrested for writing that the Republican Party would not have
been sorry if the King had died. The reformists in the Socialist Party,
such as Leonida Bissolati and Ivanoe Bonomi, on the other hand, had
gone to the palace to pay their respects to the King and congratulate
him on his escape. Shortly after the assassination attempt, on 23rd
March, Mussolini wrote in *La lotta di classe*:

> The King may happen to be the head of state, but we socialists are only the
> constrained subjects of such a state. The King may be the symbol of the nation,
> but we socialists are only the constrained citizens of such a nation. The King's
> personal qualities are not in discussion. In our eyes he is a man like any other,
> subject as we all are to the ridiculous and tragic caprices of human destinies.
> Why should the socialists be more concerned about the King than about any
> other man? On the contrary! If we introduce an objective principle – the value
> of the individual as a producer – into our subjective responses, then we see that,
> between the misfortune which befalls a king and one which befalls a worker, the
> first leaves us indifferent while the second grieves us. The King is by definition
> a "useless" citizen.[4]

Mussolini's aggressive style was unsettling his opponents within the
party. On 15th June, demanding the release of Nenni, his rebuke was
aimed at many in the party beyond Forlì; he wrote ironically in *La
lotta di classe* how dangerous it was in Italy to remain unmoved by
what had happened to the King, since "some imbecile would come
and arrest you on a charge of being an apologist for regicide". On
21st June Nenni was released on bail. Shortly afterwards the National Socialist Congress, held on 7th July 1912, turned, like all such
occasions, on factions, on who and how many sided with whom.
Mussolini couldn't count on many votes – the Forlì Federation was
small – and he had no allies. Yet the congress was an outstanding
personal triumph for him. Tactically he was careful not to arouse
the suspicions of the majority bloc in the party, while at the same
time he wanted to inflame the delegates with a powerful speech. In
the account his sister Edvige gave of the event, Mussolini entered the
congress like "someone from genuine peasant stock", a "provincial

revolutionary" – which in effect he was. She paints a picture of him as awkward and clumsy compared to the sophisticated intellectuals who frequented the Turati-Kuliscioff circle, and conveys a sense of his solitariness, due in part to the essential mediocrity of the others in the revolutionary wing of the party. She admits her brother did not have the knowledge of Marxism possessed by other prominent delegates, but finds it natural that he should still have emerged "suddenly from nowhere as a miraculous leader", thanks to his words, his fiery oratory which he had learnt at his father's knee, and with which he blew on the embers of socialism in order to make them blaze.

The congress ended in victory for the revolutionaries and the expulsion of the reformist right wing of the party led by Bissolati. In the heat of his triumph, Mussolini published his analysis of the events of the congress in *Avanti!* on 18th July: "The Socialist Congress in Reggio Emilia should be seen as an attempted rebirth of idealism. [...] What does it matter to the proletariat to 'understand' socialism as a theory? Is it after all just a theory? We need to believe in it, we must believe in it, mankind needs *something* to believe in. Faith moves mountains, because it enables us to believe that mountains can move: in the end, illusion is perhaps the only reality in life."

Anna Kuliscioff, back in her elegant drawing room in Milan, began to ask herself and her guests what kind of socialism Mussolini could possibly be advocating. But the newspapers charted the rapid rise of this new member of the party's national committee: this "bold young man" cast in the mould of "the classic revolutionary" as Amilcare Cipriani wrote in *L'Humanité* on 26th August. A fifty-year-old lawyer from Milan, Cesare Sarfatti, who had just been elected as a Socialist deputy in parliament thanks to internal party arrangements, returned from the congress full of what he had heard and seen there; he described to his wife Margherita the forcefulness and energy with which Mussolini had addressed the delegates, the passion which stirred him and the sense of optimism he managed to convey. A leader like that communicated the sense that something could be done, that violence could be used to transform socialism into rigorous hard realities. "'Remember his name – he's the man of the future,' he told his wife. Sarfatti had been filled with enthusiasm listening to Mussolini's speeches to the congress, by what he praised to Margherita as his 'explosive seriousness of purpose'. Although he and his wife led largely separate lives, they shared a hunger for power."[5]

Margherita Sarfatti, née Grassini, decided she would like to get to know this young man – and ended up going to bed with him out of pure sexual curiosity, on a mere erotic impulse. She was very beautiful, very rich and very liberated. She only needed to invite him to her house and in he came, with his customary air of truculence and brusqueness of manner and arrogant conviction that yet another woman was ready to succumb to him. And yet, in his meeting with Margherita Sarfatti, something more complicated had begun: for the first time Mussolini found himself dealing with a woman driven by a desire for power. He didn't realize, at least at the outset, the cultural and financial resources his new mistress could call upon in her pursuit of power.

As a fifteen-year-old girl back in her native Venice, Sarfatti had been named "the Red Virgin" after she published an article in *Avanti!*. Her father, Amedeo Grassini, was a wealthy member of the city's middle class, with right-wing views; his Jewish roots meant nothing to him and he was a close associate of the city's archbishop. He had started life in the ghetto, but had bought Palazzo Bembo, where he had had a lift installed, the first in a private residence in the city. Margherita was taught by a Swiss governess at home. Every now and then she would escape from the house to go and find out about the poverty in which the working class had to live, and she picked up the rudiments of socialist teachings from pamphlets sold on the streets. She sent her article to *Avanti!* under a pseudonym, but her identity was discovered and caused a scandal at home: her father's business interests could be threatened by having a militant socialist for a daughter. Margherita was still a young girl. She realized she had one way out of her situation and pursued it with cynical determination. She picked out a man, a Jewish lawyer aged twenty-nine, fourteen years older than she was (he seemed even older with his old-fashioned moustache and heavy build), made him fall for her and then told him she would marry him only on the condition that he became a socialist. So she escaped from her father. The couple had three children in quick succession; when her father died in 1908 she inherited a vast fortune, enough to allow her to live as freely and as independently as was possible for a woman to do at the time. She and her husband moved to Milan, where they found the city's political life was dominated by another Jewish woman.

Anna Mikhailovna Kuliscioff, née Rosenstein, was the *éminence grise* of Italian socialism. In her apartment on the fourth floor of a palazzo in the heart of Milan, in Piazza Duomo, she held a salon which was frequented by intellectuals, artists, philosophers, writers and young men hoping to make a career in politics. She resembled a little the high-ranking women who ran influential salons in Enlightenment France. Meetings, debates, cultural exchange, intelligence and talent filled the rooms – and she oversaw it all, making sure that the rules of good behaviour and courtesy were respected and harmony prevailed. In this refined atmosphere no references to money or to violence were allowed. Political careers were made or broken here; strategies and tactics were planned and advanced. The Kuliscioff salon certainly helped to lend polish and urbanity to Socialist Party politics and enable the party's leaders to acquire knowledge of art and culture, but at the same time it was a closed circle. The attraction which Italian socialism felt for the elitism and snobbery of such ambiences has been a perennial failing of the party throughout its long history.

In the early twentieth century, the Kuliscioff salon in Milan was the epicentre of the left; its influence extended far beyond Milan. Kuliscioff was always dressed in a black skirt and gleaming white blouse, and smoked continually; you only needed to take one look at her to appreciate her determination and willpower. "The blonde Russian" was a figure of irresistible fascination for all prominent socialists. She and Andrea Costa had been lovers, and she had borne him a daughter, Andreina. From Costa she had learnt Italian and acquired an understanding of the politics of her adopted country; for him she became a source of inspiration.

On 6th May 1898 street rioting broke out in Milan because of a rise in the price of bread. The army general Beccaris ordered the demonstrators in the city to be surrounded and shot: eighty-four people died, according to the government, but the Socialists, who had not organized the demonstrations, estimated the number to be more than three hundred. Anna Kuliscioff was among the people arrested. Since she wasn't an Italian citizen she risked expulsion: the leading Socialist Filippo Turati, who was her lover at the time, offered to marry her in order to enable her to stay in the country, but Kuliscioff turned him down scornfully – marriage was a bourgeois arrangement. Their relationship had to stay true to the socialist principles of free love.

Sarfatti has left us a malicious portrait of Kuliscioff, though one which also reveals how much she was in awe of her:

> She had once been blonde and beautiful and now was faded; her face was wrinkled and her hair dull. She was crippled with arthritis, but her sheer strength of will enabled her to radiate a magnetic fascination. Inside her tortured body, which had suffered in the prisons of Russia, France and Italy, her pure and cold intelligence shone out like a multifaceted diamond. [...] She was idealistic and stoical; free of weakness but also of human warmth; only sensuality and the life of the mind moved her; there was a mystical strain in her Russian soul and a Russian harshness in the exercise of her intellect. She was full of proud ambition, yet without any personal vanity. It was so natural to her to get where and what she wanted by tortuous routes, she was quite incapable of acting straightforwardly. With her natural superiority she dominated the masses from the shadows, through parliament and the press, leaving the glory of action to the men who surrounded her...[6]

At the time Margherita Sarfatti and her husband moved to Milan, Kuliscioff was in a relationship with Filippo Turati and shared his pursuit of political power. The pair of them were in effect the leaders of Italy's first modern political party. And in her salon Kuliscioff could extend her influence over many other men.

The young Mussolini – dishevelled, with his black clothes coming apart at the seams, the pockets of his coat out of shape because of the newspapers he kept stuffing into them, with his provincial manners and abrupt gestures – was also one of her guests. He was too raw a recruit to hold his own in the elaborately analytical conversations that filled the rooms of Kuliscioff's apartment. Mussolini came from a background where he did without meals in order to buy newspapers. He was permanently short of money; he went about dressed in the same rather dirty outfit; he had the air of being out for a stroll on his travels about the province, but the truth was he had to walk from place to place, sometimes barefoot to save on shoe leather.

But in Kuliscioff's drawing room he needed to walk on tiptoe, and he couldn't. Kuliscioff observed the awkward and uncouth young man attentively and was unable to make him out. "For Mussolini it would have been a great triumph to win the admiration of the circle round Kuliscioff, but he never succeeded. Only occasionally did he manage to make Kuliscioff look on him indulgently, as if she were benevolently waiting to find out what he would make of himself. [...]

Turati never budged in his implacable dislike and contempt for this *agitateur* who'd struck lucky and who in his view had nothing to do with genuine socialism..."[7]

Margherita Sarfatti on the other hand could move with ease in Kuliscioff's political circle: she was fascinated by her and tried to imitate her. From Kuliscioff she learnt that a woman's path to power depended on men. As women, Sarfatti and Kuliscioff couldn't stand for parliament or even vote, but they could still play a prominent political role, albeit from the sidelines, by influencing their husbands and lovers and helping them practically in their careers by gathering information and by writing speeches full of literary and historical quotations. Margherita felt the need to find such a man whose career would become her project, and it wasn't going to be her husband Cesare. Like Kuliscioff, she herself couldn't go into politics, but politics, like being in love, was a passionate activity. She already had beauty and wealth on her side; in order to obtain the power she lacked and wanted she could exploit the passion of a man in love with her, guiding him towards the right doors he had to force open in order to make a political career.

On inheriting her father's vast wealth, she decided to start another political salon in Milan:

> She was beautiful, rich and young, and she knew how to exploit these qualities to the full. She admitted, with an air of scorn, that Anna Kuliscioff had certainly been a great beauty in the past. She observed the declining sex appeal of the older woman with the satisfied air of a younger one who knew her opportunities had still to come. The older woman herself was aware, with a pang, that the blonde Margherita was being praised for her winning beauty; she envied the new arrival's attractiveness, her wealth, her carefree demeanour. Anna had tightly constrained her restless life; the sight of Margherita was a painful reminder of how immobile her existence had become.[8]

In the new circle which formed round Margherita Sarfatti, Mussolini found the woman who could inspire him, who understood his potential and dedicated herself to developing it. He took advantage of what she offered him to the full, and when the time came to discard her he took the decision with his usual cynicism, completely untroubled by any moral misgivings. Shortly before the racial laws against the Jews were declared, on 2nd September 1938, he had one of his usual long, rambling conversations with his young mistress Claretta Petacci, who had just pointed out to him, gleefully, that she had been born the year he started his relationship with Sarfatti. By this time Petacci was well aware of the rules of the game of sexual initiation Mussolini was playing with her; with her obsession for writing things down, she recorded everything he said to her. It is true that her diary needs to be read with a certain caution; nevertheless, significant details are mentioned in it which are confirmed by other sources, such as Mussolini's sensitivity to smells and to women's perfume. Strong disturbing odours could influence his behaviour. He tells Petacci that Jews (against whom his new racial laws were about to unleash a tide of anti-Semitism) "stink". Because of her smell, he couldn't manage to penetrate Sarfatti the first time they slept together: "I just couldn't do it, because of this terrible smell they have. Perhaps it's to do with their diet, I wouldn't know. But I couldn't manage to do anything."[9]

After the National Socialist Congress had ended, Mussolini returned to Forlì and his daily routine, but his work as secretary to the Federation was now livelier, full of meetings and political assemblies, which were always followed by dancing and drinking. The revolutionary wing of the party was newly energized and focused round the figure of Mussolini. In Milan the party leadership had managed to delay a decision on the vacant post of the editor-in-chief of their official newspaper *Avanti!*. Three months after the congress, factional pressure from the tendency which had won a victory there forced them to accept Mussolini as a candidate. At a meeting of the party's national committee on 10th November 1912, the decision was unanimously taken to appoint him to the job. Mussolini moved to Milan, without his family, to take up his post on 1st December. He immediately marked the change of editorial regime by announcing that his predecessor Claudio Treves's salary of seven hundred lire had been too high: he would take a reduced figure of five hundred a month. The two men's dislike of each other became an open conflict which not even a subsequent duel between them managed to resolve.

1. Benito Mussolini in 1922,
shortly after he had become head of government.

2. A view of Predappio, the birthplace of Mussolini (above).
3. The house in which Mussolini was born (below).

4. Letter of 8th September 1895 from Rosa Maltoni to the Prefect of Forlì asking for a subsidy for her son Benito, "who – according to his teachers – shows some signs of promise".

5. Rosa Maltoni and Alessandro Mussolini, the Duce's parents (above).
6. Rachele Mussolini, the Duce's wife (bottom left). 7. Presumed photo of Ida Dalser and
Benito Albino, the son born from Dalser's affair with Mussolini (bottom right).

8. Bruno and Vittorio, the two elder sons of the Duce (top left). 9. Mussolini with his daughter Edda when she was seventeen (top right). 10. Mussolini and his family: his wife Rachele, Anna Maria, Romano, Edda, Bruno and Vittorio (below).

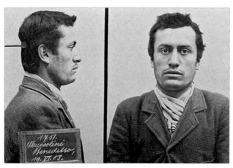

11. Letter from Mussolini to a friend dated 3rd September 1902 from Lausanne, which begins: "Dear friend, what I am about to write down are the sad memories of a disillusioned youth for whom everything is fading away – even the ideal. You mustn't tell anyone about the contents of the following pages: a woman alone knows my pain, and once you've read this, you'll know too (top left, above). 12. Mugshot of "Benedetto" Mussolini after his arrest in Switzerland in June 1903 (top left, below). 13. Mussolini the revolutionary in Lausanne, October 1904: "To my mother – grateful and mindful" (top right). 14. Mussolini as a Bersagliere during his early service as a soldier (bottom left). 15. Mussolini in 1910, when he was appointed editor of the newspaper *La lotta di classe* in Forlì (bottom right).

16. Mussolini in 1913, when he became editor of *Avanti!* (top left). 17. Mussolini in 1915, as a Bersagliere on Mount Javoršček during the war (top right). 18. Mussolini, on the right, in the Kras trenches with his comrades (bottom left). 19. Mussolini posing as a member of the Arditi during the First World War (bottom right).

20. The military hospital in which Mussolini stayed,
shown after being bombarded by the Austrians in 1915.

Chapter 8

Scent of a Woman

There was a smell of incense and sandalwood when you entered, then a faint trace of citrus followed by the sensation there was a bowl full of apples nearby; once you turned the corner of the hallway, a sudden intense fragrance assailed you – a combination of thyme, lavender, rosemary, mint. Then, at the door of the drawing room a sharp smell of varnish which gave way to a gentler smell of mild tobacco. Meanwhile the scent of roasting coffee wafted nearer. Waves of perfumed air, now acute, now subtle, drifted round them as they made their way towards the sofas and cushions in the room. "Blessings on the guest who comes to my house," Leda murmured. Her mouth was large, and her eyes were black and shining; as she shut the door the illusion of being transported to the East was complete. The long robe she had wound round her showed the soft curves of her figure as she moved; her warm presence was disquieting. The windows faintly glimmered with the last light at dusk; a pierced brass lamp had already been lit and threw its curious shadow patterns on the walls. There was no doubt that strange dreams could be dreamt on those sofas. Some scented leaves were scattered over a low table; Leda brushed them aside, releasing a brief fragrance of honey and violets. Then she put the coffee pot down and proceeded to pour it into two small cups of Arab design. She handed him his coffee and their hands touched. A quiver darted through them. "Muslims drink coffee together as a sign of friendship," she said. "Friends who have drunk coffee together are incapable of treachery."[1]

Leda Rafanelli was three years older than Mussolini, not that this mattered to either of them. She had anarchist and socialist leanings and was a committed Muslim. Writing came easily to her: as a very young girl she had published a poem in *Avanti!*. Her family had moved to Alexandria in Egypt; while there she had come into contact with some of the anarchists who belonged to the large Italian community in the city. She had also travelled extensively in the country in order to find out more about its history and traditions. She became fascinated by Sufism and decided to become a Muslim. She saw her conversion as a form of protest against Western culture and its repressive colonialism. When she returned to Italy she began to write regularly for *Avanti!*. She was married very briefly to an anarchist by the name of Ugo Polli; after they separated she had relationships with several men, including the Futurist painter Carlo Carrà.

She waited patiently, in silence, for Mussolini to emerge from his embarrassment. It was his first visit, and all the scents and smells he had encountered had turned his head. He needed some time to focus properly on the woman now sitting opposite him. He eventually noticed that round her neck she wore a pendant on a simple string which formed a "V" shape over her breasts. Leda saw his glance and explained that the pendant was made of sandalwood and combined the two basic streams of the life force, yin and yang. Her visitor gave no sign of wanting to leave; in fact, he started to recline on the sofa. Rafanelli thought good Muslims should not show their tiredness in the presence of a guest, so she let him stay stretched out on the sofa while for the next three hours she told him stories of her life and travels. The next day she received a letter from the new editor-in-chief of *Avanti!*: "Visiting you in your house was a revelation and a surprise for me. You made me feel I was in the marvellous and mysterious Orient, with its intense perfumes and its mad, fascinating fantasies, and for this I want to thank you. Please forgive me if I seemed ill at ease and untalkative – that is what I am like. But I will keep a sweet memory of the afternoon spent in your company. Nor will I mention it to another living soul."[2]

Mussolini became a frequent visitor to Leda Rafanelli's "oriental" house, often staying until the small hours, lulled by the perfumes and the tales she told him. She was struck by how easily he gave way to her in all their discussions; he was always quick to give up on an opinion – even one he had just expressed – in order to agree with his new friend's point of view. In her memoirs, written after the Second World War, Rafanelli dismisses Mussolini as someone who, far from being tough and intransigent, switched opinions and changed his mind easily. And it is true that in politics he frequently and rapidly abandoned positions which only a moment before had appeared to be unchangeable beliefs. With Leda Rafanelli, on the other hand, it was a mere tactic to reach his goal, the usual goal, the only one which mattered to him – and one which could be consummated on the very sofa on which he was sitting, breathing in deeply the strange aromas. She too deployed tactics of her own, making the process of courtship as complicated as a maze in which at every turn she could disappear and reappear at a whim. Mussolini grew impatient and tried to undermine such a tortuous construction by speaking bluntly of free love, of sex, of jealousy – but he was too hasty. Leda began to regret welcoming him to the warm fragrant sitting room with its atmosphere of erotic disturbance and desire. It would have been better if they'd met in his office at the newspaper, after she had given him her new article.

She asked him if he was married, and he told her he wasn't, which was true. Then did he live with someone, did he have a partner? Intent on reaching his goal, Mussolini said he hadn't. Leda found herself increasingly pushed back into a corner where her only choice was either to yield to his pressure or react violently against it. He asked her if she was jealous. No, she retorted, she wasn't jealous of him. Why on earth should she be?

"Very well, since you're not jealous of me, I can tell you a secret: there are two women who are passionately in love with me but I don't love them. Can you guess who they are?" "I'm not interested in knowing who they are," I replied – and I remember that I was genuinely indifferent – and added, "Besides, it's not very gallant of you to tell me another woman's secrets – two women's secrets." "No, it's because you're truly my friend and you wouldn't be jealous… One is really ugly, but she has a noble and generous soul. The other one is beautiful but she's deceitful, avaricious, even sordid. […] The woman who's ugly and good-natured is Angelica Balabanoff." I gave a start – I knew her well, knew her to be a strong and courageous socialist, I had greeted her many times after speeches she had given brimming with revolutionary ardour, and I admired her. The thought of her suffering the pains of unreciprocated love grieved me. But immediately another thought struck me: Balabanoff was different from other women: she was a Slav by temperament, used to life's struggles, she was widely travelled and knew socialists in many different countries; she certainly wasn't the sentimental faint-hearted type who'd be plunged into despair because a man didn't care for her. "What about the other woman?" I asked, almost against my will but wanting to change the subject away from the brave Angelica Balabanoff. "The avaricious beauty? That's the writer Margherita Sarfatti, as sly as Balabanoff is honest."

"You mean the wife of the lawyer Sarfatti?" "That's her... her love is obsessive, but I'll never be able to return her feelings."[3]

The tactics Mussolini used with women who hadn't surrendered to him within a few hours or, at most, a few days were not over-refined. They were the usual techniques of the "hunter male", cynical and banal. But during his period as editor of *Avanti!* Mussolini found himself up against strong-minded and determined women who left a mark on him. In her essay which was appended to Balabanoff's book on him, Maria Giudice, perhaps wishing to dismantle what she saw as the central element of the myth, describes Mussolini in these terms:

> Benito Mussolini, with his physical and cultural shortcomings, his lack of mo-
> rality, his unsteady temperament often subject to rapid changes of mood – he
> often openly admitted he was an opportunist – closely resembled the clay-footed
> giant mentioned in the Bible in connection with Nebuchadnezzar. He always
> knew his feet were of clay, he was aware of this weakness inside him with a kind
> of obsessive fear, so he was always searching for a reliable support. He found it
> in two women: Angelica Balabanoff during the period he still called himself a
> socialist, and then, later on when he became an interventionist and subsequently
> a Fascist, Margherita Grassini Sarfatti. Both women were highly cultivated, both
> exceptionally intelligent.[4]

So the editor of the leading socialist newspaper prowled Milan in search of his usual short-lived adventures; the new women in his life were now firmly centre stage. An increasingly angry and impatient Rachele had stayed at home, back in Forlì, together with their small daughter Edda; she was well aware of what the man she called her husband would get up to if left on his own in Milan for too long. Angelica Balabanoff was indispensable to him for her help with managing the paper and contributing to the editorial work; Margherita Sarfatti was introducing him to the world of culture and art, and gradually teaching him, with her own sense of style and the money at her disposal, how to dress and behave; Ida Irene Dalser had followed him to Milan from Trento, and it is probable that he still enjoyed being in her company. Leda Rafanelli also contributed to *Avanti!* and Mussolini was only too willing to let her exotic perfumes weave their coils around him.

He stood up to go. For the first time his visit had been brief. I didn't ask him to stay. [...] At the door of the room he suddenly and unexpectedly – it was so sudden and unexpected I didn't have time to react – embraced me and kissed me. I felt his face burning as if he had a fever. I didn't have time to withdraw from the embrace, but I didn't return his kiss. During his previous visits I had realized what he wanted and had always been careful to avoid giving him any opportunity, but the gesture now came so unexpectedly that I had to submit to it.[5]

So Leda had submitted to the kiss, the kiss had taken place and she either failed to extricate herself or found herself incapable of doing so. For Mussolini it confirmed his conquest. At twenty-nine he found himself occupying the most influential position a revolutionary could hold; when he wished to conquer a woman, he regularly triumphed.

Now that he was the editor of *Avanti!*, he and his opinions were prominent on the national stage; he didn't lead the party, but he was its most publicly visible exponent. He fired off some broadsides: what he called the "inert masses" of socialism must rapidly become a strategic force to bring about change, otherwise nothing could be achieved. As soon as he'd been given the editorship he asked for Angelica Balabanoff to work alongside him as his deputy – not because he felt insecure in his new post, as she herself and various historians have surmised. Renzo De Felice sees it as a tactical manoeuvre:

It is my considered opinion that Mussolini wanted the collaboration with Balabanoff – which because of her rigidly held Marxism was an uneasy and turbulent partnership – in order to "compromise" so to speak, at least in the early days, the whole revolutionary wing of the party, to force it to share in the responsibility for the direction in which he intended to take the newspaper, so that he wouldn't be seen as the only proponent of a change which was bound to cause a rift between the majority and minority tendencies in the party.[6]

Mussolini exploited his success in the classic way and used Balabanoff to get rid of the reformist journalists who had been working for the paper. He also came into conflict with some of its leading contributors, beginning with his predecessor Treves. Treves had signed a contract to continue contributing articles to the paper and immediately submitted three pieces which Mussolini as promptly rejected. On leaving the editorship, Treves had the right to severance pay, but Mussolini insisted he shouldn't get it and accused him of greed. Kuliscioff, a close friend of Treves and a fellow Jew, had to mediate between the two men. "Kuliscioff's worth a lot more than most men, even the best," Mussolini commented to his family, much to the amazement of his sister Edvige. "There was no love lost – and not much contact – between the new, prickly, turbulent editor of *Avanti!* and the circle round Kuliscioff in her apartment in Piazza Duomo, where she and Turati worked on some form of politics which attempted to remain true to Marxism and be post-Marxist at the same time, all the while dispensing hospitality to friends and followers with a style which was both typically Milanese and also cosmopolitan."[7]

In the end Mussolini agreed to let Treves have his severance pay, but only on condition that he donated it to a fund which supported the newspaper. Kuliscioff, defeated, was alarmed by the situation; she even wrote to Turati suggesting a bomb should be placed in the new editor-in-chief's office. She tried to enlist the support of the party's executive committee to no avail. In the meantime Mussolini was busy filling the place with journalists who were loyal to him as well as engaging some prominent writers, such as Gaetano Salvemini and Sergio Panunzio, as contributors along with various revolutionary syndicalists. The party's executive committee decided to approve the new line the paper had adopted. Mussolini's observation was a shrewd one: Kuliscioff was "worth more than most men" and was the only person capable of opposing his rapid takeover of the party, but fortunately for him, she wasn't a man and wasn't in a position to muster and manoeuvre others to support her.

The beginning of 1913 saw a series of bloody massacres in the course of political demonstrations throughout the country, from Sicily to the Po Valley. The clashes were particularly severe in Roccagorga, in the Ciociaria region, around sixty miles south-east of Rome, where on 6th January seven agricultural labourers were shot dead by army troops. The following day Mussolini joined the fray with a hard-hitting article under the headline "State-Sponsored Murder"; the government reacted by bringing an accusation of incitement of class hatred against him. He was unconcerned. Before he appeared in court, the thought crossed his mind that a trial and possible condemnation might win the sympathy of some of the women he was pursuing. He wrote to Leda Rafanelli:

So what do you say? When can I come round and see you? I come back from Rome on Tuesday morning, but on Thursday the trial begins and I've no idea how long the grotesque charade will last. Let's hope the Milan jury are intelligent enough to find me guilty. Wednesday afternoon is the only time I'm free. What about then? Spring is in the air, the capricious weather of March is over, and you can buy bunches of violets from the Milan flower-sellers. But they're not scented. Do you think even the spring violets are on strike?[8]

Angelica Balabanoff observed Mussolini and his behaviour closely, even down to small details, so she must have realized how sensitive he was to perfumes and to smells in general. In her memoir, she examines this aspect of his personality, deriding his obsession with smell and interpreting it as a form of hysteria.

One evening I was working alone in the newspaper offices when Mussolini came in. I hardly recognized him, he seemed to be in pieces, tottering as if carrying a heavy weight... he threw himself down in an armchair, buried his face in his hands and started to sob. I shut the door so that no one who came into the office would see this spectacle and asked him, with the calm which is the only proper response to hysteria, what had happened to him. "What do you mean, can't you smell it?" he replied in a hoarse voice, lifting his face towards me. He seemed hardly human, and I felt pity for him. "What smell?" "You mean you don't smell the ether," he replied irritably. "The doctor had to take a blood sample. I fainted, and since then I can't get rid of the smell of the gas." He started to swear.[9]

Margherita Sarfatti also recalls the episode in her memoir *My Fault*, written after the fall of the regime: Mussolini had fainted when Dr Pini, a fellow socialist, had taken a blood sample from him: the results of the test were not promising, and her lover had angrily cursed the young free-living woman who had infected him in Switzerland.

Mussolini's extreme sensitivity to smell could on occasion induce an uncharacteristic faint-heartedness in him: an example is his seduction of Cornelia Tanzi when he was already installed as Duce. Tanzi was a bewitchingly beautiful brunette; her mother ran a brothel in Rome, and there were rumours that her daughter every now and then helped out. After her affair with Mussolini had ended, various leading Fascist Party officials enjoyed her favours; she boasted of her conquests. After the war she was sentenced to thirty years in prison by the special tribunal set up to weed out ex-Fascists and the regime's collaborators: providing sex free for Fascists was obviously seen as a more serious offence than shooting Partisans or deporting Jews, given that most of the men responsible for these crimes were given lighter sentences than Tanzi. But Mussolini had problems with Cornelia Tanzi's smell, as he confided to Claretta Petacci:

> She's got long legs, she's slender, light, tall, dark-haired. Yet she's frigid beyond belief. She never feels any pleasure, not even with me. She arrived, undressed, took her slip off, showing her long legs, then lay down on the bed to begin, without a flicker of interest. She would lie there showing complete indifference and then would get up, dress and leave. It took less than half an hour. Let me tell you something else: the last time with her was really an effort, I couldn't manage to do anything, I wasn't in the mood. And then she'd put on a particular perfume which smelt disgusting... I'm sorry, you know how sensitive I am to these things. No, I never loved her; whenever I went with her, I always felt like a poor wretch, I shouldn't have done it. I can't think why on earth I did, I'm an animal. [...] Afterwards, I felt nothing but disgust. I wanted to beat her up, throw her on the floor.[10]

Having seen off the challenges to his editorship and taken control of the workings of the newspaper, Mussolini threw himself into a violent political campaign, without forgetting the need to attack the enemy reformist wing within the party itself. Treves and Turati countered with brilliant articles on the theory of socialism, but they lacked Mussolini's energy and impetus. On 3rd February the revolutionary wing of the Socialist Party in Naples declared a strike against the government; even Giacinto Menotti Serrati distanced himself from Mussolini on this occasion, criticizing him. In April the car workers of Milan went on strike. The General Confederation of Labour refused to support the initiative which they thought was counter-productive at a time of national crisis, but Mussolini and *Avanti!* sided with them. The strike started to spread: there was an atmosphere of unrest, violent clashes, and after a few days the city's transport workers decided to join their fellow strikers from the car factories. There was a fear of harsh reprisals from the government. An editorial in *Avanti!* warned the government not to intervene with armed force, since if they did "the sympathy we feel for every class struggle, even when it doesn't conform to the strategy we have proposed, would become full solidarity with the strikers, at which point... the entire working class would take up arms."

Mussolini began to seem to many, including Salvemini himself, to be the man who was needed to lead the Italian revolutionary movement. The reformist camp within the Socialist Party now openly spoke of his populist aims and accused him of ill-defined nationalist-socialist positions which exalted the disorganized and directionless masses who had turned out to celebrate Italy's invasion of Libya. To no avail, just as their attempt to spread the view that Mussolini was not really a socialist came to nothing. It is true he was an autodidact in political matters, his theoretical grounding was full of lacunae, his uncertainties were manifold, but in terms of his general cultural background he was certainly not inferior to the vast majority of his local comrades in the party, a state of affairs which reflected the general backwardness of Italian socialism. As De Felice has remarked: "How many real socialists were there in Italy at the time, taking socialism to mean something more than the commonly accepted definition of the time, i.e. more than someone with a basic belief in social determinism and class struggle?"[11]

Kuliscioff, Treves and Turati made another attempt to ambush Mussolini at a meeting of the party's national executive on 13th July 1913, but his editorial policy was approved by seven votes to (their) three. But Mussolini wanted an outright victory, and he got it by resigning, at which point the whole executive, including the minority who opposed him, were forced to reject his resignation and confirm their support of his editorship. He had the party firmly behind him and felt free to change tactics. He suddenly withdrew the newspaper's support for the Milan strikers, declaring there was no point in continuing the struggle; he turned his attention instead to the coming general election and launched a fierce campaign in support of the Socialist Party candidates. On election day, 2nd November, the party had nearly a million votes and won fifty-seven seats in parliament. The campaign waged by Mussolini allowed him to claim responsibility for the success and present it as proof that the intransigent line followed by the party's revolutionary tendency was the winning strategy, because it was supported by the country's proletariat.

Mussolini's daily life had never been quiet, but now it became frenetic: he wrote all day and every day articles, notes for lectures, political briefings for party colleagues. He was also writing letters, especially to Leda Rafanelli, with whom he continued a complicated relationship. He tripped up in one of them by writing hastily that he was off to take his "domestic tribe" to the seaside. Rafanelli seized on the phrase: "So he had a family? What kind of family? His mother was dead. Perhaps there was a sister? Two people... A wife and a son? So he had lied to me when he told me he was 'as free as a bird'?"[12] It can be difficult for a liar to keep track of his lies. Rafanelli's sudden coldness towards him made Mussolini realize he had made a mistake, and he tried to recover ground in his next letter:

> Monday evening, nine o'clock. My darling Leda, you haven't written to me for three days. Why ever not? But I can guess the reason. I thought you were stronger, more "human" than that. So we're finished? Our love which promised to be so marvellous is over? And all because of a stupid involuntary mistake? You cannot know how much your silence hurts me. Write to me, even if you only want to curse me, but write to me I beg you. Tell me everything. It's ridiculous for lovers to keep secrets from each other. I'm waiting for you today, Tuesday. Your grief-stricken and passionate Benito kisses you.[13]

But she kept him dangling for a long while. The passage of time, however, didn't help to calm her down. After three days she wanted to end their relationship, if possible, conclusively. She could never have a relationship with a man who had a wife, even if he wasn't legally married to her, and a daughter waiting for him at home. As a Muslim, she thought this was the typical subterfuge adopted in the West's approach to relationships: "In the West a man swears he'll be monogamous and wants to be loved exclusively and for ever... we should accept the wise law of the East: a man may take, freely, publicly, two or even three wives, and this produces order and peace within the family, because men are polygamous by nature."[14]

Yet Mussolini's simple ploy was proving effective. It was "just" a matter of getting Rafanelli to interrupt her stand-off. Whatever she said or wrote, even if it were a stream of abuse, could be used to put things back together between them and start again. However, when he finally got to meet her, outside the protective perfumed refuge of her house, this strategy came up against his more urgent desire to get her into bed as quickly as possible. He stammered a series of excuses and then tried to kiss her; she pushed him away. He started to justify himself again and made another attempt. Writing in her memoirs many years after the event, Rafanelli describes how their conversation continued, in a dark Milan street. Mussolini said to her:

"All right, let's speak about us. Now that we're alone together... how long can you stay with me?"

"Half an hour at the most."

"That's not much, hardly any time at all. Listen... why stay here in the dark? I want to look at you. Let's go to the Diana, it's near here."

"To a hotel? Out of the question! Anyway, you owe me an explanation, that's the important thing... Your 'domestic tribe', who does it consist of exactly?"

He suddenly started and let go of my hand.

"My what?..."

"Your 'domestic tribe... the two of them'. That's what you wrote, remember? I should know you by now. Who are these two people?"

He stayed silent for a moment or two. Then he said in a low voice:

"My wife and my daughter."

There was an even longer pause. I said:

"Why have you always lied to me?"

"You always told me you knew anyway..."

"But you always denied it... You told me that if I knew you had a wife or you were living with another woman I would break off our friendship."

"But it's an obsession! It doesn't matter whether I've got a wife or not. She's used to my infidelities. She's a good woman..."[15]

The good woman Rachele, who knew nothing of what was going on but was guided by some kind of survival instinct, hurried to Milan. There, with the little Edda in tow, she unexpectedly turned up in front of Mussolini and demanded they resume a normal family life. Subsequently, in her memoirs, she romanticized the episode, describing how Mussolini went to Forlì to take her back with him and also mentioned how he'd taken a reduced salary – five hundred lire a month in contrast to the seven hundred which his predecessor Treves had earned – in order to help the party's coffers. The news angered her: she reminded him who had to do the shopping, look after their daughter, what her own requirements were. "Benito had a job calming me down, but in the end we set off hopefully for Milan, having sold some possessions to pay for the journey and for a few days' stay in a cheap *pensione* once we arrived. As the months passed, our situation improved. We could afford to rent an apartment in Via Castel Morrone in a working-class suburb of the city; I could start to believe that our hard times were over and done with for ever..."[16]

Mussolini's rediscovered family life in Milan didn't stop his adventures. Relations with Rafanelli remained tense, but he managed to heal the rift to the point where he could write to her in a letter from his office: "My dear friend, just a moment ago, completely exhausted after a long detailed discussion, the strong perfume I know so well told me a letter from you had arrived, and I shouted for joy. That's right, I shouted for joy. [...] You know what a strange magical power a perfume has over me – your perfume, so intense and intriguing, so strange and so remote."[17]

Apart from the few women who managed to exercise a fascination over him or who impressed him with their intellectual superiority, Mussolini's general attitude to the female sex is soon summed up. Silvio Bertoldi described it thus: he never wasted time, even with women he'd just met. They didn't need to be beautiful. His approach was basic: "If he succeeded, all well and good; if it failed, too bad. This was his method and this was what women were for. Hadn't he once remarked to an acquaintance: 'All you need to do with women, old chap, is beat them and give them babies'?"[18]

Maria Giudice tells the story of a provincial schoolmistress who made a trip to Milan in order to deliver an article she had written to the offices of *Avanti!* and to see Mussolini. Giudice felt sorry for the shy young woman and decided to accompany her into the editor's office. She writes that Mussolini's frowning expression was even grumpier than usual: he was in one of his black moods. He showed no politeness towards the poor young woman and didn't stand as she came in. He hardly looked at her but planted his fists on the desk and leant towards her, as if about to devour her alive, and said fiercely: "'Do you know what I think about women? I think they should stay at home to do the housework, obey their husbands and, every now and then, be given a good beating.' It's easy to imagine how the unfortunate woman reacted, what she did and what she said, but it's immaterial since we've told the story simply to show what kind of man Mussolini really was."[19]

The women he encountered for short-lived adventures left no trace, but the strong decisive women in Mussolini's life – like Sarfatti, Balabanoff and Rachele herself – must have had some effect on him to judge from remarks he wrote – in *Pensieri Pontini e Sardi* (*Thoughts from Ponza and Sardinia*) – much later, on 16th August 1943, when he had been imprisoned and was tired and demoralized:

"*Chercher la femme* – people will try to do this when they interpret my destiny. But women have never had the slightest influence on my political life. Perhaps that was a disadvantage. Women's sensibilities are more finely tuned than men's, and that sometimes makes them more far-seeing."[20]

Under Mussolini's editorship and the aggressive style of journalism he adopted, *Avanti!*'s daily circulation soared from the 34,000 it had been under Treves to an average of 60,000, on occasion reaching 100,000. At the National Socialist Congress, held in Ancona from 26th to 29th April 1914, the increase in the paper's circulation and the success of its campaigning in the elections attracted much attention, as did the man responsible for them, Benito Mussolini. He became in effect the real leader of the party. The socialist press reporting the congress described his speeches as fascinating and compelling; the man who gave them seemed like "an ascetic", his voice like a forest murmur, his gestures like someone haunted by a nightmare. If there had been a vote, the party's militants would have chosen him as their leader, but congresses depend on the votes of the delegates, not of the members, and it was the delegates who voted in the new executive committee. According to Pietro Nenni, Mussolini was received with thunderous applause at the congress; he couldn't recall anyone who had achieved such prestige and power within the party. He reported from the congress in the journal *Lucifero* on 3rd May: "The party has the good fortune to be led by a man who is upright and honest. Benito Mussolini is neither a great intellect nor a great speaker, but he has incomparable moral force, driven, like all such moral forces, by ruthless logic." Nenni adjusted his view in the years after the First World War: in Russia Lenin had emerged to put into practice the revolutionary will of the working masses, while Italy had Mussolini, revolutionary in temperament but unprincipled, someone who pursued action for action's sake, whose burning ambition impelled him forward in the effort to ensure his own personal success at all costs.

The Ancona congress led officially to a kind of triumvirate leading the party, composed of the new secretary Costantino Lazzari, Mussolini as the editor of *Avanti!* and Oddino Morgari, the leader of the Socialist Party group in parliament. It was perfectly clear to everyone, however, that the real leader – the man who could make or break a strike, get a candidate elected, confront the police head on and mobilize the socialist masses – was Mussolini. It was merely a question of seeing where his political tactics would take him. Mussolini had in the meantime founded a magazine, *Utopia*, which was intended to contribute to the theoretical and ideological debate. Margherita Sarfatti was one of its leading contributors; she later emphasized the journal's importance as a link between Mussolini's socialism and his subsequent Fascism:

> A careful reader of *Utopia* can see, from the very first issue, that the orthodox line was being criticized. Some of its fundamental assertions were clearly heretical from the outset, however hedged about they were with sophistries and qualifications, such as: "A desperate enterprise. The socialists fell victim to a grave illusion. They believed that capitalism had reached the end of its historical development. But capitalism is capable of continuing. [...] The socialist revolution is not an intellectual scheme or a political calculation; it is above all an act of faith. I believe in the socialist revolution." [...] In its convictions, methods, ideas, the Fascism of today is the fulfilment of the most vital part of the revolutionary socialism of the past. Many people see beyond the labels and realize this is the case and that is why they adhere to Fascism.[21]

"Faith and revolution" – the verbal pairing became a standard slogan during the twenty years of the Fascist regime. In his interview with Mussolini, the journalist Ludwig asked him about the phrase:

> "You've written that 'if Fascism weren't a faith, how could it inspire courage and ardour?' But doesn't communism do this?"
>
> "That's no concern of mine."
>
> "Then is it the element of faith – which both you and the Soviet leaders encourage and find in the masses – that distinguishes your systems from other political systems?"
>
> Mussolini agreed. "There's an even greater resemblance between us – in all the things we're opposed to. We and the Soviets are against liberals, democrats, the parliamentary system."[22]

Barely two months after the National Socialist Congress in Ancona, on 28th June 1914, the pistol shot fired by Gavrilo Princip changed European politics. In Sarajevo, the car that was carrying the heir to the Habsburg throne, Franz Ferdinand, took a wrong turning. As the driver was reversing to change direction, Princip found himself unexpectedly in front of the royal couple sitting in the open-topped car and fired. The first bullet hit Sophie, the wife of Franz Ferdinand. Her husband was wearing a bulletproof vest under his uniform, but the second bullet hit him in the neck. He remained upright on the back seat of the car as his life drained away. Two rapid shots, only apparently fired by chance. Archduke Franz Ferdinand was destined not to leave Sarajevo alive: only that morning he had narrowly escaped a bomb attack. The pretext was now in place for the long-threatened outbreak of a European war.

At the meeting of the party's executive committee, which had been delayed until 3rd August 1914, Mussolini advocated the hard line of the Socialist International in calling for a general strike and popular insurrection if the Italian government decided to bring the country into the war. He wrote in *Avanti!*: "May the masses cry out with one voice and may their cry resound through the streets and squares of Italy: 'Down with war!' The day has come for the Italian proletariat to obey its vow of old – 'We won't send a single soldier, we won't give a single penny – whatever it takes!'"

But for all its emphasis and show of resolve, Mussolini's line was not especially effective as a political move, given that the Church had also come out against the war, the Italian government had immediately declared neutrality, and the socialist International was utterly divided on the issue, with the Belgians against the Germans, the French determined to defend their country, and the Austrians ready to come in to support them. In Italy too, positions began to shift. Bissolati publicly demanded a change in the view that a policy of strict neutrality was the only option for the country's workers; at best it was a tactical move, intended to preserve military strength before entering the conflict in the defence of democracy. Salvemini too came out against a hard-line policy of neutrality, arguing that in order to combat the rising tide of nationalism Italy needed to take part in a conflict of national interests and should not let the war play itself out without resolving the problem of the Italian population of Trento and Trieste who were still under Austro-Hungarian rule. Even the revolutionary trade-unionist Alceste De Ambris, speaking on behalf of many in the trade-union movement, openly asserted that the socialism represented by the International had failed in the face of the war; what was needed now was to prevent the victory of Austria and Germany. These were men of impeccable socialist credentials; their outspoken views caused an outcry. On 6th September yet another prominent socialist, Filippo Corridoni, who had just been released from prison, announced that neutrality was a policy of the weak; Italian socialism could not be seen to ally itself with a government secretly intent on supporting the Austrian side.

On 12th August Cesare Battisti arrived in Italy from Trento; he was a member of the Austrian Socialist Party but his influence was strong among Italian socialists, including the man who had formerly worked for his newspaper and was now the editor-in-chief of *Avanti!* – Mussolini. Once in Milan Battisti began a campaign to persuade the Italian public to come out in favour of entering the war against Austria. In public Mussolini held to his policy of strict neutrality, although he allowed differing points of view to be expressed in the newspaper, but in private his thinking started to waver. In various private meetings, including with French and Belgian socialists, he commented that a change in the party line was possible, and his remarks, which contrasted with the official position, were noticed in wider circles. He had a long meeting with Cesare Battisti in the headquarters of the regional journalists' association in Milan, not the most appropriate place to hold a private conversation. Many of the journalists who were there that day overheard him saying that neutrality was nonsensical, that the Italian Socialist Party couldn't allow itself to give complicit support to the imperial powers in the pursuit of their own interests, that the Italian Risorgimento needed to be completed. Battisti publicly reported how pleased he was to hear the editor of *Avanti!* expressing such views, even if only in conversation.

Angelica Balabanoff's misgivings were aroused. In an alliance with one of the senior editors on the paper, Eugenio Guarino, she made sure that the public pronouncements of the man who had been her protégé were kept under control. Some other socialist magazines started to talk of "two Mussolinis" and asked themselves which one would come out on top. Leda Rafanelli was opposed to the war and wrote a series of articles in support of the policy of maintaining strict neutrality. Mussolini told her she had his "unconditional" support and asked her for an opinion on the articles he was writing. All the time, as part of a spreading breakaway movement, the number of Socialist Party members who were coming out in favour of Italy entering the war was growing; in many newspapers and journals there were frequent calls to fight alongside the French and the Belgians.

The situation must have been tormenting for Mussolini; he was a step away from his main political goal of being recognized as the leader of the Socialist Party. He confided his concerns in a letter to Rafanelli (which also included a ploy to get her to meet him):

> I am feeling sad and downcast. It's as if everyone around me is drunk. Even men who never used to drink, now they too are like this. I soon won't be able to trust you, or even myself. [...] It's terrible – Ciardi, Corridoni, Rygier coming out in support of the war! It's like a kind of contagion affecting everyone. But I'm determined to fight to the finish. I'll come and visit you next week – it's been so long since we've seen each other. I know no one in Milan – I could almost say no one in Italy – whom I feel I can confide in. I need encouragement. The proletariat seems to me deaf and confused and remote...[23]

Mussolini was losing his grip on the party, which a few months earlier had seemed so firm. The increasing number of those who were advocating Italian intervention left him without room to manoeuvre, as if he were a prisoner of the neutralist approach he'd adopted even though there were better and more convincing spokesmen for it in the likes of Treves, Turati and Balabanoff herself. He was trying to find a way of escaping the impasse which would otherwise wear him down. It wasn't just a matter of airing different views in private conversations held in bars or in clubs. Sarfatti writes that he referred to his growing doubts in a public speech he gave:

> One evening in September, the Socialist Party in Milan decided to debate the choice between absolute and relative neutrality. Mussolini was asked to speak as the – hitherto – leading proponent of maintaining a position of absolute neutrality. So it came as a bolt from the blue when he spoke frankly to the audience of his tormenting doubts. [...] His usual eloquent flow of speech was halting, anguished, hesitant with introspective anxiety, now that it was a question of general ideas, a problem of conscience, a position which would have grave implications for the future. At one point he exclaimed: "Yes, the poet's words have now become ours: *We who loved you, O France.*"[24]

That Mussolini was in difficulties did not escape the notice of Filippo Naldi, the editor of the Bologna daily newspaper *Il Resto del Carlino*, which was financed by major landowners and had come out on the side of intervention in the war. When Leda Rafanelli went to the

Avanti! offices one day to hand in yet another article she had written opposing the conflict, she found all the editorial staff in uproar. Naldi had laid a trap for Mussolini. One of the journalists showed Rafanelli an article which had been published in *Il Resto del Carlino* criticizing Mussolini. The headline left the reader in no doubt as to its contents: "The editor of *Avanti!* is a man of straw!" On 7th October 1914 Naldi, in agreement with the newspaper's owners, had published an open letter from Massimo Rocca, writing under the pseudonym of Libero Tancredi, in which Mussolini was attacked for duplicity, bad faith and betraying his own country. Rocca-Tancredi presented himself as an outspoken outsider who couldn't prevent himself saying exactly what he thought. He addressed Mussolini in these words: "You are the only person among the small group who lead the Socialist Party today who is capable of making a stand. I have already told you, in private conversation, how saddened I am to see a party representing a vital force in Italian politics led today, at such a tragic time, by people who are not up to the job – Lazzari, Vella, Ratti and Balabanoff, a Russian proponent of German socialism..." The author mentions the widespread reports in socialist circles in Milan of Mussolini's remark that he would willingly support going to war against the Austrians and continues:

> Let's put our cards on the table. The line adopted by your newspaper went against your own feelings and your own private opinions on the matter. [...] It's now an open secret. [...] The truth is that, under the pretext that Italy was militarily unprepared, you began to hand over control of the paper to the journalists who worked for you and your fellow members of the party's executive; then, when Italy was ready to go to war and you could not go on using the excuse that it wasn't, you no longer could or would change the newspaper's line so as not to contradict the stance it had previously been taking or admit that up until then you'd been a mere front man for the opinions of others. [...] All along you've been discreet with the truth, which, in journalism, is tantamount to lying. Come on, call a halt to it! since in any case the mediocrities who surround you will kick you out now that they've been able to use you, with the excuse you're willing to say anything as long as you get paid at the end of the month. [...] You know better than I do that it's no longer a question of choosing between war and revolution, but between war and a disastrous peace that will lead to German domination. [...] Your behaviour at present is an act of political dishonesty.

Leda Rafanelli read the article carefully as the tense and worried journalist who had given it to her looked on. Then she handed it back to him: Tancredi was lying, she reassured him, she herself had spoken to Mussolini only the day before about all this and he had shown no signs of wavering. He would need to be a consummate actor to play a double game like the one of which Tancredi accused him. The journalist didn't seem convinced. Rafanelli decided to accept Mussolini's invitation in his letter to meet up so that she could get to the bottom of what he was really thinking. Many years later, she told the story of their encounter in her memoirs. Mussolini said to her:

> "I know you're loyal – Muslims value loyalty. But you must promise me that you won't take part in the debate, at least at the outset. It's true that your contribution would add a note of dignity, as it always does, but I don't want to see you mentioned... will you promise me?"
>
> "I promise you."
>
> "Thank you, Leda. Now please leave."
>
> He let go of my hands and stayed leaning against the wall, looking down at the ground. I said, "You're not feeling well... come with me, let's go back to the offices. Or at least go back home. Get a taxi... Where is your home? Shall I call a taxi?"
>
> "No... I'll walk home... but you go... and remember what you've promised me."[25]

It wasn't clear to Rafanelli what debate she should keep out of, given that Mussolini's reply to Tancredi, published on the following day in both *Avanti!* and *Il Resto del Carlino* was an unruffled denial of all the accusations which had been made against him. This reply opened up a volley of articles urging Mussolini to have the courage of his real convictions, to inject vigour into the editorship of *Avanti!*, to clear the road ahead for socialism by sweeping away the deadweight of its official policy of neutrality. In various articles published in several different newspapers, including first and foremost *Il Resto del Carlino*, Cesare Battisti also revealed the indiscreet remarks Mussolini had made to him.

One day in the offices of *Avanti!*, Balabanoff and Guarino, the editor-in-chief, came across Filippo Naldi deep in conversation with Mussolini, much to their alarm, which was perhaps the effect Mussolini wanted the scene to have on them. There were, after all, dozens of places in Milan where he could have arranged to have a private conversation with Naldi; to meet him in such a public way could only mean that Mussolini wanted to send a strong signal to the newspaper and to the party: the image of Mussolini as a "man of straw", an indecisive Hamlet-like figure, was wrong; on the contrary, he was the one who was in control of the game and moving the pieces. De Felice's comment on Mussolini's character in this respect is relevant here: "There was little of the hero, in the Emersonian sense, about Mussolini – even a populist hero – just as there was very little of the statesman, though he was undoubtedly a remarkable politician. At all the crucial moments in his life he proved incapable of coming to a decision; it could be said that all his important decisions were either imposed on him by circumstances or achieved tactically, by degrees, by adapting himself to reality – which more or less amounts to the same thing."[26]

So circumstances forced Mussolini to follow a high-risk strategy; he had to remain the target for increasingly ferocious criticism until he found the political solution which seemed to him to work best. A real political solution required a detailed ground plan, adequate means for its implementation and a sufficiently strong dose of cynicism to enable him to abandon ties of affection, of habit, of old alliances. He took the party's executive committee by surprise when they met in Bologna on 18th October by leaving copies of that day's *Avanti!* on the table as they came into the room: it contained a long article by him entitled 'The Choice: Uncompromising Neutrality or Engaged Neutrality?'. The committee members were completely taken aback; the article was long, and some complained that they had not been told about it in advance. In setting out his new position, Mussolini started by attacking the weak points in the party's adherence to a neutralist position. For example, the fact that none of the leading members of the party had replied when Mussolini had declared in *Avanti!*: "If the Italian government is intent on breaking its neutrality in order to come to the aid the central empires, then – let there be no misunderstanding about this – the Italian working class have one duty, and one duty alone: to rise up in opposition!" Mussolini tabled a motion before the executive committee to amend the party's line, using the arguments he had set out in the article:

As socialists we have condemned warfare, understood as a universal phenomenon, but this has never prevented us from distinguishing – logically and historically and in terms of socialism itself – between different individual instances of war. [...] The Socialist Party has given its tacit approval to the call from those classes who would guarantee Italian neutrality in the face of possible reprisals following an Austro-Hungarian victory. [...] A policy of uncompromising neutrality has threatened to leave the party without any other options, to restrict all its possibilities of manoeuvre in the future. [...] A refusal to examine wars on a case-by-case basis, an insistence on opposing them all on identical grounds – if this is a sign of "political intelligence", then it's indistinguishable from stupidity. [...] The question of the Trentino region must make even the most diehard advocate of neutrality think again. If the "Italian people" in that region had risen up against Austria, how on earth could we as socialists – who have declared our solidarity with the uprisings among the Armenians or in Crete – have had the temerity to prevent Italy from military intervention? [...] If the idea of "the nation" has been superseded as well as that of the working masses coming to the defence of the nation – since there would be nothing for them to defend – then why don't we have the courage of our convictions and condemn the socialists in Belgium and in France for coming to the defence of their nations? [...] If we want to keep our freedom of movement, we must not allow ourselves to be chained to a formula. Reality is moving – and moving fast.

Mussolini was confronted by a chorus of criticism from the committee, none angrier than Balabanoff. At this point, the other woman in his life, Leda Rafanelli, with whom he'd spent so many evenings, simply disappears. She continued to write, but the years of Fascism saw her reduced to earning money by fortune-telling and giving Arabic lessons to ward off poverty.

Mussolini's reaction to the attacks of the leaders on the party's committee was swift and harsh. After the meeting had lasted well into the night, one of its members, Arturo Vella, suggested that he should take three months off as sickness leave; in the meantime a solution would be found. Mussolini brusquely refused: "I'm not going to report sick." The meeting continued the following morning when a vote was taken on Mussolini's motion: it was rejected, with one vote in favour, his own. He immediately offered his resignation, which was accepted. They offered him a severance payment, which he refused, before leaving Bologna immediately. He returned home tired and depressed but also, according to Rachele, burning with rage. He told his wife brutally that it was all over and they would have to start again because the Socialist Party had sacked him from the editorship and shown him the door. Rachele was worried for the future of the family. Mussolini spoke about money, but not about the money they would need to survive so much as the money he would try to find in order to set up another newspaper. The time had come, he told Rachele, to have a newspaper of his own where he could write what he wanted, independently of anyone else.

But Mussolini had already found the money he required. No one can set up a newspaper in less than a month, and Mussolini's was already being sold in the newsagents in Milan and other major Italian cities on 15th November. It was a great success: on the first morning all copies had sold out by ten o'clock. Naldi's manoeuvring – with, it seems, the backing of certain government politicians – had paid off: the two men had clashed, not without provocation on both sides, but in the end the ebullient editor of *Avanti!* found it impossible to resist the prospect of having his own newspaper. Filippo Naldi had given him the money for all the immediate expenses involved, had arranged for the transfer of various journalists over from *Il Resto del Carlino* to the new title, and had even made sure that there was a supply of paper at the same printers his own newspaper used in Bologna. Once the immediately available money ensured that the new paper could be rapidly launched on the market, Naldi had taken Mussolini over to Switzerland to sign a contract with a well-known advertising agency. Mussolini wrote to his sister:

Dear Edvige, I've come to Switzerland for a day to arrange publicity with the firm of Haasenstein and Vogler. Perhaps it'll work out. But in any case, as you'll have seen from the announcements in other papers, the first issue of *Il Popolo d'Italia* [*The Italian People*] will come out next Sunday. People are waiting for it. You know what I think: it's time to put an end to this idiotic stance of neutrality which will only prolong the massacre indefinitely and make us all die of hunger and shame. Affectionately, your Benito.[27]

Whatever the size of the sums involved, there was no shortage of finance to back the new paper.

Who was responsible for putting up all this money? A group of Italian and French backers. Among the former, there was Alceste De Ambris, Manlio Morgagni, Ugo

Clerici and others, who'd all been in Paris recently. [...] And in Paris itself, who was financing the initiative? In effect, there was only one man, Georges Sembat, the Socialist member of parliament for Clignancourt and a minister without portfolio in the "Union Sacrée" government, with a responsibility for "the press and propaganda". His private secretary, a certain Dumat, had the job of providing support for the newspapers – especially the left-wing ones – in various countries which were advocating military intervention in the war.[28]

One final step remained: a general meeting of the Milan Socialist Party was called for on 24th November. In accordance with party rules, only they could decide whether to expel Mussolini from the membership. Insults and chairs were thrown around; amid all the yelling, some hurled coins at Mussolini, shouting at him that he'd sold out. His oratorical skills failed to save him on this occasion, although certain passages of his speech, shouted out over the audience's heckling, have remained famous: "You think you are losing me. But you are wrong. You hate me because you still love me." More menacing, in the light of his subsequent political career, was the following declaration: "Let me tell you that from this moment onwards I'll show no pity or forgiveness for anyone who refuses to commit himself, for the hypocrites and the cowards." And he ended the speech, now that it was obvious he would be expelled from the party, with a rhetorical flourish: "You can tear up my membership card, but don't think I'm pleased to lose it. You won't stop me fighting in the front line for the cause of socialism. Long live socialism! Long live the revolution!"[29]

Two days after Mussolini had been expelled from the party, three hundred of the Gioventù Socialista (Socialist Youth) movement in Milan had defected. Over the next few months there was a gradual reduction in the number of members in all sections of the party. Small groups would leave, sometimes following some local leader. *Il Popolo d'Italia* continued to sell well. The paper's header always carried two quotations. One was by Napoleon: "Revolution is an idea which comes armed with bayonets". As Duce, Mussolini cancelled his reference to Napoleon in the proofs of his interview with Ludwig, but the journalist reinstated his words in the edition he published after the war: "I learnt something extremely important from Napoleon. He destroyed in advance whatever illusions I might have cherished about men's capacity for loyalty. Nothing has ever subsequently changed my mind about this."[30] The second quotation that appeared every day underneath the title of *Il Popolo d'Italia* was from Blanqui: "The man with a weapon in his hand gets to eat". And underneath the title and the quotations, still in large enough type to be visible: "Socialist daily newspaper".

Chapter 9

More Weapons, More Mistresses

Killing your rival in a duel was out of the question; better to leave him alive, with a scar to mark his defeat. Dead, he was a victim and a hero at the same time. Think what happened to Felice Cavallotti, the founder of the radical left in Italy, a former *camicia rossa* ("red-shirt") who'd fought in Garibaldi's troops, a prominent Freemason, the man responsible for getting the statue of Giordano Bruno put up in Campo de' Fiori in Rome – there was even a popular song about it.

> Poor old Cavallotti
> His first name meant "Happy",
> but he didn't die happy;
> he shouldn't have followed you [...]
> A precious life
> cut off in a duel
> by evil chance
> it shouldn't have turned out like this...

Cavallotti fought many duels, and his last one proved fatal. His opponent was Count Ferruccio Macola, a right-wing member of parliament, who'd been one of Cavallotti's admirers at the outset of his career. It was perhaps Cavallotti's twentieth duel, so he was experienced, but Macola was twenty years younger. On 6th March 1898, in the garden of the villa belonging to the Countess Cellere in Rome, Cavallotti was struck in the face during the third round of the sword fight. The sabre cut across the face and the throat, slitting it open. The line of mourners who followed his coffin when he was buried by Lake Maggiore stretched for over a mile. The newspapers were full of articles in his memory; Giosuè Carducci wrote the funeral oration. The fact that Macola had won their duel didn't bring him any advantage. In striking the blow that killed Cavallotti, his honour had certainly not been vindicated. He had to flee to escape arrest; an object of hatred and a fugitive, he ended up shooting himself in 1910.

The chivalric code for duelling didn't provide for one of the duellists getting killed. But it was always a possibility, even in the early years of the twentieth century. Adrenalin filled the veins of the two contenders at the thought that one of them might die; it excited them, brought the anger they had nursed for days to boiling point, to a ferocity which sought to appease the insults and humiliations which had passed between the two men by trying to inflict physical wounds on each other. A report published in *Il Popolo d'Italia* on 23rd February 1915 gives an example of the events which could lead up to a duel. A trial was under way in the law courts in Milan. Between Benito Mussolini and the socialist lawyer Libero Merlino there had been a tense relationship for some time:

> As soon as he entered the courtroom where the case against our newspaper and against *Il secolo* was being heard, Benito Mussolini found himself by complete chance facing the lawyer Merlino...
>
> "Are you the author of the letter which appeared today in *Avanti!*?" Mussolini asked. And the other replied: "Yes, I wrote it."
>
> "So when you speak about the 'Duce', you mean me?"
>
> "That's right..."
>
> At which Mussolini exclaimed: "Then you're a real bastard! You're scum!" letting fly with his hand and slapping the dapper little anarchist lawyer in the face.
>
> Merlino tried to react, more out of an instinct for self-defence than from bravery, but didn't have the time to land a blow before Mussolini unleashed a series of punches which drove the lawyer up against the radiator, pinning him there under a continuous volley for several minutes, until the policemen, lawyers and journalists who were in the room rushed up to separate the two men."[1]

It was decided to resolve the men's argument with a duel, but when Mussolini, along with his seconds, the editor-in-chief Alessandro Giuliani and his friend Manlio Morgagni, turned up at the chosen place they found several plain-clothes policemen waiting for them. Their sabres were confiscated and a report filed, but this setback didn't deter them. They arranged to meet again shortly afterwards on the outskirts of Milan, under the supervision of the lawyer Vittorio Gallarati. The duel was stopped after the second bout, because the doctors who were in attendance judged the wounds the two men had given each other to be too severe to allow the duel to continue according to the traditional rules of chivalry.

A deserter and a coward, untrustworthy, malicious, coarse, a sordid money-grubbing opportunist, the thought of whom made one want to throw up: Mussolini lambasted the former editor of the *Avanti!*, Claudio Treves, with all the insults in his vocabulary. "He used to be known as Claudio Tremens, but from now on we'll call him 'threepenny bit', because that's all he's worth," he wrote in the paper on 24th March. Once more he targeted what was presumed to be Treves's avarice and greed. Margherita Sarfatti had a hand in the attack on Treves; it was she who'd suggested to Mussolini that Treves had married the Venetian heiress Olga Levi for her money. All Venice knew how rich Levi was, and Sarfatti kept her ear close to the ground in her native city. Mussolini didn't let up his attack, writing that Treves disliked taking risks and only cared about his salary and acquiring more money. Treves responded in kind, calling Mussolini a louse, and went on to describe him as:

> Bitter, sterile, empty, meretriciously avid for praise, ready to flatter the masses only to betray them, intent on climbing the ladder of power at any cost – being a turncoat just seemed to him the quickest way to achieve his ambitions. But he was mistaken; his vanity betrayed him. Far from carrying the party with him, the party threw him out, like a piece of old rubbish. [...] And to think I have to reply to this envious toerag, this dog's turd, who sets himself up to judge the way I carried out my responsibilities for the Socialist Party, even as far back as 1898, when he hadn't even started his career![2]

The two men's respective circumstances had changed a lot since they clashed over the severance money which Mussolini had refused to pay to his predecessor as editor of *Avanti!*. Now he too had moved on; he had changed his policy to one of advocating Italian intervention in the war; and he was in charge of a new paper with substantial financial backing and a mass circulation. Both men called themselves socialists, but now viewed each other with implacable hatred. The Socialist Party was officially against the fighting of duels but, after receiving yet another insult from Mussolini, Treves sent his seconds to him to issue a challenge. Just one month after the encounter with Libero Merlino, at 3.30 p.m. on 29th March 1915, Mussolini once more took up his sabre. The person chosen to arbitrate the duel,

Leonardo Pracchi, an accountant by profession, got the two men to walk towards each other; when they'd got to within a sword's length, without waiting for the traditional cry of "Have at you!" which began the duel, they threw themselves at each other. In a burst of excitement and trepidation, fury and fear, the two men's blades clashed swiftly together, now held high, now low. The situation had to be brought under control so that the rules could be respected, otherwise the duel would have no formal value – on the contrary it would be a scandal involving all the men who were present. Leonardo Pracchi had been chosen by the seconds of the two contenders because he knew a lot about weapons, he was cool-headed and sharp-eyed, and finally because he had arbitrated at many duels always with rigorous impartiality and a fierce adherence to the rules. Even Pracchi found it hard to separate the two men; when he did, he reiterated his instructions and warned that they should be obeyed to the letter. In the meantime, Treves's seconds, Giovanni Allevi, a doctor, and Angelo Lanza, a journalist from *Avanti!*, took a look outside the room to check everything was under control, while Mussolini's – Manlio Morgagni and the editor-in-chief of *Il Popolo d'Italia* Giuseppe De Falco – did the same on the other side. The lookouts who had been posted outside the Villa Bicocca in Milan gave the all-clear – there were no police or inquisitive members of the public to be seen. The doctors who had been called to the duel to operate on either Treves or Mussolini if need arose had not wished to be present at the fight and were seated in another room.

The milky-white light of the cloudy sky filtered through the tall Gothic windows of the room, weakly illuminating the duellists' white shirts. The shining sabres pointed downwards; the seconds withdrew to the sides of the room; when Pracchi called out "Have at you", the two men flung themselves anew into the fight as if they hadn't been interrupted for a sermon on the rules of duelling. Treves was tall and technically adroit; Mussolini was agile and experienced. The seconds had assessed the two contenders and had agreed that it was a well-balanced match. As such, they had deemed it possible for the two men to fight "without exclusion of blows", which meant that the duel did not have to be stopped as soon as the first blood was drawn, as was the usual practice, especially after the Cavallotti affair. Pracchi's main instruction had been that the two men should drop their swords as soon as he called out for them to stop. There was a first round of violent sword blows, after which Mussolini and Treves disengaged and stood apart to take stock. Then there was a second bout followed by a second stand-off. The third round began; by now it was clear that it would only take a single maladroit sword blow and one of them could lose his life. Pracchi yelled out "Stop!". Mussolini's sword had been bent by the clashes. He was panting, out of breath, like Treves. A cold sweat soaked their shirts. Pracchi ordered new swords and a minute's rest. Mussolini took advantage of the pause to slip his hand inside his pocket, where he kept a piece of sticky resin which enabled him to keep a firm grip on the sword handle. The fourth bout began, even more violent than the preceding ones; the duellists' swords suddenly slipped, wounding both of them in the right forearm. Pracchi again called out for them to stop, but had to repeat his command before they did. He took a look at their wounds and decided there was no need to call the doctors. The fifth round began; Mussolini struck Treves under the right armpit. Pracchi called the doctors in to see, but they all said it wasn't serious and the duel could continue. A new attack, with thrusts and parries; Mussolini's blade grazed Treves's forehead. The doctors were again called in; they needed to bandage the wound to stop the bleeding, but said the two men could continue fighting. A sixth, seventh, eighth round was fought; Treves struck Mussolini's right ear. The two men's shirts were now stained with blood; this time the doctors' opinion was negative; the seconds consulted among themselves and declared the duel could not continue. Under the rules of duelling, the authority of the seconds is absolute – they can decide whether a duel takes place or not in the first place; for instance, when Pio Schinetti, an elderly journalist on *Il secolo* called Mussolini a "cheapskate adventurer", and Mussolini formally challenged him, Schinetti's seconds forbade him from fighting on account of his age – and the duellists were duty-bound to respect their decisions.

The rules of duelling required a report to be drawn up immediately after the duel was concluded. Before sending the two men to have their wounds treated, Pracchi asked them, as was customary, if they were now reconciled. Both answered in the negative. The seconds and the referee then wrote their report:

The Honourable Claudio Treves has suffered a wound to the right temple, with bleeding, a wound to the right armpit, a wound on the forearm and multiple bruising in the deltoid region. Professor Mussolini has suffered a graze to the right forearm, bruising and a wound to the right ear. Swords were changed at the end of the third round, since their blades had been bent in the fierceness of the fighting. The duellists separated after twenty-five minutes fighting with no reconciliation. The first to leave the villa was the Honourable Claudio Treves; the editor of *Il Popolo d'Italia* preferred to wait until the report had been written before leaving the villa with his friends.[3]

All this too was part of the ritual and served to show the outside world how slight were the wounds which the antagonists had received. The day after his encounter with Treves, Mussolini sent a telegram to his sister Edvige reassuring her that his own wounds were nothing serious, while on the contrary those he had managed to inflict on Treves were. In Rachele's account of the episode, her husband returned home holding a piece of his right ear and with his shirt soaked in blood. She let off steam by scolding him about the costs involved in duelling: each time he needed to buy a new shirt, he had to pay for lessons from a fencing master, the doctors received a fee for attending, and the seconds had to be given gifts; even the men who were posted on lookout so that there was no danger of arrest had to be tipped.

> On another occasion, the two duellists, in order not to be disturbed, had rented a room and locked themselves in. They pushed all the furniture to one side and started to fight. In the middle of the combat one of the lookouts told them the police were arriving. Still holding their swords, Benito and his adversary rushed out to find another place, but the police started to pursue them. Then, just like in a gangster film, the two of them jumped into a taxi to escape them and asked to be taken to the railway station. There they climbed on board a goods train and got off in a small village, where they finished the duel they had started in a room.[4]

Up to 1922, Mussolini was frequently challenged by the men who were the object of his abuse. According to his wife, he fought duels on at least ten occasions. His flunkey, chauffeur, valet and general factotum Cirillo Tambara would be sent off to the drugstore to buy some resin and would make sure he had some ready for use in his trouser pockets. So the battles he fought on paper, with their floods of insulting invective, were transformed into physical combat in remote places well away from prying eyes, although everyone must have known about the encounters, even though they weren't allowed to talk about them.

The ritual was always the same. Each time Mussolini would prepare to face his new opponent by taking a fresh course of fencing lessons. His attack was full of energy, but his technical prowess left something to be desired. Missiroli, the editor of the newspaper *Il secolo*, challenged Mussolini to a duel after the latter had called him "a perfidious Jesuit and a rank coward" in an article he published on 10th May 1922. The duel was fixed for four o'clock in the afternoon; the blades broke in the ferocity of the first round. The referee called a halt to allow them to change swords; then the duel continued for a further forty minutes. Mario Missiroli said that Mussolini's swordplay was not bad, but he held the weapon badly – this didn't mean of course that he was less dangerous an opponent. Even for the army officer Cristoforo Baseggio, who was highly experienced in handling swords, fighting against such a fiery adversary must have been no easy task. "The night before his first duel, I couldn't sleep a wink, I was so afraid; I had read many novels with terrible fights to the death, and I already saw my husband covered with blood... When I saw him leave at dawn, accompanied by the seconds, I was convinced it was the last time I would see him alive, especially because his opponent was an officer, Colonel Cristoforo Baseggio, a socialist who had split with the party and who was in all probability a much better swordsman than Benito. On the other hand, my husband was very calm and confident."[5]

Avanti! was against duelling on principle, but despite this still sneered at Mussolini's abilities by describing him as a ridiculous counter-revolutionary d'Artagnan. After the March on Rome and the beginning of the establishment of Mussolini's dictatorship, Claudio Treves repeatedly lamented to his son and his close friends how one day he had had Mussolini at the end of his sword and had wasted the opportunity.

What was probably Mussolini's last duel took place in 1921: the editor-in-chief of *Paese*, Francesco Ciccotti-Scozzese, challenged him to a duel because Mussolini had described him as being "morally confused". The two men had difficulties in arranging their duel. The police were onto them, and they had to resort to various stratagems before they could finally meet on 27th October. In the fourteenth round Ciccotti collapsed, out of breath. His seconds put him in one of the beds in the villa where the duel was being fought; the doctors injected him with camphor oil and said the duel could not continue with Ciccotti in such a condition. "Colonel Basso and the Hon. Finzi [Mussolini's seconds] together with their duellist declare that they are at the service of the Hon. Ciccotti's representatives. They are of the opinion that the encounter cannot be allowed to proceed since it is not possible – and never has been – to continue a duel in the absence of medical assistance."[6]

These sword fights were a regular occurrence throughout Mussolini's tumultuous journalistic career. *Il Popolo d'Italia* was continually full of threats, challenges, insults, polemics. "Only a bullet in the head can silence me," he wrote in an editorial; the newspaper's readership – which increased every day – was inflamed by his rhetoric. Later on, Mussolini expressed his opinion on duelling in his long interview with Ludwig: "Duelling is certainly a more chivalric form of conflict – I fought duels on many occasions. But war is an extraordinary experience: it's a school where you learn about life, when you see men in all their naked reality."[7]

War was Mussolini's new and overriding goal. He took ample advantage of the weaknesses of Italian democracy, which could easily be overrun by determined partisan initiatives, by using his newspaper as the focus for the creation of the Fasci di Azione Rivoluzionaria (Leagues for Revolutionary Action), which brought together a heterogeneous group of volunteers who were in theory prepared to go to war against the central European empires. Margherita Sarfatti asserts that by January 1915 these groups or, as she called them, "nuclei of the brave and willing" totalled around five thousand members throughout various Italian towns and cities. They were not properly organized: they followed no rules and didn't have a political programme; their single goal was to make sure Italy entered the war. Renzo De Felice has calculated the number of these early Fasci: there were 105 of them with around nine thousand members overall. Together with other groups of intransigent republicans, Mazzinians and left-wing supporters of Italian military intervention, they were intent on provoking the situation with a sudden attack which could provide a *casus belli* – for example, by invading Austrian territory and attacking one of their army barracks. They had built up secret stockpiles of arms and drawn up plans. "Mussolini's role in all this was a double one. He was responsible – with the evident aim of keeping personal control of the developments – for maintaining contact with a Russian agent working in Italy by the name of Matvei Gedenstrom, who could provide the funds needed to organize a military sortie into Austrian territory, and he was also working to keep all the revolutionary groups in favour of Italian intervention together in a united front..."[8]

Money was forthcoming, but not from the Russians. The activities of the early Fasci were kept more or less under wraps, but in the public political arena Mussolini soon carved out for himself a key role as the main proponent on the left for Italian intervention in the war, in the process weakening considerably the appeal of the Socialist Party. Indeed numerous leading figures from the party, together with revolutionaries and republicans, joined sides with Mussolini; many would go on to become his bitterest opponents during the Fascist regime. Pietro Nenni had been friendly with Mussolini when they were in prison together, as we have seen, and he now joined him as a passionate advocate for Italy's participation in the European conflict, which he believed was necessary if the country was to complete the work of the Risorgimento and become truly unified. Mussolini struck Nenni as being more interested in the war in terms of internal politics, as a means of acquiring power, but his misgivings did not prevent him from starting to contribute regularly to *Il Popolo d'Italia*. The newspaper was glad to welcome him to its pages: his first article, published on 20th January 1915 and entitled 'Which War?', was actually printed in place of the usual editorial. With its new contributors the newspaper soon moved to the centre of the contemporary debate on Italian intervention, necessary reading for supporters and opponents of the policy alike. In the eyes of the Allied powers' intelligence services the paper was a useful tool, and they funded its campaign to convince the country to enter the conflict. Gaetano Salvemini has also shown how Mussolini obtained financial backing from the French and the Belgians by using a network of contacts in their respective socialist parties, consisting in a large initial payment of perhaps as much as 100,000 lire followed by monthly deposits of about 10,000 lire. In her memoirs, Rachele Mussolini tries to defend her husband's activities in this period by maintaining that the sums of money which were supplied did not amount to as much as was reported; she also points out that the regular salaries of journalists were often paid with considerable delay. She admits that the leading French socialist

Marcel Cachin was a frequent visitor to the their home, but writes that she had no memory of his ever having brought money with him. Her naivety here may be excused: on the perhaps erroneous assumption that envelopes containing banknotes passed hands on these occasions, no one would have bothered to show Rachele the packet. Their apartment was a suitable place to hold private meetings. Rachele recalls one exceptional visitor in particular: Lenin. She was no linguist and her conversation with their Russian guest cannot have been very extensive but she seems to have understood from the few words she managed to exchange with him that Lenin wanted to encourage her husband to "reunite the Italian Socialist Party and fight against the reformers from within the party. [...] Many years later my husband remarked to me that 'Lenin had one stroke of luck in life – he died before Stalin could do away with him'."[9] *Il Popolo d'Italia* would later welcome the revolution in Russia in 1918 with enthusiasm, announcing the event with a banner headline: "Victory of Russian Revolution over Germanophile Reactionaries". The historian Peter Martland, whose work is included in Christopher Andrew's history of the British secret services *Defence of the Realm*, has recently shown that Mussolini was also financed by the British, after discovering documents among the private papers of Sir Samuel Hoare, Viscount Templewood (known as the Templewood papers) in Cambridge University Library. Hoare had worked for the British intelligence services in Rome during this period and was in close contact with Captain Vernon Kell, the head of the external affairs department of the secret service. Mussolini received £100 a week in cash from Hoare in return for his promise to unleash the Fasci and keep the pacifists out of the picture.

When Italy finally entered the war on 24th May 1915, the Fasci were dissolved so that their members could enlist as regular soldiers in the armed forces. The experience of organizing the Fasci would prove useful to Mussolini after the war. On 27th May Pietro Nenni was sent to join the third coastal-artillery regiment; Mussolini, however, was blocked by new military measures which put him in a category which was excluded from volunteering. He decided to show up anyway at the Bersaglieri barracks, but his request to enrol was turned down. He wrote of his disappointment in the newspaper, but also stated that he was certain he would eventually be called up – only the naive, the foolish and the hardliners for neutrality could believe that the war would be over quickly. On 31st August 1915 he was called up and sent to join the Bersaglieri troops. He applied for officer training, and on 6th November his divisional commander received a telephone call instructing him to send Mussolini to do an intensive course in Vernazzo. After he had completed his first week, a courier on a motorbike brought a counter-order: Mussolini was to return to his regiment. It appears that he did so without undue protest – as we shall see, he had other matters to worry about at the time.

The same treatment was meted out to Nenni and other left-wing leaders marked down as subversives. General Staff had received a confidential report which informed them of a plot to spread revolutionary propaganda among the troops: Mussolini was one of the leaders of the plot and had to be blocked from becoming an officer, along with his fellow extremists, whether they were socialists, republicans or radicals. Mussolini planned to exploit the new military and political situation brought about by Italy's entry into the war, but his plans involved more than merely drumming up support among the soldiers. He asked for permission to send reports back to *Il Popolo d'Italia* from the front, thus turning himself into a war correspondent on active service. On 25th December 1915 the newspaper carried this announcement: "In the next few days a new feature will appear in our pages: the 'War Diary' of our chief editor, Benito Mussolini. This will show us the war as it is experienced from day to day, in all its strange fascination and all its horror. These pages are written in the heat of battle, with machine guns firing and cannon thundering – they're not about fine writing, but about the truth."

There were many writers on the war's front lines: some were there as soldiers while others, like Ernest Hemingway and Edith Wharton, were there to assist the troops, living among them and above all writing about what was happening. But Mussolini didn't set out to be a writer in this sense. His reports from the front, fifteen in all, were a journalistic coup which enabled him to live in the midst of the ranks, one of the men in this new mass army, but recognized by all. He didn't need or want to propagandize for the revolution by trying to convert his fellow soldiers, which is what the senior army command feared. General Cadorna had instructed all the divisional commanders to keep an eye out for the revolutionary socialists who had enlisted and who would spread their cause within the ranks with the aim of carrying out the revolution after the war. Cadorna's concerns were well founded, but he didn't and couldn't understand the methods that might be used, above all the new forms of mass communication such as the popular press and also cinema, since the first filmed reports from the war were made in this period. Mussolini as a journalist, on the other hand, was quick to grasp the importance of the new techniques of communication and was willing to put the day-to-day running of the newspaper at risk in order to experiment with them. Although Mussolini tried to dedicate the few days of leave he was granted to running the paper, the publication soon ran into problems, especially financial ones.

The first instalment of his war diary appeared in issue No. 359 in December 1915 and covered the period from the 9th to the 17th of September. He started off by highlighting his role as the editor on active military service: "While we were queuing up in the mess for our rations, a medical officer picked me out and said: 'I'd like to shake the hand of the editor of *Il Popolo d'Italia*.'" A few lines later he writes: "A Bersagliere from Mantua came up to me and said, 'Signor Mussolini, we've seen how courageous you are and how you led us on the march while grenades were being thrown – we wish we were under your command...'"[10]

Mussolini frequently puts himself in the spotlight, a journalistic device aimed at convincing his readers that the reports they were reading were important: "My squadron leader is a Calabrian by the name of Lorenzo Pinna, from Nicastro. His father is a civil engineer. He said to me, 'Who'd ever have thought I'd be fighting side by side with Mussolini, as two ordinary soldiers together. I must write and tell my father – he's often mentioned your name to me.'"[11]

Mussolini was certainly no Hemingway, and in any case he wasn't interested in literary effects. Yet all his reports, even the banal ones, are intended to play on his readers' nascent nationalist sympathies: "We soon reached the line of the old frontier. By the road there was a house and a sentry post; the Austrian flags had all gone. It was a moving moment for me as I remembered being expelled, in October 1909, from 'all the territories of the Austro-Hungarian Empire'. The lieutenant shouted: 'Long live Italy!' I was at the head of the column and echoed him, whereupon I heard four hundred voices shout out in unison: 'Long live Italy!'"[12]

Or this passage, from the entry for 18th October: "No soldier who's been wounded wants to show weakness and fear in front of his comrades. But there's a deeper reason behind this reluctance: you don't groan about a wound when you're constantly in danger of death. Being wounded is not so bad as getting killed. But to see these young lads, the humble sons of our motherland, proudly refusing to cry out and complain as the surgeon's hot steel cuts into their flesh is a proof of the magnificent determination of our nation's race."[13]

On 25th and 26th November 1916, while he was on sick leave and grappling with a series of personal problems to do with his mistresses, Mussolini published two articles in *Il Popolo d'Italia* which broke up the united front of those on the left who were in favour of Italy's intervention in the war by coming out in support of the nationalists. Fiume must belong to Italy, he declared in the second piece, a reference to the fact that the strategically significant Adriatic port, currently under Austro-Hungarian rule, had not been included in the list of territorial gains promised to Italy by the terms of the secret 1915 Treaty of London. His socialist convictions were receding, as is also apparent in some offhand remarks he makes in the reports sent from the front. Colonel Giuseppe Beruto, the new commanding officer in charge of Mussolini's regiment, had asked to see him. Mussolini's account continues:

> I presented myself and greeted him. We shook hands warmly. "I asked to meet you in your rest break after you've been on sentry watch in the trenches all day and night. I've heard you're a good soldier and I've never doubted it." The colonel continued: "I've often been on military picket duty in Milan because of you and your friends." "Well, that's all in the past," I replied. The colonel lived alongside us, like an ordinary soldier, putting up with all the discomforts of an ordinary soldier's life.[14]

The articles Mussolini sends back from the front respond to a broader political and communicative strategy, but he never forgets that he's a journalist, and on occasion uses his reports to win the support of the factory workers and agricultural labourers who made up the army's rank and file, sometimes at the risk of provoking military censorship:

> When rations are handed out unequally, the men start to shout "*Camorra!* We don't want the *Camorra!*" It's unfortunately true that the *Camorra* exists in the army. Only a very small part of what soldiers fighting on the front line – the men who should be seen as "sacred" – are entitled to, as stipulated by army regulations,

ever reaches them. Coffee, chocolate, wine, grappa – all these supplies pass through the hands of too many drivers, corporals, orderlies. The "*Camorra*" is a fact of army life, but it infuriates the rank and file, especially in wartime. You sometimes hear them muttering that the government is a bunch of thieves. The "*Camorra*" can end up lowering the morale of the troops.[15]

Mussolini's military career – and his articles from the front line – were brought to an abrupt end by a fairly serious incident in battle, as was reported in every newspaper in Italy, and also by some abroad. On 23rd February 1917, during some troop exercises, a grenade exploded next to him. Five Bersaglieri were killed on the spot; Mussolini had dozens of shrapnel wounds and was taken to hospital. The medical officer who operated on him, Dr Piccagnoni, described the operation:

I extracted the first two pieces from the right thigh.

On 27th February I carried out a further operation to extract a fairly large piece from the back of the left hand. It was extremely painful – the piece had lodged itself between two bones and proved very difficult to remove – but Mussolini bore the operation with great courage.

Two more pieces were removed from the right shoulder and another from the right tibia. [...]

Two days after this operation the patient's temperature reached forty; the pain in his leg had become atrocious. I was alarmed and decided to operate again; this time I managed to extract three more fragments with the use of an electrical vibrator. They varied in size from a grain of rice to a grain of maize. Most of the pieces were found in the right leg; there were just two in the region of the left Achilles tendon."[16]

Twenty years later, in 1937, Mussolini recalled the incident in conversation with Claretta Petacci:

I can still hear the noise of the explosion. I was seriously wounded. I remember doing one thing which not many people know about: when the bomb fragments hit me and cut into my skin the first thing I did was to touch myself here (he pointed to his...). I touched myself there while I was still just conscious, and as soon as I felt everything was still there I fainted. All the soldiers were scared of losing their testicles. Many had them blown off completely or damaged. He laughs. Yes, I touched myself to make sure and then I felt OK.[17]

While he was serving with the Bersaglieri, Mussolini had been in hospital once before, for paratyphoid fever, and the King, Victor Emmanuel III, who was a fairly assiduous visitor to the areas behind the front lines, had asked to see him. On hearing that he was in critical condition after the grenade explosion, the King asked to be taken to visit him again. On 7th March he went to the hospital; he walked along the wards watched by the other patients who had by now become used to the bustle and the visitors around Mussolini's bed. The King's visit was reported in *Il secolo* in a piece written by Raffaele Garinei:

> The King approached Mussolini's bed and asked: "How are you feeling, Mussolini?" "Not too well, Your Majesty." [...] The King kept his eyes on Mussolini's face and listened. "Not being able to move must be very painful for an active man like you!" "It's indeed a torture, Your Majesty, but I must put up with it." Then the King asked Mussolini to tell him what had happened, and the patient gave him a detailed account.
> "What do you think caused the explosion?" he asked.
> "The mortar's barrel was overheated."
> "Yes, perhaps it had been pulled too quickly," the King added.
> Then, changing the subject, he said:
> "Do you remember I came to visit you six months ago when you were in the hospital in Cividale?"
> "I remember it very well – I was being kept in hospital for observation—"
> "And now," the King interrupted, "after so many brave deeds, you've been wounded."
> A short silence followed. Everyone looked at the valiant soldier who had led his men under Austrian fire the better to defeat the enemy and had fallen in the attempt, just as heroically as the soldier in the trenches who falls to a sudden enemy charge.
> The King continued.
> "The other day, at Debeli, General M. spoke very highly of you to me..."
> "I've always tried to do my duty, obeying orders, like any other soldier. The general has been very good to me."
> "That's the man, Mussolini!" the King interjected. "Try to be patient and put up with not being able to move and the pain."
> "Thank you, Your Majesty."
> The King rose and went to visit other wounded patients.[18]

Margherita Sarfatti went to town embroidering this episode of Mussolini's fortitude in constructing the myth of the Duce in her biography *Dux*. She wrote that when the surgeon's scalpel made the first incision, Mussolini clenched his jaws and cursed through his teeth. The sight of the operating theatre seemed to energize rather than depress him. In depicting her lover's stoical and detached reaction, Sarfatti uses a feminine analogy: "Ask a young woman, two hours after she's given birth to her first child, to describe the pain. Her tired smile will tell you that she can hardly remember what it was like. In common parlance, the pains of childbirth are called 'the pains soonest forgotten': to sufferings like these it can do nothing to alleviate, nature induces a kind of stupefaction resembling indifference and a state of oblivion – which works like an anaesthetic. Experience belongs to the spirit; it is not the mechanical product of old age."[19]

While he was at the front Mussolini was elevated to the rank of corporal – not an especially remarkable promotion, but Sarfatti exalts the official reasons given for the recognition: Mussolini had shown the true fighting spirit of the Bersaglieri, had stayed cool-headed under fire, had proudly shed his blood in the battle for Trieste.

A photograph had been published in *Domenica del corriere* showing the Austrian destruction of a military hospital which the magazine identified as the one where Mussolini had been taken – his presence there was justification enough for the Austrians to bombard the place. Sarfatti describes in detail the inferno of falling bombs, the cries of pain and terror, the thick clouds of smoke and the wounded bodies rolling down the stairs; she adds the picture of Mussolini, in the silent twilit aftermath of the attack, still in his bed since his wounds meant he could not be carried, surrounded by doctors, the hospital chaplain and the nurses.

Sarfatti was a skilful verbal painter, but trying to describe what was going on in Mussolini's private life during this period would be beyond even her capabilities. Ida Irene Dalser had made a statement to the police that she had sold her beauty salon in order to raise funds in support of Mussolini's new undertaking, *Il Popolo d'Italia*. A son had been born from their relationship: Benito Albino, on 11th November 1915 in the maternity hospital in Via della Commenda in Milan. Thus the baby had been conceived in February 1915, at the time when Mussolini had become the spokesman for all those on the left who supported the campaign for Italy's intervention in the war and the circulation of *Il Popolo d'Italia* was increasing daily. Ida Dalser must have had a special attraction for him. His sister Edvige wrote: "I think he liked her, because although she was older than he was and was not particularly good-looking she gave him a son. That said, what attracted my brother to certain women – that blend in their characters of insouciance and daring which I've tried to analyse in writing – remains a mystery to me."[20]

The day after his son was born, Mussolini was withdrawn from the intensive training course for officers and sent back to the trenches. It can certainly be assumed he had other things on his mind that day: he was under pressure and not only because he had to fight. In December 1915 he was taken to a hospital in Treviglio for suspected paratyphoid and associated jaundice; his commanding officer sent a telegram with the news to "Signora Ida Dalser Mussolini", the mother of his son. Rachele too, as the mother of his daughter, although not yet his wife, was informed. She always tried to keep a watchful eye on Mussolini's various mistresses; at this time she regarded his relationship with Dalser as particularly threatening, while she was less concerned about Sarfatti. In her memoirs she writes that up to 1918 she was certain that there was nothing going on between Sarfatti and Mussolini, although it's not clear what her conviction was based on. "Nothing going on" might conceal a number of casual sexual encounters, which nevertheless Rachele chose to ignore as nothing serious.

Ida Dalser was different, however, and it was a kind of proof that she represented a serious threat when she turned up suddenly one day at the front door when Mussolini was away in Genoa. "I thought her ugly, older than me, and wearing too much make-up. She wouldn't tell me her name, but claimed to know all about our life together, what my husband did, and so on. I was taken aback by her audacity. She even had the impertinence to ask Edda if her father was kind to her and if he got on well with me!"[21]

When told about the visit, Mussolini reacted with his usual cynicism. He freely admitted that he and Dalser had been lovers, and dismissed her by describing her as a crazy Austrian woman. There was some justification for his description: Ida Dalser had once set fire to a room in the Hotel Milano in a fit of hysteria. It was 15th November 1914, the day the first issue of *Il Popolo d'Italia* had come out. Seeing it on sale at the news-stands exacerbated Dalser's fury at having been exploited and then abandoned by Mussolini. The fire was put out and the damage assessed and a police investigation was started. One day two policemen called at Rachele's house; she was out shopping, Mussolini was away in the war, but Rachele's mother, who was still living with them, opened the door. The two police officers announced that they had been ordered to sequester the family's belongings. It was only when she went to the police station that Rachele understood the situation. When the policemen had asked her if she was the Signora Mussolini, she automatically said she was. Then one of the officers said in that case it was clear she was guilty, since the hotel managers had accused the Signora Mussolini of setting fire to one of their rooms. It took a while to sort things out. Rachele had to prove that she had never set foot inside the Hotel Milano. Finally, by comparing statements taken from witnesses, it became clear that the person guilty of arson was another Signora Mussolini.

Rachele immediately realized there was no time to lose. She set off to find Mussolini. On 17th December they were officially married.

As good socialists we decided to get married with a civil ceremony only. It was a very simple affair and took place in a room in the Treviglio hospital. Benito was in bed, recovering from paratyphoid but still unable to get up because of jaundice. He had a woollen beret pushed down on his nose and he was unshaven. He cracked jokes with the friends who had accompanied me on the journey from Milan, but it was obvious he was nervous. When the moment came for him to say "Yes", he said it, joyfully, in a loud clear voice. When my turn came, I at first didn't reply, pretending to be lost in thought, but watching Benito from the corner of my eye. When the presiding officer repeated his question, I remained silent. Benito had raised his head and was looking at me in amazement. At the third attempt I finally and joyfully said "Yes". He gave a sigh of relief and sank back on the pillow as if having to wait for my reply had been too much for him.[22]

There may have been other reasons, apart from Rachele's silence before she said "Yes", for Mussolini's suddenly being overcome: he was weakened with jaundice, she had told him she was pregnant again (with Vittorio, their first son) and, possibly, he had realized that he had just committed bigamy. The accusation has never been proved with documentary evidence. We know that when he was wounded during the troop exercises in February 1917, Ida Irene Dalser came to visit him in hospital and, to gain entry to the ward, showed a document proving she was his wife. Then Rachele arrived and all hell broke loose. The two women at first ignored each other, but when they realized they were both claiming to be Mussolini's wife, they rushed up to his bed, each shouting out that she and only she had the right to stay by his bedside. "The other soldiers in the ward were highly amused. Then something in me snapped and I threw myself at her. I even managed to put my hands round her neck and started to throttle her. Benito, all bandaged up in bed like a mummy and unable to move, made vain attempts to stop us. He even threw himself down from the bed. Luckily some doctors and nurses intervened before I strangled her. She fled away while I burst into tears."[23]

Ida Dalser continued to maintain she was Mussolini's legally recognized wife for the rest of her short unhappy life; she declared that if she had no official documents to prove it, it was because once he had become the country's leader he had had all the evidence destroyed. One document survives in the archives: a certificate signed by the mayor of Milan testifying that the family of Benito Mussolini, on military service, was composed of "his wife Dalser, Ida and one child (male)". This certificate gave Dalser the right to a financial support consisting in an initial payment of seven lire and seventy cents, followed by two lire forty-five cents on every following Monday.

According to Alfredo Pieroni, who has done some careful research into the question, Mussolini "was aware that he was leaving a pregnant woman on her own without any resources. The document is not necessarily a lie told for the sake of officialdom. It is possible that soldiers were given the possibility of indicating the name of a woman who was pregnant by them and whom they had not been able to marry before being called up for military service. Whatever the significance of the document, no such certificate was ever drawn up for Rachele."[24]

We can add that Mussolini was also aware he'd taken all Dalser's financial resources to pay for the launch of *Il Popolo d'Italia*. While Mussolini was away at the front, the acting editor-in-chief, Manlio Morgagni, had instructions to give five hundred lire from the newspaper's funds every month to Rachele. There was only one solution for Ida Dalser, left to survive on two and a half lire every week: to force Mussolini into a binding agreement whereby he would provide support for their son. There were lots of letters between them she could show, but she must also have had other arguments that "clinched" the matter, since she succeeded in securing a commitment from the editor-in-chief-cum-soldier.

On 22nd December 1916 Mussolini obtained permission to take a long period of sick leave, until 16th January. A few days before he was due to return to his regiment, on 11th January, Dalser got him to sign an official document, drawn up by a notary, Vittorio Buffoni, acknowledging Benito Albino as his son, in the offices in Via Passarella of a Milanese lawyer, Guido Gatti. The document was witnessed by Carlo Olivini from Brescia and Irma Marcosanti from Viareggio.

Despite having to deal with this complicated situation, Mussolini was still able to use the period of sick leave to pursue other women. It was probably while he was in Milan on this occasion that he met a twenty-three-year-old woman who would go on to become one of his longer-lasting mistresses. Alice De Fonseca Pallottelli was intelligent, cultivated, beautiful, fascinating, high-spirited and, with the typical Florentine wit she had inherited from her family, amusing. She had lived in London, could speak English fluently and was called "*l'inglese*". A police dossier on her stated, but only on the evidence of hearsay and anonymous letters, that her origins had been modest and that she'd started out in life employed as a chambermaid by a wealthy foreigner. In 1916 she was travelling throughout Europe with her husband, who had a well-paid job as the agent for one of the leading piano virtuosi of the period, the Russian Vladimir de Pachmann. From comparing the information we have, it is also possible that she and Mussolini met not during his period of sick leave but while he was on active service, but there's no firm evidence either way. In 1917 Alice gave birth to a son, Virgilio, who as an adult would become one of the members of Mussolini's inner circle, the associates he trusted most. She also had two other children, Duilio and Adua, and, according to Claretta Petacci, claimed that Mussolini was their father. Even if their relationship did begin in 1916, it remained secret and only became known after Mussolini had seized power. On 2nd April 1938 Petacci called at the elegant villa belonging to the Pallottelli family on Via Nomentana in Rome and found out Mussolini was inside and that his liaison with Alice Pallottelli was continuing. On the following day she angrily told him what she had found out and asked him to justify himself, transcribing his reply in her diary: "You must be patient with me, I won't make you suffer any more. I'm an animal. She wrote to me asking me to help her and her husband, since he had been arrested. So I brought her 5,000 lire. Yes, it's true, I could have sent her the money. But she's also got two children she says are mine..." "Or her husband's," Petacci replies angrily. In the end, as always, he simply admits to having had intercourse with her: "It was very quick. She's past it nowadays, you know."[25]

Some months later, the topic returns in Petacci's diary, since Mussolini has had other meetings with this long-standing mistress. "Pallottelli has written to me saying she's got no money, she doesn't know what to do, and asking me for such a small sum that I think she must really be on the breadline. Her husband's left her in bad circumstances." Petacci wanted to eliminate all her rivals in Mussolini's bed, starting with the longest surviving mistresses, with whom naturally he felt more at ease sexually. The lovers who could play on his affections by claiming he was the father of their children were the most threatening. Driven into a corner by Petacci, on 29th October 1938 Mussolini owns up: "Yes, it's true. I called Pallottelli, yesterday or the other day, to find out if she was back in Rome. She told me her son Duilio was very ill, with amoebiasis. He'll have to go into hospital. She told me he's at school while Adua is still very pretty and is at home. I think she's got real problems, but she didn't want to tell me about them. She's really at the end of her tether, the poor woman. The children are mine – it's true."[26]

So, according to what Petacci writes in her diary, Mussolini was convinced he was the father of Alice De Fonseca Pallottelli's children. There was no actual proof, but he tells Petacci a small detail he somehow remembers from one occasion he made love to the beautiful *inglese*: "I wanted to see the children that she says are mine. It's true I remember something about Duilio: when she had her orgasm she gripped my arms tightly. A month later she told me she was pregnant. It was April, so it could be true. In any case, the poor woman now is really down-at-heel."[27]

Ida Irene Dalser, on the other hand, despite being the only woman who got Mussolini to acknowledge paternity of her son, never became one of his habitual mistresses and never enjoyed the advantages which came from belonging to the circle of the women with whom he enjoyed sexual relations. She was left burnt out by her own passion for the man. He demoted her to the status of former lover and, partly because of the war and his own financial problems, both at home and with the newspaper, failed to send her the sums they had agreed for the maintenance of their son Benito Albino.

On 15th February 1916 he was once again far away from Milan and his giddy womanizing, on the Italian battle lines where, however, he was putting his pen to more use than his bayonet. Together with the rest of his Bersaglieri regiment he was on the march through a small Slovenian town which had been occupied by Italian forces, Caporetto – a name that would leave an indelible mark on Italian history the following year. Ida Irene Dalser employed the lawyer Bortolo Federici to take on her case. Edvige Mussolini wrote to her brother to tell him that the documents had now been sent to the magistrates and to urge him to appoint his own lawyer to represent him. He replied to her on 16th August 1916: "My dearest Edvige, I have received your letter. I too believe that, for the time being, I need to follow my lawyer's advice. I hope there won't be any repeat of this: if there is we'll need to act decisively."[28]

On 19th May 1916 the Milan magistrates had charged Mussolini with failing to fulfil the undertakings he had agreed before the notary; he was bound to pay Dalser the monthly sum of two hundred lire, even though the court denied granting her the status of "victim of moral coercion" – that, in other words, she had been seduced and abandoned. Then as now the time such conflicts took to go through the legal system was very different from that required to meet the urgent needs of the people actually affected by the problems. Ida Dalser only received the first monthly contribution from Mussolini nearly a year after the court case, as we know from a letter he wrote to his sister on 18th February 1917, in which he tells her that Dalser had been to his lawyer's office to collect the money and to promise to stop harassing him. There then followed a period of calm, when it seemed that the mother of the Duce's first-born son had indeed decided to leave him alone. But getting the agreed monthly sums proved increasingly difficult: a new storm loomed on the horizon.

Chapter 10

A Corpse in the Naviglio Canal

After he'd delivered the morning's mail and newspapers to the various offices, the office boy was dozing by the stove. The cleaner was dusting the desks, careful not to move a single sheet of paper as she did so. Heaps of brown files, articles and short pieces, books precariously piled up, cuttings the size of postage stamps, bundles of proofs, everything was in unchangeable, untouchable order. When she'd finished her dusting, the cleaning woman began to wipe the worn floor tiles in the long corridor with a wet cloth; the office boy just about managed to lift his feet to let her clean round the stove before getting back to enjoying the warmth and resuming his nap. As in all newspaper offices, the staff worked until late at night and didn't start coming in until the middle of the morning. Outside the city was bustling, the school day had started an hour ago, you could hear a woman shouting from the street below. One of the journalists arrived, gave a curt greeting to the cleaner, tiptoed near the skirting to avoid dirtying the tiles she had just washed. It was warm in the office; he took off his overcoat and threw it over his chair. Warm?... He gave a sudden shout which made the office boy jump and rushed to the stove. Burning his fingers, he managed to turn it off and open it. It was full of hand grenades. Holding the wet cloth so he didn't burn himself again, he gently lifted each grenade out one by one and placed them on the chief editor's desk.

The office boy tried to excuse himself, stammering that he'd lit the stove because he knew the editor always felt the cold since he had fought in the trenches – and after all he hadn't known about the police inspection which had taken place the evening before and where they'd had to hide the grenades. The journalist continued to shout what a crazy fool he was – he could have set off an explosion which might have wrecked the building and half of Milan along with it. Eventually he calmed down and the cries could be heard again from the street.

The day had begun badly: he'd come in early hoping for some quiet in which to take another look at an article he'd drafted, but there was no hope of that now. He opened the window and looked down into the street: there she was again, that half-crazed woman from Trento who kept shouting for Mussolini and calling him a corrupt traitor and a coward. He ran down the stairs and approached her, but she pushed him away. He tried to tell her that she was wasting her time standing there and shouting because the editor was not in the office – and no, he told her repeatedly, he didn't know when or even if he'd come in today. From the building opposite the newspaper offices someone leant out and shouted angrily at the woman; Ida Irene Dalser calmed down a bit and decided to talk to the journalist. She promised him she wouldn't keep shouting. She had brought a letter to give to Mussolini. He said he would give it to the editor-in-chief in person. He also agreed to persuade Mussolini to call her. When would she like him to call her? As soon as possible, as soon as he had a free moment.

Dalser was removed from Milan by police order in May 1917, because of her continual harassment and threatening behaviour towards Rachele, who was by now Mussolini's legal wife. She was not supposed to leave Florence, where she went to live, but Mussolini's abandonment of her continued to torment her, and once more she returned to Milan and started to attack her former lover in public, denouncing him, laying siege to him. One Sunday evening, towards supper time, she stationed herself once again outside the newspaper offices, holding her small son Benito Albino in her arms. The street was quiet. "You coward, you pig, murderer, traitor," she screamed out. Some of the customers in a local bar came out; two policemen also arrived. "Trying to hide, are you, you coward? Come out if you dare!" Some journalists came running out to try and calm her down. Then Mussolini leant out of the window and shouted: "That's it! I've had enough! I'm going to deal with you once and for all!"[1] He raced down the stairs holding a revolver. Dalser went on screaming, but the journalists who were trying to restrain her now had to deal with their enraged boss as well. It took some time to calm them both down. Mussolini was infuriated a woman could call him a coward and also that his journalists were trying to defend him from her in a public street. He only agreed to go back to the office when he saw the two police officers escorting her away.

Rachele got to hear about this episode. Cesare Rossi wrote long afterwards that "once all the fury aroused by Fascism and its leader has died down, and an objective historical account can emerge of all the political and personal events which occurred in Mussolini's life and career, then it won't be hard, I think, to find someone who will put in a word of praise for Rachele and for all she had to put up with."[2] Rachele indeed tried to react to her husband's excesses with good sense and restraint. No one has ever sung her praises because the fury aroused by Fascism has never abated. The years following the First World War were full of violence, while after 1945 Italy was riven by fierce political conflict and by both left- and right-wing terrorism. Fascism is still a current political term today, although it is often used loosely and inappropriately. No one bothers to examine the figure of Rachele Mussolini, what kind of person she was and what she did. What would be the point? Margherita Sarfatti also gets overlooked, or when she is mentioned at all it's only as Mussolini's mistress, with the fact of her Jewishness occasionally being added.

"There was a heart-warming bohemian atmosphere at *Il Popolo d'Italia* in those years," Sarfatti wrote, "where we all lived like one big family of comrades and brothers; the offices were in a wretched street in one of the most run-down areas of old Milan, but our high spirits and enthusiasm and laughter kept us going in the midst of so much work and so many worries!"[3]

The atmosphere at the newspaper must indeed have been fairly anarchic: Sarfatti must have smiled as she read the notice pinned to the office doors: "Colleagues are kindly reminded not to leave for the day before they have arrived". In Mussolini's eyes, Sarfatti was his prize capture. He even believed that it was the force of his intellect which had led her to abandon her socialist beliefs, which was not at all the case. She was beautiful, blonde, wealthy, intelligent, without inhibition and, at the outset of their affair at least, not intrusive; on the contrary, she was somewhat reserved. It was she who was convinced that in Mussolini she'd found the embodiment of her ideal man. She could respond gratifyingly to his fiery sexuality, making him believe his prowess was irresistible. In 2009 several of her letters to him were sold at auction in London for 25,000 euros. They were written in 1922 and give us an insight into their personal and sexual relationship on the eve of the March on Rome. She tells him that she thinks of herself as a Fascist, fighting in one of the Fascist squads, "part of Mussolini's army – the public one and the secret one. And I vowed myself to you, and confirmed my vows, as your friend, your woman, your bride: I vowed myself to you, my lord and husband, my chief, my lover. With the unwavering faith and loyalty of a firm follower of the cause, as an Italian woman, citizen, mother and lover… I am proud of you for all this, but for what you are, not for what you appear to be. My pride in you is fanatical, it borders on frenzy, but not with the fetishism of the masses, but because of the value of what you inwardly are."

In another of the letters she writes that there is no limit to her passion for him, aside from her feelings as a mother: "My thrice-adored man, I will do whatever you want me to. I am yours. You will not ask me to do anything which is incompatible with my dignity and my duty, and with the sacred and inviolable rights which my offspring, whom I also adore, claim from me." There can be no doubting, it seems, the intensity of the physical, erotic attraction which, in addition to their shared intellectual interests, brought the two of them together and kept them together as a couple for many years. Shortly after the March on Rome, Sarfatti writes to him: "May God allow me to serve you silently, by your side, hidden in the shadow cast by your light; so you may taste some repose and some sweetness, and rest in the certitude of my boundless love. Anchor yourself in me, my great and glorious ship; from my harbour set out to cross the oceans; you will be safe even in the midst of tempests since, if God so pleases, a tenuous but unbreakable bond will keep you rooted to firm land. May God bless you. I love you. Amen."

There is a curious remark in another letter – No. 10 in the lot in the 2009 auction catalogue – which might allude to their use of drugs: "Your divine bewitchments make my blood burn with strange ferments". Cocaine and morphine were widely used among assault troops and warplane pilots in order to overcome the extreme dangers they had to face, as well as cold, tiredness, hunger and fear. Compare Sarfatti's reference to cocaine in her memoirs written after the war, when all her ties to Mussolini had ended:

I still have a packet of cocaine which I managed to seize from him – we wrestled over it – in Milan in 1930. He had turned up at my house, his face pale and his eyes bloodshot, and swaying as though he were drunk. I thought he was tired or ill or indeed that he'd had too much to drink, and I made him a cup of very strong coffee. He gradually told me what had happened. He had started to frequent a place he called the "house of the three witches", some lowlife den run by women who obligingly supplied him and other clients with cocaine.[4]

Sarfatti must be wrong about the date here: it stretches belief too far to think that in 1930 Mussolini as Duce paid clandestine visits to squalid dives in Milan in order to procure drugs. Getting hold of cocaine was fairly straightforward, especially for the powerful. Mafia godfathers like Vito Genovese kept the upper echelons of the Italian "market", including the regime's leading authorities known as *gerarchi* or "gerarchs" and other prominent officials, well supplied; they didn't have to run any risks. As we have seen, after a certain period Mussolini was careful not to touch a drop of alcohol, and it therefore seems improbable that Sarfatti would have assumed he was intoxicated. If the episode is true, then it must have taken place over a decade earlier, in the immediate post-war years and during the early stages of the relationship between the elegant and cultivated Venetian and the raw, uncouth ex-soldier and newspaper editor.

But when Mussolini returned from the war and from active service, after his long convalescence, it wasn't Sarfatti who helped him up and down the stairs with his crutches, but rather another blonde: the reassuring and familiar figure of Rachele. Although his health was still precarious, he took over again the running of the newspaper, looking for financial backing so as to improve its prospects. The war was still being fought; he had often written that it would be a long-drawn-out affair, and events were proving him right. Nothing much happened at the fronts, then all of a sudden there was a burst of fighting, followed once more by a lull. The crisis arrived unannounced on 24th October 1917. The news at first was confused, but it soon became clear that Italy was facing defeat. For two whole weeks it seemed as if the entire country would collapse, that the army would be routed and the enemy would arrive in Venice and even reach as far as Milan. The government fell, and for over a month it proved impossible to form a new one. A "Fascio Parlamentare per la Difesa Nazionale" ("Parliamentary League for National Defence") was set up within parliament, which had the aim of bringing together all those people who were willing to fight for the defence of the fatherland. The two chambers held secret meetings to minimize the risk of any information reaching the enemy's ears. The Socialist Party retreated even further into isolation, refusing to join the Parliamentary League. Mussolini swung between moments of depression at the thought of the impending catastrophe and writing enthusiastic articles in praise of the valour of the Italian troops. His sister Edvige wrote that he would return in the evening completely downcast after a day at the newspaper: "His face was grey and drawn; in his talk he would switch suddenly from anger and defiance to the utmost gloominess."[5]

Mussolini's drawn face also reflected what was happening to his mistress. A grief-stricken Margherita Sarfatti had watched her eldest son Roberto leave for the front; he was just seventeen. Seeing him off on the train she tried to be cheerful while all around them the mothers and fiancées of the departing men were weeping. She had tried to persuade him not to volunteer for the special assault troops known as the Arditi, but to no avail. How could she have succeeded in persuading him anyway – a woman who had been expelled from the Socialist Party for claiming that her sex had a vital role to play in the war, who had written that the nurses in the trenches tending wounded soldiers were a honour to all women? She had travelled through wartime France and had been impressed by the patriotism she had found among the country's women. Serving one's country – this was the new message which was coming from the feminists in England and in France: by serving their country they drew nearer to their goal of emancipation, to the acquisition of their full rights as citizens, starting with the right to vote. In this way patriotism was an important factor in the international women's movement: the right to vote would eventually be achieved, but only for some – British women were granted it after the war, while those in France and Italy still had a long time to wait.

Margherita Sarfatti's husband, lover and now her son as well were all on active military service. On 30th January 1918 she "received in the post a lock of bloodstained hair. One of Roberto's fellow soldiers had cut it before they buried his corpse. [...] As night was falling, he had attempted to storm the hiding place of a rifleman armed with a machine gun. As he leapt onto the enemy soldier, a bullet hit him in the face. He died instantly."[6]

During the course of the war Sarfatti's attitudes towards women's emancipation grew increasingly distant. Women's role in society was changing, even the way they dressed; they were dynamic, they began to have a collective voice. Though Italian women did not immediately achieve the right to vote, they were wooed more and more by political parties, all of which, including the early Fascist Party, put women's suffrage as one of their aims. Sarfatti's opinions started to move in the opposite direction, instead, and it was her views which would become characteristic of the regime when it came to power. For Sarfatti, both as a mother and as a supporter of Italy's intervention in the war, although women had active roles to play both in their own families and in society more widely, they should keep away from the sphere of politics. In her view, women no longer had the right to claim equal treatment as citizens; their role lay at the roots of the new state, by providing children for their country:

> For Sarfatti the issue of women's suffrage was not about their emancipation so much as enabling women to contribute a vote of confidence in the state, its decisions to go to war and while it was at war, and in the men who were responsible for the political sphere. The only women who had the right to express their opinion on the state and its future destiny were, just as in 1915, mothers, since they were the guardians of the species, of the family, of the primary cells of the state as it grew and developed.[7]

The revolutions in Russia in February and October 1917 and the arrival of over a million American troops in Europe backed by American financial resources, altered the overall development of the war. Italy's defeat at Caporetto led to a temporary swing to the right, while Mussolini changed position definitively. "Between the end of 1917 and the end of 1918, between Caporetto and the final victory, Mussolini's political positions underwent what I would argue was an extremely important change, one which would determine the rest of his life. In the course of three years he moved from socialism to Fascism (in the full historical sense of the word as I am using it here): within another four years a Fascist dictatorship had been established in Italy."[8]

This process of change incubated over several months, up to the summer of 1918, during which Mussolini left behind him his position as a "sleeping" socialist, to use the term De Felice borrows from Freemasonry to describe his status. He took the first steps in December 1917 when, writing in *Il Popolo d'Italia*, he came out in support of the newly formed Parliamentary League, declaring that the old parties and their old leaders would soon belong to the past, since there were now only two great factions in Italian politics: "Those who went to war and those who didn't; those who fought and those who didn't fight; those who produce and the parasites who don't."

Ansaldo, the important engineering and armaments firm in Genoa, started to show interest in Mussolini; they saw the potential usefulness of his newspaper as a barrier against "red" propaganda and its "subversive and defeatist" message. In the wake of the debacle at Caporetto there were increasing fears that revolutionaries had infiltrated the country's armaments industry. According to an intelligence report on Mussolini drawn up at about this time by the chief of police in Milan Giovanni Gasti, Ansaldo signed a contract worth half a million lire to buy advertising space in the newspaper.

Mussolini made several visits to Genoa, on occasion travelling there by aeroplane. He wrote an article praising Ansaldo and the Italy which fought, worked, produced; he also spoke enthusiastically of his experience of flying. He became a fanatic for this form of travel; when he heard that the author and poet Gabriele D'Annunzio was organizing a long-distance flight from Rome to Tokyo, he did his utmost to try to join it. His trips were a source of concern to his wife, who writes that he was the first politician to use an official aeroplane for getting around. It was an old warplane which had been converted for civilian use and it enabled Mussolini to move around speedily and carry out many more public engagements. His enthusiasm for flying was later imitated by Hitler, who used aeroplanes to move from town to town and hold several political meetings in the same day.

Just over three years after the grenade explosion in the war which had almost killed him, Mussolini was involved in a flying accident. On 2nd March 1921 he had signed up for a low-altitude flying lesson; the instructor was an ace pilot, Cesare Redaelli. Mussolini took up his position at the controls.

> The first flight passed off smoothly, but on the second, while coming down to land, the engine suddenly cut out. The aeroplane immediately lost speed, and the steering went out of control; it winged forward and then suddenly lost altitude and dropped forty metres to crash. The whole right side was shattered. Redaelli sustained bruising on his forehead, while our editor-in-chief received several cuts to the face, which according to the doctors should heal over in two weeks' time, barring complications, and several painful contusions to his legs and arms.[9]

Mussolini was unable to walk; a haemorrhage in the knee kept him bedridden. Rachele, who had had a premonitory dream of the accident, supervised her husband's recovery. It was during this period that she realized his relationship with Margherita Sarfatti was something more dangerous than a rapid, casual sexual encounter.

> One day, in 1921, while Benito was convalescing from the plane crash with Redaelli, Sarfatti came to the house to see him about work. I pretended to know nothing about their relationship. She behaved impeccably, and yet I was annoyed she had dared to come to my house. After she'd gone, while I was adjusting the bed for Benito, I said as if absent-mindedly: "The cheek of some people! They deserve to be thrown out of the window..." I could see Benito's conscience was uneasy; he didn't pursue the argument, merely remarking, with not much conviction, that I was always getting the wrong end of the stick.[10]

Mussolini's curt reaction was characteristic, made more so because he was on crutches and didn't want more problems. His priority was to get better and recover the physical strength which would become such an important element in the myth that grew up round him. In his report, Giovanni Gasti remarked on Mussolini's "strong physical constitution, despite his syphilis, which allows him to work uninterruptedly for long periods". He writes that Mussolini had a fifteen-hour working day, from about midday when he left his house for the office to three in the morning, after he had checked the final edition of the paper for the presses. "His nature is sensual", Gasti continues, "as is shown by his many sexual affairs of which the most important are with Sarfatti and with Dalser." Gasti uses many adjectives to describe Mussolini's character: emotional, impulsive, suggestible, persuasive, sentimental, disinterested, prodigal, intelligent, shrewd, measured, reflective, a good judge of men, quick to take for or against people, capable of self-sacrifice, a harbourer of long-term grudges and hatreds, brave, daring, well organized, highly ambitious. Gasti's conclusion was that all these qualities added up to a character which was capable of attracting many people and had made him an acknowledged political leader. Mussolini knew that he was kept under observation by the authorities, but can have had no idea that he was being studied in such detail. The richness and precision of the report's analysis owe everything to the intelligence of its author, who also remarked on Mussolini's tendency to change his opinions according to his prevailing interests: "As I have already pointed out, Mussolini's political aims are changeable. It would not be difficult to make him collaborate, at least to some degree, but it is also quite possible that in certain circumstances – because of the turn of events or in order not to be overtaken by other parties or for some other external or internal motive – he will change direction and help to undermine institutions and principles which he has hitherto supported and advocated."[11] Later Mussolini would attempt to justify his tendency to "change direction" by describing it, with a daring rhetorical flourish, as "absolute relativism".[12]

In response to the advertising contract from Ansaldo, Mussolini decided to close *Il Popolo d'Italia*'s offices in Rome and move them to Genoa to start producing a local edition there. The announcement of the change was carried in the issue for 1st August 1918: "Genoa, 31st July, evening. We remind our readers – although such is the expectancy there's no need to – that tomorrow evening the new offices of *Il Popolo d'Italia* will open in Genoa, in Via Palestra 2, on the ground floor. Correspondents, journalists and a few specially invited friends will gather at the newspaper's head offices at 7 p.m. for the war dinner to be hosted by Mussolini at the Fiaschetteria Toscana in Via Ettore Vernazza."

There were also opportunities in Genoa to form links with the associations for mutilated and disabled ex-servicemen. If we are to choose one date to symbolize Mussolini's definitive change of political direction it would be the same day – 1st August 1918 – on which the first issue of the Genoese edition of the paper was printed, for the usual subtitle "Socialist Daily Newspaper" had been removed. The alteration was announced the following day: "As from yesterday the word 'socialist' has been removed from the newspaper's subtitle, replacing it with a new one which all who read us and also those who don't will appreciate for its actuality and stirring commitment: 'The Daily Newspaper of Combatants and Producers'."[13]

In the first issue's editorial, Mussolini declared that all the forces were in place for a new politics, it was only a question of recognizing them. They were the masses who had fought in the Great War, the "men of the trenches", the workers and peasants who had answered the call-up and now, on their return, were asking for a better life. Shortly afterwards, another article by him appeared which explained the use of the word "producers" in the subtitle. It was no longer a question of class struggle, of the proletariat against the bourgeoisie: engineers and mechanics, entrepreneurs and workers were all "producers". "Producing" was the fundamental activity: only by producing could the proletariat improve its living conditions. In saying this Mussolini was using some of the ideas which had struck him while listening to Pareto's lectures during his time in Switzerland: Fascism stemmed from a handful of superficial concepts.

Perhaps no period in Italian history has been studied more than that between the Italian defeat at Caporetto in 1917 and the March on Rome in 1922; hundreds of books have been published, but you'd read them in vain to find a coherent line of development, since it does not exist. Mussolini was not following a deliberate strategy with the personal aim of acquiring power; on the contrary, he was pushed forward by a train of events which unfolded too rapidly for him to stay in control of by taking the decisions. When Italy was declared one of the victorious powers at the end of the war on 4th November 1918, Mussolini was above all a journalist, confident in his communicative abilities, an editor-in-chief aware of the potential which a well-established and widely read newspaper offered and prepared to ensure its survival by any means. He was sure his cynical adroitness would enable him to stay in control of any alliance of convenience he might be obliged to make as well as the vested interests of any financial supporter. He believed that a newspaper which enjoyed a wide circulation was the best way of obtaining political influence, but he didn't have a clear idea when or how he'd acquire political power. While the war was still continuing, although activity on the Italian front had been at a standstill for months, he wrote that the important thing was to win the war, to come out of it victorious, and – brushing aside the criticisms of the nationalists – if that meant thanks to the French or the Americans, then so be it. In a way events proved him right. Italy won the war at the Battle of Vittorio Veneto, which some historians do not even consider to be a proper battle. The war was not won solely by the sacrifice of the lives of soldiers, sailors and airmen; it was the clash between two different economic, industrial and financial systems. One of them, backed by the capital which arrived from the United States, managed to hold out a day longer than the other. The Austrian-Hungarian Empire imploded, the Kaiser in Germany no longer had the capacity to defend himself, let alone his country, Italian troops marched down into the plains without encountering any resistance. In southern Europe, a third great empire, the Ottomans, crumbled.

On 22nd April 1918, while the war was still being fought, Rachele Mussolini gave birth to their third child, Bruno. She was still having to breastfeed the new baby when, at the beginning of 1919, she came down with the Spanish influenza, which was then sweeping Europe. In Italy alone more people died in the outbreak than had during the war. Many ex-soldiers who had survived all the hardships of trench warfare and enemy fire in battle succumbed and died from fever, coughs, pulmonary bleeding, in hospitals and at home. The outbreak eventually killed more than fifty million people, and already by the time the powers assembled for the peace conference in Paris in January 1919 it was a pandemic which was out of control. The Italian delegation was snubbed by the others round the table: the request to annex Fiume was turned down, despite the agreement which had been made in the 1915 Treaty of London before Italy entered the war. The Spanish flu virus had been brought over with the American troops, but no one knew then that this was the cause. President Woodrow Wilson presented the bill for American participation in the war; he became the new leader in international politics.

Back in Rome, meanwhile, it was proving difficult to form a government with a stable majority. The political situation was full of uncertainty; the government headed by Francesco Saverio Nitti declared an end to the war and started to demobilize the army. *Il Popolo d'Italia* was, to all intents and purposes, the expression of the political line adopted by Mussolini, although "line" is to exaggerate its consistency: there was no long- or even medium-term project and no unifying vision. The immediate aim was to use the newspaper to acquire a political role in the new circumstances; just as war had been the theme of the paper's interventionist campaign back in 1915, so it was the focus of its efforts to speak to the feelings and the needs of the ex-servicemen returning to their homes. Mussolini wanted to play on the mood of these men, especially the men who had belonged to the assault troops, the "Arditi", the so-called "daring ones". He had the right cards to play, and the game was made easier by the extreme anti-war position of the Socialist Party. He had been intransigently, fanatically in favour of Italian involvement in the war, he had fought against the enemy, he had been wounded and in danger of death: if from one point of view these experiences had served to demolish his socialist ideals and principles, from another they were exactly the credentials he needed in order to speak convincingly to the mass of ex-servicemen now returning home. His own experiences at the front gave him an understanding, even if it was only an instinctive one, of how the men from the assault troops must be feeling. Today we know a lot about the state of dependency which can be created in those on active combat; even "embedded" journalists who've covered the fighting in war zones have been known to become affected or addicted, and have difficulties when they need to go back to normal life. The Arditi were trained to operate behind enemy lines; only the bravest men were selected to join them, those who'd passed severely demanding tests of endurance and courage and who'd shown notable sangfroid in the face of death. They underwent intense physical training sometimes under conditions of real artillery fire – on several occasions men were killed. They needed to know how to fight at close quarters, sometimes with their bare hands. They learnt to slide forward on the ground with a dagger between their clenched teeth in order to attack enemy positions which ordinary troops would find impregnable. They threw themselves down into enemy trenches, often with bayonets unsheathed, and then would defend them until the regular troops arrived in support. Powered by adrenalin and frequently cocaine, they had complete freedom of action in a war that by the standards of the time saw particularly unrestrained fighting; now these men were being demobilized and sent back to resume their ordinary tranquil pre-war lives. But the freedom they had enjoyed in war was now their natural environment; they found the limitations of peacetime life unendurable. No emotions of homecoming were aroused in them as they saw again the places they'd left years before; while not yet asocial or maladjusted, they were well on the way to developing the potential to become so. No psychological help or counselling was available then to help them through the traumas caused by living for so long within sight of bloodshed and the sound of gunfire. In normal life they stood out as violent and undisciplined, a set of anarchic individualists. Their very physical existence was ill adapted to the tranquil routines of everyday life; they needed the constant stimuli they'd become used to during the war.

In the pages of *Il Popolo d'Italia* Mussolini called for the formation of *"fasci di combattimento"*, "combatants' leagues". Many ex-combatants responded eagerly to the call. Filippo Tommaso

Marinetti, who, along with other Futurist artists and writers, had fought with the Arditi, also signed up. A shrewd move was to offer a sum of money to all those who agreed to join; the financial support for this was provided by some of the bankers and industrialists who had grown rich during the war. Writing from her particular and somewhat privileged point of view, Edvige Mussolini describes the "enrolment" of the Arditi in the new Fasci: "By joining the 'Fasci' all those who felt dispersed and out-of-step were enabled to re-enter national political life; these men had been ignored by all the major established political parties, a huge mistake on their part because it condemned them to sterility, an impoverishment of energy and imagination. Their pointless good sense left them helpless in the face of the new barbarians."[14]

Mussolini also had a hero he could hold up as a model to the Arditi who joined the new Fasci: the eldest son of his mistress, Roberto Sarfatti, who had himself been one of the Arditi and had fallen while trying to carry out the impossible task of attacking a machine-gunner. The boy's memory provided him with useful political capital. Margherita Sarfatti wished she had died instead of her son: she felt she was to blame for his untimely death; Mussolini's focus on him, the ceremonies with all their paraphernalia of flags and daggers which he organized to exalt his memory, gave her new energy. She had developed a hatred for pacifists, socialists and other politicians who refused to praise the victory for which her son had sacrificed his life; she only valued being with Mussolini, and she was moved by the sight of him surrounded by Roberto's former comrades. For his part Mussolini relished his association with them. Surrounded by them, he thought he struck fear into the hearts of others, a useful effect for a movement which freely exploited violence to achieve its ends.

The militarization of political life began with the Fasci: the black flames and fezzes and pennants, the skulls with a dagger between their teeth – Fascism's leading symbols were borrowed from the Arditi as was the party anthem, 'Giovinezza' ('Youth'). Over the course of a few months, Mussolini found himself in possession of two inestimable weapons: a well-funded newspaper with a wide circulation and squads of ex-servicemen highly skilled in the handling of arms of all kinds. Every former member of the Arditi knew how to fire machine guns, pistols and rifles; in wartime they always carried a dagger and twenty hand grenades. The daggers, the grenades and the firearms would be employed again in the Fascist squads' attacks. Mussolini hoped that the ex-members of the special assault forces who had joined the new Fasci would attract the allegiance of the vast majority of ordinary ex-servicemen.

On 21st March 1919, the "Fascio Milanese di Combattimento" or the "Milan League of Combatants" was founded. *Il Popolo d'Italia* convened a general assembly of the Fasci or squads in the great hall of the building which belonged to the organization known as the Alleanza Industriale e Commerciale (Industrial and Business Alliance) in Piazza San Sepolcro in Milan: "On 23rd March an anti-party will be founded: the 'Combatants' Leagues', which will lead a crusade against two impending dangers: the right with its hatred of the new and the left with its yen for destruction. The political goals of the Leagues will be few, but they will be precise and radical". Those who assembled on 23rd March were asked to join a movement which would be anti-bourgeois, anti-socialist, anticlerical and anti-monarchist. Its political manifesto had an improvised, confused air; it did not so much anticipate the future regime as rehash former radical left-wing issues – an eight-hour working day, the state confiscation of property belonging to religious orders, the abolition of the Senate, universal suffrage including for women. Nor, in the gathering in Piazza San Sepolcro, was Mussolini seen as their leader or "*duce*"; he was merely one of the leading exponents of the new movement, perhaps the one who spoke with the most authority, but whose views nevertheless were open to discussion and on occasion contested. *Il Popolo d'Italia* added the further clarification that it remained Mussolini's newspaper and was not the official mouthpiece of the Fasci. Those who gathered in Piazza San Sepolcro on 23rd March were not all men: there were also nine women, none of whom would play any part in the regime as it was established from 1922 onwards – "predictably, given Mussolini's continual changes of conviction, his sudden tactical switches, his readiness to form expedient alliances and to make what turned out to be merely face-saving concessions, and his declarations of firm-as-a-rock principles which crumbled to pieces when put into practice. And predictably too, given the political background of these nine women activists, all of whom were committed to the fight for women's rights."[15]

The best-known of the women was the socialist – and secretary of the Unione Femminile Socialista (Socialist Women's Union) – Regina Terruzzi; she was twenty years older than Mussolini, an unmarried mother who, long before it became a general cause, battled for the legal recognition of children born out of wedlock. Terruzzi had been part of the editorial team, along with Margherita Sarfatti, of the periodical *La difesa delle lavoratrici* (*The Defence of Women Workers*), founded by Anna Kuliscioff in 1912. After war started she sided with the interventionist movement. Joining Mussolini in the gathering in Piazza San Sepolcro must have come naturally to her, although later she withdrew when she saw the violence committed by the Fasci. Much later, in 1932, she once again drew nearer to the regime, accepting the presidency of the Federazione Nazionale Fascista delle Massaie Rurali (National Fascist Federation of Rural Housewives); she resigned a year later with the excuse that she had to follow her son who had gone to live in Nice.

Cesare Rossi was given the task of summarizing the various speeches made by the so-called "*sepolcristi*", those who were present at the first general meeting of the Fasci. Rossi was one of Mussolini's leading collaborators. In his later memoirs he revised his view of the meeting given in his original report: he describes it as insignificant in terms of the numbers attending and the level of discussion, and points out that at least a third of those who turned up later became anti-Fascists. He also writes that Mussolini had no real sense of political direction at the time, given that at the very moment he was calling for the Fasci he was also testing the ground for a possible return into the Socialist Party fold.

> Several veteran Socialists who were active in the party have confirmed to me that in 1919, especially in Milan, there were rumours that Mussolini was making cautious approaches about rejoining the party. Pietro Nenni has also confirmed the rumours, adding that Mussolini had approached [Bruno] Buozzi; Buozzi had mentioned this on several occasions to more than one socialist comrade during their years in exile. [...] It wasn't at all a question of Mussolini simply rejoining the Socialist Party; in my opinion, he was angling to rejoin in agreement with the reformist and federal wings of the party – it is not by chance that his initial contacts were with Buozzi – in the hope of creating together with them a breakaway movement.[16]

Whatever Mussolini's vague intentions of rejoining the Socialist Party might have been, an abrupt stop was put to them on 15th April 1919, when a Milanese Fascist squad made up of former Arditi (together with various Futurists), attacked and burnt down the main offices of the Socialist Party newspaper *Avanti!*. It was the day the Chamber of Labour had declared a general strike. One of the nine women who had been present at Piazza San Sepolcro – Luisa Rosalia Dentici – also took part in the attack. In reaction, several Socialist Party activists swore undying hatred towards Mussolini and threatened to kill him. But Margherita Sarfatti was full of enthusiasm for the attack, which she saw as a just revenge for the death of her son. In the attack the Fascists had killed four people, but Sarfatti openly defended their actions, while Mussolini's response was more guarded, saying that the attack had been carried out spontaneously. In interviews at the time he declared that even if the Fasci were not responsible for the assault on the offices of the Socialist Party newspaper he would still accept the moral responsibility for what had happened. As we have seen, the attack went against the tactics he was secretly pursuing, but nevertheless he was obliged to brazen it out, as he had to so often on later occasions. But there was one immediate tangible result: everyone was talking about Mussolini and the Combatants' Leagues. The nature of the struggle in politics was changing: it was no longer merely a question of meetings and rallies, of speech-making, of manifestos and newspapers. Now military considerations prevailed: the organization of attacks needed physical strength and careful planning just as if you were going over into enemy trenches. The destruction of the offices of *Avanti!* worried Pietro Nenni – who would go on to become the leader of the Socialist Party after the Second World War – but it didn't make him change his position at the time: only a week before the attack took place, on 9th April, he had proposed himself as a candidate to be one of the leaders of the Combatants' League in Bologna. A summary of his speech on the occasion was printed in *Il Popolo d'Italia*: Nenni wanted the "*fascio*" to be anti-Bolshevik, anti-monarchist and strongly republican.

A noteworthy point in these years when Mussolini's politics were changing and developing is the support he gave, as early as June 1919, to the anti-Semitic view on the hidden manoeuvres of Jewish international finance and the alliance between Bolshevism and Zionism. Seeing the Jews as a "lobby" intent on damaging the country's interests was an attitude which would emerge at several points over the course of the twentieth century (and indeed beyond).

Mussolini and the writer and poet Gabriele D'Annunzio had exchanged letters between December 1918 and January 1919 on what had been described as the "truncated victory" in the war. Both men were intent on sounding each other out. When, under the leadership of D'Annunzio, volunteers started to flock to add their support to a military action aimed at ensuring the city of Fiume became part of Italy, Mussolini wrote to the warrior-poet that he was ready to fight under him. On 12th September D'Annunzio, at the head of an army consisting of about 2,500 men, occupied Fiume. Sarfatti described the event: "With a bard's intuition, D'Annunzio saw that the redemption of Fiume would in its turn redeem Italy. Fiume was the Holy Grail, the mystical chalice filled with the blood of the martyrs, round which this High Priest, ardent keeper of the sacred mysteries, gathered the flower of Italian military prowess. Fortune and victory smiled on this Holy Grail by the shores of the Adriatic Sea."[17]

Mussolini had assured D'Annunzio that *Il Popolo d'Italia* would lend its active support to the occupation of Fiume. Many Arditi from local Combatants' Leagues went to join D'Annunzio's forces, among them the revolutionary syndicalist and renowned war hero Alceste De Ambris. All of them saw D'Annunzio as their real leader or "*duce*", to Mussolini's discomfiture: he described his rival as a man of letters playing at politics, trapped in his own world of high-sounding words. Nevertheless, D'Annunzio's high-sounding words, the distinctive way he harangued the crowds, made political meetings into spectacular, emotionally overwhelming occasions and introduced a new style of political communication. Mussolini couldn't counter the powerful effects of D'Annunzio's spellbinding oratory, but he knew that in the long run they would fade and real politics – where D'Annunzio was a clumsy tactician (he wanted to lead a march on Rome on condition the Socialist Party gave him a guarantee they would remain neutral) – would resume its rightful place. D'Annunzio was a poet who wanted to turn his life into a work of art – he was above all concerned with the figure he struck, with the exaltation of his own successes, with becoming the "*duce*" of "his greatest poem", the one he was writing with his actions, in seizing hold of Fiume; Mussolini was a politician, without, for the moment, a plausible strategy, but attempting to construct one by any means which suggested themselves, such as an electoral alliance with those on the left who had been in favour of intervention. D'Annunzio wrote to him criticizing him for his hesitations and wavering; Mussolini responded by launching an appeal in the newspaper for funds to support the attack on Fiume. However, when D'Annunzio first floated the vague idea of a march on Rome from occupied Fiume, Mussolini realized that the poet was overtaking him and that he risked being left behind. He replied endorsing the idea, but also trying to gain time by arguing that they needed to secure the support of the army before they made a move. Mussolini's response irritated D'Annunzio, who saw it as more the product of indecision and incapacity than political foresight. Mussolini tried to reassure him by sending one of his most loyal journalists, Michele Bianchi, to let him know that as soon as the weather was good Mussolini himself would fly to Fiume and join him. His aim was to persuade D'Annunzio to draw back from doing anything hasty and to evaluate the changing political situation in the country: parliament had been dissolved, the march could not go ahead unless other events intervened first, it would be better to wait until after the general election on 16th November.

The election took place in an extremely troubled period for the country. Reports of D'Annunzio's government in Fiume spoke of an idiosyncratic social experiment, a city-state ruled by an artist whose approach mixed right-wing militarism with avant-garde and for the time outlandish social policies. The whole of the continent was in ferment. The alliance of victorious European powers had turned their attention on Communist Russia and attacked it; international socialism attempted, without success, to organize protest strikes in various countries to force their governments to withdraw their troops. In Italy the Dalmine factories were occupied and there was a series of demonstrations in the leading industrial cities which heralded the so-called "*biennio rosso*" ("two red years"), the period from 1920 to 1921, when the left seemed to be in the ascendant. Sarfatti sums up what this period felt like to her, describing how Mussolini would shout angrily he wouldn't "join the race, no, in God's name, he wouldn't, to become redder than red! [...] But the race to be redder than red was happening all around us: the socialists, the Third Internationalists, the communists and all the supporters of the Moscow soviets... The priests were red – the reverend Don Sturzo – the conservatives blushed pink, making the democrats turn beetroot and the republicans deep-dyed crimson. It was like walking along a street lined with bars, each one claiming they sold the best wine."[18]

Mussolini would have liked to forge a single alliance from his Fascist squads and the various forces on the left who'd been in favour of Italy's intervention in the war, but the attempt failed. When we look more closely at his own development in the context of the overall picture of Italian politics in this period, we can see that he remained an isolated figure, while his armed squads, although violent, were no more than small minority groups. When Mussolini stood as a candidate in the general elections of 1919, he was on his own: he was supported only by Marinetti's Futurists and by the ex-Arditi. "Their electoral campaign was more like a carnival than a political movement: gunfire, war songs, torches flaming in the breeze, trucks disguised to look like assault tanks. The Milanese electorate remained unimpressed by this Futurist war show on wheels."[19]

Mussolini did pull off one coup: he managed to get the world-famous orchestral conductor Arturo Toscanini to agree to add his name to his list of proposed candidates. During the war Toscanini had organized an orchestra to play for the troops, on the front, often in inaccessible mountainous places where fierce battles had only just been fought. During the debacle at Caporetto he had insisted on continuing to rehearse with his musicians (despite the wartime conditions, he demanded flawless performances from them), and it was only at the last moment that the army generals persuaded him to pack up and retreat before he and the orchestra fell into the hands of the advancing Austrians. Mussolini admired Toscanini's energies in conducting and the way he exercised an absolute authority over his musicians which seemed to meld their individual qualities into one compact unity. In exile Toscanini would become one of the most intransigent and outspoken opponents of Mussolini's regime, but his agreeing to stand as a candidate alongside Mussolini in 1919 should not unduly take us aback. We are now able to see Fascism clearly for what it was: a violent right-wing reaction, anti-unions, anti-socialist, anti-democratic. But in 1919, at least from the outside, the "Combatants' League" looked like a progressive movement – dynamic, energetic, intent on modernizing Italian political life and opening it up to the masses.

The first name on the list of candidates for the Combatants' League was Mussolini himself, who was described as "combatant, wounded in action"; the second name was Toscanini's, followed by the simple description "orchestral conductor"; while Emilio Filippo Tommaso Marinetti appeared in the seventh position, "volunteer recruit, wounded in action, awarded a War Cross and recommended for two silver medals". The fourteenth place was occupied by Giacomo Macchi, an "aviation captain from Gallarate, deputy commander of Gabriele D'Annunzio's Squadron, three times silver-medallist, twice wounded in action, and awarded military honours on a total of twelve occasions".[20]

The political isolation of the Combatants' League was evident during the election campaign. Their hustings were poorly attended, while those who spoke at them and the main offices of *Il Popolo d'Italia* itself had to be protected by ex-Arditi and other former servicemen from over Italy, including Fiume. On one occasion, because of the usual pressures of his private life, Mussolini was unable to attend a meeting of the Fasci in the main hall of the Institute for the Blind. At a meeting which was held three days later he spoke about the need for the League to differentiate itself from the old political parties and their traditional constituencies:

> He didn't manage to carry his audience, who kept interrupting him, until a brusque interjection from one of the combatants annoyed him and managed to turn the situation to his advantage: "Why didn't you come and tell us all this the other evening?" The question provoked Mussolini, and he replied violently: "Because one of my sons was dying!..." Bruno, still only a baby at the time, had had an attack of croup and had almost died. Mussolini's reply revealed the anguish he was feeling as a father and moved the audience to the point they rose as one to their feet to acclaim him. After which at least half of the people present didn't feel up to voting against his proposals...[21]

Bruno had caught diphtheria and recovered from it, only to fall ill again immediately with bronchial pneumonia or "croup", an extreme form of laryngitis. Rachele wrote that "Bruno's illnesses had exhausted the two of us – Benito especially, and not only because he couldn't bear illness, either his own or when others fell sick, but because the sight of children who were ill disturbed him profoundly."[22]

Mussolini's list of candidates in the 1919 elections in Milan obtained just 4,657 votes; other constituencies returned equally dismal figures. Only in Liguria did a single candidate from the Combatants'

League manage to get elected. "We have neither won a victory nor suffered a defeat: we have made a political statement," Mussolini wrote in *Il Popolo d'Italia*, obeying as if by instinct one of the golden rules of political communication, which is that you must continue to defend your image and that of your movement come what may. When he called home on election night, however, his assessment was a lot bleaker: "Benito telephoned that evening about eleven o'clock. 'It's a complete fiasco,' he announced. 'We haven't won a single seat. People are demonstrating against us in the centre of town – especially the Socialists.'"[23]

Two days after the election, *Avanti!* was full of comment on the Socialist Party's remarkable success, but also found time to dent Mussolini's image by publishing an insultingly brief notice: "A corpse in a state of putrefaction has been found in the Naviglio canal. It is believed to be Benito Mussolini." The author of what reads like malignant wishful thinking was a Socialist Party city councillor, Ippolito Bastiani, who later, as Cesare Rossi reminds us, would become an enthusiastic Fascist journalist, just as so many Italian Socialists did in many different walks of life.

And on the same day as Bastiani's announcement, 18th November, Mussolini suffered a further setback: the police raided the headquarters of the Combatants' Leagues and the offices of *Il Popolo d'Italia*, confiscating pistols, bombs and knives and putting him and Marinetti under arrest. That same evening the senator Luigi Albertini called the Prime Minister Nitti advising him to release Mussolini speedily. The *Corriere della Sera* reported the news the following day:

> The editor-in-chief of *Il Popolo d'Italia* got into a car along with his brother and followed the officers. He arrived at San Fedele unobserved and was led into the office of the deputy chief commissioner Stivala for preliminary questioning. The editor of *Il Popolo d'Italia* was calm and unmoved. He said with a smile that his arrest would certainly give the Socialists further cause to celebrate their success. He added that if his temporary detention put a stop to civic unrest and allowed the re-establishment of law and order, then he was pleased to have been put under arrest.

The *Corriere* condemned Mussolini's arrest, declaring that it would seem like "an act of submission to the victorious Socialist Party", "a concession to Mussolini's worst enemies at the moment he appeared to be most vulnerable", and that his continuing detention represented "a persecution out of proportion to the actual reasons for his arrest". The magistrates took the view that the twenty revolvers found on the premises of Mussolini's offices were not sufficient cause to warrant his arrest, and the police failed to find any compromising documents: Mussolini spent a total of twenty-two hours in a police cell. On the 19th he was released, and on the 20th he was writing in *Il Popolo d'Italia*: "A whirlwind has been unleashed on the Fascist movement, but it won't succeed in uprooting it." He wrote another letter to D'Annunzio, sent to Fiume via his friend De Ambris, in which once more he temporized, by telling him they needed to take into account the fact that hundreds of Fascists had been arrested, those who were left would have to be reorganized, they should wait until the members of the Leagues could all take up their posts again. If D'Annunzio thought this painted too discouraging a picture of their situation, then too bad – it was the truth. It was a difficult juncture in Mussolini's career: even Margherita Sarfatti began to think that the man to whom she had committed herself completely might not succeed. Both physically and intellectually their relationship had grown more intense since their days together at the offices of *Avanti!*. "The curves of her body, her blonde hair, her sense of herself as a woman were ever present to him. Both Margherita Sarfatti's body and intellect challenged him."[24] But Sarfatti grew more jealous as their intimacy increased: the problem was that the man she loved continued to have eyes for the curves of other women's bodies besides her own.

Chapter 11

A Military Encampment

The important guests had all arrived. The drawing rooms of Margherita Sarfatti's apartment were thronged with artists, painters, writers, celebrated academics, wealthy entrepreneurs and ambitious journalists. Among them were the poet Ada Negri, Filippo Tommaso Marinetti and Guido Da Verona, but one guest, surrounded by a court of elegantly dressed women, stood out: the great conductor Arturo Toscanini. Normally at an event like this the celebrated musician would have picked out the most beautiful and fascinating woman among the female guests and spent the rest of the time with her, but on this evening at the end of 1919 he'd come with other intentions. He wanted to give his hostess and her guests a surprise, one which filled him with pride. He had brought along to the party a nineteen-year-old violinist from Bohemia, Váša Příhoda. The young man had ended up in Milan after a series of misadventures and was playing in a small café orchestra in order to earn a living; one evening, in the room packed with customers, Toscanini had spotted his quality immediately.

The maestro called the guests to attention and even succeeded in gaining Mussolini's, who was sulkily sitting on a sofa by himself, licking the wounds of his recent electoral defeat. Their lack of success had not discouraged Toscanini who, despite the defeat, made a donation of 30,000 lire to Mussolini, which he had promised him before the election. He called for silence, and all the guests turned to look at him expectantly – although they couldn't have foreseen the tense situation which would soon develop. Toscanini presented Příhoda to them, praising his talent to the skies, much to the amazement of the guests, since the conductor had a reputation as a tyrannical perfectionist who didn't hesitate to sack reputable orchestral players if he didn't think them good enough. He was extremely grudging with his praise, yet here he was pouring commendations on a young refugee whom he had spotted by chance in a café. Příhoda played a short piece and was thunderously applauded by the guests; he indeed deserved Toscanini's high esteem. Then the hostess of the evening, Margherita Sarfatti, asked Mussolini, in front of all the others, if he would care to play to them. There was consternation among her guests: here she was, asking a self-taught amateur violinist to play in front of Toscanini and the exceptionally talented young man they had just listened to – it must be some kind of cruel joke. "All eyes turned on Mussolini, who muttered something about being indisposed. But he clearly hadn't realized what Margherita was capable of, since she went on to ask him to agree to play if only for her sake."[1] Mussolini furiously hissed at her to stop and left the party without having had to take up the violin. Their quarrel continued the next time they met. Sarfatti was taking her revenge for his continuous infidelities with other women. She showed him that a mistress could be more jealous – and much more perfidious – than a wife. This was another problem among the many at this time on Mussolini's plate. He had been defeated in the elections. *Il Popolo d'Italia* was also facing a financial crisis: the funding which the paper had received from the British and the French during the war had stopped. A certain amount of financial support came from Genoa, but only just enough for the paper to keep on publishing. Many of the Fasci had been dissolved, while others had only a very small number of members. The left-wing supporters of the movement started to melt away, such as Pietro Nenni, who left the Bologna League. The Fasci still attracted new members, but they were younger and firmly on the anti-populist and anti-socialist right. Moreover, they were frequently asocial, maladapted types in search of violence.

Many books have been written about Mussolini's rise to power, but the report on him drawn up Giovanni Gasti in 1919 when he was the chief police officer in Milan still stands out for its lucidity and intelligence. His analysis of Fascism is remarkable when one thinks that it was written when Mussolini was making his initial moves. Gasti writes that the political programme of the "*sepolcristi*" was aimed at blocking the spread of Leninist ideas by official Socialists, as much as to say, in Gasti's opinion, that the Fasci were made up for the most part of "non-official Socialists". One figure who stands out in the report is Ida Irene Dalser: "A reference to Mussolini's relationship with her will not be out of place". According to the report,

Dalser was the daughter of the mayor of Sopramonte, a village near Trento. She was three years older than Mussolini. She had worked as a housekeeper in Milan and then had gone to Paris to take a diploma to become a beautician, although Gasti writes that all she learnt was the job of manicurist: "In 1913 she returned to Milan, where she set herself up as a so-called 'specialist in aesthetic hygiene and massage' with a beauty salon in Via Foscolo 5." She had a relationship with a well-off sales agent for the Erba company, and when it ended gave the first signs of the threatening and outrageous behaviour she was prone to. Gasti then says she started to work for *Il Popolo d'Italia*, but he doesn't add in what capacity. Dalser was receiving – though only irregularly, as we've seen – a monthly sum of two hundred lire every month from Mussolini, sent via the lawyer Ermanno Jarach, who had an office at Via Santo Spirito 7 in Milan. Gasti points out that he was the brother of the banker Jarach, whose bank held the account where Manlio Morgagni kept the supporting funds for *Il Popolo d'Italia*. On one occasion, during a police interrogation, Dalser had accused Mussolini of selling himself to the French: she said that on 17th January 1914 in Geneva Mussolini and Naldi had received the sum of a million lire from the former French prime minister Joseph Caillaux, which they had deposited in an account in the Jarach bank in Via Santo Spirito in Milan. She added that she had contributed to setting up the newspaper with the not unsubstantial proceeds from the sale of the beauty salon. Dalser's accusation was detailed, and the details intrigued Gasti. How did this former mistress know that the early discussions on starting the newspaper were held in the Bella Venezia hotel in Milan? And that a certain Commendatore Iona had deliberately been excluded from the discussions by Mussolini and Naldi so that he wouldn't find out about where the supporting money for the newspaper was coming from? Dalser was undoubtedly "neurotic and hysterical and driven by a desire for revenge on Mussolini", but subsequent police checks on her statement showed that the only slip in the details she gave was a date. Mussolini and Naldi had certainly been in Geneva, at the Hôtel d'Angleterre, but ten months later, on 13th November 1914; while there they had not only signed an advertising contract with the publicity firm Haasenstein and Vogler, but had also met with leading French politicians, as mentioned in a report drawn up by the Italian consul in the city. Mussolini's briskly dismissive description of Dalser as crazy and hysterical didn't quite fit: she knew a lot. From what she said, one has the impression that the "not unsubstantial" sum she'd given her lover was actually a considerable amount of money, and that it represented a lifeline at a crucial moment when the financial survival of the newspaper was in doubt and Mussolini's other contacts had not yet produced any cash. Dalser knew enough to single out certain men who collaborated with Mussolini – Ugo Clerici, for example, whom Gasti was also investigating. Clerici had entered Mussolini's circle as a lowly sales agent for coffee, but he was working in partnership with Angiolino De Ambris, the brother of the revolutionary syndicalist. He soon abandoned this job and started trafficking in Switzerland, where he appeared to have had "ample financial resources". In any case, Gasti's report continues, "it is public knowledge that Mussolini has received money from the Fascio delle Associazioni Patriottiche [League of Patriotic Associations] under its director Candiani, from Freemasonry and from the Republican Party…"[2]

Once her hysterics were over and she could reason more calmly with the police officers who were questioning her, Dalser pointed out how much Mussolini's style of life had changed. He'd left the editorship of *Avanti!* without a penny, scornfully refusing to take any redundancy payment, but not long afterwards he was publishing his own newspaper, was able to pay the journalists who worked for him good salaries, moved into a fine house in the Foro Bonaparte area of the city, lunched and dined in restaurants, owned several cars, could pay for a network of informers and also, in fear of reprisals after the attack on the offices of *Avanti!*, for a team of bodyguards – made up of twenty-five ex-Arditi, each of whom received fifteen lire a day – stationed permanently outside his office as well as accompanying him wherever he went. From the middle of May onwards, their number was reduced to five. Dalser was right – 1920 had seen a sudden and marked improvement in Mussolini's personal finances – and Gasti duly continued his investigations in the wake of her accusations. Mussolini had purchased a new car, a four-seater Bianchi Torpedo fitted with jumpseats. He had also moved the newspaper's operation to a new and well-appointed building, where he had a large office as well as a special room for his fencing lessons and training. He started to dress elegantly, in grey or black suits, stiff-collared shirts and beautiful ties. This was also true for Rachele as she herself notes: "I followed the fashions of the day and wore beautiful dresses, wide in the skirt and narrow at the waist. I also liked to wear buttoned-up boots, like those worn by elegant ladies in the nineteenth century – they really suited me. A bit later we started to employ a chauffeur; we were indistinguishable from any other middle-class couple in Milan."[3] What Rachele didn't know was that there was another reason for her husband's new sartorial elegance – the smart gaiters, the white handkerchief sported in the breast pocket, the bowler hat and the straw boater. Margherita Sarfatti was also responsible for Mussolini's new dress sense; in a sense she was re-educating him.

Dalser's hysterical anger is understandable: in Trento she had formed a relationship with a man barely able to keep himself, she had sold her beauty salon to support him, she had given him his first son, she asserted she was his legal wife, and now that fortune was smiling on him all she had to show for it was two hundred lire a month, and even that didn't always arrive on time. On 3rd October 1919 she went once more to the main police station in Milan to lay new charges against Mussolini. In a torrent of accusations and insults, she let slip that she was receiving some financial support from the Ministry for Internal Affairs; the police chief immediately sent them a telegram. The historian De Felice discovered two letters in the Nitti papers which seem to show that Dalser was being used by the Ministry as a possible means of blackmailing Mussolini. Nitti had sent a friend to make approaches to Mussolini and soften him up; the friend had found that Dalser might be a useful way to do this and wrote to Nitti: "You should use Signora Darsen [sic]. Up to now she's been under court orders, but there's a possibility you could get Mussolini to stay quiet by offering to remove her from Milan. Let me know what you'd like to do."[4]

The situation grew embarrassing for Mussolini. Dalser's continual disturbances were causing people to talk. A friend and follower of his, Cesare Berti, felt obliged to write and tell him that Dalser, by dint of sheer persistence, was persuading several people of her point of view. Berti had first met Mussolini in Trento and had followed him back to Forlì, where he later founded the local league in favour of Italy's intervention in the war. He went back to Trento after the conflict was over, when he became the official representative there for the so-called Ministry for the Liberated Territories. He knew all about Mussolini's relationship with Dalser and realized the damage she could cause him back in her home town of Trento. Mussolini

reacted with alarm to Berti's letter and didn't mince his words when
he replied:

> Milan, 15th February 1920. My dear Berti, the person who is the subject of your
> letter is a dangerous and unbalanced criminal, a blackmailer and fraudster. I
> had a relationship with her, I've acknowledged paternity of her son, but she has
> never been – and will never become – my wife. During the war she was put under
> house arrest and never stopped hounding the authorities. You are not deceived in
> calling her unhinged. Let me know what she's doing now, where she is and how
> she makes a living. She must be kept under observation and put in prison, where
> she belongs. Unfortunately I have to send her 200 lire a month. I'll wait to hear
> from you with the information I've asked for. Yours, Mussolini.[5]

It was probably difficult for Mussolini to understand why Dalser
was so angry, though it's worth remembering that he was paying
out 375 lire a day for his twenty-five strong bodyguard, and that she
knew this. Luckily for him, the other women he was having relations
with – or had had in the past – were a lot less trouble. With Bianca
Ceccato, for example, he had had a son and she didn't make any
fuss about it. Bianca had been a secretary in the *Il Popolo d'Italia*
offices. We don't know how long she worked there before she caught
his eye. She gave birth to a son in 1920, who was later to become
a famous writer and screenwriter. Mussolini never acknowledged
he was the father. Edvige always maintained that Dalser's son was
the only case where Mussolini admitted paternity, since this was
the only child he had outside his marriage, but Edvige obviously
wasn't privy to the admissions her brother made to his last mistress,
Claretta Petacci, as transcribed in her diary. On 19th December
1937 the latter mentioned to Mussolini that the whole of Rome
was talking about an illegitimate son he had had with Romilda
Ruspi. He admitted that the sensual and determined Ruspi indeed
believed her son was his. He also brought in Bianca Ceccato, saying, as Petacci reports it:

> I never actually had full relations with her, I always pulled out before coming,
> which really wore me down. One morning in Via Rasella she told me she hadn't
> had her period. "How's that," I said, "when I've always been so careful?" [...]
> Her sister told me later she'd given birth to a boy. I wasn't much moved. I've seen
> the lad twice – he's now eight years old. To be honest, I felt nothing at all. But it

was different with Ceccato's son, who's now eighteen – I felt he was mine. But it hardly matters, she's of absolutely no interest to me now.[6]

It was against this backdrop – Dalser's manic and suffocating pursuit of him, his seduction of his tranquil employee Bianca Ceccato, his fascinated cultivation of the wealthy and accomplished Sarfatti, and his attempts to reassure an increasingly alarmed Rachele – that the political and social situation in the country started to disintegrate. On 1st December, during the King's traditional speech on the opening of parliament, the Socialist Party deputies left the Chamber *en bloc* singing an anthem to the socialist republic. In 1920, at the start of the *biennio rosso*, a wave of strikes started in factories and in the countryside. The factory owners reacted by imposing lockouts, taking on thousands of non-strikers or scabs, and obtaining army intervention against the strikers. Mussolini organized a second national congress of the Combatants' Leagues in Milan; the date he chose to hold it was significant: 24th May, the anniversary of Italy's entry into the war. Many years later, in a reply he gave during the interview with the German journalist Ludwig, he said: "We celebrate the 24th of May – when the war began – not our victory over the defeated. You'll find the whole of my political programme summed up here. We regard the date of Italy's entry into the war as a revolutionary beginning. It was the people's decision against the will of parliament. The Fascist revolution began that day."[7]

The nature of the movement intended by Mussolini had changed, as had many of the men who belonged to it. The first congress had been made up of groups all vaguely coming from the left; now when the editor of *Il Popolo d'Italia* rose to speak he faced an audience which was explicitly right-wing. The movement needed to reorganize itself if it was not to remain isolated. There was an armed wing, and it had a newspaper with which to undertake the political struggle. On 13th July, against a backdrop of increasing trade-union agitation and strikes, Fascist squadrons set fire to the Balkan Hotel in Trieste, the headquarters of the city's Slovene associations, while in Rome they wrecked the printing works responsible for producing *Avanti!*. The various forces of order – the police, the *carabinieri* and the Regia Guardia per la Pubblica Sicurezza (Royal Guard for Public Safety) – derided and insulted, as they frequently were, by anarchists and subversives, attacked as they patrolled the streets or wounded in clashes with demonstrators, began to have some sympathy for the Fascist squads. Moreover, many of them, like the men in the squads, were former soldiers. As for the army, if it had to be called in to deal with strikes, it's natural to suppose that the soldiers felt a fraternal bond with the ex-military men and former Arditi who belonged to the Fascist squads. Mussolini had a long meeting with General Pietro Badoglio, the head of the country's armed forces, who was quick to understand the potential of the Fascist fighting bands. The heads of the prefectures of several large cities warned the government of the widespread sympathy in which the Fascists were held. Following the massacre at Palazzo D'Accursio in Bologna, Cesare Mori had been appointed as head of the prefecture in the city (the same man who would later be asked by Mussolini after he had come to power to deal with the problem of the Mafia in Sicily through military intervention); in a report drawn up for the government in Rome, Mori indicated that the police did not always obey his orders, or at least obey them in full, in countering the squads. The prefect in Florence, Carlo Olivieri, also mentioned the sympathy felt for the Fascists in the army, among the *carabinieri*, the Royal Guards, town-hall officials and the magistrature, while his colleague in Pisa pointed out that not only did many officials in the local administration belong to the movement, their daughters did too. It should also be remembered that while the forces of order were capable of suppressing strikes and countering left-wing street disturbances, they were not so well equipped to deal with the kind of attacks carried out by the highly trained former Arditi who fought in the squads.

In trying to understand how rapidly the situation was developing, a note which was circulated on 24th September 1920 to all commanding officers from Colonel Camillo Caleffi, in charge of the Office of Information of the General Staff, is significant: "It is clear from information being received on the activities of the Combatants' Leagues that they are playing an increasingly important role in the general political picture and could eventually be used to counter the unpatriotic and subversive elements in the country." Caleffi could only have issued such a statement with the full knowledge and backing of the entire high command of the armed forces. It must also have had tacit if not explicit approval from the head of the armed forces, the King. At the same time, Giovanni Giolitti, who on 15th June became prime minister for the sixth time in his career, was seeking out allies and support among right-wing forces. He was either unaware of Gasti's report or didn't take it seriously, given that his attempts to harness the forces of Fascism for his own political ends stemmed from a fundamental misreading of the phenomenon.

Mussolini now found himself in the kind of situation for which he was best suited. The two weapons in his armoury – the newspaper and the armed gangs – enabled him to wield the political power he had failed to obtain through the ballot box. It wasn't even necessary to incite the squads to take action. On 21st November in Bologna the installation of the new Socialist Party-controlled city council was being celebrated in Palazzo D'Accursio; the Fascists stormed in and a massacre ensued – nine people were killed and more than fifty wounded. A month later three Fascists died in clashes in Ferrara on 20th December, which led to harsh retaliation from the squads, backed up by the official police forces. As for the events in Fiume, time had played into Mussolini's hands. D'Annunzio's adventure had reached a dead end, and politicians decided to call time on his "rule" of the city. Italian troops attacked on 24th December, and there was a battle over what became known as "Bloody Christmas". On 18th January D'Annunzio handed over his power to the national council for Fiume and left. Mussolini condemned the attack on the city, but at the same time it meant that his principal rival, the alternative "*duce*", had been removed from the scene to return to his writing.

In January 1921 a split in the Socialist Party led to the creation in Livorno of the Partito Comunista Italiano (Italian Communist Party). In an editorial which appeared in *Il Popolo d'Italia* on 27th January, Mussolini held out the possibility of a truce between the warring factions: "We are equipped for war; we are ready for peace." In the meantime, the increasingly frequent attacks on the part of the Fascist squads, added to the fact they were protected by the army and often found themselves fighting alongside the forces of order, led to a growth in their numbers. According to their own records, there were 249,036 signed-up members by the end of 1921; the Ministry of Internal Affairs calculated the figure in May 1921 as 187,098. Whatever their accuracy, the figures show how rapidly a new and aggressive political force had emerged. Far from creating an atmosphere of fear, the Palazzo D'Accursio massacre led to an increase in membership. On 28th February the Fascists destroyed the Chamber of Labour in Trieste as well as what had become their favoured target, the Milan headquarters of the Socialist Party newspaper *Avanti!*. In the countryside, the Socialist Party made little headway; the striking day labourers were hit hard by the organization of the Fascists among the agricultural population; they armed and financed gangs of brutally violent thugs and murderers. For Mussolini, taking control of this phenomenon spelt the definitive abandonment of any of the vague ideals he might have held; he did so in the belief that it furthered his political strategy. He praised the violence of the squads, especially their attacks on the *Avanti!* offices, and declared himself to be "reactionary and or revolutionary, as circumstances dictate"; he was beginning to see the road ahead that would lead him to power. When the metalworkers occupied the factories, he momentarily adjusted his political balance to lean slightly towards the left, but De Felice comments that

> it is hard to believe he seriously thought he could deceive anyone, if the metalworkers' occupation had turned into a real act of revolution. Even if he had given them total support, the rift between him and the Socialist Party was now so deep that he would have become the revolution's first victim. It seems more probable that he wanted firstly to emphasize Fascism's socialist "aspirations", to show the workers he was on their side in their battle for fair pay… and secondly to present himself as a mediator between the factory owners and the metalworkers.[8]

Mussolini had a meeting with the Socialist Party deputy and trade-unionist Bruno Buozzi to reassure him that as long as the factory occupations were the result only of trade-union action there would be no Fascist attacks on the workers. His aim was to sound out the possibility of mediation, and he also wanted to show his opponents how easily he could control the armed wing of the movement, which was where his real political strength lay. Furthermore, Mussolini was also aware that his room for manoeuvre was threatened if the movement fell under the sway of the agricultural landowners: he duly launched an attack on the phenomenon of "*rassismo*", the power of the various "*ras*" or gang chiefs who were responsible for the attacks in the countryside (the word "*ras*" comes from the Ethiopian term for "chieftain").

In the midst of the highly unstable political situation, Giolitti as prime minister dissolved parliament with an incontestable argument: Italy's newly annexed territories should be allowed to vote in an

election. The 15th of May was fixed as the date for the vote. Little
more than a month before polling day, an anarchist attack played into
the hands of Mussolini and his Fascist squads. On the evening of
23rd March, at a theatre in Milan, a bomb explosion killed twenty-
one people and wounded two hundred. The aim of the anarchists
behind the attack was possibly to kill the police chief Gasti – the
same man who'd written the report which, as we've seen, provided
the most perceptive analysis of the new movement. There were many
women and children among the victims. Mussolini saw the electoral
possibilities in the attack and declared that it represented a challenge
which the Fascists would not hesitate to accept. He tactically changed
course, perhaps to confuse his enemies, by talking of a truce when he
addressed the crowds at the funeral for the victims. At the same time
he ordered the squads to increase their attacks, while he also made
the first moves towards forming an electoral alliance with Giolitti.
In his report, Gasti had warned the authorities about Mussolini's
skill in political manipulation and also given a psychological analysis
of the man, but his remarks had fallen on deaf ears. But even Gasti
can't have realized how many opportunities Mussolini was able to
find, in the midst of his activities as a journalist and a politician, for
the sensuality he had noted in him.

Numerous instances can be found in the biographies which look
at these aspects of Mussolini: for example, the incident which took
place in May 1921, when Mussolini was opening the office of a new
section in the Porta Vittoria neighbourhood in Milan. He gave his
usual rabble-rousing speech, after which Gigi Lanfranconi, a lawyer
and an enthusiastic Fascist who was in the audience, came up to greet
him. Mussolini barely acknowledged Lanfranconi, but couldn't take
his eyes off the young woman who accompanied him; Lanfranconi
quickly understood the situation, so that when he subsequently went
to the newspaper offices to request an interview with Mussolini, he
took the young lady along as well. Within fifteen minutes he was
ushered in to Mussolini's office. They spoke about the situation in
Lanfranconi's local Fascist branch, after which the lawyer made his
excuses and left. "As soon as he was left alone with Lanfranconi's
wife, Mussolini wasted no time in small talk, but went straight to the
point by asking her if she would like to spend the evening with him."[9]

Another person who asked to see Mussolini in the spring of 1921
was Giacomo Cucciati, the son of prosperous landowners. Mussolini

could not deny his request, since Cucciati was an old companion from his Socialist Party days who now had a serious family problem. He came with his daughter Angela, whose husband was Bruno Curti, the son of a bronze industrialist. Curti was in prison facing a charge of murder. He belonged to a Combatants' League that had attacked a certain Professor Gadda who subsequently died from his injuries. The fact that firearms had been used in the attack made it impossible for the police investigators to dismiss the case. From his prison cell Curti was appealing to Mussolini to intervene, so his wife Angela went to see him, accompanied, in the proper middle-class way, by her father. On entering the private apartment in Via Paolo da Cannobio which was used as the newspaper's offices, the journalists pointed out to the couple the door to Mussolini's study. That first meeting was friendly – but the friendliness was soon to intensify.

The relationship between Mussolini and Angela Curti lasted, on and off, for more than twenty years. Curti bore him a daughter, Elena, very early on in their relationship, on 19th October 1922. Elena later described her mother's regular meetings with Mussolini:

> I see my twenty-two-year-old mother, a pretty 'coquette' to use one of the French borrowings typical of the *belle époque* which she liked to use, wearing the fashions of the day, waiting for Mussolini on the bridge over the Naviglio canal. My brother used to accompany her, because a woman should never wait alone on the street. [...] In Rome, my mother would go always to the same hotel – at first the Quirinale in Via Nazionale, until she was pestered by a man who had followed her and guessed her secret, when she started to go to the Minerva near the Pantheon.[10]

There must have been something in Mussolini which attracted women, and, remembering what her mother used to tell her, Elena Curti believes she can identify what it was: "There were certain moments when his face seemed like that of an overgrown boy. At others his gaze took on a special luminosity."[11] Even a woman like Angela Curti from the wealthy and sophisticated middle classes fell for Mussolini's usual seductive tricks. All the women, married or unmarried, saw first the famous orator, the rough-mannered revolutionary, the aggressive journalist, the successful editor-in-chief, the hardbitten soldier who commanded the ex-Arditi, the legend in his own lifetime everyone was talking about; then, with a suddenness that made them dizzy, they found themselves close up to him. Without their realizing it was happening, he broke through that natural and invisible social barrier which protected their honour and was busy whispering phrases like "my sweet little girl... I want this moment never to end... I could look into your eyes for ever... you are the only thing I live for..." and so on. Most women probably couldn't resist. It was unlikely that their boyfriends or husbands lavished such attention on them, or perhaps they were in difficult marriages where the couple's problems were not aired for the sake of preserving appearances. Angela Curti was beautiful, and when she met Mussolini she already had a two-year-old son. She and her husband Bruno had married too young and were now paying the price. And suddenly Mussolini appeared on the scene, who was inflexible with everyone but unexpectedly gentle with her, ready to dedicate precious time from his very busy life just to be with her. Bruno Curti got out of jail. The bronze industry went bankrupt, so Angela Curti stepped in and opened a dress shop. Elena grew up surrounded by the mirrors, fur coats, lace trimmings, coat dresses and chiffon of her mother's shop without ever finding out who her real father was. She met him for the first time only in 1929, but neither he nor Angela ever gave the slightest hint of their involvement. She became a fanatical Fascist supporter and never asked why she, out of all the others, was always close to the Duce. She didn't even pose the question when she found herself in one of the cars which accompanied Mussolini on his final attempt to flee across the frontier into Switzerland and then the Valtellina, on 25th–27th April 1945. In this final act, like that of a Greek tragedy, amid the mountains and the clouds which shut in Lake Como, Elena's mother, fearing that they might all end up in front of a Partisan firing squad, told her who her real father was. By strange coincidence, also in the line of cars which threaded their way along the lake was a young pilot who was particularly close to Mussolini: Virgilio Pallottelli, the son of his long-standing mistress Alice De Fonseca Pallottelli. "Whether Pallottelli was yet another of his illegitimate offspring or not, it is certainly the case that Mussolini regarded him as especially loyal, employing him at his headquarters during the Republic of Salò. It is unsurprising therefore that on 26th April 1945 Virgilio was in the escape motorcade organized by a leading Fascist, Antonio Pavolini, as it drove to Menaggio. Another passenger in his car was Elena Curti, the daughter of Angela Curti Cucciati and Benito."[12]

With the self-confidence which derived from the education they had received from their cultivated and wealthy families and from the fact that both their husbands had recognized and accepted their illegitimate children, Angela Curti and Alice Pallottelli had no qualms about meeting Mussolini for more or less secret assignations. They would go to meet him wherever he required them, without making problems, and only bothered him with requests for small favours, often on behalf of friends and acquaintances. Angela gave birth to Elena nine days before the March on Rome; during her pregnancy she had made no demands or protests, never complained or betrayed any sign of jealousy. If anything, it was Mussolini who became agitated when he learnt she had spent time on her own with another man. It's also quite possible that he gave her some financial help during 1922, since his own circumstances were much improved. Angela was a perfect mistress, in that time spent with her was pleasurable and relaxing; she never threatened to disrupt his busy life.

And Mussolini's life was at the time full of problems. He was playing a game of tactics with Giolitti, but the men in the Combatants' Leagues hero-worshipped D'Annunzio and hated the prime minister. So Mussolini was obliged to mend bridges with the great poet who, after Fiume, had withdrawn from active political life. At a rally in Bologna attended by a huge crowd of Fascist supporters Mussolini paid eloquent tribute to D'Annunzio and was thunderously applauded. The episode enabled him to renew contact with the poet and to go to visit him at his house in Gardone on 5th April; spreading his net carefully, Mussolini succeeded in bringing about a reconciliation and in getting D'Annunzio to agree to support him. Another element in Mussolini's trap was a tactical alliance with the so-called Blocchi Nazionali (National Blocs), a right-wing parliamentary coalition led by Giolitti. During the month of April there was a notable increase in the number of Fascist attacks, which Mussolini defended as being a transitional but necessary violence, stressing that the Fascists were a party of order and that he would never allow the squads to run "out of control", and taking care to leave the door open for a future collaboration, at ministerial level, with Giolitti. Mussolini's moves were deft, Giolitti's clumsy: the prime minister misinterpreted the Fascist phenomenon, thus allowing Mussolini to enter parliament at the head of thirty-five Fascist deputies among the 275 elected for the National Blocs. The Socialist Party lost thirty-four seats, while the Communists entered parliament for the first time with a small group of sixteen deputies.

The 15th and 16th of May saw a sudden intensification of Fascist attacks which killed many people, although the wave of violence, paid for by the landowners, had already led men like Pietro Nenni, the future leader of the post-war Socialist Party, to distance themselves from the movement. On 23rd March, the day of the attack at the theatre in Milan, Nenni offered his support to *Avanti!*. His experiences in the Bologna Combatants' League had disappointed him, and he had made a decision to abandon journalism, but when *Avanti!* suggested he take on the job of their Paris correspondent he accepted the offer immediately. The political situation made it clear that the newly elected Fascist deputies in parliament would not agree to become part of the broad front which Giolitti thought he could somehow control. Mussolini remarked to his sister that, among the heterogeneous political creatures who made up the alliance, he was the one who remained "a completely unknown beast to the eyes of that old explorer Giolitti".[13]

On 18th May in Milan the city's chief of police, who was still Giovanni Gasti, had twelve Fascists arrested. The squads protested and, faced by their threats of violent retaliation, the prefect in Milan, as the main authority in the city, decided to release the twelve men. In carrying out his political strategy, Mussolini could now draw on the resources of a vast nationwide movement, a large group of deputies in parliament, a newspaper with a healthy circulation and financial backing, and a strong private army. On 21st June, in his maiden speech as a deputy, he continued with the tactic of blowing hot and cold, this time turning to the left, by suggesting a realignment with the Socialist Party in some kind of political truce. The idea of calling a halt to the continual clashes had been proposed by four parliamentary deputies, all of them former combatants in the war: two Fascists, Acerbo and Giurati, and two Socialists, Zaniboni and Ellero. Mussolini described the Fascists as the new party of order, but at the same time did nothing to stop the violence which was being wreaked by the armed squads. In conversations with his family, however, he was careful not to appear to praise the use of violence. His sister Edvige wrote her memoirs immediately after the Second World War, when the full extent of the Fascists' atrocities had been made public, and she naturally felt obliged to diminish, as far as she could, the personal responsibility borne by her brother; she maintained that he disliked the violence of the squads, regarding it as a kind of fever which had to be undergone if the body politic were to return to health, which may strike us as a somewhat spurious justification. In this context she writes a revealing passage: "Whenever I spoke to my brother about the phenomenon of the armed squads, there was always a kind of shadow or reserve in his words, which went from outright and bitter denunciation of the cruelty and ill-advisedness of certain incidents to the lightly condescending irony with which he spoke of the type of certain regional and provincial *condottieri* who were emerging within the Fascist squads."[14]

These *condottieri* were the local *ras*, the bloodthirsty leaders of the local squads who were responsible for torture, mayhem and murder. When one reads the newspaper reports of the assaults and the attacks on vulnerable individuals, frequently involving violent sexual abuse, from raping women to pushing sticks up men's rectums, an attitude of "condescending irony" is entirely out of place.

Against the backdrop of continuing violence, Giolitti resigned, on 27th June 1921, to be followed by an ineffectual government led by Ivanoe Bonomi; Mussolini thrust himself forward with the aim of making sure the democratic process did not leave him high and dry. On 13th July the Fascists destroyed the headquarters of the Republican Party in Treviso; in Sarzana, on the other hand, when they occupied the railway station and tried to march into the town, they were forced back by the *carabinieri* acting in conjunction with left-wing groups calling themselves "Arditi del Popolo" ("Arditi of the People"), which had been formed with the aim of countering the Fascist attacks. Eighteen Fascists were killed and thirty were wounded in the confrontation in Sarzana. The episode gave Mussolini food for thought: quite unexpectedly, even to the surprise of his own deputies who were listening, on 23rd July he gave a speech in parliament proposing an alliance of the Fascists, the Partito Popolare Italiano (Italian People's Party) and the Socialist Party, which would adopt a basic, minimal programme of measures all three parties could agree on. Two of the most prominent *ras*, Dino Grandi and Roberto Farinacci, fomented the unease felt by the rank and file in the squads and cast doubts on Mussolini's real intentions by reminding them that he was a former member of the Socialist Party. They knew that the real power lay in their hands: without them and their weapons all the tactical toing and froing in the parliamentary hothouse would come to nothing. Mussolini might think he was the leader of the movement, but they were the men who organized and carried out the military attacks.

Fascism was by now irrevocably a right-wing movement. Those members who had come to it from the left had either abandoned it or were increasingly isolated within it. Only Mussolini was still trying to adjust the balance – with his support, for example, on 8th June, of pay strikes within the country's public sector. When negotiations opened to reach some kind of truce or compromise agreement among the divergent political forces, many of the *ras* rebelled, but Mussolini won them over with a right-wing line of reasoning they had to accept: he was the founder of the movement, he was their leader, what he wanted and said went; it was their duty to discipline themselves and obey him.

The signing of the agreement was fixed for 2nd August in the office of the Leader of the Chamber Enrico De Nicola. In the arrangements for the small-scale ceremony, the Socialist Party asked De Nicola to avoid any formal act of greeting between the two delegations. They refused categorically to shake Mussolini's hand, since he had been expelled from the party as someone who was morally and politically unworthy of membership. Cesare Rossi, who was involved in the planning, realized the Socialist Party would be unmoveable on this point; he gave orders that Mussolini was not to be told about their refusal in order to avoid a controversy over status which might have caused serious problems. Unaware of the Socialists' demand, Mussolini went to the ceremony and signed; at which the local Fasci rose up against the agreement. In Bologna they even threatened to split away.

On 18th August, Mussolini staked everything on one last gamble: he announced his resignation from the executive of the Fasci. The effect was like an electric shock to the exposed nerves of the Fascist movement. The whole of the national press followed the developments of the crisis. *Il Popolo d'Italia* printed a series of telegrams which had been sent in support of its editor-in-chief. From Bologna, one of the most powerful of the *ras*, Italo Balbo, sent a letter to the paper in which he tried, with the help of some contorted reasoning, to calm the situation down by maintaining that while the

Bolognese "*fascio*" were against the agreement, they also realized that Mussolini was not personally responsible for it, but had agreed to sign only because of his overwhelming desire to see the political reconstruction of the country. The executive committee of the Fascist movement rejected Mussolini's resignation. At a meeting of the parliamentary party on 7th September Mussolini decided not to take a hard line on the issue, instead giving his listeners to understand that his opportunism would override any residual sense he might possess of political ethics. He completely ignored the agreement signed before the Leader of the Chamber and acted in such a way that its provisions were never put into practice. Rossi described the agreement as "stillborn. Most of those who signed it did so with so many private reservations and conditions as to leave it in moral and practical terms quite worthless. The Communists besides were violently opposed to it and attacked the Socialist Party ferociously for signing up to it. But even the Socialist Party had only agreed to sign it out of tactical necessity and to mark themselves out from the Communists."[15]

With no principle to guide him any longer, interested only in action, or rather enamoured of action for action's sake, Mussolini closed off all overtures to the left and turned to the right – after all, he believed that Fascism was an "absolute relativism" to which the categories of right and left, reaction or revolution, no longer applied. Hannah Arendt's words on him are relevant here:

Everything which was useful for the so-called productivity of the individual, in other words the completely arbitrary play of that individual's "ideas", was transformed into the centre of a total vision of the world and of human existence. The cynicism which is inherent in such a romantic cult of personality has given rise to certain attitudes among modern intellectuals. Mussolini, one of the last to spring from this tradition, is a typical example: he boasted of being at one and the same time aristocratic and democratic, revolutionary and reactionary, proletarian and anti-proletarian, pacifist and anti-pacifist. At the heart of romantic individualism in all its ruthlessness has always been the sole belief that "each of us is free to create his own ideology" (a quotation from an article by Mussolini). What distinguished Mussolini from other romantic intellectuals and from many of his contemporaries was that he devoted all his energies to putting his ideas into practice.[16]

On 7th November the "Partito Nazionale Fascista" ("National Fascist Party") was founded in Rome. At the time Dino Grandi was a very young man, so young that his election to parliament had been annulled because he was found to be under the age of majority. Right up to the eve of the establishment of the party he had been regarded as the leader of the revolt against the peace agreement and, as such, the movement's new man, the only figure who could rival Mussolini. Instead, at the congress which founded the party, Grandi embraced Mussolini, to the wild applause of the delegates, after he declared his sincere fraternal wish to "work alongside" the party's leader. This was Grandi's attempt to replace Mussolini, and it failed; his second, on 25th July 1943, when he proposed a motion to unseat the Duce, succeeded: "Twenty-two years later he was successful, but only after twenty long years spent in servile fawning and flattering and being rewarded with leading positions in the regime, honours and fat emoluments."[17]

More than thirty thousand men from the local Fascist squads attended the new party's congress in Rome, and among them there were those who suggested seizing the opportunity to overthrow the state by taking control of the city's strategic centres and wresting power into their own hands. Mussolini said it was too early to make such a move, but the mass of Fascists in the capital gave rise to clashes which led to six deaths and more than a hundred people wounded. Such an outcome suited Mussolini: he wanted these new and increasingly violent attacks from the armed wing of the party to destabilize further the country's already fragile democracy. The message had to arrive loud and clear to all the politicians: without the Fascists Italy could not form a government, and only the Fascists could restore stability to the authority of the state.

In January 1922 Mussolini launched a new publication, the magazine *Gerarchia* (*Hierarchy*), and asked Margherita Sarfatti to become its editor. Sarfatti was already a contributor to the cultural section of *Il Popolo d'Italia*. Now Mussolini had his brother Arnaldo as his right-hand man on the newspaper, and his mistress and muse leading the new political magazine. Sarfatti continued to publish occasional articles in *Gerarchia* under the pseudonym "El Sereno" ("The Serene One"); her friend and protégé the painter Mario Sironi frequently designed the cover illustration; and many of the intellectuals who frequented her salon contributed over the ten years she edited the review. In his interview with Ludwig, Mussolini once declared categorically that "women have no influence over men who are strong"[18], only to cancel the remark in the proofs, perhaps because he regretted making such a dogmatic statement. But several times in the course of his life Mussolini denied that he had ever been influenced by a woman, although his relationship with Sarfatti and, in part, with Balabanoff, suggests otherwise. It is interesting to hear the point of view of a female historian, Karin Wieland, on this subject: "Mussolini was not a man who loved women, but nevertheless they were the only people he really trusted. His ideal conception of virility meant that he could not take criticism from a man or reveal his own weaknesses to one. Only with someone who was not an actual or potential rival could he share his own doubts. And that meant only with women, because a woman, precisely on account of her sexual status, was excluded from political power while still being capable of understanding its rules."[19]

At the beginning of 1922 Mussolini travelled to France where, in Cannes, he met his old political comrade Pietro Nenni, now a member of the Socialist Party and the Paris correspondent for *Avanti!*. They had been in prison together, their wives had been friends, Nenni had held the little Edda in his arms – a reunion was inevitable. They conversed a lot, sometimes deep into the night. Nenni later reconstructed from memory some of these conversations:

One of us [Mussolini] said: "The state of civil war has been a tragic necessity. I take all responsibility for it. The failings of the state meant that there had to be a party which was capable of facing up to Bolshevism, restoring a sense of authority, saving the fruits of the country's victory in the war."

But the other [Nenni] retorted: "You've become a tool in the hands of the classes for whom the right of the workers to organize themselves to defend their social interests and take power is called 'Bolshevism'; authority equals the police, and 'saving the fruits of victory' means maintaining the dominance of a military ethos over a civil one."

"I'm not at all unaware of the feelings and resentments of the classes you're referring to. But I'm not their tool. I've never hesitated at the right time to declare that we must leave the spiral of violence behind us."

"Leaving yourself isolated."

"Whenever I've spoken about peace, they've laughed in my face. I have had to accept a situation of war."

"Your individualism leads you astray. I've no idea how you'll turn out, but I'm certain of one thing: everything you do is going to be marked by the iron brand of will, because you lack a sense of justice. The peace you hold out to my comrades in the Socialist Party means that they would have to give up the ideals they pursue. The bourgeoisie is always ready to come to an agreement if this is the price demanded. And then, you're forgetting a lot."

"?"

"You're forgetting those who have died, you're forgetting you once led the Socialist Party, you're forgetting that the workers who are now being attacked by your Blackshirts probably became socialists because of your call to join the party." [...]

"There's no room for sentimentality in life. Those who died cannot be dismissed. I often remember my past with profound sadness. But it's not only a question of the dozens who died in the streets in political clashes. There are the hundreds of thousands who died in the war. They too must be defended..."

"The working class, the object of your attacks, defends the dead by struggling against war and against materialism. It might get some details wrong, but the general thrust of its struggle is always the right one."[20]

It's hard to believe that during this trip to France, as on previous visits, Mussolini didn't pursue sexual contacts, even though there's no surviving evidence or reports of any encounters. This could be because his over-direct approach to women led to them turning him down, which he would hardly want to talk about. Or he "restricted" himself to visiting brothels. Either hypothesis is compatible with the coarse and racist description of French women found in Claretta Petacci's diary: "French women – not the working-class women who are all sordid, filthy and sweaty – but those a bit higher up the social scale, they really are all the most unbelievable whores. Full of vice, just like real whores. They come after men. Did you know French women like Negroes? It's said that Negroes' cocks are not like white men's, standing up thick and firm, but are long and thin. This gives French women a real thrill. Yes, they're all crazy for Negroes, all of them."[21]

When, in 1922, the government fell for the third time in succession, Mussolini wrote in an editorial in *Il Popolo d'Italia* on 12th February: "In the light of the recent political and parliamentary developments, the eventuality of a dictatorship is one which must be taken seriously."

For ten days in early March Mussolini visited Germany, accompanied by his political secretary. Violently critical articles on him

214 IL DUCE AND HIS WOMEN

appeared in the left-wing German press. He had meetings with various prominent right-wing politicians. There is however, according to Renzo De Felice's researches, no evidence that he met Hitler during this period. De Felice goes on to add, however, that "it is not at all unlikely that Mussolini met leading Nazis in Berlin in 1922. However, in the absence of evidence to the contrary, I think it probable that such contacts did not go beyond a simple exchange of ideas and information."[22] This is borne out by Mussolini's subsequent criticisms of Nazism as well as by the unsuccessful efforts Hitler made in the following years to establish contact with Mussolini once he was installed as Duce.

Mussolini left Germany because he needed to be present in parliament to support the vote of confidence in the new government led by Luigi Facta. In May the military actions undertaken by the Fascist squads took on a new dimension: now there were plans for thousands of armed militants to muster with the intention of occupying entire towns and destroying associations, clubs, party headquarters, Chambers of Labour, cooperatives. During the summer the situation deteriorated. In July the Fascists launched attacks the length and breadth of the country, in Apulia, in Umbria, at Cremona and Novara, Magenta and Ravenna.

Once the Fascist squads' military machine was set in motion, it continued almost with its own momentum, achieving unprecedented "military" targets but descending to a level of truly bestial violence (in the second half of July, after Mussolini and the executive committee of the PNF [National Fascist Party] had already intervened to try to stop outbreaks of "excessive" and counterproductive violence, the squads in Magenta behaved so "barbarically" that the party was forced to order an inquiry) and frequently making its own decisions without any reference to the party leadership. Yet it is beyond doubt that the party leadership and Mussolini himself were willing to be carried along by the train of events and, casting aside all considerations of political prudence, believed they could exploit the military success of the Fascist squads for political ends.[23]

On 28th July, the Socialist Party's members of parliament called for decisive action to defend freedom and the rule of law. A general strike, or "*sciopero legalitario*" ("constitutional strike"), was called for 1st August. The country was once again without a government at the helm, and negotiations to form a new one were rushed through, resulting in Luigi Facta being asked for the second time to become prime minister. On 31st July Mussolini had a meeting with the leader of the (Catholic) People's Party, Giovanni Gronchi, who agreed that his followers would refuse to join the strike. Many on the left, beginning with Salvemini, criticized the decision to call a strike, saying that it could only alienate once more that sector of moderate public opinion which was disturbed by Fascist violence. On 1st August Mussolini called on the squads to oppose the strike: he declared that with the backing of his own army he was ready to step in and replace the state. The strike was called off after one day: it was a defeat for the Socialist Party and the entire trade-union movement, but not only for them. Italian democracy lay in ruins. The failure of the strike meant the road was now clear for the March on Rome. Now that his opponents had been routed and their weakness revealed to the country, all Mussolini had to do was choose the right moment before public opinion once again turned and began to demand peace and tranquillity.

The Fascist squads' reprisals against the strikers were immediate. On 3rd August in Genoa the headquarters of the socialist newspaper *Il lavoro* were destroyed. On the 4th the offices of *Avanti!* were attacked and the seat of the city's Socialist Party-majority council, Palazzo Marino, was occupied. The leaders of the squads saw the occupation as a *coup d'état* or something close to one, and wanted to celebrate it. By chance D'Annunzio was in Milan to visit his publisher. A Fascist delegation led by Cesare Rossi called on him, and after repeatedly insisting got him to agree to give a speech to the crowds from the balcony of Palazzo Marino.

In August 1922, during the Fascist mobilization to counter the *"sciopero legalitario"*, the author of the present lines expressed a wish that the occupation of Palazzo Marino should be marked by a speech from D'Annunzio, full of his glittering eloquence... [...] Mussolini deeply resented this revival of erstwhile Fascist enthusiasm for D'Annunzio, but he was brusquely told that the old adage that "those who stayed away from the party were in the wrong" had never been more true – he was in fact in Rome, lusting after some easy-to-get woman.[24]

Under Rossi's stage management, the Fascists decked the balcony from which D'Annunzio would speak with the red flag which had flown during his brief rule of Fiume next to the black pennants of the Fascists. The poet's speech was somewhat generic. "We were expecting a fiery harangue in favour of right-wing extremism. But, although it was full of patriotic rhetoric, the poet appealed to 'the victory of the good', to the 'affirmative and creative' virtues of all those who were prepared to put aside any partisan interests in the supreme name of Italy and its well-being."[25] Only a few phrases could be heard in the crowded and noisy piazza in front of Palazzo Marino. Amid the general celebrations after their victory, the Fascist squads hung on a few expressions – "a fraternal bond... nothing against the nation" – and were otherwise pleased that D'Annunzio had honoured their success with his presence. The fact that Mussolini was absent from Milan, on some amorous escapade in the countryside outside Rome, shows, in De Felice's view, that both he and the party's executive had played no part either in the involvement of D'Annunzio for propaganda purposes or more generally in the revolutionary aims of the Milanese "*fascio*". Mussolini returned to Milan only on 12th August: "Rossi's explanation that it was a love affair which kept Mussolini in Rome doesn't hold water. This was a period when his love life never interfered in his political career. His adventures with women were rapid and uncomplicated; his other interests were never subordinated to his affairs."[26]

Today, however, after many books have appeared on Mussolini's mistresses, new light has been shed on Mussolini's sexuality and love life, and it no longer seems so implausible to suggest that he decided at such a critical juncture to spend several days with a new woman. If the woman in question had a particular sexual appeal for him, it is even probable that this is what he did, especially if, at the same time, passing time in enjoying himself sexually in some villa or castle in the countryside outside Rome also meant that he was away from the insurrection in Milan, which was clearly destined to end in failure. The affair would also have provided him with a convincing cover, especially for the men who surrounded him, behind which he could work on his own plan in secret. He had suppressed the rebellion of the *ras* and he had put paid to every potential rival within the movement. His real rival, the only man who might become an alternative "*duce*", was external: Gabriele D'Annunzio. The poet had distanced himself from the Fascist movement; his initial reluctance to speak from the balcony of Palazzo Marino is just one proof of his detachment. Mussolini could not overlook D'Annunzio, because otherwise he risked finding the latter against him when he least expected it. The plan he devised was a bold one: to organize a top-secret meeting involving himself, D'Annunzio and Francesco Saverio Nitti with the purpose of forming an alliance to set up a strong and stable government, capable of restoring the state's authority. It's enough to recall how the whole of Italy had been amused when D'Annunzio, during the assault on Fiume, had contemptuously nicknamed Nitti "the snail" to see that Mussolini's plan to bring the two men together required a certain stretch of the imagination.

The meeting was fixed for 19th August in the Tuscan villa belonging to the baron Romano Avezzana. The country was in such a dire state that Nitti, who as a former prime minister had had the power to release Mussolini and his fellow Fascists from prison, had to get a permit from Mussolini and be driven in a Fascist-chauffeured car to get to the destination. Nitti was just about to leave when he received a telegram telling him that D'Annunzio had fallen out of a window and was in a critical condition. The meeting was called off. "A rumour went round that Mussolini was behind it... which was neither true nor even plausible. It seems it was all the result of a quarrel between the poet and one of the new recruits among his mistresses, who happened to have a younger sister – a much younger sister well below the age of consent: her youthful charms had attracted the great man, whose lusts were insatiable and not inclined to admit defeat. The elder sister in her irritation pushed the impenitent D'Annunzio off the window sill."[27] The lover in question was Luisa Baccara and the little sister who attracted D'Annunzio's attentions was called Jolanda. While Luisa was playing the piano, D'Annunzio began to molest Jolanda. The most likely version of the story is that the girl was annoyed and pushed him too hard on the balcony where they were sitting. The medical report speaks of a fracture to the skull and contusion. Yet the French translator André Doderet tells a different story: "By the beginning of September there was no trace of a fracture or bruising on Gabriele's skull, easy to note because he was bald. We can assume that D'Annunzio, like 'the great mythomaniac' he so notoriously was, had invented the whole story of the fall from the balcony in order to get out of a meeting which he regretted agreeing to attend, since he had realized he wouldn't be able to dissuade Mussolini from carrying out his plan to march on Rome."[28]

Whether it was by deliberate political choice or by chance, D'Annunzio's exit from the scene was a boon to Mussolini. If their meeting had gone ahead as planned, it would only have increased the poet's standing and turned him into the leading protagonist of a project which was supposed both to bring peace to the country and at the same time help to establish a new government. Mussolini saw D'Annunzio in a secret meeting in the latter's home in Gardone on 11th October. It was the last thing he did before giving orders for the March to begin. The situation had changed, and the prospect of D'Annunzio taking over a prominent role no longer worried Mussolini. The armed squads had all been brought into line: the rules and regulations governing them had been published in three instalments in *Il Popolo d'Italia*.

Entire provinces in the country were in the hands of the Fascists. In Bolzano the mayor had been expelled after the town hall was attacked; in Trento the governor of the region had been forced to resign, and the city was now under military control. Mussolini hadn't bothered to inform even the party's executive of this latest coup, and they were resentful of the high-handed treatment. But his aim was to show them that he and only he was the leader, the Duce. With a series of articles and speeches spelling out and guaranteeing a programme for a future government, he had won the support of the industrial and financial sectors in the country. The movement's former anti-monarchist stance had been allowed to fade away; Mussolini had also encouraged the otherwise fortuitous cultivation of the man who was second in line to the Italian throne, the Duke of Aosta, who was known to sympathize with the movement's aims. As early as 1919, Gasti had noted in his report that the Fascist squads "would welcome the King's abdication and his assumed replacement by the Duke of Aosta as regent".[29]

Despite his antipathy towards Freemasonry, amply demonstrated at the Socialist congress in Ancona when he succeeded in getting Freemasons expelled from the party, Mussolini succeeded in obtaining the support of the Italian obediences – Piazza del Gesù and Palazzo Giustiniani – thanks also to the numerous Fascist leaders who belonged to Masonic lodges. And he had got D'Annunzio's tacit assent: after paying him the tribute of making him the principal and last person he spoke to before the March went ahead, he called the leaders of the armed squads together and told them the time had come for action.

On 21st October the party's national executive ceded power to a so-called *quadrumvirato*, four men chosen by Mussolini: Italo Balbo, Emilio De Bono, Cesare De Vecchi and Michele Bianchi. Mussolini's actions during the March on Rome often seem to contradict each other, but it should be remembered that there were also differences of opinion among the four men appointed to oversee the March, while the political situation itself was constantly changing and possible developments along with it. There was no one who enjoyed Mussolini's complete trust. He had delegated the practical organization of the March to others, but he sought to keep for himself the main role as the man in control of all the moves. "Without Mussolini, the March on Rome would not even have been attempted, just as D'Annunzio never attempted it, despite all the plans and repeated declarations of intent. Many leading Fascists feared it or wanted to prevent it, and even after it had begun continued to shuttle between the Quirinale and Viminale palaces in the hope of agreeing some compromise solution with the more conservative and reactionary political forces."[30]

On 24th October in the San Carlo opera house in Naples a Fascist conference was held which was attended by leading representatives from the city's administration and its universities. In addressing the conference Mussolini launched a new tactic: he declared that only three ministers serving in Facta's weak government were against the Fascists, thereby extending an implicit invitation to the others to start manoeuvring themselves into the good books of the soon-to-be-victorious party. Before returning to Milan, he put the final touches on the plan for the March in a meeting in the Hotel Vesuvio: it would set off at midnight on the 26th. The following evening, back in Milan, he went to the theatre, making sure he was noticed as he took his seat in the stalls. There are differing interpretations of why he acted like this. Perhaps he wanted to reassure the middle classes of Milan by this display of normality. Or he was keeping his distance in case the March was a failure, so he could restart his political manoeuvring more easily. According to his wife Rachele, he did it because he wanted to avoid a test of strength with Facta, the prime minister, who was prepared to introduce a state of emergency:

On the evening of the 27th, Benito suggested we go to the Manzoni theatre to see [Franz Lehár's] *The Merry Widow*. The suggestion irritated me. "How on earth can you go and see *The Merry Widow* with everything you've got on your mind?" I asked. He didn't reply, but started to whistle as he buttoned up his shirt collar. This surprised me even more, because he was always annoyed if he caught an errand boy or one of the maids whistling. It was only when we were on our way that he explained to me why he was behaving so oddly. "Everything's ready for the March on Rome," he said. "If I'm seen at the theatre, that will throw the police off the scent. They'll think that nothing can be happening if I can spend time amusing myself." And so it was: he made sure people noticed him, Edda and me, like any ordinary middle-class family out for a night at the theatre, and twenty minutes later we quietly left the theatre.[31]

Other contemporary witnesses, however, claim to have seen Mussolini at the theatre, but accompanied by his mistress and colleague Margherita Sarfatti and her daughter Fiammetta. In the short justificatory memoir she wrote after the end of the Second World War, *My Fault*, Sarfatti wrote: "The 26th in the evening, the Duce in Milan goes to a Wagner opera at the theatre, the first night of *Lohengrin* at the Dal Verme theatre. [...] On the evening of the 27th we are surprised to see him, an unexpected guest, enter our box at the Manzoni theatre."[32] It is hard to reconcile these differing versions of the events, even more so because Sarfatti has provided us with yet another one, again written after the fall of the regime and the end of the war: in this, on the evening of 27th October Mussolini went to join her at her country villa in Cavallasca, very near the border with Switzerland, in order to escape but, as they sat by the fireside, she managed to calm him down and persuade him to wait and see how events would turn out. His wife's account seems more reliable: she goes on to write that Mussolini spent the rest of the evening holed up in his office at *Il Popolo d'Italia* and glued to the telephone. He knew of course that his telephone was being tapped and made sure that no word he uttered betrayed any sign of weakness.

The armed squads met with no resistance in the various towns and cities they passed through on their route; they would occupy prefectures and railway stations, the civil authorities would withdraw and hand over power to the army, and then, bringing the process full circle, the military authorities would enter into negotiations with the Fascists. On Mussolini's instructions, Cesare Rossi, Aldo Finzi and Manlio Morgagni paid calls on the editors-in-chief of the various newspapers to suggest they wrote nothing which might impede the Fascists' path to power. At the *Corriere della Sera* Rossi spoke with

Eugenio Balzan, the managing director, and Finzi contacted the newspaper's co-editor, Alberto Albertini, by telephone. They spoke to Mario Missiroli at *Il secolo*, who was sceptical about how successful the March was actually proving in practice. As for *Avanti!*, Nenni described their visit:

> I received the Fascist delegation in the main office in the *Avanti!* building in Via Settala, where broken bits of furniture and charred books remained from the last incursion of the Fascist squads. The delegation was made up of Finzi, Cesarino Rossi and Morgagni, who would all go on to hold important posts in the new regime a few days later – unluckily for the first two, since they soon fell out of favour (Morgagni went on to prosper, but he committed suicide on the day Mussolini was arrested in 1943). A fourth person was there at the door: Amerigo Dumini, the man who would assassinate Matteotti.[33]

Clearly the delegation sent by Mussolini was not going to get any firm undertakings from *Avanti!* that they wouldn't come out against the Fascists, so the alternative option was adopted: a squad was dispatched to destroy their offices as soon as possible in order to prevent them publishing the paper over these crucial days. Facta and the government he led resigned, at the same time suggesting that the King sign a decree declaring a state of emergency. The King refused. Cesare Rossi recounted the episode: "The prime minister Facta chose to resign rather than oppose the sedition – a very bad mistake which both justified and facilitated the Fascists and induced the King to refuse to sign the declaration of the state of emergency on the morning of Saturday 28th October. He said to Facta: 'You're an expert in constitutional law, yet you've forgotten that a government which has resigned no longer has the moral authority to impose such a serious measure.' And he handed the decree back to him."[34]

Antonio Salandra was asked by the King to form a new government, but his efforts came to nothing after only a few hours, whereupon, on the morning of 29th October the King summoned Mussolini. That day's edition of *Il Popolo d'Italia* carried the announcement that victory was in sight and that the government would be largely made up of Fascists. Rachele Mussolini writes that the news sent their household wild. The only person who managed to sleep on, as the others tried to read the newspaper, was Mussolini: the imperturbability he displayed on this occasion and by going to the theatre two evenings before fed into the construction of his myth. Cirillo, the family chauffeur, was so overjoyed, according to Rachele, that he started to strum the piano and sing: "We're on our way to the top..." In the general confusion, the two children, Edda and Vittorio, decided they could safely skip school. Before leaving Milan to be officially received by the King at the Quirinale palace in Rome, Mussolini demanded a telegram be sent to him confirming the King had asked him to form the next government. When he left the house to go to the station, Rachele came out with a characteristic remark: "Who would've believed it? My husband's going to be the next prime minister!"[35] The train Mussolini took for Rome left at 8.30 in the evening. It was an express, but it arrived in the capital only at 10.50 the following morning, since it had to stop at all the stations on the way which were occupied by the Fascists, who wanted to see and acclaim their leader. At 11.15, after arriving in Rome, Mussolini had a meeting with the King which lasted an hour. The school history books which were published under the regime always told the story of how Mussolini's first words to the King as he entered his office were: "Your Majesty, I bring you the Italy which fought at Vittorio Veneto." Rachele remembers reading these words in her small daughter's school textbook and was surprised when Mussolini told her he had said no such thing. After his fall from power, during the twilight period of the Social Republic in Salò, Mussolini gave his final reflections on the March on Rome: "Was it an insurrection? Undoubtedly. It lasted more or less about two years. Did it bring about a revolution? No – if you define a revolution as changing, by force, not only the system of government but the institutional framework of the state. Seen from this point of view Fascism did not initiate a revolution in October 1922. There was a monarchy already in place, and the monarchy remained in place."[36]

The squads, known also as "Camicie Nere" ("Blackshirts") as a result of their adoption of the sombre look of the Arditi, marched on parade in front of the Quirinale palace; it would have been better, as Mussolini intimated in the remark just quoted, if they'd been able to march into the palace itself, but that was not possible. The March on Rome came to a halt before the head of the Italian state, the King. A diarchy was born. Even though the Fascist squads were under the control and leadership of former officers from the Arditi regiment, they remained in effect the same disorderly, undisciplined and aggressive gangs they had always been, nothing like a real military force. Any army worthy of the name could easily have routed them – if it had received an order to do so, but the order in this case was never forthcoming. "The 'March on Rome' is one of the most interesting political events in modern times," wrote Emilio Lussu in 1945.

> As they read the following passage, non-Italian readers should refer to a map of the kingdom of Italy. The decision to undertake the "March", as envisaged by the new plans, was taken in Naples on 26th October. The Fascists started mobilizing over the next two days, between the 26th and the 27th. The March would start on the 28th. Rome or thereabouts would be the place where Italy's destiny would be decided. Mussolini leaves Naples by train to return to Milan; the train goes via Rome. Milan is six hundred kilometres from Rome, at the other end of the country. If Mussolini had stayed in Naples, he would have been much closer. It was, in short, a curious choice of battle positions. Even with the conveniences of modern warfare, six hundred kilometres from the main theatre of action is a long way off. On the other hand, Milan has the advantage of being only a few kilometres from the frontier with Switzerland. The Fascists mobilize as far as they can. Most regions in the country remain completely unaffected by their mobilization. It is not easy to attack a state which is prepared to defend itself. All over Italy people were saying that the marchers would end up behind bars. But then the government threw in the towel and resigned.[37]

A king who acted like some unresponsive bureaucrat, a prime minister trapped by his decision to resign, an array of lily-livered political parties, a paralysed opposition and innumerable mistakes and miscalculations committed by the leading figures in the crisis – all these factors played straight into Mussolini's hands and helped him carry out his plan. Those who bear the real responsibility for his success in October 1922 were the leaders of Italy's democratic and liberal state. They in effect chose to commit political suicide. And the responsibility falls most heavily on the left-wing parties who were incapable of organizing even the most minimal resistance to the advancing Blackshirts. Mussolini was careful to remain at a prudent distance from the plot he was hatching, only, suddenly and surprisingly, to reappear at the centre of power before the squads on the March had even reached the outskirts of Rome. He knew very well that if he had arrived when the capital was invaded by hordes of armed Blackshirts, his room for manoeuvre would be severely reduced. He had to quell the squads he had mobilized for the March, tame them and turn them into just one of the many cards he could play. The Fascist squads were and had to remain his own private army. Margherita Sarfatti describes, without personal comment, the first day of Mussolini's government:

> At midday he leaves the Quirinale palace surrounded by excited crowds and goes to his hotel. There he spends the time until three in the afternoon making all the important decisions for government while not losing sight of the small details which, if overlooked, can often wreck large-scale projects. He sends a group of Blackshirts dressed up in full ceremonial rig as a guard of honour to keep an eye on the ex-prime minister Facta. He sends others to keep watch over all the main places of strategic importance as well as the offices of opposition newspapers both in the capital and elsewhere in the country. He communicates precise instructions to civil servants and prefects, appoints the ministers in his government, who by seven in the evening have already been sworn in by the King and taken up their offices, and then summons the head of the railways to his hotel room. Nothing untoward must be allowed to cause disruption. "Starting from eight o'clock this evening, I want you to organize the departure from Rome of the forty thousand men in the squads who are under orders from me to demobilize and send them back to their localities within twenty-four hours." "But, Your Excellency, that is impossible! Not even in wartime could we do such a thing. We'll need at least three days." "I said in twenty-four hours. I do not accept the word 'impossible'. Please make sure my orders are followed to the letter." Then, swiftly changing demeanour, from authoritarian to benevolent, he gives the man a smile.[38]

The Blackshirts, who thought they would take over the capital as they had Trento and other towns, had to swallow their disappointment and, as soon as their parade was over, get on the trains – there were sixty of them, with extra carriages attached – to go back home. It was impossible for them to disregard the demand for obedience and discipline. Many of them had never seen Rome before: underneath their brash triumphalism they hid the abashed amazement of first-time visitors to the Eternal City as they wandered round its sights: from the Piazza del Popolo they went to pay tribute to the Tomb of the Unknown Soldier, then climbed towards the Quirinale Palace; a short distance away was the station where the trains were waiting to take them back home.

On 1st November, the following announcement appeared on the first page of *Il Popolo d'Italia*: "From today the new editor of *Il*

Popolo d'Italia is Arnaldo Mussolini. I wish to thank warmly the journalists, contributors, correspondents, employees, workmen – all those in short who have worked so hard and so loyally with me to produce the newspaper for the benefit of our motherland. Mussolini." Three swift moves: the formation of the new government, the assertion of control over the armed wing of the party, the handing-over of the newspaper to his brother, the only man he trusted without reserve. After this, he calmly went to parliament to obtain the vote of confidence in his new administration. "He entered the Chamber, at the head of his ministers, striding triumphantly. It seemed as though he were entering on horseback. From the benches and galleries on the right a huge storm of applause greeted him. The Fascists rose to their feet and started to sing their military marching songs. Mussolini stiffened as he stood to attention and repeatedly raised his arm in a Roman salute."[39] His speech began with a few formal phrases of introduction before he swelled up and launched himself: "With three hundred thousand young men armed from top to toe, determined for action come what may, ready, with almost mystical intensity, to respond to my command, I could have unleashed reprisals on all those who have slandered and blackened the Fascist movement." But, he went on to say, although he could easily have routed his enemies, he had refrained from doing so. The reaction of the Chamber to these words was described by Emilio Lussu, who was a parliamentary deputy at the time and present at the scene: "A certain wave of relief ran round the room. Many a deputy nodded with approval, just like a man who is threatened with violence by someone who's got a weapon placatingly nods and tries to calm him down..."[40]

Mussolini probably didn't even hear the muttering coming from the opposition benches. He took breath and jutted out his jaw and with his eyes blazing with menace threw out another challenge: "I could have turned this grey and out-of-touch Chamber into a military encampment. I could have shut down parliament by force and formed a government made up entirely of Fascists." At this point, Lussu recalls, "the Leader of the Chamber lowered his gaze. A chill crept through the benches. A sudden vision hovered before us of Napoleon's grenadier guards storming into the French parliament in the coup on the 19th of Brumaire. Consternation seized the dyed-in-the-wool lovers of public order and private tranquillity. There was a long silence."[41] Rolling his head back, with his chest puffed out,

Mussolini suddenly continued: "I could have – but I have decided not to, at least for the time being." "Again a sensation of relief ran round the benches, subsiding melancholically," Lussu's bitter account continues. "Once more there were nods of agreement. The 'Duce' was enjoying himself. Just like a cat which catches a mouse between its paws and, though it could crush it to death without more ado, holds it first delicately, then grips it hard, then releases it so it thinks it's free, only to seize it and start all over again. Like the cat intoxicated with its drawn-out killing game, so the 'Duce' played with the Chamber."[42]

Mussolini could not have shut down parliament by force, not yet at least. He needed the votes of the deputies, but all who were listening to him took him at his word and believed him – or, it would be more accurate to say, surrendered their belief to him. Many years later, in Ludwig's interview with him, the journalist, perhaps thinking of the mass mobilization of the young Fascists Mussolini had described as ready to obey him "with almost mystical intensity", asked him whether, as he travelled on the night train to Rome, his sense of triumph felt more like an artist's or a prophet's. He thought for a moment about the question and then answered curtly: "Artist."[43]

Chapter 12

A Woman's Influence

The attendant had finished his stint in the park of the Villa Borghese, where his boss in the city's parks department had had him posted as a punishment. That would teach him to get caught relaxing in a warm bar when he should have been on duty outside. After just a few days there he'd already had his fill of the dogs who did their business wherever they wanted, their rude owners getting their leashes in a tangle, the gangs of screaming urchins and mischievous girls – it only needed the most trivial incident to put him in a bad mood. So just imagine what he felt when he saw this bizarre-looking type at the steering wheel of a Torpedo with the silencer off, who wouldn't stop roaring up and down the main avenue which crossed the park. Next to him in the streamlined sports car was another person who looked even odder. The previous Sunday the two had driven round the tree-lined avenues of the park with a lion on the back seat. Not just a very large cat, but a lion, or rather a lioness, to the amazement of all the people out strolling. Luckily she seemed fairly placid. Now once again they were roaring along in their convertible Alfa Romeo 20/30 HP. They must be super-rich to have a car like that, the warden thought: it cost at least thirty-five thousand lire, could go at a speed of 130 kilometres per hour, and consumed... who knows how much, with its 4,000-cc capacity. A short moment of peace and quiet as they disappeared, then back they were again, with that irritating exhibitionist at the steering wheel. Everyone in the park turned to look at him, especially the women and the young girls. He did a circuit three, four, five times – he seemed to keep his eyes fixed on that brunette with the big tits who looked at him adoringly every time he drove past her, as if she just wanted to run behind the car with her tail wagging. She was elegantly dressed, obviously from a "good" family, the warden thought. He was confident he could judge people by their appearances, he was used to seeing all types in his job. As he was crossing a patch of wet grass, he wondered what made a girl like that slaver after those two louts. Who knows how they'd made their money. Then he decided to intervene. He walked up the avenue while the two men in the sports car, a bit farther down, had slowed to an almost complete halt practically in front of the young brunette. The sound of the motor echoed among the trees. Suddenly he heard its roar getting louder behind him. It had started on another circuit of the park, perhaps the final one, which would succeed in hitching the brunette on board. The moment had come to get his own back for the month he had had to pass in the damp park of the Villa Borghese. He turned round sharply to take his revenge and signalled to the driver of the car to draw in to the side of the avenue and stop. He gestured again to make him switch off the engine. Then he made his way calmly and deliberately over to the Alfa Romeo. A silence finally descended. It seemed as if all the people strolling in the park had come to the top of the avenue to watch the scene unfold. He gave a quick glance at the strange type at the steering wheel, who had one arm slung ostentatiously out of the window, while the man in the passenger seat was twisting and turning to get out of the car to meet the warden. The warden paid no attention to him. He took the pen out of his pocket and opened his pad of penalty forms. "Kindly give me your personal details," he demanded of the driver. The answer momentarily stunned him. He lifted his gaze: his heart felt as if it had stopped beating, his hands were icy and his legs were tottering. No doubt about it, the driver was Benito Mussolini. The man who was accompanying the head of the Italian government in the car had made every effort to avoid this scene, but he'd been too late. Now he was talking rapidly to the warden, who was too astonished to hear him. He gave him his documents and introduced himself: Ercole Boratto, an official government chauffeur in the personal service of His Excellency Benito Mussolini, they were just taking the car for a spin, for a little relaxation in the middle of all His Excellency's commitments – the government, the ministers, the reports, that kind of thing... Yes, the noise of the engine had been too loud... but His Excellency wasn't to blame, no, it was his fault, the chauffeur's, he should have remembered to put the silencers on before they set out. But the warden remained immobile and unresponsive. Some female shrieks emerged from the small crowd of onlookers. Boratto didn't know what else to say or do. No one made a move. With one eye still on the brunette – who in the meantime had made her way to the front of the crowd to watch the unusual scene – Mussolini insisted he should pay the fine. The warden didn't even have the strength to hold his pen. It took a lot of persuasion to resolve the situation, but finally Boratto convinced the warden that if he didn't proceed to fine Mussolini the car would remain where it was. While the car was being started, he tried to reassure the warden – nothing would happen to him, he needn't worry, he had only done his duty. The warden made his way unsteadily back down the avenue. He crossed Piazza del Popolo with one thought tormenting him: how was he going to explain to his boss that he had just fined Mussolini?

Recalling his time as the Duce's chauffeur, Boratto wrote:

> I was stopped innumerable other times by the police on account of all these contraventions until I decided to ask Mussolini to let me fit the car out according to the regulations, which he allowed me to do with a bit of reluctance, since he hated luxury cars with all their mod cons. When it was a question of his own personal car, he used to maintain that bumpers and windscreens were completely unnecessary. Was Mussolini a good driver? No. His attention kept wandering, he was unaware of potential dangers, and couldn't steer skilfully, but nevertheless he thought he knew everything there was to know about cars. How many times did I have to step on the brakes just in time to avoid what would have been a certain crash![1]

When Mussolini came to power, Ercole Boratto thought that he would be transferred to another post. Right up to the day before Mussolini became prime minister, Boratto had been Facta's official driver; with the Fascists now in power he was certain some Blackshirt from one of the squads would be given his job. As it turned out, Mussolini decided to retain his services and soon grew to like him. After the regime fell, Boratto wrote a memoir of his twenty years working for the Duce, drawing also on the private notes he had occasionally jotted down whenever he feared he might forget some details of the curious episodes he witnessed. Once the war had ended, he needed a new job, and the idea occurred to him that he might sell what he had written and buy a lorry on the proceeds. He offered the piece to several newspapers in Rome.

Informers for various secret services can be found in most newspaper offices. A source named "Dusty" – a curious name for a spy

– informed agent CB 55 of the Office of Strategic Services, the predecessor of the Central Intelligence Agency, of Boratto's document. Unknown to its author, it was microfilmed, and copies were sent to Washington and London. It contained no special information, only a thoroughgoing demolition of the myth of Mussolini, but the secret services in every country are interested in everything and report on everything, producing vast quantities of documents which serve to justify their existence and their high salaries.

Boratto describes the most hidden aspect of the multifaceted Mussolini, one which the Fascist *gerarchi* didn't see and not even his wife and mistresses were privy to. Boratto's working day began at 7.30 in the morning, because Mussolini always liked to drive down the Via Appia through the countryside outside Rome. They returned in time for breakfast. Then there were the drives in the park of the Villa Borghese or the outings to the countryside beyond the city. "During these excursions, if we came across some isolated inn (and there are many in the countryside round Rome) he would stop and order a glass of white wine. He would drink a little from the glass, in little sips, as if to savour it better, insisting I drink a glass with him, and then he would order me to pay, since he never carried any money."[2]

As time went on, the seaside became the favourite destination for these outings. When Mussolini saw that the road to Ostia didn't go as far as the sea, he had one of the period's most up-to-date motorways built. As he confessed in his interview with Ludwig: "When I'm tired of men, I go to the sea. I should like to live always by the sea! Since I can't, I turn to animals instead. Their instincts are like those of humans, but they never ask anything of us: horses, dogs and, especially, cats (they're my favourite animal)."[3]

Admiration for Mussolini's sporting prowess was also part of his myth. For this witnesses were needed; solitary horse rides in the country were not much use, but the crowded riding track in the Villa Borghese was – it was where Rome's fashionable middle classes congregated. Ercole would drive him there and then had nothing to do but wait and watch: "Some of the *gerarchi* were good riders, but there were many who didn't know how to handle a horse. Mussolini belonged to the second category."[4]

In his chauffeur's severe judgement, the myth of Mussolini the sportsman was practically baseless. He could hardly stand on skis and had difficulty in completing a descent; he was applauded on the tennis court, but only because he was the Duce, not because he was a good tennis player; he was an aggressive swordsman and sometimes got the better of his opponent, but only because he was used to fighting duels – his fencing style left a lot to be desired. "In short, Mussolini was no good at sports, even though he forced himself to practise so many of them. It was obvious he was passionately interested in physical education, but he did not have the right qualities perhaps to practise himself."[5]

No one of course risked undermining the myth with some inopportune comment. Normally there would be an admiring crowd for some display of his sporting "skills", after which Boratto would pick him up in the car and take him back to get dressed for his political appointments. It was Boratto who drove him to the Chamber on 16th November 1922, when, after he had taunted the deputies with the "military encampment" speech, he won the vote of confidence with 316 votes in favour. There were only thirty-five Fascist deputies, but Mussolini declared his government was "beyond, above and opposed to parliamentary dispensation", drawing its strength instead from its popular support. Many believed him, too many surrendered their belief to him, as we have already seen. The leaders of the parties and parliamentary factions, accustomed to complicated and long-drawn-out negotiations and secret agreements, were ill equipped to deal with the sudden new rhythm of political events.

On 24th November Mussolini's majority in parliament voted to give him full power to re-establish order in the country. On 9th December he travelled to London for the conference on the German war debt and reparations. *Il Popolo d'Italia* reported:

The head of the Italian government, wearing the Fascist badge in the buttonhole of his frock coat, is introduced into the presence of King George in a private sitting room in the palace. The monarch, wearing a suit, is alone. Bukinghan [*sic*] Palace is as silent as a church; the hours ring out solemnly from a tower. All the windows are closed. The marble façade is blacker than the Colosseum or the other ancient monuments in Rome. The colonnades, the imposing architecture of the different buildings which make up the palace, the internal gates, the isolation, the sentinels standing to rigid attention almost as if in a religious trance, everything gives off an air of solemn austerity, of a closed and impenetrable place. The head of the Italian government remained in conversation with the King of

England for nearly twenty minutes; their conversation was cordial and touched on various current political issues.[6]

Mussolini's visit to London was also an opportunity for his mistress Alice De Fonseca Pallottelli to meet him. She held a joint Italian and British passport and spoke both languages fluently, and as a fervent nationalist was keen to support the Fascist cause abroad. She met him when he arrived at Victoria Station, taking her small son Virgilio along with her; Mussolini seems to have treated the little boy affectionately. During the four days he stayed in London, therefore, the new head of the Italian government was not without female company.

In the same month he also returned to Milan for the first time since coming to power, on a private visit. The purpose of the visit was, so Ercole Boratto assumed, to see his family. The chauffeur had been given orders to follow on with the official car so it was available for Mussolini's use while he was in the city; Mussolini himself travelled on the royal train that the House of Savoy had put at his disposal for the occasion. He arrived after nightfall and ordered his chauffeur to pick him up and take him to Corso Venezia. He indicated the house, got out of the car and, telling Boratto to wait for him – official drivers had to know how to wait as well as how to drive – slipped through the main entrance. Boratto whiled away the time trying to work out who Mussolini could be visiting in the apartment block. It was clearly someone important, if he was paying a call on this person first, as soon as he had arrived in the city, rather than going direct to his own family whom he hadn't seen for several months. While he was trying to work it out, Margherita Sarfatti's maid appeared. "She was German, very talkative and, I soon realized, very indiscreet. She willingly started to tell me about all the visits Mussolini had made to the house; in fact, she maintained that this was his real home, not where his family lived in Foro Bonaparte."[7]

On the following day, after meetings in the city's prefecture, Mussolini again summoned his chauffeur, but this time wanted to drive the car himself. He drove to Sarfatti's villa on Lake Como. There were several such excursions during the visit to Milan, and Boratto, silent and attentive, had always to be ready with the car. "With Mussolini and 'S.', there was also the latter's fourteen- or fifteen-year-old daughter, who was already shapely and pretty. I only realized later why she was so often with them."[8] The long periods the two lovers spent together Boratto whiled away in the company of the gossipy maid. She worked in all her mistress's various houses and knew about her private life in intimate detail. "She even told me about what went on behind their bedroom doors – all I'll say is that, if her stories were true, which I rather doubt, then what they got up to was worthy of a brothel."[9] Boratto's testimony is not entirely to be trusted: he was writing after the fall of Fascism and wanted to ingratiate himself with some new employer so he could save up and buy his lorry. Sarfatti's maid too could have exaggerated the stories about her mistress's sexual practices to build up her own importance, making herself out to have been privy to significant secrets. Yet it's worth remembering that Claretta Petacci in her diary also records some of Mussolini's unconventional sexual activities; for example, she writes that he admitted to her on several occasions that some of his mistresses – such as Romilda Ruspi – watched while he had sex with other women: "I was attracted [to Ruspi] only in a physical, sexual way, but even so not excessively. That explains why I had other mistresses, it was a kind of rota, every now and then when I felt like it I slept with her. And when I felt like it, I had sex with other women while she watched…"[10]

But we also need to treat Petacci's diaries with a certain caution. She filled the pages with accounts of her conversations with Mussolini filtered through a sentimental girlish crush; only when she copies down unflattering comments on her rivals, past and present, for his affections, does a dry matter-of-factness enter her tone, as for example when she transcribes his remarks, made in 1937, on Sarfatti: "She was an unpleasant woman. She was four years older than me. She had a kind of Jewish intelligence. I put up with her, she bored me. Just think that I had sex with women right under her nose. With Ester Lombardo and also Tessa, I had them out in the open while Sarfatti was there. She saw me doing it and she just threw a handful of pebbles against the balcony. I kept going with her only because it suited me…"[11]

In the pages of Petacci's diary Mussolini emerges as the typical figure of a mature man beginning to feel the onset of age, who enjoys embroidering the stories of his exploits with details to impress his mistress, perhaps because he fears he can't impress her in other non-verbal ways. She is clearly struck and perhaps attracted by his sexual exhibitionism, since she never fails to speak about it. She's more vague about their own lovemaking, tending to describe it through rose-tinted glasses: "His face is tense, his eyes are burning. I am sitting on the floor; quite suddenly he slides off his armchair onto me, curved over me. I can feel his body strain to unleash itself. I pull him close and kiss him. We make love with a kind of fury; he cries out like a wounded animal. Then he falls exhausted onto the bed; even in repose he looks strong."[12]

But his last mistress shows her real untrustworthiness and ruthlessness when she writes about the sexuality of his earlier lovers, beginning with Margherita Sarfatti, for whom she pretends to feel a kind of female solidarity. She was perhaps not aware of it, but the Mussolini she describes in the pages of her diary emerges as the classic kind of Latin male, like something out of a cartoon or soap opera, ready to swear undying faith, ready to say anything so long as he gets what he wants. Petacci reports that Mussolini told her he had failed to have sex the first few times he slept with Sarfatti. She omits the details almost out of some kind of empathy: "I'm leaving out the intimate details because they upset me too much."[13] A few months later, however, Mussolini returned to the topic and this time she transcribes what he tells her:

> Do you know what happened to me the first time [I slept with Sarfatti] in that hotel room [in Milan] from which you could hear the bell in the San Gottardo church striking every quarter of an hour? It sounded like some tinkling carriage clock. Seven o'clock, ding ding; quarter-past seven, ding ding; and there I was tossing and turning and not able to do a thing. In the end I had to give up. I invented an excuse, something about suddenly feeling unwell, so we got up and left. The second time was the same. I just couldn't do it, because of this terrible smell they have. Perhaps it's to do with their diet, I wouldn't know. But I couldn't manage to do anything. There was no love involved – [Sarfatti] was a fanatic, like all Jews. She used to say: "It's better to be the mistress of the prime minister than some ordinary fool's."[14]

Ercole Boratto wondered why his boss, the head of the Italian government, spent so much time with Margherita Sarfatti, but he wasn't capable by himself of searching out the complex reasons for the relationship. All he had to go on was her chambermaid's saucy tales of Boccaccio-like romps. Among the women in Mussolini's harem, Sarfatti was undoubtedly the one with least sexual inhibitions. She was familiar with the style and cunning of the great mistresses of the past: they realized that their men, their lords and masters, wanted female flesh, as much as they could handle. If their mistresses were to keep their positions of power in his private life – power which could also extend its influence into the public sphere – then they needed to keep him plentifully supplied with young girls. The most famous mistress of them all, Madame de Pompadour, had done this. As she got older, she realized she no longer had the physical attractions which had enabled her to conquer the King, so she started, on the one hand, to soothe him by providing cultivated pursuits – art, music, theatre – while, on the other, satisfying his continuing sexual needs by subcontracting out the services which she herself could no longer supply. She set up a small and exclusive brothel on the outskirts of Versailles, called Le Parc aux Cerfs, where a handful of girls in the first bloom of youth, taken out of the slums and given a good wash, were kept ready to service the King's desires.

Edvige Mussolini writes that after he became prime minister her brother, "wrapped in an aura of mystery and legend", was literally besieged by aristocratic women, but whatever amorous adventures took place, they were insignificant and "uninvolving". Besides, Mussolini hated the rigid formalities and the ostentatious "good breeding" found in aristocratic circles. According to his sister, real involvement was to be found in his relationship with Sarfatti: "Benito's love for this woman writer was – in my opinion – profound and new, as it enabled him to suppress the real inclinations of his mind and soul, because, in this relationship, he loved those female qualities and faults which previously – and again subsequently – he treated with indifference or scorn. Simple-hearted Rachele sensed that Margherita Sarfatti represented a special kind of danger, and for that reason perhaps hated her alone among all the other women who troubled her existence."[15]

Boratto was aware that Sarfatti was somehow "useful" to Mussolini, and also came to realize that she in some sense advised him. But he could not have appreciated her real importance, as the most cultivated and sophisticated member of the army of supporters with whom he had climbed to power. Sarfatti was the primary theorist in Mussolini's circle, who provided Fascism with its inner content or ideas. Her influence in this sense can be seen as early as 1913, in the magazine *Utopia*, in which Mussolini tried to sketch an outline

of his own socialist beliefs. It continued with the founding of the
Fascist review *Gerarchia* and culminated in her biography of Mussolini, *Dux*. She financed *Gerarchia* and was its editor for ten years,
from 1924 to 1934. Its main purpose was clear from the title: to create a Fascist ideology based on a scale or hierarchy of values. The
foremost value was the restoration of a social order in which the
Fascist mission would find its justification. When Mussolini went to
Milan in December 1922, accompanied by Boratto, to see her, she
was not merely his sexually uninhibited and willing mistress: she had
already set to work on writing the biography that would become the
principal building block in the myth of Mussolini and in the Fascist
state's quest for public legitimacy, its need to develop its own visible
rituals so that it could enthuse the masses. As she made love, apparently without shame or inhibition, to the "Duce's" body in various
bedrooms, she was theorizing that that same body would need to be
seen as the personification of the new state, the indispensable symbol
of the new regime. Mussolini had spoken in general terms about the
need to instil in the masses a sense of faith in the political actions of
their leader, but it was Sarfatti who created the religion of Fascism
and centred its ideology on Mussolini. She even came to realize that
there could be such a thing as a Fascist "type", which people would
imitate and which would inaugurate a trend or fashion: "It occurred
to me one day, quite out of the blue, that a certain way men had of
combing their hair, straight back from the forehead, was known as
the 'Fascist style' and was indeed typical of Fascists; a certain type
of gaze, of walking, a certain facial expression, distinguished and
still mark out a Fascist, even if he isn't wearing the party badge in
his buttonhole. A style or fashion had grown up – a whole physical
type."[16]

Sarfatti worked on *Dux* until 1925, publishing the book only when
she was certain she had succeeded in bringing off the minor miracle
she was attempting: to paint a portrait of Mussolini in which there
was a consistency and ideological substance in him which he'd never
had in real life.

It is my personal belief that if there were anyone besides Mussolini who was
capable of giving the Fascist state – precisely in so far as it still needed to be
"constructed" after Mussolini came to power – a symbolic context and meaning,
that person was Sarfatti... [...] In Sarfatti's view, symbols generate politics, so

it follows that only those individuals who know how to embody and give form to these symbols are capable of being political movers and shakers – in other words, the intellectual elite, herself above all. [...] The state needs an officiating high priest, a "*duce*"; therefore Sarfatti applies herself to forging, with the *Dux*, another symbol, an image of Mussolini which is convincing not as the picture of a new man but as the priest of a new and hitherto unknown – and therefore completely modern – conception of how the state should be organized.[17]

At first sight the careers of Sarfatti and Mussolini appear to develop in parallel, but on looking more closely it can be seen that she was always ahead of him. She always had the right intuitions and made the right choices before he did; above all, she supplied the ideological backing for Fascism which on his own he would never have been able to develop. While Mussolini was, in some sense, "overtaken" by the events in Fiume and struggled to contain and control D'Annunzio, Sarfatti never considered the episode as a serious milestone on the road to Fascism and refused to be swept up in the general enthusiasm for it. To her role as a woman who argued forcefully for Italy's intervention in the war – a position and a right she argued closely for and justified on an ideological level – she added that of the mother whose young son had heroically sacrificed his life for his country. It came naturally to her to associate with the Arditi, to sympathize with their disorientation after the war, to work to make them part of the nascent Fascist movement until she became the ideological advocate of the violence the Fascist squads wreaked on the life of the nation. The acceptance of political violence seemed to her consistent with her developing beliefs. She became convinced that the new state could only come into being through violence; that violence was the necessary foundation for the state's legitimacy and revealed its historical destiny.

Once her lover had gained power, Sarfatti no longer limited herself to the role of theorist or of a prompter off-stage. She used her considerable wealth to back publishing ventures and public events in which she could present herself as the model of a Fascist woman, the embodiment of a femininity which was above and beyond political conflict. In taking on this role she was helped by the myth she assiduously created and promoted of her son who had fallen in war. She played the figure of the courageous mother and the grieving mother in public commemorations, as she built up round the figure of her son one of the earliest Fascist rituals, one centred on the cult and sacrifice of the hero, who represented the high spiritual ideal in contrast to the low materialism of the Socialists. Mussolini supported her, and his role as high priest in these rituals suited him perfectly; it took him a long time to realize that the real figure at the centre of the ceremonies celebrating the prowess of her brave son Roberto was his mother, the sophisticated and intellectual Sarfatti.

> The legitimization of Fascism through the experience of war, the mystical cult of heroic sacrifice, became the foundation on which Sarfatti built her justification of the new state as the only possible revival of the universal Roman Empire, while at the same time being the culmination of the political process of Italian unification begun in the nineteenth century. The transformative function of the symbolism of ancient Rome must be exploited in the construction of a new state which would embody the ideals of classicism and humanism and fulfil its mission as a national religion.[18]

Sarfatti's role in helping to destroy the claims of the women's movement in Italy, especially as it had evolved in the years before the war should not lead us to diminish her importance as a theorist of Fascism under Mussolini. While he praised the tactical advantages of "emptiness" or "blankness" in exercising power and thought that the main goal was simply ensuring the continuity of the Fascist regime, she was busy filling in the blank canvas of its ideology. While on the one hand her approach crushed the prospects of women under the regime, forcing them to renounce every form of feminism, she also pursued the utopian idea of a new order, a Fascist city of the future, where the women who belonged to the cultural elite – of which of course she was the pre-eminent example – would have an important role to play. In her vision of this utopia, Fascism would have to use various cultural means to construct the new state based on order and hierarchy. In carrying out this task women would represent a point of contact between the past and the future, between tradition and modernity; in this way a new classical civilization would emerge which, in coming into existence, would demonstrate the historical necessity of Fascism.

It was thus Margherita Sarfatti who lay behind Mussolini's revival of classical Rome as a central element in Fascism and the fundamental precondition for its imperialism: "The names and the classifications which characterized the ancient Roman way of doing things were rediscovered: the legions, the squadrons, the maniples and chief maniples, centurions and consuls; the division into *princeps* and *triarii*; the rapid ordered marches, three abreast. How different from the old slow rambling and disordered processions – like those of the Socialists – which proved resistant to all attempts to give them an order and design!"[19]

Completely absorbed in daily political activity, Mussolini had no time to spare on designing an outward face for the regime so that Italians would be able to see it and recognize it. Perhaps he thought the new state would take on its own form spontaneously, as Sarfatti wrote, and therefore had no need of further high-flown theorizing to help it do so. He must also have found it bizarre that a woman was so concerned with the ideological aspects of Fascism. It took him a long time to appropriate her ideas – and only after he had vulgarized them – and it is probable that he never realized how much his dictatorship and the myth surrounding it owed to her. "Women should be passive", he exclaimed in his interview with Ludwig,

> they're good at analysis, not at synthesis. In the whole history of architecture, show me a woman architect. Tell one to build a shed, let alone a temple! She can't. Architecture is the synthesis of all the arts, but women are completely incapable of being architects – that sums up their destiny. My opinion of their role in the state is completely opposed to all forms of feminism. Of course they shouldn't be treated as slaves, but if I gave them the right to vote I'd be derided. In the Fascist regime women don't count.[20]

In the proofs of the interview he corrected "should be passive" to "must obey", but he was probably being sincere when he told Ludwig that he had never allowed a woman to influence him. In his conception of politics as a daily and ruthless deployment of tactics, a field of action unbounded by any preconceived programme, where he might choose either to assassinate an opponent or flatter him into compliance, there was no room for female influence, least of all of an intellectual kind.

Mussolini had managed to bring the People's Party on board his government, bypassing Don Sturzo and reaching an agreement even with the hated De Gasperi. He had toyed with the idea of giving a couple of ministries to Socialist Party trade-unionists from the General Confederation of Labour, perhaps including their well-known leader Bruno Buozzi. But the Socialist Party didn't even have time to consider the possibility of their members participating in the new government, albeit under the condition that their acceptance would be their own individual responsibility, before the intransigence of representatives from the squads, who threatened to stir up rebellion among the rank and file, and of the nationalists, who said they would withdraw their support, scuppered the idea. Mussolini, without putting up much resistance, beat a rapid retreat. But when the full list of the new government appointments was published, a sense of disappointment spread through the Fascist camp. Out of all the posts – ministers, deputy ministers, commissioners, etc. – only a few of them had achieved their ambitions. And when the heads of the various prefectures of the cities and towns throughout the country were chosen, Mussolini preferred to appoint army generals and senior civil servants with solid careers behind them rather than Blackshirts from the squads. He knew his choices would lead to insubordination on the part of the local *ras*, whose only option now was to nurse their resentment against the state, but he also calculated, correctly, that the conflict would wear them down and lead to their eventual defeat.

On the evening of 12th January 1923, at a meeting held in his private suite in the Grand Hotel in Rome, Mussolini founded the "Gran Consiglio Nazionale del Fascismo" ("Grand National Council of Fascism"). "The idea must have come to him out of the blue. He had not spoken of the idea beforehand with anyone, unlike all the other plans he'd come up with. He summoned us all to the very large and ornate sitting room of his apartment, without saying what the meeting would be about."[21]

Mussolini must last have come across the expression "Gran Consiglio" during his time in Switzerland, where the term – "Gran Consiglio" in the Ticino, "Grand Conseil" in the French-speaking part – is used to mean the parliaments, the legislative bodies of the individual cantons. For the meeting at the Grand Hotel he also hired a photographer: the occasion was to be recorded for posterity. Then he had it put into the school history books as one of the milestones in the history of Fascism. The Grand Council became an official organ of state in 1928. In January 1923 it was still merely a private meeting of party members, but Mussolini used his rhetorical skills to present it as the founding act of what would be the party's most important executive body. It was always he who opened its meetings. He would listen in silence to the sometimes lengthy discussions and at a certain point intervene in person again, by summing up the points which had been raised and then gathering them together in a proposal which was put to a formal vote. The Grand Council was another tool in Mussolini's hands, and it was clear from the outset, when his proposal to set it up was voted through unanimously, that he would use it to quell the rebel *ras*. "The Grand Council, in accordance with government directives requiring the disbanding of all political-military groupings of whatsoever kind by the end of the current month, declares the disbandment of all squads within the Fascist Party and their incorporation into the Milizia Volontaria per la Sicurezza Nazionale (Voluntary National Security Militia) according to the regulations to be issued by General Headquarters."[22]

The disbanding of the squads spelt defeat for the *ras*. Any resistance would have been a rebellion against the Duce and against the party. Whoever tried to prevent the disbandment of the local squads and their incorporation into the centralized Militia would have found himself automatically against the government, the party and, above all, the state. Mussolini's aim was to identify Fascism with the state – the Fascist state – and transform himself into its symbol. He would no longer be the leader of a political party, but the "*duce*" of a totalizing national identity, of a patriotic faith capable of including the entire life of the country in its grasp. Since he was the state, it followed logically that the armed forces of the state should stand over all, including the Fascist Party. When Mussolini ordered the publication of an account of the first five years of the Grand Council and its decrees, he called it nothing less than *Il libro della fede* (*The Book of Faith*) and wrote in the introduction: "All the great institutions of the Regime have emerged from the Grand Council – above all, the Militia. The creation of the Militia was the fundamental, inexorable act which placed the Government on an utterly different level to all previous governments and transformed it into a Regime."[23]

In inventing the Grand Council, Mussolini thought he would achieve two things simultaneously: the progressive marginalization and eventual elimination of all the local *ras*, as we have seen, but also the creation of an outlet for the ambitions of the more prominent members of the party that conceded no real space for autonomous political manoeuvre, but instead parcelled up power into small portions which could be handed out. The new executive body took the most important and wide-ranging decisions. It was inconceivable it would ever vote against what the Duce wanted, at least until 25th July 1943, when it was the Grand Council which forced Mussolini to stand down in an internal *coup d'état*.

In another passage from his introduction to *Il libro della fede*, Mussolini summed up the other move which laid the foundation for the creation of his personal dictatorship, over the Fascist Party itself: "There is a decree of 13th October 1923 which establishes – four years before the noted circular issued on 6th January 1927 – the position of the city prefects under the Fascist Regime: 'The functions of the representatives of the Government – the prefects – and of the representatives of the National Fascist Party are clearly distinct and differentiated. The prefect's sole responsibility is towards the Government, and he therefore has to act with complete autonomy within the limits of the law."[24] In other words, the party was free to occupy itself with organizing Fascist parades, Fascist dances, Fascist festivals, etc. The business of governing was up to Mussolini, working through the prefects he appointed.

Yet this does not mean that Mussolini was ready to delegate the organization of the various Fascist ceremonies and rituals to the *gerarchi*; on the contrary, "he occupied himself with the smallest details of such ceremonies, down to the uniforms which were to be worn and other such petty matters. Even in doing this kind of work he was indefatigable. The first Fascists who joined the movement early on, in its rabble-rousing and unrestrained years, were highly resistant to these external rules of military discipline; he had an uphill fight to impose them."[25]

But when it was a question not of the organization of Fascist parades but the ceremonies controlled by the rigid protocol of the state and the Royal House of Savoy, Mussolini found himself up against that constitutional impediment which dogged him throughout his dictatorship. In the early summer of 1923 George V and his wife Queen Mary paid an official visit to Italy. Ceremonial protocol stipulated a precise order of precedence: after the royal families came the personages of the state, the President of the Senate, the President of the Lower Chamber, then the holders of the Order of the Annunciation, who, by virtue of their office, were regarded as the King's unofficial cousins, and it was only after all these that Mussolini was placed. By the terms of the Albertine Statute, the fundamental law of the Italian monarchy, the position of head of government did not exist. By the rigid rules of ceremonial protocol, Mussolini was merely *primus inter pares* among the other ministers, who each swore an individual oath of loyalty to the King and were answerable to him, again as individuals, for their actions. Mussolini's dictatorship began with this institutional flaw unresolved and it continued like this for years until he succeeded in finding a – partial – solution.

To make up for the humiliation of having to process behind the presidents of the Senate and the Lower Chamber and obscure army generals, Mussolini spent the rest of the summer on a tour of central and northern Italy. The courtiers responsible for applying ceremonial protocol might have snubbed him, but the cities and towns he visited on his tour were keen to make him an honorary citizen. "The women in the Abruzzi region, when he was travelling there, wanted to 'touch' him, especially the widows and mothers of men who had died in the Great War, in a replica of the local custom of touching fetishistic objects or relics."[26]

Of apparently less concern to Mussolini was another institutional defect: the ideological weakness of a regime that had no principles to guide it and no precise moral and ethical points of reference. He himself, on his road to power, had progressively discarded one ideal after another, until the resulting blankness itself became the goal, since it meant he was completely free to act as he chose: "Fascism did not have a ready-made programme for implementation. If it had, by now Fascism would have failed completely, like other political parties who neatly pack their suitcases with their doctrines and think that with this they can face the complex and ever-changing reality of human life. So the National Fascist Party did not have a manifesto of fine phrases but an overriding desire for action."[27]

The Fascist "desire for action" soon manifested itself in a series of violent attacks on all the opponents of the new regime: leading Socialist, Republican and Catholic politicians were beaten up and sometimes killed even in broad daylight. The more intransigent members of the squads hated democracy and refused to accept the idea that Fascism had become "parliamentary", and that it had formed a government by allying itself with the old political parties they loathed. Mussolini's attempts to transform some of his old adversaries into supporters by offering them posts in the new government were anathema to them. Margherita Sarfatti used all her skills as a writer to try to justify the violence on ideological grounds, to minimize its effects, to present it as a merely transitional phase:

> Groups of young lads would suddenly climb on a lorry or pile into two or three cars and drive to a nearby town, taking the Chamber of Labour by surprise or the shop in the left-wing cooperative which wouldn't sell bread to non-party members, or the local Socialist association whose members had betrayed a local Fascist to the authorities or had had him beaten up; the young men would break up some furniture and smash windows, tear up registers, let fly with the occasional punch or thump... [...] It was like a practical joke or an adventure story, played out with no sense of menace, with the lads' faces uncovered for all to see, in an open-hearted crusade against petty local tyrants, who'd be "kidnapped and put in prison" briefly, as a prank, or made to drink a glass of castor oil. It was just a way of puncturing the self-importance of these local bigwigs who thought themselves omnipotent.[28]

The reality was very different. The squads who had got used to overrunning towns and rural areas more or less with impunity, since the police forces rarely intervened, now saw Mussolini's takeover of power as the signal to unleash a final reckoning. The thugs thought they'd been given the right to break into the homes of their political opponents – university professors, intellectuals, journalists and trade-union activists – where they would beat up and force their victims, as a minimum punishment, to drink a glass or a whole jug of castor oil, as, so it was thought, a purgative for the turpitude of their anti-Fascist ideas. Administering the oil was nothing less than a form of torture; castor oil is a powerful laxative, no longer used today precisely because its effects are so drastic. It also makes people vomit. The victims were not allowed to empty their bowels normally, but frequently had their trousers tied so they couldn't take them off. When they returned home – if they returned home – they would arrive in front of their family in a pitiful and humiliating state.

> Just as man, according to the Catholic Church, is redeemed from original sin by holy water, so the anti-Fascist, according to the Fascist religion, is washed from the crime of anti-Fascism – harming his own country – by being administered castor oil. If the neophyte was responsive to the initial reprimands and drank

the oil without resistance, the ceremony was soon over. If there was a show of resistance, the procedure was more complex. Because of this, many anti-Fascists were killed, since the man who resists redemption is more useful dead than alive to the faith and to the country. In the Romagna region there are many such martyrs. But in most cases such extreme measures were avoided. The rebel was rendered powerless and then his mouth was opened, often by using a special device which had been invented and patented by veteran members of the squads. The Florentine squad was celebrated, among other achievements, also for this invention. In the case of persistent recalcitrance, a tube was used, as in hospitals. The dose of castor oil was carefully measured out in proportion to the degree of the heretic's obstinacy and the extent of his heresy. In complex cases, paraffin or petrol, and on occasion iodine tincture, was added to the castor oil.[29]

After 1945, the various *gerarchi* and local Fascist chiefs did all they could to deny their responsibility for this wave of terror, deliberately trying in their memoirs and testimonies to minimize and gloss over the events. It is not by chance that Mussolini's right-hand man, Cesare Rossi, recalls only one isolated incident from the period – the attack of Tuscan squads on the distinguished and well-known liberal senator, Olindo Malagodi. In his version, Mussolini was furious when he was informed that Malagodi had been forced to drink castor oil: "He immediately sent me to visit Malagodi at home with his apologies and regret for what had occurred. I found the late senator still suffering from the after-effects of the castor oil. When he recovered he came to the Viminale to thank me, after which our relations were always friendly."[30]

Rachele Mussolini is also one of those who have tried to make light of the severity of the acts of aggression committed by the Fascist squads, which frequently left the victims half-dead and on occasion killed them outright. If we are to believe her, we must assume that Mussolini's wife never saw an attack or knew someone who was a victim of one, since she found herself able to write that castor oil was used on only "a few occasions" and was in any case a punishment restricted "to opponents of a certain social class". Unbelievably, she writes that this form of torture was considered an "honour for lawyers and public servants" and comments:

They took their victim and forced him to swallow a certain quantity of castor oil, not in amounts which could kill him, of course, but enough to keep him at home for a while with all the usual after-effects. These methods are certainly blameworthy, but, all things considered, it was better to have to remain in the lavatory for several hours than in a hospital bed with a fractured skull or, worse, in the mortuary with a bullet in the chest, as happens with the more "progressive" methods they use nowadays.[31]

But the mortuaries were frequently used, since the punishments meted out by the Fascist squads were not restricted to inflicting degradation and humiliation on their victims. The so-called "punishment" was carried out in public, frequently in front of the victim's family, after making sure they couldn't intervene to stop it going ahead. The chosen victims were dragged from their homes just as they were, with no time to dress or cover themselves. If they thought they could soon escape the wrath of their attackers by drinking a pint of castor oil, they were usually deceiving themselves. Many were forced to acclaim Mussolini and make public recantation of their own ideas and political beliefs. If they refused, they were beaten up. "The aim was the same whether they used castor oil or the method which became a favourite in Ferrara and Rovigo, in which the victim was kidnapped in the middle of the night and then stripped naked and abandoned by the side of a road or tied to a tree. [...] The opponent was infantilized; sometimes his body hair was shaved in order to 'feminize' him."[32]

In this climate of extreme violence, many newspapers and some of the most prominent figures from the democratic parties took the view that Mussolini was a kind of "transitional cure", a necessary evil to resolve the problems of the country. Others retreated into an ineffectual silence and, despite the increasing authoritarianism and violence in political and social life, refused to speak out on the developments which were taking place after the March on Rome. Then there was the increasing number of those who flocked to support the winning side, loud in their effusive praise of Fascism and Mussolini. In their view, the man had finally arrived who could sweep away the dinosaurs and scoundrels of the old order. After that, they fantasized, it would be up to a new generation to sweep away in their turn the Fascists and their leader. Circumstances such as these offered Mussolini new possibilities for manoeuvre. "If Fascism as a movement gave cause for concern and was responsible for many things which were seen as inexcusable, Mussolini was viewed in a quite different light. The myth of Mussolini the man was emerging. Many Italians who were critical of Fascism or even opposed it outright put their trust in him. The sensational course of his political career, his contradictions, his excessive reactions, tended to be seen positively or at least were regarded – more or less absurdly – as giving cause for hope."[33]

But perhaps the political insight which was most beneficial to Mussolini was his realization that the country was desperately tired after the long travails of the war years, the outbreak of the Spanish flu epidemic, the aftermath of two major earthquakes (Messina in 1908 and Avezzano in 1915) and the violent civil conflict during which his own Fascist squads had sown mayhem and bloodshed through the length and breadth of Italy. The weariness in the country had resulted in a moral and economic crisis. Public opinion was becoming increasingly passive; several massacres perpetrated by the Fascists had taken place without incurring any display of public indignation.

Chapter 13

In Bed with the Leader

Still short of his fortieth birthday, Mussolini was now prime minister: he felt young, full of energy and drive. Other politicians described him as plebeian, violent, vindictive, coarse and histrionic, but he ignored them so they would realize their criticisms fell on deaf ears. He wished to give Italy at least the illusion of the peaceful existence which, a long time ago, he had been the first to sense the country yearned for, and he wanted to reap the political benefits of being the person who gave the country the order and calm it needed. He was the head of an anti-democratic party within what was still a liberal democracy. He was responsible to the Sovereign as the guarantor of the country's institutions. He led a large coalition in which his own party was in a minority, and at the same time he was faced with an internal opposition made up of diehard Fascists. One successful stratagem was to absorb the Associazione Nazionalista Italiana (Italian Nationalist Association), thereby widening, in one swift blow, his own party's constituency to serve as a counterweight to the more intransigent *ras*.

He also succeeded in dividing various local parties and absorbing the parts which split away. One example was the Partito Sardo d'Azione (Sardinian Party of Action), which had been founded by former combatants after 1918 and was led by the parliamentary deputy Emilio Lussu. At first the Fascists and the "Sardisti" collaborated in the general election. As violence in the country increased before and after the March on Rome, the Sardisti started to take up anti-Fascist positions, and the relationship between the two parties grew increasingly tense. Using the man he had appointed as prefect to the city of Cagliari, Asclepio Gandolfo, Mussolini manoeuvred for a merger between the Sardisti and the Fascist supporters on the island which would lead to a reconstituted local Fascist Party, possibly led by Lussu. The merger foundered on the aspirations of the

Sardisti towards Sardinian autonomy. Mussolini changed tactics and started to focus instead on separate factions within the Sardisti who were more open to the idea of collaboration with the Fascists (a tactic he also adopted towards the Republicans and other parties). Emilio Lussu describes the appeal made by the prefect Gandolfo to these local leaders in the villages:

"I appeal to all those who oppose the Fascists, especially those who fought in the war. You are against the Fascists mainly because the Fascists in your village are scoundrels. Well, you're right and I'm going to send them all to prison." There was a round of applause. "Look on me as your father, not your enemy. I am your general," he said, turning to the veterans among them, "not your prefect. You say that political liberties are under threat! Very well, join the Fascists and defend those liberties. You can take control of the situation. I'll hand over the Fascists to you and you can do what you want with them. The true Fascists will be you. [...] Are you democrats? You think I'm not a democrat? You support Sardinian autonomy and a republic? Well, go ahead, no one's stopping you. Fascism is like a mosaic – all the different colours and all the different details contribute to the splendour of the whole." Several of his listeners couldn't resist the idea of immediate revenge on their enemies. In Pirri, a village near to Cagliari, one of the leaders of the opposition had been beaten up by the Fascists and forced to drink castor oil. He introduced himself to Gandolfo, joined the Fascist Party, and the very same day had the leader of the local Fascist squad given a public beating in the village square. [...] In this way, slowly but surely, the Fascism of the early days was buried. The Fascists who came afterwards burned the newspaper their predecessors had produced and then proceeded to take over the offices.[1]

While in this way Mussolini's men brought entire towns and villages over to Fascism, including the local opposition, he himself had to confront the Vatican. Taking both his opponents and his own supporters by surprise, he described his deep religious feelings and declared his readiness to establish friendly relations between the Italian state and the Holy See. One concrete sign of this new openness towards the Church was the decree passed by the Grand Council on 15th February 1923 which declared Fascism to be incompatible with Freemasonry. Mussolini was riding an old hobby horse, which he'd wheeled out when he was still a left-wing revolutionary, especially in the National Socialist Congress in Ancona, and now found could come in useful again in his dealings with the Vatican. As we've seen,

Mussolini's attitude to Freemasonry was ambivalent and changeable. He'd obtained the support of various lodges for the March on Rome, while prominent members of the party were Freemasons: Italo Balbo – one of the four men who organized the March – and the future ministers Costanzo Ciano and Giuseppe Bottai belonged to the Piazza del Gesù Lodge, the obedience which had split away in 1908, while the party's future secretary Achille Starace, Roberto Farinacci and the war hero Luigi Rizzo were members of the Palazzo Giustiniani Lodge. A month before the decree issued by the Grand Council, in January 1923, Mussolini himself had agreed to become, for no apparent reason, an Honorary Grand Master. However, Cesare Rossi, his closest associate at the time, shows no surprise in his account: "One Sunday afternoon I bumped into Palermi (the Grand Master of the Gran Loggia d'Italia della Massoneria di Piazza del Gesù) who's just come out of a meeting with the Duce. He was elated. In his hand, in a case, he was holding a document written on parchment, which he took out and unrolled in front of me. It was a message of homage from all the various Masonic lodges ratifying Mussolini's eligibility to join. At the bottom, in Mussolini's handwriting, there was his signature with the usual formula of 'I hereby accept and confirm'. I felt more scepticism than surprise. In fact, I thought to myself: 'Palermi, you're a poor fool if you think Mussolini will pay any attention to your parchment scroll...'"[2] And indeed, less than two months later, Palermi's scroll might as well have been written on scrap paper. Palermi had been used and thrown away like a squeezed lemon; the subsequent persecution he had to endure drove him to attempt suicide.

These kinds of volte-face, typical of Mussolini's character and political tactics, paved the way for the opening of secret negotiations with the Vatican in 1923 in an effort to resolve the so-called "Roman Question", which had proved so treacherous for all previous Italian governments, ever since the Bersaglieri troops had entered through the breach in the Porta Pia gate in September 1870 and the Eternal City had become the capital of the newly unified country.

According to De Felice's reconstruction of the events, a first meeting took place between Mussolini and Cardinal Gasparri on either 19th or 20th January 1923, barely three months after the March on Rome. The negotiations which followed were perhaps the most difficult and demanding which Mussolini had to face during his twenty years in

252 IL DUCE AND HIS WOMEN

power. On the opposite side of the table were no longer the worn-out leaders of spent political forces, but a centuries-old organization capable of fielding men of outstanding preparation and ability. The Vatican appointed Father Pietro Tacchi Venturi as the chief mediator responsible for relations with Mussolini during the secret talks. The priest had become Mussolini's spiritual advisor and, as a shrewd tactician, started off by asking the new Italian government to adopt some specific measures, as a token of their good intentions, which could then be shown to the Pope; such as, for example, handing over the assessment of suitability – and therefore in effect the selection – of teachers of religious instruction in the country's state schools to local bishops; or abolishing the special tax which Church seminaries had hitherto had to pay on their assets. But Mussolini too was not going to be outflanked. The Fascist press started publishing articles threatening violent attacks on Catholics, even reprisals against all the churches in Rome; such atmosphere of unrest enabled Mussolini to step in in the role of the peacemaker who could restore order. He realized that the negotiations with the Vatican would be long-drawn-out and would require a whole series of manoeuvres in order to align the two sides, including the involvement of his own family.

The first step took place on a visit to Milan in the spring of 1923; it was a private visit, but Mussolini also had an eye on its public effects. Together with his brother Arnaldo, he arranged for his three children – Edda, Vittorio and Bruno – to be baptized at a ceremony which took place in his apartment. Arnaldo and the journalist Manlio Morgagni were the godfathers, while Don Colombo Bondanini, a priest who was a brother-in-law of Arnaldo's and therefore known to the family, presided. There was also a secondary political purpose for Mussolini in establishing good relations with the Vatican and making the first moves towards what would eventually become the wide-ranging and historic agreement known as the Lateran Pacts: it would weaken the anti-Fascist stance taken by the Catholic People's Party and so precipitate it into a crisis which would leave it politically powerless. Whenever anyone mentioned the name of Don Sturzo in Mussolini's presence, he would stiffen indignantly and pour scorn on the priest turned politician. Don Sturzo was forced to resign in the summer of 1923. The Vatican marginalized him by sending him to the monastery of Monte Cassino, from where he chose to go into voluntary exile, at first in London and then the United States.

Margherita Sarfatti's influence also lay behind Mussolini's attempts to establish a rapprochement between Fascism and the Catholic Church. She believed that religion must be part of the Fascist state; by including the Church the regime would be able to assume its rightful role as the interpreter and restorer of Roman and Christian civilizations.

> For Sarfatti the ideological construction of the state, the new 'City of the Future' (not to be confused with the new Jerusalem of either the Church or socialism) had to incorporate as a central element its Judaeo-Christian roots. The 'City of the Future' embodied the political religion of the state, seen in a messianic/ Roman perspective. Sarfatti saw the *raison d'être* of the modern state (modern in so far as it embodied a political religion) as residing not only in its religious vocation but above all in the myth of Rome, which included the Judaeo-Christian roots. For this reason it was necessary for the state to avail itself of the Catholic religion, since it could not call itself a universalist state without it.[3]

Mussolini had little time to devote to the theoretical development of Fascist ideology, immersed as he was in the frenetic business of government and the need to read endless documents, keep an eye on the anti-Fascist opposition – as well as those who opposed him within his own party – and maintain sexual relations, however cursorily, with dozens of women. For a long time it was as if he delegated this task to Sarfatti, except whenever he saw the potential political uses of her theorizing and appropriated large parts of it. The shallowness of Mussolini's involvement with the ideological lucubrations of his mistress were revealed when she founded the movement "Novecento" ("Twentieth Century"), which included some of the best-known artists of the time and formed an important part of her overall plan for the development of a distinctively Fascist culture. Sarfatti hoped – for the moment at least – that thanks to the movement she would come to play a leading role in the cultural politics of the new regime. On the occasion of Novecento's first exhibition, not only did Mussolini give the event his formal support, but, persuaded by Sarfatti, he agreed to give a speech at its inauguration on 27th March 1923. The evening was supposed to confirm Sarfatti's role as the undisputed arbiter of the new Fascist culture, but in the event it only revealed Mussolini's superficiality and almost total lack of interest in her project. Mussolini's improvised remarks were faithfully transcribed in the next morning's issue of *Il Popolo d'Italia*, which didn't appear to notice that they didn't really hang together: "There is no doubt that 1900 marks a watershed in the history of modern Italy. We only need to think of the bleak unhappy days of the African campaign, before Italy lay buried under the sand on which so much valorous and generous Italian blood had been spilt. 1900 is also an important date in Italian politics."

It's easy to picture Margherita Sarfatti's frozen mask of a face as well as the embarrassed silence of the artists and intellectuals who were present at what was supposed to be a significant cultural event. No doubt she managed to excuse her lover on the grounds that he had perhaps just arrived, completely unprepared, from some tryst with a woman or an angry argument with some obtuse official, but the other guests, all those who were part of the Novecento group, wouldn't have been able to reason away their amazement and disappointment quite so easily. "Mussolini's speech showed not a trace of understanding Sarfatti's project, as is shown by the banal and comical sentence: '1900 is also an important date in Italian politics' – as if twentieth-century art were confined to 1900 or the turn of the century. [...] One might wish that this episode had planted some misgivings in Sarfatti's mind about the intellectual subtlety of her *leader*'s thought processes. As it is, she already knew his limits, but probably overestimated her ability to change him."[4]

After fulfilling his agreement, no doubt extracted under pressure, to speak at the opening of the exhibition, Mussolini showed no more interest in his mistress's new movement. The Fascist hierarchy took note of his lack of involvement and started to distance itself from her, as it waited for the right moment to strike and destroy her. Not one of the *gerarchi* understood what she was trying to do. On the contrary, they all hated her, above all for her closeness to Mussolini, which meant she knew many secrets and could in turn exercise influence over him.

In March 1923 Mussolini was still living in an apartment in the Grand Hotel; the security escort which had been assigned to him was something of a hindrance to his sexual escapades. No sooner did he leave his suite than he would find himself surrounded by a kind of itinerant circus: in the entrance halls, in rooms, alongside the Royal Guards there loitered "*squadristi*" bristling with knives and provincial *ras* who would confront strangers with pointless

pugnaciousness, gentlemen of fortune in search of a post, and fanatical female admirers prepared to do anything to see him. He could
no longer draw a curtain of discretion over the comings and goings
of his various mistresses by having them use the staircase reserved
for the hotel staff. To her increasing annoyance, even the refined
Margherita Sarfatti had to climb noiselessly up and down the service
stairs. Something was changing in the privileged relationship she had
constructed with Mussolini, and she was beginning to wonder what
she might do about it.

Mussolini's rapid and sensational political success had led to new
sexual opportunities for him: he could now indulge in as many relationships as he wanted. Obviously, with the pressures of his new
job, he could only spare a few minutes for such diversions, but this
only encouraged his preference for rapid sex at any hour of the day
or night. He called on the services of one of his mistresses at seven
in the morning. He was still attracted to Sarfatti and enjoyed his
relationship with her, both physically and intellectually, but it was a
relationship which demanded time, time he no longer had to spare.
As the months passed by, he began to realize that even when he did
have free time he didn't necessarily want to spend all of it with her.
He appreciated her advice and enjoyed the relaxing physical and
psychological intimacy she gave to him, but he felt he was changing,
that he had less need of her. Now it was enough that she came to see
him, as she continued to do, regularly and obstinately; he less and less
wanted to seek her out. Then he found he didn't mind if they didn't
manage to meet for several days but only spoke on the telephone.
Then a very significant change took place: Margherita Sarfatti could
no longer go and see him when she wanted. Even she, now, had to
wait in line to be received by him. However, on the increasingly rare
occasions when he wanted to see her and she wasn't immediately
available, he lost his temper and bombarded her with abuse. She
remained his confidante, the only person he could ask for advice
without feeling weak or ridiculous, but he wanted absolute control
over her. Even so, the intervals between their meetings lengthened,
and in the meantime he voraciously pursued other sexual adventures.

One night his loyal factotum Cirillo, who'd been the office boy at *Il
Popolo d'Italia* but had changed jobs with Mussolini's advancement,
found that his master was not in his room. He raised the alarm; the
police arrived immediately. They discovered that the head of the

Italian government had slipped out of a side door of the hotel onto Via Cernaia and, under cover of darkness, had walked on foot and alone to the Hotel Continentale, where one of his mistresses who had just arrived by train had taken a room. No one dared to disturb him; instead several policemen had to dress as hotel staff and in that disguise stand guard outside his room. Some weeks later, Mussolini again disappeared for an entire day, and on this occasion no one, not even the police, found out where he had gone. Rumours abounded among Mussolini's staff that a mysterious hotel waiter, a shady type, had managed somehow to make contact with Mussolini and take him off for an assignment in a luxury apartment with an elegant woman who was waiting to give him irresistible pleasures. It was a bad failing on the part of the security services surrounding the head of government. Investigations showed that the said "waiter" was not in fact on the staff of the hotel and was an ex-convict, but it proved impossible to find out how he had managed not only to infiltrate the hotel but above all to attract Mussolini's attention to the point that he was able to persuade him to undertake the escapade. The security services made sure the man disappeared. Shortly afterwards, however, in March 1923, "to the great disappointment of the cosmopolitan clientele of the Grand Hotel, who, each time Mussolini entered or left the hotel would crowd into the foyer to watch him and ask him absurd questions, he decided that all the party *gerarchi* should leave the hotels and pensions in the city where they had been staying and take up lodgings in private houses".[5]

Mussolini himself left the Grand Hotel and moved to an apartment in the Palazzo Tittoni in Via Rasella, the street whose subsequent notoriety in the history of Rome and of Italy was due not to the fact that Mussolini had lived there, but because in March 1943 it was the scene of a Partisan attack on a troop of German soldiers which led to the savage Nazi reprisal in the massacre of hundreds of Italian civilians at the Fosse Ardeatine.

Mussolini had ordered party officials to find private houses to live in because he realized that staying in hotels was hardly conducive to the image of stability and normality that Fascism wanted to communicate to Italians. Margherita Sarfatti had found the apartment in Via Rasella and had suggested to Mussolini that he take it. At the same time, she occupied herself with his appearance and the way he dressed. Mussolini had not added to the minimal wardrobe he had brought with him when he caught the train from Milan in the wake of the March on Rome; since then he'd been too busy to bother about such matters, and his clothes were frequently creased or crumpled. His family had stayed – or rather, had been left – in Milan and were not around to provide for his daily needs. There was Cirillo, who now also had to take on the duties of a personal valet, but he could only manage to do so much. At the Grand Hotel they were ready to fulfil their guests' slightest requests – especially if the guest in question was the most powerful man in Italy – but Mussolini, left to himself, was not even aware of the way he dressed or that anything needed to be done about it. Ensuring a continual supply of women was more important. He boasted to Claretta Petacci that he had had sex with four women every day in an alcove in his hotel suite while he stayed there – countesses, princesses, wives from wealthy bourgeois families, among others – and if they turned out to be sexually inexperienced, that was just too bad. Even if we reduce the figure in Mussolini's boast to a mere half or even quarter, the traffic in women must have caused some public embarrassment. No doubt the hotel staff, the porters and chambermaids, could be relied on to be discreet – except that the chambermaids themselves were at risk... Margherita Sarfatti realized how dangerous the situation might become and, since she also knew that Mussolini would never make a decision, took one for him: an ordinary apartment and, above all, an experienced housekeeper would solve the problem.

She soon found a suitable one in Milan. Cesira Carocci was originally from Gubbio in Umbria but had moved to the city to find work as a cloakroom attendant in a big hotel. She came from a peasant family and was a hard worker and a good cook; she kept the house as clean as a pin, had a robust and energetic constitution, was untalkative and discreet, and – last but not least – hadn't, according to Sarfatti, the slightest whiff of sex appeal about her and therefore presented no risk from that point of view. "It is natural that Margherita should bother about making the daily existence of Mussolini, who at the time was still Prime Minister and not yet the Duce, more comfortable. But as his principal mistress she was well aware of her numerous rivals – and she herself was hardly a model of fidelity – and nothing suited her purposes better than having a reliable informer to follow his every movement."[6]

Sarfatti had no intention of competing with Mussolini's other mistresses or of trying to stop his other occasional escapades, but

she wanted to keep the situation under control so that her own leading position as the favourite, the first lady of the harem, his closest
counsellor, was maintained. The ideal solution was to place in his
home a reliable person she herself had found. The comings and goings of Mussolini's mistresses were always frequent and sometimes
bordered on the chaotic. Cesira was to observe the goings-on with
maximum discretion and duly report back. She herself could certainly not be described as attractive: she was thirty-nine – well past
the age after which it was normal at the time to describe women as
"old spinsters" – but she was tall and thin, with a clear white com-
plexion; she held herself well and dressed soberly and elegantly;
all in all, she was what might be called a "handsome woman". Her
role as "guardian of the threshold" soon made her unpopular with
everyone. Mussolini's mistresses – whose arrivals and departures she
organized – spoke ill of her, and various Fascist officials criticized her,
often slanderously, when she denied them entry to Mussolini's private
rooms. She was most often attacked as a "procuress", since it was
thought she was responsible for the supply of women for the Duce's
bed. Other scandalmongers wondered what kind of relationship she
had with Mussolini. As we have seen, physical attractiveness was not
an overridingly important consideration in Mussolini's choice of
women, so it is possible that she serviced his needs in the intervals
between other lovers. "She was authoritarian and highly protective
of her role. She certainly developed a deep fondness for her difficult
and cantankerous master, who returned her affection and gradually
came to rely on her."[7]

There was a rectangular entrance hall, then a long corridor which
led to the large drawing room, after which there was the bathroom
and the dining room with two antique cabinets, where Cesira had
laid a frugal supper, according to his instructions. When Mussolini
returned from the opening of the Novecento exhibition on 27th
March 1923, the new apartment and the new routine of living in it
were still unfamiliar to him, but his housekeeper, silent and efficient,
seemed perfect for the job. It is highly improbable that Mussolini gave
any further thought to Novecento, the project that so absorbed his
mistress. There was nothing in it which he could exploit to achieve
his pressing political goals – such as weakening the People's Party or
wooing dissident factions in other parties over to the Fascists. Since
coming to power he had managed to destabilize the entire party

spectrum in parliament. This was what politics was really about, this was what he had to do. Now he turned his attention to changing the electoral system: a new one was needed, capable of guaranteeing him a solid majority, thus freeing him from the need to make alliances with other parties. The speed and freedom with which he acted left other political leaders standing. He trusted no one and kept everything under his personal control, with the result that he spent each day reading or skimming dozens of newspapers and piles of documents of various kinds – reports, memoranda, letters – as well as receiving large numbers of visitors, from ministers, leading party officials and city prefects to a queue of petitioners.

Much of this work in the normal course of affairs would have been delegated to senior civil servants and their respective staffs; he preferred to tackle it himself. Each day was tiring and, in the end, for a head of government, essentially unproductive. Mussolini placed a lot of trust in his instincts: in effect his intuitions had served him well in his career so far. By merely skimming a newspaper article or official report he was able to grasp its political implications and possible consequences. In his increasingly solitary eminence as dictator, in the attitude of distrust, bordering on contempt, he showed towards his close associates, and with his lack of friends, apart from his brother Arnaldo, Mussolini wanted to control even administrative minutiae, as though he were the mayor of some small village. He described himself as the nation's ox – or, in a letter to D'Annunzio, as its mule – overburdened with all the tasks that others failed to perform. He complained if the problems of an aqueduct or a nursery school kept him from more important questions of foreign policy, but nevertheless continued to insist he took personal control over everything. He was always short of time but spent hours on end reading hundreds of official reports on all aspects of national life and writing comments in the margins of newspaper articles. In his own hand he wrote communiqués, denials, articles, memoranda as well as résumés of official audiences or events that he had attended for publication in various newspapers, and he always checked that they all duly appeared.

In her biography *Dux*, Sarfatti presents an idealized portrait of all this frenetic activity. "How do you manage to do so much?" she asks him (using the Fascist preferred polite form of address "*voi*"), to which he replies, in words she has doubtless embellished:

You're right, it's as if a thousand different problems, all of them urgent, are continually hammering away to get in my head. I sometimes think my brain will literally burst. But now I've got all Italy in my head, like a great map of the country with all the places where there are problems marked on it: here a road, there a railway line, a bridge, a forestry plantation, docks and marsh drainage; the transport links between the suburbs and a mainline station in Milan, housing in Rome, the water supply in Apulia, residential development in Calabria and Messina, a motorway network in Sicily, the fight against malaria in Sardinia.[8]

At the top of the list of the Fascist regime's achievements can always be found the reclamation of the marshes and the creation of new towns to encourage the mining and agricultural industries, followed by various public works such as railways and railway stations, town squares, canals. The failures and the aborted projects are never mentioned. After a visit to Sicily Mussolini confided in Sarfatti: "I can't sleep for thinking of those disgraceful shacks which, fifteen years on from the earthquake, are still housing the victims! I'll burn them down one by one as I put up new houses."[9] The survivors of the earthquake in Reggio Calabria and Messina in 1908 were still living in wooden huts provided by international aid. It should be added that no democratically elected government managed to solve the problem either, although over the course of the decades various families rebuilt their houses relying on their own initiative and the money sent from relatives working overseas; even today, more than a century after the earthquake, some of the original huts are still standing and are occupied by new generations of the poor.

Mussolini frequently travelled throughout the country, stopping in places and taking rapid notes of the local problems, reassuring the inhabitants that he would deal with them, and then moving on to the next appointment. He always carried a notebook and pencil with him. If, as he drove along, he saw something that was out of order or didn't work properly, was broken or dirty, he immediately noted it down. His chauffeur writes that people feared Mussolini's notebooks as a kind of "black book". The local officials who were supposed to be responsible for the faults he had noticed – for the most part they were completely unaware he'd driven through their towns and villages – would promptly receive a personal reprimand from the head of the government himself. Potholes, trees blown over in the wind, weathered road signs which had become illegible, housing constructions left half-finished... every trip Mussolini took round Italy was a potential nightmare for the civil engineers responsible for the maintenance of the roads or the councillors of some small town or the civil servants in the Ministry of Public Works.

On his travels Mussolini liked to be recognized by people, and therefore often used an open sports car to get about. In sun or rain or harsher weather, there would always be a small crowd at every crossroads to applaud him on his way. Drivers in those days often had to wait a long time at level crossings for trains to pass through, and Mussolini was no exception; he would use the delay to get out of the car and talk to any people who were around. "On one occasion the mayor of a village in Sicily came up to the car. 'We do not ask you for anything. You will probably never pass this way again, so please take this opportunity to get out and walk on our land.' Another man, a local small landowner, wearing a magistrate's ceremonial stole over his Sunday-best suit, approached him. 'This morning at dawn my two brothers who died in the war appeared to me in a dream and told me, "Get up to go and meet the leader, kneel in front of him and tell him that we give him our blessing, we the silent dead, and we thank him for saving the country for which we died."' Taking his hat off, he kneeled on the main road, while around him women burst into tears and stretched their arms out imploringly."[10]

Such extreme, quasi-religious exaltation of the figure of Mussolini explains in part why his myth disintegrated so rapidly after his fall in July 1943. In the space of a few hours crowds started to smash statues and burn portraits of him, and rip away Fascist emblems from buildings – an inevitable reaction to the years in which Mussolini had been cloaked in a kind of religious aura – the omniscient, omnipotent and almost omnipresent Duce. Sarfatti, one of the few intellectuals who hoped to invest the figure of the Fascist dictator with real cultural significance, had foretold the danger: "This miracle-hungry state of mind can feed the legend and even create the longed-for miraculous event, but the insidious menace of disappointment lies beneath. The stature of a man can also be measured by the myth, the self-image he projects, as by the devotion he inspires in others, but there must always be a fear that the sheer accumulation of the excessive hopes which are placed in him will end by pulling him down."[11]

In addition to his frenetic activity as head of the government, managing director and mayor of the village called Italy, Mussolini also had to fit in his assignations with his numerous mistresses, even though these encounters often took no more than a few minutes, sometimes without even bothering to lie down, with Mussolini still wearing his boots. He also had to find time to write letters to the various women so they could be kept "warm" in case of future need; Angela Curti's daughter comments on one her mother received: "Mussolini had already moved to Rome, and a letter he wrote to my mother must date from that period. She read it to me from time to time, and one sentence in it struck me: 'I like being in Rome, but I'm weighed down with work here.' And he went on to say that he didn't know when or how he could return to Milan."[12]

Given that he was not going to go back to Milan, Bianca Ceccato, his former secretary in the offices of *Il Popolo d'Italia*, decided to join him in Rome. Immediately on her arrival Mussolini invited her to supper in his new apartment in Via Rasella. Moving from the dining room to the bedroom, however, now meant getting into his housekeeper's good books. Bianca Ceccato soon managed this; on occasions she brought along her little son who charmed Cesira, or gave her small presents which flattered her sense of her own importance. She even became a trusted confidante of the dour Umbrian: "The recollections of Bianca Veneziana (the pseudonym used by Bianca Ceccato) seem accurate. They confirm that if Cesira Carocci maintained privileged access to Mussolini for Sarfatti, she did the same for the young woman from Milan, which demonstrates that however great her loyalty was to the former, she was more devoted to her new employer. Bianca describes herself, naturally enough, as being a frequent visitor to the apartment in Via Rasella."[13]

It is not possible that Cesira Carocci concealed the increasing number of women visitors to Mussolini's apartment from Sarfatti. She would have had to own up if Sarfatti had interrogated her, but in any case she had no reason to act against the interests of the woman who had found her the job and was in some sense her protector. It is more probable that Sarfatti was unconcerned by the arrival of Bianca Ceccato or any of the others who made their way into Mussolini's bedroom. She felt confident that her physical appeal would continue to entice Mussolini whenever she wanted. The depth and complexity of her relationship with him – qualities that the writing of her own biography of him has served to confirm – was itself a reassurance to her. She was focused on his political activities in the attempt to see a consistency or overall significance in them (and where she couldn't, to paste over the cracks by inventing).

Mussolini's rapid and overwhelming advance to power concentrated above all on control of the press. The newspapers which supported him sang his praises, while the more moderate titles feared and tolerated him; the opposition press, however, was the object of constant pressure, threats and raids. In December 1923 a wealthy Fascist supporter bought up the building which housed the editorial offices of *Avanti!*, together with the printing works where the paper was produced. He intended, in a gesture – a kind of present – he thought would please Mussolini, to force them to move out, but Mussolini refused the offer and stopped him from going ahead with the idea. He knew how the world of the media worked and had no wish to create heroic martyrs for the opposition and potential problems for his political plans. But he also knew from his own experience as an editor how newspapers begin, flourish, and decline, and he made sure the sources of the Socialist Party daily's financial backing began to dry up.

Using all the means at his disposal – violence, blackmail, threats, undercover agreements – with the utter cynicism so characteristic of his political strategy, Mussolini won a significant victory in parliament: the new so-called Acerbo law on electoral reform was passed on 21st July 1923 by 223 votes to 123. The new electoral system would guarantee the party with the largest share of the vote – assuming that share represented a minimum of twenty-five per cent – two thirds of parliamentary seats, a secure and solid majority. The news was "celebrated" by the Fascist squads with an outbreak of violence largely aimed at the constituency offices of the People's Party and Catholic clubs and associations; its culmination was the murder of the priest Giovanni Minzoni in Agrigento in Sicily. Three days after the murder, an international incident gave Mussolini an opportunity to play the strong national leader. On 27th August an Italian military unit that was carrying out checks on the Greek-Albanian border on behalf of the League of Nations was the victim of an ambush in which its commander, Enrico Tellini, and three other soldiers died. Mussolini accused Greece of carrying out the ambush and demanded that a formal apology be sent within twenty-four hours, and that they hold a ceremonial funeral for the victims, including a formal act of homage to the Italian flag, an inquiry into the incident resulting in the death penalty for the guilty and the payment of compensation amounting to fifty million lire. The Greek government denied all responsibility for the incident. Mussolini moved with characteristic speed, leaving no time for reflection, and on 31st August bombed and occupied Corfu. It took a month of Italian and Greek diplomatic negotiations to resolve the situation, with a general secretary from the Italian Foreign Ministry, Salvatore Contarini, a man who spent his career sorting out other people's messes, making a special effort to achieve a solution. Public servants like Contarini did their utmost to protect state institutions and were often used by Mussolini in preference to Fascists who were known to be incompetent. Mussolini agreed to withdraw from Corfu only on 27th September, when he was certain he had extracted the maximum benefits from the crisis in terms of domestic politics.

Rome, 29th September 1923. Today at 13.00 the director general of the Bank of Italy has informed the Ministry for Foreign Affairs that it has received a telegram from the National Bank of Switzerland, authorizing the Bank of Italy to transfer to the Italian Treasury, on behalf of the Greek government, the sum of fifty million lire received in deposit. With this transfer of money the crisis, at least from the financial point of view, is definitively resolved. It has also been agreed that the Italian government will continue to make diplomatic efforts to persuade the Greek government to track down and punish the perpetrators of the atrocious massacre which took place at Ioannina. In proof of the fact that the Italian government, in asking for and obtaining the sum of fifty million lire, was not guided by its own financial interests but wished to impose a sanction for reasons of political morality, His Excellency the Prime Minister of Italy has issued instructions that ten million lire immediately be placed at the disposition of the Sovereign Military Order of Malta to distribute in aid to the Greek and Armenian refugees from Asia Minor who are now in Corfu and elsewhere in Greece.[14]

Public opinion and a majority of the parliamentary deputies backed Mussolini's show of strength, and saw it as evidence that Italy was beginning to play a role once more in the Mediterranean – the Romans' *mare nostrum* – as a sphere of influence which it was entitled to dominate after its victory in the war. There was a wide social consensus backing Mussolini's actions: the man of strength was seen as making the entire nation strong. "The Fascist government strives to give Italy and all Italians in the Old and the New Worlds, wherever

their energetic wanderings have taken them, a strong sense of being
Italian, directed but also supported by a strong government. The
occupation of Corfu, though the event itself played out rapidly, was
nevertheless a worthy and indispensable consequence of this new
sense of pride in Italy's reacquired dignity."[15]

The admiration for Mussolini's show of strength was marked by
his receipt of some unusual gifts. Cesira Carocci opened the door of
the apartment in Via Rasella to take delivery of one; for a moment
she didn't realize what was happening. An enormous cat leapt on
her and then ran into the house. She fainted, and it was only after
she came round that she found out a circus owner had decided to
present Mussolini with a female lion cub. The Duce called her "Italia", arranged living quarters for her in the drawing room and started
to talk about what she got up to as if she were a puppy rather than
a lion cub. The news spread through the whole country, and in his
enthusiasm Mussolini took to walking her on a lead through the
streets of Rome. He boasted he could control her merely through
the power of his gaze. Nevertheless, neither his housekeeper nor his
mistress was pleased with the gift: Cesira thought that the animal
would dirty the house, and Margherita Sarfatti thought it would
make Mussolini look ridiculous. One day Italia tore one of Mussolini's leather jackets to shreds and, finally realizing he wasn't dealing
with a puppy, he reluctantly had her transferred to the Rome zoo.
He continued to pay her visits; he would enter her cage to touch her
and come out thinking he smelt like a lion. Sarfatti added the image
to the myth she was constructing in her biography. Many years later
Mussolini recalled the lion in talking to Petacci: "She was beautiful.
When I entered her cage, pam! – she would stand up on her hind legs
and put her front paws on my shoulders and start digging her claws
in. Then I would suddenly wrestle her to the ground. There were
always people watching, they would be frightened, and the women
would scream when she jumped up."[16]

Mussolini enjoyed another opportunity to play the strong man on
the international stage when he secured, in March 1924, the definitive integration of Fiume into Italian national territory. The King
awarded him the Order of the Annunziata, the highest honour he
could bestow, for this widely acclaimed achievement. The success
not only bolstered his growing reputation but occurred on the eve
of the general election on 6th April. Mussolini had been responsible

for the idea that the Fascists should present a single countrywide list of candidates – known as the "big list" – and made sure that his approval was needed for all the names on it. Naturally much was made of his international successes in Corfu and Fiume during the campaign, while Fascist violence against the opposition parties increased even further in intensity. Democrats, Socialists, members of the People's Party and even dissident Fascists were attacked, beaten up and sometimes murdered. Hundreds of trade-union and party offices and associations were destroyed. The forces of public order were sent in to break up political meetings. In a particularly notorious incident, one of the opposition's most distinguished figures, Giovanni Amendola, was attacked and beaten to within an inch of his life.

A few days before the election, Mussolini went on a visit to Milan, officially to take charge of the local campaign in the city. Cesare Rossi paints a different picture:

> Mussolini was going through one of his not infrequent phases of sexual excitement, during which he paid scarce attention to government business and then only with the greatest reluctance. He chose to sleep in the prefecture rather than with his family in their new apartment in Via Mario Pagano. He spent every evening with Margherita Sarfatti until the exasperated Rachele decided to take herself off to Forlì, together with the little Bruno. [...] Dr Binda, a friend of the family as well as their doctor, called on me and told me without explaining why that I should leave immediately for Forlì. [...] I thought some argument must have broken out in the local party over the distribution of the preferential votes – the *ras* hated elections and always got worked up at any threat to their status and the little fiefdoms they controlled – but he then clarified: "Signora Mussolini has stormed off, you must go and bring her back."[17]

Mussolini was present in the room when this conversation took place; although he was not part of it, he immediately caught its drift and going over to the two men stopped them from doing anything to bring Rachele back. He told them not to worry, that his wife would return of her own accord. It was just one of her usual fits of unreasonable jealousy. Mussolini was completely unconcerned about any possible effects such a domestic scandal might have on his electoral prospects. He had secured considerable financial backing for an aggressive electoral campaign from industrialists and landowners. He was also using his private militia, though he took care not to be seen to be involved personally in what they got up to. He easily won the election with his "big list": out of seven million votes cast he received 4,653,488, to which he was able to add 347,000 from other Fascist splinter groups. Under the new electoral system introduced with the Acerbo law, Mussolini ended up with 375 deputies in parliament, against only 161 for all the opposition parties put together. It didn't escape Mussolini's attention that the opposition had won the majority of votes in the north of the country, from the workers in the industrial heartlands of Piedmont, Liguria, Lombardy and the Veneto. The spread of violence had served his purpose, but at the same time had strengthened the position of his internal opponents within the party, the local *ras* who sent their squads to carry out attacks and then arranged for the murderers to evade justice.

As prime minister Mussolini now enjoyed an unprecedented parliamentary majority, but he was also exposed to divisions within the Fascist Party. He started to send covert signs to the opposition parties that he was interested in creating openings for them in his government, even with a position for a leading socialist figure such as Turati. The King, Victor Emmanuel, was aware of Mussolini's efforts once more to adjust the balance of the party towards the left, as his son, the future Umberto II, in an interview given long after the fall of the regime, recalls him saying:

I knew what was going on, and I must say I wouldn't have been scandalized if he had succeeded. The future for Italy would have turned out very differently without a doubt. Nor would my father when he was king have been dismayed – the word socialism, in the constitutional sense, didn't frighten him. The entry of socialists into the Fascist government would have benefited enormously the great mass of workers, who would no longer have been vulnerable to political exploitation by revolutionaries and who would have seen their role in the country's economy recognized on a par with that of the entrepreneurs. I believe that Mussolini by then had given up all thought of revolution, except when it came in useful in his speeches, and had opted instead for a cautious process of gradual reform in order to avoid putting the fragile recovery of the country's economy at risk. It was unfortunate that not all his associates, as you know, agreed with his point of view...[18]

Mussolini's contacts with reformist socialists – in the Partito Socialista Unitario (United Socialist Party), which had split from the Italian

Socialist Party in 1922 – proceeded cautiously, with secret agreements and official denials. Some among the United Socialists started to demand that Mussolini "lay his cards out on the table", in other words that formal negotiations should be opened so it could be seen what the government's real intentions were in the matter. Unconfirmed rumours abounded as Mussolini held meetings with Bruno Buozzi and other leading Socialists and the more extremist factions among the Fascists grew increasingly restive. Other figures were brought into the party, D'Annunzio among them. A trade-union delegation went to visit him at his home in Gardone in the hope that his presence might help to bring about a reunification of the country's unions, much to the alarm of a Fascist like Roberto Farinacci, who feared the potential effects of D'Annunzio's prestige. Farinacci declared that any move towards a united trade-union front could only come about if all other political forces "unilaterally" agreed to submit to the Fascists in power.

Mussolini was on an official visit to London at the time, but was kept informed of what was going on around D'Annunzio. In September 1923 he had assigned a police officer, Giovanni Rizzi, to watch over D'Annunzio, ostensibly to protect him but in reality to spy on him and report back on his activities. The reaction of some elements in the Fascist Party to what was happening forced Mussolini to intervene before the situation got out of hand and he was no longer able to control it. While still in London, he issued an official denial that he was seeking a political agreement with the Socialists and declared that he would block any move towards trade-union unification, but back in Italy he once more started to make tentative approaches towards the opposition and even hinted at what he was doing in speeches in the Chamber. But these attempts came up against two strong opposing forces: the by now familiar intransigence of the extreme right-wing Fascists, the *ras*, and a new opposition from the left-wing, organized round the dynamic figure of the United Socialist leader Giacomo Matteotti. In the interview with Ludwig, Mussolini complained that "[he] had accepted democracy on its own terms and held out to the Socialists the possibility of their joining the government. Turati, who'd just died, might have agreed, but once again the Waldensians and the rest of them let the opportunity slip by, as they had on all the other occasions, because of their obstinate refusal."[19]

Under Matteotti's leadership the socialists' opposition to Mussolini was becoming more outspoken and defiant: it was not just a question of being prepared to fight in defence of the principles of liberty, justice and democracy; they also launched a fierce attack on the regime and its financial supporters in the business world, an attack which had the potential to become the focus for a new wave of organized anti-Fascist protest. On 30th May 1924 Matteotti made what was to be his last speech in parliament, attacking the results of the elections and demanding they were declared invalid; he put the motion to the vote amid tumultuous scenes of shouting and abuse from the deputies. Matteotti's proposal was clearly intended as a provocation, and as such succeeded: he intended to demonstrate to the Fascists that the opposition had roused itself from its stupor after the March on Rome and that he personally would block the participation of any Socialist in Mussolini's government. And this was not all: Matteotti was prepared to launch a series of new and well-founded accusations against the government and its backers. Many years later, in the final period in Salò, Mussolini recalled these days in talking to the doctor Hitler had sent to look after him, Georg Zachariae: "I hoped that the Socialist Party under Matteotti would join my government: I knew many of them, and it was my belief that with their energy they had a lot to contribute to the Fascist movement. My contacts with them were very close, so close that I hoped it was only a matter of days before I could greet some of them as colleagues round the cabinet table."[20]

Matteotti had already been attacked violently by Fascist squads. He had been subjected to torture and sexual abuse, but refused to be silenced. On the contrary he had already declared he would give a speech in parliament denouncing the links between Fascist politicians and the world of business and finance which Mussolini had created. But he never gave it: on 10th June 1924, in the centre of Rome, near the Tiber, he was kidnapped by a squad of Fascist thugs under the command of Amerigo Dumini. They were members of a newly formed secret corps which had been created in the wake of the elections on 6th April, apparently after Mussolini had remarked that the party needed an internal police force. How this internal corps was organized and who belonged to it have never been properly clarified. It was known as the Fascist Cheka, after the name of the

Bolshevik secret police. Mussolini always denied its existence while at the same time Cesare Rossi, his right-hand man – and the head of the party's press office – was secretly setting it up, recruiting its members and planning its first operations. At half-past four on that June afternoon, Dumini, one of Rossi's close collaborators, and other members of the Cheka forced Matteotti into a car that belonged to the editor of the newspaper *Corriere italiano*, Filippo Filippelli. Matteotti disappeared, never to return. The opposition rose up in protest. Many Fascists left the party. What was left of the free press launched an attack. Mussolini was increasingly isolated, his regime tottered, and the country held its breath.

Chapter 14

The Art of Power

The weather had turned bad: it was sultry, the sky was livid. And it kept getting worse. If only one of those summer storms would come – a torrential downpour, announced by a couple of gusts of wind, followed by a sudden darkness, and then echoing crashes of thunder and a deluge of rain which cleans the streets. Instead the tension remained in the air. He wished he could disappear. A chauffeur sees and hears everything, and yet must become invisible at the steering wheel when necessary. But he couldn't. He had to keep an eye on his boss, who for some days now had been going around with a grim face, as if ready for a funeral or a fight, sitting alone on the back seat. The police escort car behind them kept a discreet distance, disappearing for a moment every time they went round a corner and then suddenly reappearing. The policemen placed at regular intervals along the route looked bored, but always turned to take a close look at the car as it sped by. As soon as he opened the door for his important passenger to get in the car, Boratto had smelt his bad breath and put it down to problems with digestion. He'd been like this for a week; the halitosis was strong enough now for Boratto to smell it from his seat in front. As the car drove towards the parliament building, turning the first bend in the Via Veneto, he looked in the rear mirror and no longer saw him in the back. He slowed down so he could turn round and take a proper look. Mussolini had slumped to his knees with his face barely raised. His skin was grey, his mouth was set and his eyes squeezed tight as if in pain. He tried to get up, pressing both hands down on his stomach. Boratto stopped the car, the police escort drew up alongside immediately. Mussolini didn't even see his chauffeur's hand stretched out to help him. As he slowly fell to his knees again, he vomited. He tried to hold back but couldn't. Boratto saw he had vomited blood and realized he needed to be got home as soon as possible. He gave him his own handkerchief, placing it over his knees, got back in and drove off. It was difficult to get him out of the car as he was bent double – Boratto called Cesira down to help him. Under the protection of the police escort, the chauffeur and the housekeeper practically carried him up to his bedroom, where he lost consciousness. His condition seemed serious, and two eminent specialists were called to the house, Giuseppe and Raffaele Bastianelli. When Cesira had called them, they had told her not to wash anything and to leave everything as it was. When they came, they carried out a thorough examination – of the handkerchiefs, his faeces, which were as black as coffee grounds, and the traces of blood in his vomit. They pronounced that he had a duodenal ulcer. Margherita Sarfatti, the only woman apart from Cesira who'd been allowed by his bedside, asked for a second opinion from another specialist, Professor Aldo Castellani, who was also a senator, and wrote off alarmed letters to the minister in charge of Internal Affairs, Luigi Federzoni, telling him how anxious she was. She also brought a famous Jewish doctor, Bellom Pescarolo, to come and see him, another senator. "The problem was his digestion, which he always maintained he had ruined by eating tinned meat during the First World War. After lunch, tea or dinner he would literally be bent in two with stomach cramps. He used to say that the only way to alleviate them was to stretch out on the floor."[1]

Mussolini suffered from ulcer problems for a long time. In the search for specialists to treat him, Alice De Fonseca Pallottelli also became involved, as Gianni Scipione Rossi has shown: "It is somewhat curious that on 26th November 1926 it was Alice and not Margherita who asked Castellani to intervene. Both women seem genuinely worried and express their concern in very similar terms, almost as if – but it can only be speculation – there had been some communication between them. [...] It is obvious that Alice's concerns, like those of Sarfatti's, are both personal and political. But it is not easy to penetrate the mystery that surrounds her."[2]

Mussolini did not really cure himself from this illness, its after-effects and its returns, until he was treated by the German doctor Hitler sent to tend to him in 1943. On first meeting him, Georg Zachariae describes him as being pale, grey-skinned and painfully thin, with sunken cheeks and jutting cheekbones:

He had had a stomach ulcer twenty years before, and from 1940 onwards the disturbances had returned more strongly than ever, despite all the treatments he had undergone. He suffered bad stomach cramps, particularly two or three hours after meals and during the night – they felt as if someone was pressing a fist down on his stomach with all his force. The result was he could hardly sleep and became almost scared to go to bed at night. He also suffered from very bad constipation, which could only be treated with powerful laxatives.[3]

Mussolini wasn't squeamish in complaining to Petacci about the laxatives he had to take. Emptying his bowels had become one of his major preoccupations. He thought having to do so was humiliating, saying that he felt he was nothing more than a digestive tube. "He thinks about the laxative and its effects, with his usual air of amused disgust: 'The good Lord ought to have made us differently, he shouldn't have given us guts. He should have created us to live on air, or made us so that we just absorb the food we eat rather than having to get rid of it...'"[4]

Boratto also had views on Mussolini's relationship with food. "I think Mussolini's illness stemmed from his irregular eating habits. Whenever we travelled in the car, he preferred to eat by buying a packed lunch in one of the railway stations, which he would eat as I drove."[5] In reality, Mussolini was paying the price for the Matteotti crisis with an acute psychosomatic reaction that exacerbated his ulcer, as he explained to Petacci: "Ulcers have psychological causes. I developed an ulcer after the Matteotti affair. It was a terrible period – accusations, suspicions, anxieties, conflicts, moments of outright tragedy. I couldn't sleep at night, the work was so intense. I began to feel pain, and once the episode was over I continued to feel it. One evening I felt ill in bed and vomited blood, then it stopped. I got up to go to the bathroom and vomited up more blood. I fell unconscious to the floor and didn't come round for twenty minutes."[6]

The murder of Matteotti was certainly not the first case where extreme violence had been used against an opposition leader. The Fascist squads had knifed and beaten many politicians, intellectuals, trade-unionists, journalists, even priests. The list of those who had been killed was long, and not one of them had caused Mussolini to lose any sleep. He'd always managed to come out on top, sometimes by playing down the political consequences and sometimes using them to his own advantage. What then was so different about the

"Matteotti affair" that it had such an extreme psycho-physical effect on him? Matteotti's murder was not like one of the by now normal attacks carried out by the squads, which frequently took place more or less on the spur of the moment. It had been carefully planned and had several serious consequences, both direct and indirect, among which was the complete cessation of Mussolini's overtures to the left, leaving an unbridgeable divide between the Fascists and the opposition. The principal aim of the murder was to prevent the United Socialist leader from revealing publicly the secrets that lay behind the regime. Amerigo Dumini, a political killer who used to boast in public of the murders he'd committed, led the small group sent to carry out the assassination. He'd been born in St Louis in the United States and had lived for a certain time in Chicago, long enough to pick up some of the techniques used by the Italo-American Mafia gangs, such as the lightning kidnapping of a victim on the street by bundling him into a car. He had then served as an Ardito in Italy during the war, and at the end of it used his experience in the army to deal in the trafficking of decommissioned weaponry, in which job he made a lot of money for himself, for his protector Cesare Rossi, as well as for the Fascist squads and the Fascist press. This fact alone should dispel any lingering nostalgic view of the Fascist ceremonies in commemoration of war heroes, such as the cult that grew up round Margherita Sarfatti's son, Roberto: behind the rituals and the pennants there were illegal business dealings. The state sold cars and other military equipment, still in very good condition, at discounted prices – or rather at rock-bottom prices – to cooperatives or war-veteran associations that had frequently been set up for the sole purpose of receiving the goods. Behind the veterans associations there were racketeers who appropriated the material and, after cleaning it up a bit, sold it on the market. Behind the racketeers – but not so far behind, since many of them intervened in person – were, often, the Fascists. "In this way Fascism continued to finance itself from the trade in decommissioned weaponry even during the early years of the regime. And it is our conviction that not only Fascism, but Mussolini personally, once he had taken power, did not hesitate to use the proceeds from several sales of war munitions in order to finance himself and his newspaper, especially during the period when Torre was acting as the provisional administrator for the state railways, in other words from early March 1923."[7]

In this context it's also worth recalling that Mussolini's first aeroplane was decommissioned after the war. So Dumini was a trafficker, and behind Dumini there was Rossi, and behind Rossi there was Mussolini, who took good care however not to become too involved in the grey area where politics and illicit business dealings meet and merge. On the other hand, all the people who were moving the money around and distributing it in cash payments – the racketeers, the traffickers, the more or less concealed financiers – wished to be sure that it ended up in the right hands so they obtained the results they wanted. One person alone could provide the guarantee that behind him lay the guiding will and desires of the man at the top; his presence and his name were enough: Arnaldo Mussolini. As Mauro Canali writes in his study of the Matteotti affair, it is hard to find evidence of the business dealings for which Mussolini's brother was acting as a frontman, but "the inclusion of his name on the management board of several businesses shows how willing he was to exploit his family connections".[8]

When the Fascists came to power, their finances took on another dimension. The thought of being in charge of the nation's entire economy had not entered the heads of Mussolini and the men around him. On his return from a visit abroad, which he had taken in Belgium, London and finally Paris, Matteotti had plunged into the study of the complex political and economic background to Italian oil production, and while engaged on this had realized that it would be possible to deal Fascism a mortal blow. Industrial production – in particular car production – was growing rapidly in Italy. In 1922, the year of the March on Rome, Italy had a requirement of 716,000 tonnes of oil, but only produced 10,000. The rest – and it was easy to predict that demand would go on increasing – was supplied by two oil companies, behind which lay the real giants of the oil-production industry: Standard Oil in New Jersey, which controlled eighty per cent of the Italian market, and the Dutch-English company Royal Dutch-Shell, which controlled the remaining twenty per cent. Through a new company, the Anglo-Persian, which had acquired the rights to the oil extracted in Iran, the Royal Dutch-Shell was able to make some advantageous offers to the Italian government, thereby threatening to reduce the American share of the market. As the overall picture gradually grew clearer, Matteotti was able to fit in significant pieces in the jigsaw of complex relations, such as the appointment of Orso Mario Corbino to the post of Minister for the National Economy. The appointment was a clear demonstration of the power of the international oil industry. Corbino had voted against Mussolini's first government but that was now irrelevant. He had ties to American interests: his first act was to scupper the proposal to create an oil company that would function in the international market to defend Italy's real interests. The objective was to keep Italy dependent on external suppliers of oil – in other words, to maintain the profitability of the century's most important business. The threat from Anglo-Persian was countered by a small American company that presented itself as "independent": Sinclair Oil, created from the merger of several individual producers. In signing a contract with this company, it was easy for Mussolini, his minister for the economy and the Fascist *gerarchi* to declare its independence, but the reality was that major American capital lay behind it, since Standard Oil was using the smaller company as a front to protect its own business interests. "Sinclair Oil's request for concessions for exploratory drilling in Sicily and in Emilia was part of a larger, more complex plan of Standard Oil's to maintain its monopoly of the Italian market, threatened by the arrival of Anglo-Persian. To be more precise, it is highly probable that Sinclair Oil was operating in Italy as a front for Standard Oil, as the higher Fascist echelons and Mussolini himself clearly knew."[9]

The powers behind the large oil-industry companies, described by Enrico Mattei in 1945 as the "seven sisters", which operated like transnational governments, were preparing for war among themselves: what was at stake was the control of the rapidly growing Italian market. The top-secret American plan was detailed and bold: Italy must not become a producer of oil, and Sinclair Oil had to reach an agreement with the Fascists whatever it cost. The regime was ready to sign a contract with Sinclair Oil which granted the company exclusive rights to the exploration of vast parts of Italian territory, in effect handing it a stranglehold over the industry – a curious policy for a government which vaunted its nationalist credentials. It was obvious that Sinclair wouldn't find a drop of oil. To win a space in the markets Sinclair paid large bribes to politicians; in the United States an inquiry had been carried out into sums it had paid out during the Coolidge presidency. The American press was on to the affair, and articles appearing there started to raise concerns in Italy over the agreement which was near to being signed. At this point the new Italian ambassador to Washington stepped in; this was the prince Gelasio Caetani, a mining engineer who was still relatively young; he had two degrees from Columbia University and had worked for many years for the Guggenheim family, who were shareholders in Sinclair Oil. He gave his reassurances that the agreement with Sinclair Oil could go ahead. Mauro Canali comments:

> It is curious that the head of the Italian government was so keen to sign an agreement with Sinclair Oil as to neglect some of the basic rules of political prudence. It might be supposed that there were external pressures on him, but if so it is not clear who was in a position to exert such pressure on the Fascist leader to sign an agreement about which in private he expressed serious misgivings, to the point that he refused to meet a representative from Sinclair. The only power at that time which could bring pressure to bear successfully on Mussolini was the monarchy, but it seems improbable that members of the court circle or even of the royal family itself would risk bringing such pressure on a head of government who was still an unknown quantity and who was also notoriously quick to take offence.[10]

Matteotti was venturing into unknown territory, bringing to light the illicit business deals which lay behind the regime, the *gerarchi*'s corruption, the source of the hidden funds which had suddenly financed the Fascist press. The United Socialist leader had discovered the way to bring Mussolini down, and in making his denunciation he would also transform the opposition to the regime, which was increasingly trapped in a sterile political antagonism based on the defence of abstract moral principles. But what Matteotti had discovered made him an enemy not only of Mussolini, but also of the large oil companies. He probably realized this, but decided to go ahead all the same. On the morning he was kidnapped, Matteotti was not due to deliver the usual outspoken criticisms of Fascism for which he had become famous among the opposition ranks. His attack was going to be a new one. Peter Tompkins – the Europe correspondent of the *New York Herald Tribune*, NBC and CBS, and a former secret-service agent who was sent to Rome during the final months of the Fascist regime in order to work with the Resistance – was convinced of this too. Tompkins was not a professional historian, but his investigations are characteristic of the solid intelligence training he had received. According to Tompkins's reconstruction of the events that surrounded the murder of Matteotti, Sinclair Oil had paid bribes to various powerful figures in the regime, from Gabriello Carnazza, the minister for Public Works, and Orso Mario Corbino, the minister for the Economy, to the men who acted as intermediaries between the company and Mussolini, such as Cesare Rossi. In Tompkins's view, their aim was twofold: to maintain the American hold on Italy's demand for oil and to prevent the discovery of oil in Emilia, Sicily and the Italian colony of Libya, and the risk of an upset in the Italian market and the emergence of autonomous oil production. It is true that any hypothetical identification and exploitation of the Libyan oil fields lay a long way in the future, but oil companies are used to taking the long view and ensuring their interests are protected over the long term.

An Italian geologist and geographer, Ardito Desio, had discovered oil in Libya, although he had not guessed at the extraordinary quantities that lay beneath the soil of the Italian colony. In 1938 he brought a bottle of crude oil that he had managed to extract himself back with him to Italy, still preserved by his daughter today in memory of an opportunity which was lost by her father and the whole country. In his reconstruction Tompkins discovered that all the *gerarchi* to whom bribes had been paid were members of the Piazza del Gesù Lodge, the branch which had split away in 1908 and so was no longer "obedient" to the English Lodge. It was men belonging to the English Lodge "The Lion and the Unicorn" who defended the interests of the Royal Dutch-Shell company, and it was probably these same men who gave Matteotti, during his visit to London, the documents revealing the secret dealings which would enable him to launch his attack on the regime. Tompkins is also convinced that the Italian royal family, the other power in the country's diarchy, was directly involved in the affair, an argument which has been sustained principally by Matteotti's son, Matteo, who was only three years old at the time his father was murdered and who later fought with the Partisans and became a deputy in the first post-war parliament in the newly founded Republic. If true, the involvement would explain the King's subsequent actions. Emilio De Bono, one of the four leaders of the March on Rome, a monarchist and at the time of the Matteotti affair the director of the department for Public Security, may have informed Victor Emmanuel of the documents in Matteotti's possession. Tompkins acknowledged that this hypothesis had been made first by Giancarlo Fusco, a journalist who worked for the

newspaper *Stampa sera*, who had based it on a remark made by the
Duke Aimone of Savoy-Aosta in a interview which Fusco published
only in 1978, many years after the Duke's death.

> Aimone had told a small group of officials in 1942 that the real reason Matteotti
> had been killed was because he was carrying important documents proving that
> the King, Victor Emmanuel III, had become a large shareholder in the Sinclair Oil
> Company in 1921, without having to pay a single lira for the shares. In exchange,
> the King agreed to keep the huge deposits of oil which it was thought existed in
> Libya "covered" – in other words, unexplored and unexploited. […] But the real
> plot was devised by Standard Oil using its dependent company Sinclair Oil to
> obtain an exclusive ten-year contract, renewable for fifty more years, to search
> for oil in Italy. The contract was signed by Mussolini and Victor Emmanuel III
> but repudiated by Mussolini when an article by Matteotti was published in the
> English magazine *English Life* a month after his murder, revealing the plot.[11]

At the end of the Second World War, the Duke Aimone of Savoy-
Aosta (the father of the present Duke Amedeo) was trapped by a
British secret-service agent posing as a journalist into making some
indiscreet revelations; for this his family sent him away into a kind of
exile or "internment" in Argentina. He died in obscure circumstances
shortly afterwards. In the second trial for the murder of Matteotti,
which took place in 1946, the Socialist prosecuting lawyer Giuseppe
Paparazzo declared that the man who carried out the killing, Amerigo
Dumini, first buried the documents that Matteotti was carrying
with him under a tree and later sent them to an American lawyer,
Martin J. Arnold, in San Antonio, Texas. Among the documents
Dumini sent to Arnold was also his own memorandum on the affair
that he wrote in 1933. Thanks to an agreement between William J.
Donovan, head of the US Office of Strategic Services (OSS), and J.
Edgar Hoover, head of the FBI, a team of FBI agents photographed
the Dumini dossier in the offices of Arnold & Robertson in San
Antonio and had them classified as secret. The lawyers would have
been in the right to refuse the agents permission to see the files, but
got round the breach in professional ethics by leaving the room for
a while, during which the dossier was left unattended. After Arnold
had died, Tompkins contacted his widow, who remembered the so-
called "Italian file", but couldn't find it any more among the other
papers belonging to her husband which had been stored in the garage.

Tompkins was certain that the file contained not only Dumini's 1933 memorandum, in which the main responsibility for Matteotti's killing was laid at the door of Arnaldo Mussolini, but also proof of the King's involvement. Tompkins died before he could go to Texas to initiate a personal search for the missing file.

Mussolini found himself in the position of an actor having to perform from a script he was not familiar with and in which he had difficulty identifying who the other characters were. Too much was at stake: the hidden manoeuvres of the giant oil companies were beyond his power to control. He saw that he was being increasingly indicated as the person responsible for ordering Matteotti's murder, realized that a solution was beyond even his gifts for political escapology, but in the effort to find a way out fell seriously ill. Once the men in the Fascist Cheka unit had been identified, the investigating magistrates started to trace the close links some of them had with Cesare Rossi, the head of the government's press office, and the Undersecretary of State in the Ministry of Internal Affairs, Aldo Finzi. Both, as close associates of Mussolini, could lead the investigators' trail nearer to him; Mussolini immediately jettisoned them. On 14th June he sacked both Rossi and Finzi – the former was given no right of appeal, but Finzi was asked to go as a scapegoat with the possibility held out of an eventual reinstatement. He also dismissed Caetani as the Italian ambassador in Washington (Caetani was the only one Mussolini re-employed, many years later, as the head of a new Italian oil company, AGIP). Rossi reacted by accusing Mussolini of losing control of the situation. He might escape being identified as the person who ordered Matteotti's killing, but he nevertheless was morally responsible for creating and fomenting the climate of intolerance and violence in which the murder had taken place. In particular, certain remarks Mussolini had let fall, such as "that man shouldn't be allowed to walk free", had easily been interpreted by others as giving a tacit green light to the assassins.

Right from the start Matteotti's disappearance had made Mussolini's position difficult. All the structural elements he'd put in place to underpin the regime were under threat. There was a general impression that he had betrayed his promise to bestow peace, tranquillity, order and security on the country, but to his great good fortune, there was no one capable of transforming this impression into a concrete strategy aimed at bringing down his government. Matteotti was the one man who could have done this, and he'd been removed, a sacrificial victim of the oil conspiracy. The opposition decided to withdraw from parliament in the so-called Aventine Secession, so condemning itself to a policy of non-intervention while it waited for some external event to overturn the political situation, which, however, remained in a stalemate. The King was on a visit to Spain, and his return was eagerly awaited by the anti-Fascists. "What was Mussolini's mood like during these days? We know from several people who saw him on the 14th and 15th of June that he appeared to them deeply depressed and at the same time full of anger, and scared by the sudden absence of support around him. On the afternoon of the 16th, however, Finzi found his mood completely transformed; he was once more full of self-confidence."[12]

A meeting between Mussolini and Victor Emmanuel took place on 17th June and was a disappointment for the opposition. The King limited himself to confirming Mussolini's tactical appointment of Federzoni, the former leader of the Italian Nationalist Association, which had merged with the Fascists, as minister for Internal Affairs. No other business was dealt with. The silence on the Matteotti affair clearly signified that the King had no intention of putting the blame for it on Mussolini. Thus Mussolini was sure that the King would not abandon him to his fate, but would stand by him during the crisis. A second stroke of luck was that he had gained time to work out a new strategy. And a third was that he had immediately offered up plausible scapegoats, deliberately chosen, to pay the penalty for the crime. Rossi realized that he was going to be offered up to placate public opinion when he saw Mussolini's secret police were following him. He escaped in order to avoid arrest and then wrote a blistering attack on his former boss which he sent to the opposition leaders in the Aventine Secession through the offices of the Grand Master of the Palazzo Giustiniani Masonic Lodge (the Piazza del Gesù rival lodge continued to support the government). It is probable that in his meeting with the King Mussolini had agreed that it would be necessary to schedule a parliamentary debate on the Matteotti affair, in the Senate at least. In the course of the debate, held on 24th June, he insisted that the government would remain in place and that he would "implacably" seek for justice to be done. The Senate approved the vote of confidence with 265 votes in favour and only 21 against, leaving the way clear for Mussolini to act.

Mussolini summoned all the deputies who belonged to his majority bloc in the parliament to the Palazzo Venezia and got them to sign a document confirming their support for him. Once he had informed the King of the vote in the Senate and the support of the deputies, he carried out an extensive reshuffle of the government. Yet the crisis showed no signs of abating; even though the opposition had withdrawn from active engagement, there were still signs that in the country at large the regime was haemorrhaging the support it had obtained at the outset. The internal opposition to Mussolini within the Fascist Party, especially from the extremist factions, who regarded him as inept and trapped in the web of his own pointless politicking, was also growing restive. Roberto Farinacci took centre stage by declaring himself to be the representative of the revolutionary Fascism which, starting out from the provincial grassroots, had wanted to conquer the state. Farinacci happened to be a lawyer – by no means a distinguished one – and agreed to act as Dumini's defence counsel in the trial in which he was charged with the planning and execution of Matteotti's murder. Mussolini duly availed himself of the weapon he had already made sure was in place for such an eventuality – he summoned a meeting of the Grand Council in which he declared his support for the "irreconcilable" factions in the party. He declared that in order to resolve the crisis it was necessary to silence the political opposition and also the Italian people. It was an astute move, since it stole Farinacci's thunder by borrowing his views, thus leaving his main rival within the party and the other *ras* grouped around him only limited room for manoeuvre. At the same session of the Grand Council he also made the celebrated assertion – echoed by many subsequent dictators over the course of the twentieth century – that "History" would be the only judge of the regime, adding that if anyone were so foolish as to insist on putting the regime on trial, the entire Fascist movement would rise up in insurrection.

Mussolini's new strategy was still developing when events took another turn with the discovery of Matteotti's corpse on 16th August. The opposition parties stirred again into action. The regime wanted to prevent the funeral taking place in Rome, since it might become a flashpoint for protests which it would be hard to control; however, his widow chose to hold the ceremony in Matteotti's birthplace, the small town of Fratta Polesine, far away from Rome and the centre of political power. A new wave of violence from the Fascist squads broke out in the provinces. During the violence, Armando Canalini, a Fascist Party deputy and representative of the trade-union movement, was shot dead, triggering an uncontrollable Fascist reaction. The second anniversary of the March on Rome took place in an atmosphere of conflict. A delegation of industrialists visited Mussolini to ask him to intervene to normalize the situation and guarantee the freedom for trade-union organization. With the country in crisis and Mussolini's majority threatening to break up, the Chamber of Deputies resumed on 12th November. The opposition, still in purdah, refused to make any countering move; it continued to believe that the regime would collapse because of the moral scandal arising from the various reports and memoranda which were being sent to the King. But the King, who was perhaps less an impartial referee in the game than a secret player, declared the lower and upper chambers of parliament served as his "ears", and without a vote from them he could not act. Thirty years later his son, the future Umberto II, explained: "[The opposition] was wrong in hoping that the King could intervene in the political struggle, it would have been inconceivable! They should not have abandoned parliament, which is the only place where deputies can speak on behalf of the nation, since outside the Chamber they are speaking only for themselves."[13]

In the United States the press had for some time been linking Matteotti's murder to Sinclair Oil's use of bribes. Normally Mussolini is depicted as paralysed during this crisis, but in reality he was wriggling desperately in the effort to find a way out of it. He proposed a new electoral reform which would introduce the system of single representation for individual constituencies, in a bid to see off both the official opposition and the Fascist extremists. The thought of losing their seats caused many deputies to tremble.

The only real countermove of the anti-Fascists was to publish, on 27th December, the first extracts from Rossi's memorandum with his accusations directed against his former boss. The publication caused an uproar. The *Corriere della Sera* suggested Mussolini give up his parliamentary immunity and hand himself over to the judiciary. Even the cabinet discussed the possibility of having to find a successor. But once again, at this climax of the crisis, no one was capable of transforming these feelings into concrete political action. The simmering discontent within the Fascist Party led to a plot being formed. Some of the "consuls" in the National Militia and various extremist groups fell in behind Farinacci and dared to speak out against Mussolini, warning him that his mandate for power rested on the local Fascist sections, and that therefore his actions should follow their bidding. They even quoted the Fascist motto back to him – "*o con noi o contro di noi*" ("either with us or against us") – with the reminder that it also applied to him. In Tuscany ten thousand armed men threatened to revolt; Mussolini was forced to send a group of local *ras* to hear their grievances: either he abandoned his political games or they would withdraw their support for him.

Rossi's memorandum had focused public attention entirely on Mussolini, and the King took advantage of this. Free from attack, he played his part by remaining silent. The opposition failed to find a new leader who was capable of bringing together all those who were prepared to fight the government. In the general paralysis Mussolini once again was the only one who was making the moves. He tried to persuade the King to let him dissolve parliament, as a way of putting pressure on the deputies, but the King was determined to stay on the sidelines and refused to sign the decree, although he implied that he would support the move if parliament voted in favour. Mussolini then decided to take the bull by the horns and resolve the issue with the one weapon in his armoury which had never yet failed him: his oratory.

His speech given on 3rd January 1925 was hard-hitting. He came straight to the point in confronting the deputies. He asked if any of them intended to invoke Article 47 of the Constitution, which gave the Chamber the right to lay formal charges against a government minister. The opposition remained silent, while the Fascists broke out into wild applause. Mussolini continued:

> People say that Fascism is a barbarian horde which has invaded the nation; that it is a movement of bandits and predators! The question of morality takes centre stage, but we're all too familiar with what happens in Italy every time a question of morality arises. You might as well go and catch butterflies under the arch of Titus. Well then, let me tell you this, before this assembly and before the entire Italian people: that I and I alone assume all political, moral and historical responsibility for what has occurred. If saying something which then gets distorted is enough to hang a man, then get the rope and gallows ready! If Fascism is nothing more than castor oil and truncheons rather than being the proud, enthusiastic expression of the finest of Italy's young men, then the fault is mine! If Fascism is merely a gang of criminals, then I am the head of this gang![14]

Once again he had carried it off. As with the March on Rome, the determining factor in Mussolini's victory was the paralysis of the political opposition. After the speech the political climate throughout the country changed rapidly. Mussolini issued a series of strict orders to Federzoni, the Fascist colleague he had put in charge of the Ministry of Internal Affairs, which had the ostensible aim of maintaining public order. Before night had fallen, the prefects in the various regions had closed down 110 clubs and 150 public meeting places, had placed 111 "subversives" under arrest and carried out 655 unannounced raids on private homes. All the opposition parties were affected: the regime had started to place a tombstone over them. They survived for two more years, continuing to hope in some miraculous event which would change the situation. But that day, 3rd January 1925, was the real turning point, the resolution of the long-drawn-out crisis, the watershed marking the end of the first phase of the regime, which had begun with the March on Rome, and inaugurated the second, which would lead to the installation of Mussolini as the country's undisputed dictator.

After she had fled Italy, twenty years on from the events in 1923 and 1924, Margherita Sarfatti, in her memoir entitled *My Fault*, maintained that she had played a significant part in the Matteotti crisis. She decribes Mussolini as being "weak, confused, contrite", even "grief-stricken". In her view, these reactions prove that he had not been informed of the conspiracy to kill Matteotti. After the United Socialist leader's body was found, she says that Giolitti sent the anarchist Virgilio Panella to visit her in order to try and get her to use her influence over Mussolini to persuade him to resign, although such a move seems uncharacteristic of such an astute and sophisticated politician as Giolitti. It is more probable that Sarfatti used her influence to push Mussolini into taking action. Her advice might have helped him in important ways to plan the speech he gave on 3rd January: "You must take up a clear, determined position on this issue; you mustn't hesitate." And she continued to urge Mussolini to take this line: "Keep on saying you're not guilty, that on the contrary Matteotti's murder was carried out as part of a treacherous and sinister plot against you. Make sure the perpetrators are punished like the criminals they are. But, as far as the political consequences are concerned, you can't go on acting the part of the poor innocent who didn't know anything about what his wicked associates were up to. You must clarify your position vis-à-vis the crime, but at the same time accept responsibility for the [Fascist] revolution."[15]

The aristocrat Countess Martini Marescotti, née Ruspoli, tried to take advantage of the uproar surrounding Mussolini during the Matteotti affair to exact her own vengeance on him. She was one of Rome's great ladies of fashion during the Fascist era, and had had no difficulty in getting intimate access to him. She knew nothing, however, of the behaviour which was well known to a restricted circle of *gerarchi* and other close associates: "Mussolini had a fairly contemptuous view of the opposite sex. Once he told me: 'Women prefer men to be brutal, like cavalry soldiers.' So he treated them brutally."[16] The Countess Marescotti found herself the object – like so many others – of Mussolini's rough-and-ready approach to sex; alarmed and disappointed, it seems she decided to take her revenge by putting poison in his food, but he fell ill before she could do anything – with the same illness which the anti-Fascists were hoping would carry him off, since they had failed to defeat him politically.

But the other opposition to Mussolini, the internal one, was more active. Farinacci now presented himself not only as the *gerarca* who had saved Fascism by insisting that Mussolini betray neither himself nor the March on Rome, but also a potential new leader who would lead the way to the real revolution. In the face of Farinacci's pressures, Mussolini seemed to cede ground to him and in a decree issued by the Grand Council appointed him to the leading position of party secretary on 12th February 1925. In reality the intention was to give Farinacci enough rope to hang himself. The ruse threatened to go badly wrong, since on 15th February Mussolini was struck down again with a severe relapse of the duodenal ulcer. The regime's propaganda tried to cover up what was happening. Rachele, who was kept informed, decided to join her husband in Rome. She quickly packed and left for the station in Milan, where she found the city's police chief waiting for her. "He made a proper little speech to me, explaining that if I rushed to the Duce's bedside it would be interpreted as a sign his illness had got worse, which would in turn provoke a new political crisis. In the interests of the country, therefore, it was my duty to stay in Milan. I accepted, somewhat sceptically."[17]

Rachele might be able to accept "reasons of state" for keeping away from her husband, but the fact that he was in the hands of Margherita Sarfatti and of her representative, the housekeeper Cesira, was harder to swallow. Rachele was allowed to visit Rome only in the following year, and before she returned to Milan she extracted a promise from Mussolini that he would stop seeing Margherita Sarfatti as a lover and also that he would have her dismissed as a journalist. Rachele knew about the others – Bianca, Giulia, Paolina, Virginia, Gigia, Fernanda, Eleonora – she had counted over a dozen of them – but they didn't bother her. However, the situation was rather "livelier" than she thought. In an effort to show Claretta Petacci that despite his advancing years his virility remained untouched, Mussolini recalled the period in Via Rasella: "Look at your giant, your big naughty boy, go on, touch him, look at his big hairy chest. I've told you I like screwing around – it's true, I used to be like that. I don't have women any more, I'm chaste by comparison with what I was then. When I lived in Via Rasella, it was like a whorehouse, I had four or five women a day. I can remember almost all of them, like Mercedes who was so ugly you wanted to throw up. She wrote to me the other day, she's working for the Party in Milan."[18]

Bianca Ceccato too, the young secretary who'd worked at *Il Popolo d'Italia*, was a frequent visitor to the apartment in Via Rasella. She and Cesira had now become very familiar with each other to the point that Bianca could ask the housekeeper how frequently the sheets were changed on Mussolini's bed, worried how many times other mistresses had slept in them. "Every three days," Cesira told her – perhaps not often enough given the number of women passing through. Ceccato often brought her little son Glauco with her. Mussolini would give him a moment's attention, but it was enough. Cesira then confided in Bianca that she had noticed Mussolini had tears in his eyes every time he kissed the little boy before he left. By dint of bringing Cesira little gifts, like a blouse from Milan, showing her a certain deference, and spending time in chatting to her, Bianca soon became such a normal part of the household that she took to having long hot baths there, with Cesira to wait on her, and was often invited to lunch, with meals cooked specially for her, given that Mussolini's own diet was spartan. Bianca Ceccato's importance was now such that Sarfatti could no longer easily control her. In any case, Mussolini's relations with the wealthy writer were gradually growing more distant. It is curious that this cooling-off coincided with the publication of the biography of him she'd been working on for over two years. The first edition came out in English in 1925 with the title

The Life of Benito Mussolini, published by Thornton Butterworth. A year later, it came out in a slightly revised Italian version, with the new and more striking title *Dux*. It was an immediate best-seller. It was also translated into French and sold well everywhere. Helped by a Jewish friend and associate, Lisa Foa, Margherita Sarfatti was personally responsible for the book's publicity. She paid special attention to its distribution: she knew that if it were to sell as widely as possible people should be able to buy it not only in bookshops but also in newsagents, especially in stations, where crowds of travellers would come across it. It was not the first book on Mussolini, but the intention behind the writing of it made it more than a straightforward biography: "Compared to the earlier books, *Dux* was the first piece of Mussolini propaganda to have been carefully worked on and put together by means of the author's continual and active promotion of the subject. A close analysis, however, of the book's structure, made up in part of a skilful collage of Mussolini's sayings, reveals more ambitious aims than merely creating an icon of the new man."[19]

Sarfatti skilfully juxtaposes her heroic portrait of the self-made working-class man with a sense of the Duce's erotic dynamism, sensing rightly that this was the central element in his myth and the one which attracted most attention, certainly the one which would lead most people to buy the book. The details in its well-written pages which sketch a priapic cult of the Duce were intended to absorb readers, who would also be aware of the rumour that the book's author had first-hand experience of Mussolini's sexuality. The myth justified the Duce politically, and the Duce, confirmed as supreme leader, justified the state which was based on his person. The aura of political mysticism surrounding the leader is reinforced by elements taken from Catholic religious mysticism. From the sacrality of the Church to the sacred reality of the state: in Sarfatti's view, the religion of Fascism embodied the universal mission of Roman and Catholic civilization. The icon of Mussolini as Sarfatti paints it is not only modern and dynamic, but also spiritual and classical. Having identified this central focus of the new ideology, Sarfatti herself converted to Catholicism in 1928, followed by her daughter Fiammetta in 1931, and two years after that, by her son Amedeo. The rumour circulated among the Fascist *gerarchi*, perhaps started by Farinacci, that she belonged to some powerful and mysterious Masonic lodge or the so-called "Jewish conspiracy". Yet, despite the signs of increasing anti-Semitism, Sarfatti's conversion does not appear to have been dictated by opportunism, but rather undertaken in a spirit of ideological coherence.

> Sarfatti's interpretation of the ideology surrounding Mussolini is so close to the view of the Duce proposed by recent historians that one is tempted to ask a provocative question: how much of this doctrinal apparatus was due to Sarfatti's influence on Mussolini? How much instead is owed to Sarfatti's acute perception of the contradictory but effective ideological compound of elements in Mussolini which recent historians have also begun to submit to analysis? Or, as is often the case, were the two aspects of her talent – the capacity to reinvent and the capacity to read between the lines – combined?[20]

Once the myth of Mussolini had been ordered hierarchically and his sexuality identified as its dominant element, Sarfatti was free to invent and reinvent the character she had created by tracing patterns and forming combinations among the numerous images now available to her. So one episode has Mussolini shifting in a trice out of the image of the "sports-car driver" into the juxtaposed one of "the blacksmith's son". After giving a daring display of his skills in driving dangerously, the Duce's car develops a mechanical fault. In the middle of the Po Valley he needs to find a blacksmith to help him mend it – and Sarfatti then describes the blacksmith's shop where the fire is extinguished and describes how the politician-journalist-aviator starts to work the bellows, the skill with which he handles the iron on the anvil and wields the hammer, to the amazement and admiration of the blacksmith who is looking on, culminating in the triumph when, after no one manages to screw the soldered piece back on, Mussolini takes it and turns it smoothly into place. Margherita Sarfatti knew that the myth needed to be continually nourished with such scenes.

On 23rd March, after he had started to recover from his illness, Mussolini appeared in public to make a short speech. He continued to work, seeing ministers, *gerarchi* and prefects in his apartment. His real return to the political scene took place on 2nd April 1925, by which time his prolonged absence had threatened his hold on power. His thoroughness in keeping tabs on every element in political life benefited him. Farinacci tried to reconstitute the Fascist squads, but came into conflict both with the directives which had been issued by Federzoni as the Minister for Internal Affairs and the chiefs of the National Militia, who resented any challenge to their own power.

Now fully recovered, Mussolini allowed the violence of the extremist groups to create a climate of increasing unease not only among the public at large, but also within the Fascist Party. He played Farinacci like a fisherman plays a catch, gradually showing that the party secretary was by no means free to act as he chose, but was completely dependent on Mussolini's wishes. As Duce and head of the government, it was his orders which had to be obeyed. After having isolated and worn Farinacci down, he pulled in the line with a jerk and had him dismissed from his position on 30th March 1926, although he allowed his adversary to save face by announcing he had chosen to resign. On the same day the Grand Council accepted the resignation and appointed a new secretary, Augusto Turati – no relation to the celebrated former Socialist leader – who was in effect a mere stooge who carried out the Duce's wishes. Mussolini happened to remark one day that "the problem with revolutions is that once they're over the revolutionaries are still around",[21] and Turati duly proceeded to eliminate all the remaining revolutionaries from the party who had become not merely irrelevant but potentially harmful. In just three years 60,000 members were expelled and, according to Renzo De Felice's calculations, a similar number left the party voluntarily.

Mussolini succeeded in warding off the political threats posed by the wave of violence by dealing with it either tactically or uncompromisingly, as well as choosing to intervene as circumstances dictated. In the end the tension, the clashes, the assaults proved more useful for him than for Farinacci, giving him the opportunity to steer ever more forcefully towards a dictatorship which was entirely focused on his own charisma. Each fresh outbreak of violence served to increase his personal power.

One of the most serious episodes took place in Serravalle Pistoiese, where one of the numerous Tuscan squads attacked Giovanni Amendola once again. The deputy was severely beaten up. He took refuge in France, but died less than a year later as a result of the injuries he had received. By giving the squads of thugs and assassins a certain freedom of action and allowing the *ras* to think they could regain their individual autonomy, Mussolini managed to hold off for a year the pressure from the rebellious provincial factions. In addition, by letting Farinacci go ahead and vent his aggressiveness, he achieved a kind of public demonstration that the man was an extremist without any of the skills to become a politician, let alone an alternative leader of the regime capable of gathering and holding together the different forces which converged in Fascism.

While Farinacci strangled himself with the rope Mussolini had given him, the latter was now manoeuvring to concentrate power in his own hands. He was in exuberant form when he spoke to the Senate on 2nd April, putting a definitive end to any hopes the opposition still harboured on the outcome of his illness. The United Socialist leader Turati was forced to admit that Mussolini was "a ham actor of genius". The other Socialists resigned themselves quickly to their hated opponent's good fortune. Quinto Navarra, Mussolini's valet – although it would better to describe him as his personal assistant – writes that during his master's illness "there were rumours that [he] was dead and the truth was being concealed from the country. During that period Cesira was indefatigable and stayed by his bedside for thirteen consecutive days without once going to bed herself."[22] Mussolini's opponents, who had done nothing in the hope that he would die or at least retire from politics, could not have guessed that his new-found strength was due to his housekeeper's tenacity. "Sister Health-Bringer" was the nickname for her which D'Annunzio wrote on a photograph portrait of himself he signed for Cesira. A visit from Mussolini had been arranged to see the poet in his home in Gardone at the end of May 1925. D'Annunzio had been informed that his guest would be bringing his housekeeper with him; familiar with Mussolini's sexual appetites, he assumed this could only mean one thing, and had a large bedroom prepared for the couple, but when he actually met the rather plain Cesira he realized he'd jumped to conclusions and had a separate bedroom arranged for her instead.

Together with Cesira, the chauffeur Boratto was also invited to take the obligatory tour of the vast garden of the Vittoriale, D'Annunzio's residence, which he had turned into a monument to his life and deeds. As you entered the villa a large inscription in block capitals on the façade warned visitors: "Clausura et Silentium" ("Seclusion and Silence"). D'Annunzio was capable of anything, even of imposing monastic rules on his guests. Next to the door there was a curious tabernacle-like construction built into the wall. Seeing the puzzled faces of Mussolini, his housekeeper and his chauffeur, D'Annunzio explained. "He enlightened us over the mystery of the little door in the wall. He pressed a button, at which the door automatically opened and a huge phallus sprang out, much to our surprise and amusement. D'Annunzio told us that he only gave this welcome to his true friends."[23] Mussolini could now afford to be amused by the poet's bizarre behaviour; D'Annunzio no longer threatened to become an alternative *duce* or indeed have any further political involvement.

Before they had to cross a small wooden bridge in the gardens, D'Annunzio stopped them and asked to pay a toll. Mussolini had to borrow the five cents because, as we've seen, he never carried cash on him, either because it gave him the sensation he was superior to everyone else or perhaps out of some strange superstition.

Mussolini tended to be very superstitious. One day he suddenly became angry, seized the tray his valet was handing to him and threw it to the floor: on the tray were the visiting cards of two people who had the reputation of having the evil eye. Another incident occurred when the Duce was presented with boxes sent from Egypt containing reproductions of statuettes and wall paintings. The tomb of Tutankhamun had recently been discovered, and there had been much talk of the misfortunes which had befallen the archaeologists who had violated the pharaoh's sacred space. One night Mussolini couldn't sleep and suddenly remembered the gift; he immediately phoned round his associates and ordered them to get rid of it. Rachele writes that, like many Italians, even educated ones, he refused to sit down to eat at a table where there were thirteen guests; on occasion one of his children would have to go and eat elsewhere to avoid the number. She also mentions that "he used to place his hand over a certain private part of his anatomy, even in public, as a way of warding off misfortunes and jinxes".[24] According to Cesare Rossi, Mussolini was superstitious to the point that he would refuse to associate with many people who would otherwise have been able to make an important contribution to the regime, either because of their professional skills or their enthusiastic support.

After his illness was over, Mussolini started to travel again both on official visits and unplanned ones to various parts of Italy. He would insist on leaving even if the police warned him of possible attempts on his life. Boratto frequently had to drive the car through enthusiastic crowds who wanted to get closer to the legendary figure. While Quinto Navarra confirms that when he was in Rome Mussolini "received" at least one woman a day, he rarely had sexual adventures while he was travelling. "When he travelled his need to approach women disappeared. I noticed this and started to observe this aspect of his behaviour with interest; I became convinced that in addition to the normal attraction a man feels for a woman Mussolini had an even more powerful desire – for the crowd. His triumphal tours across the country responded to this need of his. His interest in women diminished: the continual contact with crowds of admirers fully satisfied his desires."[25]

Mussolini had a constant need to appear in public. His travels, which occupied an extraordinary amount of his time, far more than any other head of state in the period, were the best way to show himself physically to the Italian people: the body of the Duce was displayed for all to admire. Usually a cameraman was present to film the event. "The Duce would stand up in the car and give the Roman salute to the cheering throngs around us. He kept his other hand on my shoulder, and used to guide me through the crowds and tell me when to accelerate or slow down."[26] Boratto was told he should never come to a complete halt – not easy to do when the car was surrounded by a mass of people and some unfortunate person risked getting run over.

In rapid succession, Mussolini assumed interim responsibility for the Ministry of War (on 4th April) and those of the Navy (on 8th May) and the Air Force (on 30th August). All the military ministries ended up under his control. On 14th June he announced the so-called "Battle for Wheat", or the drive to increase wheat production in the country. The campaign was the opportunity for further propaganda and added a new dimension to Mussolini's multifaceted public persona: the "Duce harvesting in the field" with the peasants, his broad chest gleaming under the blazing sun. Mussolini hadn't forgotten that in the middle of the Matteotti crisis a delegation of industrialists had tried to dictate what his political agenda should be; he coolly took his revenge on their presumption with a new proposal: a Fascist trade-union movement.

He told the prefects in the various regions that they were to expect protests for higher pay and other unrest among the workers, and asked them not to intervene, but on the contrary to support the action of the Fascist trade-unionists. A number of so-called "Fascist strikes" took place, especially among the car workers. The industrialists who had come to see him with their claims for autonomy now had to deal with direct action taken by Fascist trade unions. Mussolini was in the position both to confront the industrialists by letting them suffer the consequences of the strikes and at the same time offer himself as an indispensable mediator between the two sides.

The result was the agreement known as the Palazzo Vidoni Pact, signed on 2nd October, in which the industrialists recognized the "Confederazione delle Corporazioni Fasciste" ("Confederation of Fascist Corporations") as the only organization representing their workers and their sole interlocutor in their relations with the unions. For the Socialist and Communist trade-union leaders and the hitherto leading union organization, the General Confederation of Labour (CGL), it was the beginning of what would spell their total extinction during the regime.

Having settled his accounts on terms which were advantageous to him with three of the main interests in Italian society – the armed forces, industry and the Church – Mussolini turned to the press. Threats, expropriations, the closing-down of entire newspaper offices: in a very short time the opposition press was silenced and news of the anti-Fascist cause could no longer reach the militants who continued the battle from the margins and the mass of the Italian people in general. In *Dux*, Sarfatti managed to paint a positive picture of what Mussolini was doing to Italian journalism: "'Journalism' – declares this former journalist who has never completely ceased to be one – 'journalism formed me and helped me to know the humanity, which is the very stuff of politics. [...] You know that I respect journalism – I've shown that I do. I only wish that journalism would take more account of historical necessity, show more awareness of certain historical inevitabilities. I would like journalism to work in collaboration with the nation."[27]

Mussolini instructed the prefects to close down all those newspapers which did not show sufficient awareness of historical inevitabilities. At the same time he ordered the activities of the Fascist squads which were still operating outside the National Militia to be stopped. On 15th May 1925 he conceded himself the luxury – most of his deputies in parliament were against it – of a law which gave the vote to women in local elections. Shortly afterwards local elections were abolished. By now there was a widespread opinion that the only way to have a "moderate" Fascism, envisaged as an alternative to the extremism of men like Farinacci and the *ras*, was to place power entirely in Mussolini's hands and follow on behind – wherever his impulses and decisions and extravagant behaviour led.

Chapter 15

Beyond Good and Evil

"Everything within the state, nothing outside the state, nothing against the state." The practical consequences of the totalitarian formula on which the state – personified in Mussolini – was based soon became apparent to the Sicilian Mafia. The story goes that during an official visit from the Duce to Piana dei Greci (now called Piana degli Albanesi), the mayor-cum-godfather of the town, Francesco Cuccia, introduced himself to Mussolini by telling him that he could be certain of not being disturbed while he was there, because the subversives had already been dealt with. "Your Excellency," Cuccia is supposed to have said, "there's no need for all these security men. You're under our protection here." The popular story might well have some truth in it since Mussolini's reaction after his visit proved to be devastating. During a rapid tour of the island he had grasped the nub of the problem, which was that this was territory controlled by the Mafia. The godfathers ruled there, not the Italian state. The issue at stake was quite clear to him: the Mafia was – as it still is today – a state within the state, a parasite state living off the legal state, a subterranean anti-state. In the small sunny town the *duce* was not Mussolini, but the local boss Ciccio Cuccia. This was intolerable.

Once he had returned to Rome, he summoned Cesare Mori, one of the more energetic prefects, and the same man who had had no hesitation in suppressing the Fascist squads in the period leading up to the March on Rome. Perhaps it was precisely this unquestioning loyalty to the state which led Mussolini to choose him, since he was now the state and he could therefore be confident that Mori would be ready to serve him. Shortly after the meeting Mori was sent to Sicily with full powers to stamp out the Mafia. And he used those powers: he put whole towns under a state of military siege and used torture whenever he thought it was needed, which was often. For the

Mafia, it was the worst time in their history. *Picciotti, capidecina* and godfathers were arrested, beaten up, tortured, executed; their families were persecuted and the survivors forced to flee abroad.

"*Calati, juncu, ca passa a china*", so says a Sicilian proverb well-known to the Mafia: "bend over, reed, and let the tide pass you by". Like the reeds, the Mafia bent over as the full tide of Fascism swept over their heads and waited for it to pass; while waiting they had time to reflect on the superior conveniences of dealing with a democracy and all its apparatus of laws rather than with a brutal dictatorship.

The troubles with the ulcer were over for the time being; the Matteotti crisis had been resolved; Mussolini persuaded a reluctant Rachele to undergo a religious wedding. Neither was a believer, but it was a necessary step to take in the long and tortuous secret negotiations to reach an agreement with the Vatican. The ceremony took place in private, at Easter 1925, in the family apartment in Via Mario Pagano in Milan. According to Boratto, the wedding made no difference to Mussolini's habits: his visits to Milan remained few and far between and always followed the same pattern: a brief drive in the car with his wife and children so they could be seen in public, followed by the evening spent in Margherita Sarfatti's house. During the summer Mussolini wanted to enjoy his two main enthusiasms: women and the sea. "I soon came to realize that Mussolini, when he came to power, had at heart not only the concerns, if we can call them that, of the Italian population as a whole, but also those of a large number of women who needed satisfying."[1]

Margherita Sarfatti moved to Rome – a fortunate change for her. Sometimes Mussolini would take her to dinner at the Casina Valadier, or on a tour of the city's monuments, when they almost always stopped for a long time to gaze at St Peter's Square, while Boratto waited with the car just beyond Bernini's colonnade. On some evenings Mussolini would hurriedly enter Sarfatti's apartment block by the service entrance, while Boratto looked on amused and curious. A few seconds later a furtive figure would leave quickly by the main entrance: the new secretary of the Fascist Party, Augusto Turati. Boratto would often pass the time waiting for Mussolini to reappear by chatting with Sarfatti's chambermaid. She once told him that her mistress was losing some of her physical attractions for the still comparatively young head of government. When Boratto asked her why in that case she thought the Duce still called on her, she replied: "He remains attached to the mother because he's in love with the daughter, who's also crazy about him."[2]

The chambermaid had clearly not understood that Mussolini's interests were aroused by any woman who came within close range of him – whose mother, wife or daughter she was, how old she was, what her social background was like, even whether she was good-looking or not hardly mattered to him. In the space of a mere hour, a war widow had managed to see him, had expressed her fervent gratitude in the manner he could appreciate, and, shortly after leaving his office, obtained the pension she had originally come to see him about – bureaucratic efficiency indeed. But what the chambermaid and the chauffeur couldn't have known as they gossiped was that Mussolini's friendship with Sarfatti was already in decline on a political and intellectual level even before their physical relations had started to wane. With five editions over the space of a few months and its adoption as a school text, *Dux* was bringing in a fortune for its publisher Arnoldo Mondadori. Mussolini and his mistress had made a friendly arrangement to take equal shares in the very large royalties on the book, which also brought in foreign currency from its sales abroad. Yet, despite this, the events of 1925 and 1926 gradually spelt the end for Sarfatti. The first Italian edition of the book had been delayed because Mussolini had lost – or rather deliberately wasted – time by annotating the text with irrelevant comments and withholding his permission to publish. This was an early sign of a growing displeasure on Mussolini's part – which at the time, however, few people succeeded in seeing, so much did Sarfatti's star seem to be at its zenith.

Dux was translated into nineteen languages and became a world-wide bestseller. Perhaps what most disturbed Mussolini in the book was how strongly it conveyed a sense of Sarfatti's qualities and personality. She did nothing to disguise the influence which she exercised over so powerful a man. When she brought out Mussolini's sexual attractiveness, she emphasized at the same time her own sexuality. Cunning, violence, sex, a self-made man who'd built himself up from nothing and the rich and cultivated woman who'd become part of his life: it was a fantastic formula for success, especially as nothing was done to discourage readers from rounding off the picture by imagining the biographer in the arms of her subject. Sarfatti felt that she had created this legend; the politician as artist was her invention – the politician who used power as though it were the supreme art form, the artist who worked with a living material, difficult, shifting, delicate: human beings. "She secretly felt superior to him because she was responsible for what he had become. She was elated and flattered when he took once again to playing her serenades on the violin over the telephone. Her dreams became more and more grandiose. At times she felt like Mussolini's muse and, posing in her robes, saw herself going down in history as the woman who started the second Italian Renaissance. [...] She felt she was the dictatrix of Italian culture."[3]

Margherita Sarfatti was a powerful woman but, under Mussolini's dictatorship, her power proved to be as unsubstantial as a dream. In reality the Duce grew increasingly dissatisfied with her biography of him. He told Petacci that it was the greatest mistake of his life. The transcription of Petacci's diaries in Mauro Suttora's edition published in 2009 contains some omissions, and the edition as a whole suggests there was a certain haste to get the volume into the bookshops in the well-founded expectation it would become a bestseller. No doubt cutting entire days and, here and there, individual lines from the diary was done to shorten a very long book, but often the omissions are a matter of a few words in the middle of a sentence. While Petacci's thoughts are not misrepresented and the contents of her diary are on the whole respected, given that a historical document is being published, a full transcription of the passages which relate directly to politics would have been more useful. Mussolini's comments on Sarfatti relate to his anti-Semitic policies; for this reason it is better when citing them to quote from Giorgio Fabre's critical essay on the subject, which transcribes them fully from Petacci's pages, where she probably wrote them down shortly after the conversation in which they occurred took place. "That woman was the biggest mistake I've ever made. To have allowed her to write a book on me – it's beyond comprehension – I don't know how I could have linked my name to the name of that woman for ever. It'll go down in history not only as my biography, *but as something else.*"[4]

In an attempt to compensate, in 1928 Mussolini agreed to the publication of another biography of him in the Philadelphia *Saturday Evening Post*. The proposal reached him through the offices of R.W. Child, a former American ambassador to Italy. He got his brother Arnaldo to write it, revised it himself and entrusted the translation to Child. The new biography was also serialized in various European newspapers and was published as a book in a popular edition which sold 100,000 copies; however, Mussolini remained dissatisfied and undecided about the book, blocking the Italian version and even prohibiting the distribution of the English edition within Italy. He was unconvinced that either of the biographies – the one written by his intellectual mistress or the one by his journalist brother – were adapted to a regime which now needed with some urgency to develop a popular-nationalist political culture to accompany its wholesale institutional reorganization. It was certainly necessary to eliminate any image of him as coarse and ignorant, but Sarfatti didn't help here. There were other methods he could adopt, such as using the Grand Council to clarify the regime's attitudes to art and the intelligentsia. Decrees were duly issued which proclaimed the need to support the partnership of Fascism and culture. Thanks in part to the collaboration of celebrated figures such as the philosopher Giovanni Gentile, the regime had organized a congress of leading intellectuals in Bologna in 1925. It was a deliberate occupation of the territory over which Sarfatti, as the self-proclaimed high priestess of Fascist art, had up until then held sway almost alone. She spoke at the congress, but made very little impression. Following the congress, the Istituto Nazionale di Cultura Fascista (National Institute of Fascist Culture) was set up, with Gentile as its president. Shortly afterwards another institution was founded: the Reale Accademia d'Italia (Royal Academy of Italy). A guild or corporation for the intellectual professions had already been established in 1924, which within four years had been transformed into the Confederazione Nazionale dei Sindacati Fascisti dei Professionisti e degli Artisti (National Confederation of Fascist Unions of Professionals and Artists). Sarfatti was excluded from all these developments, and the spaces where she could be present increasingly restricted.

Her evening strolls with Mussolini became less frequent, and it was harder for her to gain official access to him in Palazzo Venezia. She tried to accompany him when he went on holiday, but with increasing difficulty. At some risk, she had even followed him to the Adriatic seaside resorts he frequented with his family. And it was not only his family who got in the way on these occasions; if he crossed the beach, he was mobbed by all the holidaymakers, who were eager to get close to him in such an unusual setting. If he swam in the sea or hired a pedalo, he would be surrounded in the water by hundreds of people.

He enjoyed his popularity, but it also spoilt the restful holidays he'd planned, especially when the police had to take special measures to protect him. In such circumstances it was hard for Margherita Sarfatti to share Mussolini's passion for the sea. When he went to the beach at Nettuno, near Rome, it was the same: the eyes of the crowd would follow him around; as he entered the water, so did all the others, trying to swim closer and closer to him. The problem of protecting Mussolini on holiday was finally solved by assigning two police officers who were expert swimmers to stay in the water with him whenever he entered it.

One summer Mussolini suddenly ordered Boratto to prepare the car to leave straight away for Carpena, just south of Forlì, where Rachele and the family were holidaying. Boratto realized that this wasn't the usual seaside jaunt. He crossed the Apennines without stopping, with an unspeaking Mussolini by his side. They had got as far as Predappio, a short distance away from Carpena, just before midnight, when something happened. Boratto learnt about it later from one of his usual conversations with a gossipy chambermaid: "She confided in me that a few minutes before our arrival, a mysterious telephone call had warned Rachele that her husband was on his way to the villa, so giving a certain 'V.' the time to leave the house and avoid an unpleasant encounter."[5]

Rachele is usually seen as a humble woman from peasant stock, but she had a strong character and on this occasion had decided to get her own back on her husband's infidelities. Mussolini had found, out and the news had caused his ulcer to flare up again. He had found out in the middle of a violent argument with Bianca Ceccato, who had aroused his jealous suspicions. Not knowing quite how to defend herself, she had retorted that it was all very well for him to be jealous with her when he should be paying rather more attention to what his own wife was up to.

Italy was now a country full of informers. The regime had enlisted even the porters in apartment blocks. Mussolini easily found out what had been going on. He no longer loved Rachele, but his dignity, his pride and above all his myth was at stake. He identified the man who had been carrying on with his wife: a certain Corrado Valori. "You don't have a man sleeping in your house without a reason. The excuse was that he was running the household, looking after the kids. And he was always with my wife. There was a lot of evidence for what was going on, though obviously she always denied it, but then why was he always with her and why did he sleep in the house? Why did he spend the night in Villa Carpena when his own house was only three kilometres off and he had a car? She said he stayed over because it was raining. But it wasn't as if he had to drive thirty kilometres, it was just three. [...] I'd heard some rumours, but I didn't believe them. Then, once I entered her bedroom by chance and found perfumes, cosmetics, dyes, lots of refined things that she'd never bothered about before because she was just an ordinary rough peasant woman."[6]

Rachele may well have been simple and comparatively uneducated, but she had a peasant shrewdness; she had succeeded in forestalling Mussolini's midnight irruption, proving that she had her own network of informers. Whether or not Corrado Valori was her occasional lover, Rachele managed always to behave with an almost austere dignity, uninterested in status and worldly success, reserved and devoted to her children. Mussolini, on the other hand, in the verbal ramblings which Claretta Petacci transcribed, talked in the most intimate detail about his relations with his wife, telling his mistress how the love he'd felt for her twenty years before had become nothing more than a kind of conjugal duty: "She's completely indifferent whenever I sleep with her, about seven or eight times a year. I think she no longer feels anything with me, or almost nothing. All sexual desire is finished, unless in her it's finished as far as I'm concerned. [...] It's true I've treated her badly, very badly. I've had illegitimate children, mistresses, I blame myself a lot and think very badly of myself. But there are excuses for the way I've behaved. Basically, a man like me, with the opportunities I've had, the kind of life I've led... How could I have stayed on the straight and narrow? All men are unfaithful to their wives, even barbers' assistants. All of them, for no reason and with no excuse. But I've got excuses."[7]

Mussolini now lived constantly surrounded by plain-clothes policemen. He used to spend his birthday in Predappio together with his family, and the village would regularly organize a public dance in his honour. "What sluts!..." Rachele would murmur to herself as she saw the women queuing up to dance with her husband. She didn't know the jokes which were circulating secretly among people. Her husband ended up by dancing with policemen dressed as village housewives, the athletes at sports festivals who thronged around him were policemen, the sunbathers who applauded him as he walked along the beach were policemen. The rough miners who accompanied him down the mine with their lamps and the group of burly car workers he was photographed with, a comrade among comrades, were also policemen. A special team of police agents known as the "Presidenziale" also accompanied him wherever he went, with the support of the local police in the places he visited. Paolo Monelli tells a story which occurred at Acireale, in Sicily, which he claims to have heard from someone who had actually witnessed the episode. "Surrounded by a celebrating crowd of villagers in picturesque costume, Mussolini grew suspicious of one of them and angrily accused him of being one of the 'Presidenziale' men. The man nervously stammered out a denial, at which Mussolini calmed down and smiled at him, pleased to find he'd been mistaken. But, thus encouraged, the man continued and, swallowing hard, told him: 'I'm on duty from the Acireale police force.'"[8]

The suffocating security which surrounded Mussolini, however, helped to prevent various attempts on his life. The first incident was the discovery of a plot organized by the former opposition deputy Tito Zaniboni on 4th November 1925, who was arrested in a hotel room in the centre of Rome, which he had booked under a false name.

> The door of the room opened, and there was the honourable Zaniboni posing as a certain Major Silvestrini. He was taken aback by the visit of the police agents, but composed himself and asked them what they wanted. But one of the police officers, Belloni, pushed his way into the room, followed by the others; two of them held Zaniboni down, while the others went straight to the window, next to which there was a panel from the shutters which had been taken down. Behind the shutter a gun had been concealed with its barrel leaning against one of the slats. It was a powerful rifle, made in Austria, with a telescopic sight – the kind used by snipers in wartime. The barrel, as I was saying, was leaning against a slat of the shutter and was turned in the direction of the balcony of the Palazzo Chigi. Besides the rifle, the honourable Zaniboni had three leather suitcases and a box of the kind used to carry military kit in the room.[9]

Mussolini was adroit in using the press to project the views he wanted: the newspapers wrote that the opposition was finished, because it was no longer using political means but assassination instead. Those who opposed Fascism therefore were trying to take the country into a period of violence, conflict and bloodshed. Mussolini was not overly concerned by Zaniboni's plot. It was advantageous to him in political terms, and the personal danger to himself had been minimal, given that the police had been keeping the former deputy under surveillance and had been able to stop him while he was still in his hotel room. In subsequent attempts on his life, the level of risk increased, but Mussolini still succeeded in using them to create an atmosphere of tension in the country which only encouraged a strengthening of the dictatorship. With a clever journalistic sleight of hand he convinced the Italian people that it was all right to give up certain freedoms, since the attempts on his life meant that national security was also under threat.

On 7th April 1926 in the Campidoglio in Rome, Mussolini stopped to greet a group of students. As he raised his arm in the Fascist salute, he moved his head back slightly, which was enough to save him from the bullet fired at him at that instant by Violet Gibson, which merely grazed his nose. Gibson, of Irish nationality, turned out to be mentally unbalanced; she was also planning to shoot the Pope. As it turned out, of all his would-be assassins, Gibson was the one who came nearest to succeeding. Mussolini had his nose bandaged and continued on his way. The best propaganda coup was to be seen to go about his business as if nothing had happened. Later that day, after the failed assassination attempt, he coined a new Fascist slogan: "If I advance, follow me; if I retreat, kill me; if I die, avenge me." The slogan was not in fact original; the words had resurfaced, who knows how, from one of the history books he liked to read. They had originally been spoken by a leader of the Vendée revolt during the French Revolution, the Catholic general Henri du Vergier, comte de la Rochejaquelein, on 13th April 1793, after the victory over the revolutionary republican army at the battle of Les Aubiers. Gibson was certified insane and sent back to Britain in a gesture of clemency, which was favourably reported in the international press.

At eight in the morning on 11th September 1926, Mussolini was being driven to Palazzo Chigi. The street was lined with the usual plain-clothes policemen standing around pretending to read the newspaper. It was hot, and the car windows had been lowered. As they reached Porta Pia, Boratto heard something bang against the car door. He turned and saw an object rolling away in the road. Like any former soldier, he knew immediately what it was – a hand grenade of the SIPE type, in the shape of a lemon, its case like a tortoise shell. Mussolini was reading in the back seat and asked if someone had thrown a stone at the car. "No, Duce, it's a bomb," replied Boratto pressing the accelerator down. The grenade exploded, but the car was already thirty metres away. Eight passers-by were wounded, and the windows in nearby apartment blocks broken; the grenade had missed entering the car by only a few centimetres. Mussolini thanked Boratto and praised his quick thinking, adding that he was certain his lucky star would have protected him in any case. One of his visitors that day was Duchess Hélène of Aosta. As she made her way among the crowd of *gerarchi* and other officials, the Duchess, who was extremely tall, identified Boratto and went over to congratulate him. The chauffeur modestly thanked her, but Mussolini, disliking the idea Boratto might be seen as a hero, interjected: "It was nothing to worry about. Even if the grenade had entered the car I'd have been able to throw it out – after all I served with the Bersaglieri."[10]

The grenade attack, the third attempt to assassinate Mussolini, had been organized by Gino Lucetti, a stonemason and an independent anarchist who had emigrated to France. Lucetti had a second grenade, but didn't have time to throw it before the security police seized hold of him. Four days later, Mussolini received a letter from his brother Arnaldo. Arnaldo looked after Mussolini's business affairs, and the letter was enclosed with the tax files for *Il Popolo d'Italia*, of which Mussolini had remained the proprietor. His brother urged him not to encourage extremist reactions to the attack, but rather to eliminate the extremists: "May God give you his help and may he make the security forces who protect your precious life always on the alert and aware. [...] If I might be allowed to express my opinion on the current political situation, I would advise you to take over the running of the Ministry of Internal Affairs in the next few days. I like and respect Federzoni, and regard him as a loyal and devoted follower. But your authority is needed to put all those detestable rebel Fascists with their factiousness and refusal to compromise in their proper place..."[11]

Arnaldo had also become responsible for keeping the still-furious Ida Dalser under control. He had had to deal with her in January 1925 while his brother was in the middle of the Matteotti crisis. With a notary in Trento he had an agreement drawn up which transferred the considerable – for the time – sum of 100,000 lire to the young Benito Albino Mussolini, to be made available to him when he reached the age of majority. Until then the money was to be held in the safekeeping of the Paichers, the couple who were the little boy's legal guardians. No one has ever been able to discover what happened to the money.

The assassination attempts on Mussolini's life, the consequent abolition of some basic civil freedoms and the constant state of alert in which the regime's forces of repression were kept made their effects felt also on the unfortunate Dalser. She was compulsorily sectioned in the psychiatric hospital in Pergine on the night of 19th June 1926. She was forty-three years old. Alfredo Pieroni in his research into her story discovered a letter from her in which she recounts what happened to her: "When they saw me, I was seized, beaten, tied up, drugged, insulted and bundled into a car with my mouth gagged until we got to the police station. After coarsely searching and tormenting me, they threw me on the floor in a straitjacket and tied me to a couple of filthy boards by my hands, feet and waist, hurting my teeth and covering me with extremely painful bruises."[12] This was the beginning of the end for her. Psychiatric asylums at the time were certainly not places where the mentally ill went to get better; on the contrary, they reduced them definitively to a state of madness. Nonetheless, Dalser was able to recover some of her calm and determination after her forced internment. She was able to speak to the hospital medical staff. They saw the bruises resulting from her capture, but no one was concerned about them, since the use of force on "an uncontrollably mad person" was considered standard procedure. The psychiatrist who visited her in the hospital a few days after her arrival, a certain Dr Satta, was convinced she was telling the truth about the manner in which she had been seized, and wrote in his case notes: "These people have tried to use the methods of the Viminale on her, they wanted to kill her as they killed Matteotti, but they didn't take account of her or of Mussolini, who's too good-hearted to think that evildoers might betray him. She knew what these thugs were really like and what they were getting up to, and she never stopped warning her Benito about what was happening, to try to advise him, to get him to see what the outcome would be."[13] Satta was clearly one of the millions of Italians who were naive enough to fall for Mussolini's confidence trickery and believe that he was the great mediator and peacemaker who could alone bring the thugs and the extremists under control.

The fourth attempt on Mussolini's life took place little over a month later, on 31st October, in mysterious circumstances in Bologna. While Mussolini was returning to the railway station, someone in the crowds lining the streets shot a pistol at him, which again grazed him, or rather the ribbon of an order medal he was wearing round his neck. In the confusion which followed, a fifteen-year-old boy, Anteo Zamboni, was identified as the perpetrator. He was lynched on the spot by a gang of Fascists. Once again, Mussolini immediately announced that he would stick to the prearranged schedule of his appointments. "Continuing the Bologna visit as if nothing had happened became, from the point of view of psychological propaganda, another fundamental building block in the construction of his public persona: nothing could disturb the imperturbable Duce, nothing could make him deviate from the path he had chosen, not even an attempt to kill him."[14]

Mussolini was far ahead of his opponents and rivals in his use of the new means of mass communication. As a former journalist, he was already familiar with the traditional press. Radio was born with him, so to speak, and he immediately used it to propagate his myth. In 1924 he had granted a monopoly of radio broadcasting to URI, which three years later was transformed into EIAR or the Ente Italiano Audizioni Radiofoniche (Italian Radio Broadcasting Corporation). The number of programmes increased rapidly while radios started to appear in Italian homes; on important occasions, they were also installed in the squares of towns and villages. The radio became a megaphone for the regime, its master's voice. The cinema, in the meantime, was emerging from its beginnings; Mussolini saw its potential and took control of the industry. When he transferred his residence to Villa Torlonia, he had a private cinema installed where he watched all the films issued by the national film institute, the Istituto Luce, before they were released. It was better than looking in the mirror; he gave orders to cut out of the newsreels all the expressions and movements of his own that he didn't like. At the same time the projections gave him an opportunity to perfect, obsessively, the ones he thought were successful. His attention to the photographs of himself taken for public display was equally obsessive. Early on in the regime he preferred the photographs in which he appeared hard, rigid, his shoulders squared and his jaw jutting; after the invasion of Ethiopia he started to modify his stern and truculent image by choosing photos in which he was portrayed smiling. Newspapers and magazines, the cinema and the radio – all the means of mass communication were put to propaganda uses: "If we understand this, the construction of his myth can be seen as a rational strategy, on a par with all the other political strategies he followed during these years."[15]

Once he had the means of communication under his complete control, Mussolini could go on to eradicate what vestiges still remained of the now superseded liberal democratic state. Nothing must be allowed to disturb the tranquillity of "his" people. The opposition parties were suppressed, and their newspapers closed down; the death penalty was introduced for opponents of the regime; a special court was set up to try anti-Fascists together with police internment; all passports were restricted and made subject to inspection before they could be renewed. The King gave his approval to all these measures, without the slightest protest, even when all the opposition deputies in parliament were dismissed. The dictatorship at this point became a reality. The talk at court and among the nobility was that the King had become a "prisoner" of the Duce's.

Yet if the King was Mussolini's prisoner, then Mussolini was in his turn a prisoner of the diarchy which formed the Italian state. In his path to dictatorship, he had in a certain sense underestimated several of the possible consequences of the legal organization of the new state – or, at least, had assumed too easily that the primacy of politics, of his own political abilities, would always prevail in the control of real power. He delegated the task of constructing the new state to a conservative politician who did not come from inside the Fascist ranks, Alfredo Rocco, and continued to support him even when the party criticized his choice. Naturally Mussolini saw that the legal architecture of the emerging new state was not ideal for the exercise of his absolute power, but he was confident that he could continue to act as he'd done so far, modifying the laws whenever it suited him to do so, and that he could always influence events to his own advantage. This was how Rocco, as the Minister for Justice, was able to get parliamentary approval for his law of 24th December 1925, which redefined the role and the prerogatives of the head of the Italian government. On the one hand, Mussolini became a head of government in the true sense of the word, given, in another sudden raft of new laws, quite enormous powers; on the other, a clause in Rocco's bill emphasized that "the government of the sovereign is an emanation of the power of the sovereign and not of parliament, and as such must therefore have the confidence of the sovereign" – a few words which would come to have a determining impact on the future course of events. At the time, as people acclaimed Mussolini's dizzying rise to power, they seemed trivial, a mere restating of what had always been the case. The Duce's authority was not affected in any way by the clause, while it served to reassure the circles close to the House of Savoy that the monarchy would be left untouched. This was indeed how things functioned for the next eighteen years, until 25th July 1943, when Victor Emmanuel III decided to use "the power of the sovereign" which the Rocco law had confirmed was his and withdrew his confidence from the head of what was, again by the terms of the 1925 law, his – the King's – government. But back in December 1925, according to Mussolini himself, no tensions between Fascism and the monarchy existed, and the diarchy was absorbed silently into the regime.

The only serious clash occurred when a further law made the Grand Council the supreme institution in the state and gave it the power to intervene in the question of who could succeed to the throne. During the period of the Social Republic in Salò, Mussolini still recalled this confrontation with the Royal House. "From this time on Victor Emmanuel began to detest Mussolini and to nurse a hatred of Fascism. 'The regime', he said, 'cannot intervene in an area which a basic law has defined. If a political party in a monarchic system wants to decide who can succeed to the throne, then the monarchy is no longer a monarchy. The only rule of monarchic succession is the cry 'The King is dead! Long live the King!'" [16] In the face of the King's hostile reaction, Mussolini hastened to explain that the proposal was only intended to enable the Grand Council to intervene in the eventuality that there were no successors to the throne – a feeble attempt at justification, made even more so by the fact there were numerous princes in the House of Savoy who by the terms of Salic law were in line for the throne. To avoid a crisis over the issue, Mussolini was obliged to confirm that the King's son Umberto, Prince of Piedmont, was the official heir.

In reality the insertion of the Fascist Grand Council into the constitutional architecture of the state represented a potential risk to the Duce's power, but this did not concern Mussolini, who thought it inconceivable that any form of internal opposition could emerge from an institution which he himself had created. As his dictatorship grew in strength he took to snubbing its decisions, and its meetings took place less and less frequently.

Despite errors and vacillations, despite the division of constitutional power with the King, the regime, now without any official opposition, embedded itself among the Italian masses thanks to the particular relationship – personal and direct – which the Duce strove to create with them. It was an insubstantial construction, not destined to resist the harsh events which put it to the test, like the bombardments and the rationing which came with the Second World War – yet, so long as it stood in place, it provided the extensive but precarious scaffolding for the Fascist system and the myth of Mussolini. "I consider the nation to be in a permanent state of war," Mussolini declared in a speech to the country's industrialists in 1926, which he concluded with the assertion that "this political regime and the current climate are, as far as we humans can foresee the future, unchangeable".

In Mussolini's Italy strikes and lockouts became crimes punishable by law. No one objected – because it was no longer possible to object – that if there were no strikes there would be no lockouts or pointed out the absurdity of treating both as if they were the same phenomenon. The country's economy had to be run according to the principle "everything within the state, nothing outside the state, nothing against the state".

Mussolini was aware that the factory workers in the industrial heartlands of northern Italy, faced by the unfolding spectacle of Fascism, were unenthusiastic, if not downright hostile to the regime. "In early 1924, the elections which were held in the factories in Turin produced a clear victory of the Federazione Impiegati Operai Metallurgici [Federation of Metal Industry Workers] which obtained eighty-one per cent of the votes against the mere fifteen per cent which went to the [Fascist-led] Corporations. The employers themselves were unfavourably disposed towards the Fascist trade unions, well aware that they were hardly representative of the mass of workers and also of their organizational limitations."[17] Mussolini took immediate practical measures to bring this situation under control, but knew that the problem could only be resolved completely over time. The regime had to maintain its grip on power and wait. A new generation would gradually replace the old working class; the new workers who would emerge would all have been born and brought up under Fascism. The fact that as children they had had to wear the uniforms prescribed by the two Fascist youth movements, the Balilla and the Avanguardisti, meant that, when the time came for them to do so, they would put on the blue overalls of the factory worker in a very different spirit from their predecessors.

Yet beneath the slogans, the violence and the parades, Fascism had no original content: there was nothing new in the regime to justify Mussolini's belief or hope that it would prove enduring. Its underlying themes were the familiar ones of patriotism and nationalism; the only "serious" part of its whole ideological framework was the idea that the class struggle preached by revolutionary socialism had been superseded, and this was "serious" only in the sense that the historical justification for Mussolini's dictatorship resided in his capacity to supersede what he himself had been in the past. As he followed his political instincts, taking all power into his own hands, he increasingly thought of himself as an artist. On 24th February 1926 he declared in a speech: "There is no doubt that politics is an art. It is certainly not a science. Nor is it merely empirical. It is therefore an art, also because it requires a high degree of intuition. 'Political' creation resembles artistic creation in being a combination of slow elaboration with lightning flashes of divination. The moment comes when the artist creates by inspiration, the politician by decision. Both the artist and the politician work with and upon matter and spirit."[18]

One outcome of the measures Mussolini took to resolve the problems with trade unions was to close down the General Confederation of Labour, the main Socialist union. On 4th January 1927 it issued a brief statement: "The National Council of the General Confederation of Labour... declares its functions have terminated and asks the Executive Committee to proceed to the liquidation and settlement of the Confederation's remaining interests." Bruno Buozzi and other exiles re-established the union in France, while several Communist trade unionists worked to support a clandestine organization in Italy. After making some concessions to the industrialists, Mussolini drew up a formal Fascist Workers Charter, which won some favourable recognition from European socialist leaders, causing problems for the anti-Fascist cause.

While the King refused to intervene in the course of political events in the country, he was more disposed to do so when it was a question of Mussolini's personal interests. Whenever the two men had a disagreement, the King did not fail to follow up with some conciliatory gesture designed to appease his head of government. The problems the Duce was having in organizing a tranquil trip to the seaside came to the King's notice, and he saw the situation as a good opportunity to make a placatory gesture which might sweeten Mussolini's mood. "The King came to hear about Mussolini's increasing enthusiasm for the seaside and, since he was always eager to satisfy his whims, decided to put at his disposal the private beach of Tor Paterno, part of the vast royal estate at Castel Porziano."[19] The estate, still reserved today for the private use of presidents of the Republic, consists of a large wooded tract of land, enclosed on its inland side by a wall thirty kilometres in length, and with fourteen kilometres of coastline. Boratto, together with some employees from the Ministry of Internal Affairs, built a wooden beach hut, consisting of three rooms. Beach huts on stilts near to the shore were common in Italian resorts at the time, and Mussolini used his for the same activities as any other Italian holidaymaker – to change into his swimming costume, to take his meals, to go to the toilet and take a shower. In addition, it was a place where he could entertain the women who had permission to enter the estate and visit him. The room which was intended to be a study he also used as a sitting room. Here, finally, he found freedom from the public gaze and solitude inside a well-protected refuge. A small straw hut accommodated Boratto, who controlled the comings and goings of visitors during the day using two telephones, one for normal use and one with a direct connection to the Ministry for Internal Affairs. The guards at the entrance to the estate called him every time a car arrived which was on the list of authorized visitors, thus enabling Boratto to make sure Mussolini only ever had one mistress in the beach hut at any one time. One of Boratto's duties was driving the motorboat for excursions out to sea, one of Margherita Sarfatti's favourite pastimes. "The first woman who visited Castel Porziano to alleviate the Duce's solitude was 'S.' She arrived punctually at midday. They swam together and then, at one o'clock, ate lunch. Immediately afterwards they sunbathed. They spent most of the afternoon reading the books which 'S.' had brought with her or the newspapers and magazines which had been sent from Rome."[20] When Mussolini and Boratto were at the beach, two lunches would always arrive at midday for them, but the chauffeur often had to give up his meal to whichever mistress was visiting on the day. To have asked for three might have aroused suspicions. At times the situation started to get out of hand. Margherita Sarfatti took to bringing her daughter, who had by now turned eighteen, with her. The three of them would swim together. Then the daughter started coming by herself. She only needed to lift her little finger to get Mussolini to give her whatever she wanted. One morning she persuaded him to take the motorboat to the port of Anzio. Boratto objected that it was too far, but the Duce insisted and Boratto had to steer the craft. As they were returning, the engine cut out three miles from the coast. The petrol had run out. No one back at Castel Porziano was aware of the problem, because the staff on the estate had strict orders never to disturb Mussolini while he was there. It's easy to panic in such a situation, but Mussolini gave a show of amused unconcern while Boratto kept thinking he couldn't swim and the girl looked around to see if she could come up with an idea. "We tried to row back to the shore, but we couldn't move the motorboat an inch. In the meantime, a light northerly wind was blowing us farther out to sea. [...] We were getting cold (because we only had bathing costumes on) and seeing it was pointless to wait further, the young lady, who was a good swimmer (whereas the male members of crew certainly weren't) dived into the water to reach the shore. It was thanks to her that, towards ten at night, we were towed back."[21]

After this misadventure, Boratto asked to be excused from the duty of driving the motorboat again, a request which was granted – a stroke of good luck for him because over the next few years Mussolini took to spending much of the summer in Castel Porziano, from early May to the lingering warmth of early autumn, with many trips in the motorboat, with or without one of his numerous mistresses.

One day an unexpected visitor arrived and asked the guards if she could be received by Mussolini. It was up to Boratto to decide whether he should give the message to Mussolini or not. Once he knew the identity of the visitor, he made his way over to the beach hut with a sense of foreboding. Mussolini didn't like to be disturbed. He'd once shouted at the head of his press office, Lando Ferretti, because he had dared to disturb him by calling him on the telephone while he was sunbathing naked on the beach. Ferretti wanted to speak to him urgently about a news item in the Vatican newspaper the *Osservatore romano*, which reported the publication of Pius XI's anti-Fascist encyclical; the Pope's views would soon be making headlines all over the world, and Ferretti didn't know how to respond. Mussolini told him to go to hell, adding that while the Pope might have gone mad, he, Mussolini, most certainly hadn't.

Boratto arrived at the hut. Mussolini was annoyed, but he too, once he'd been told who the visitor was, couldn't deny her request. The visitor in question was Maria José of Savoy. She was well known for her anti-Fascist views, and it is difficult to understand why she'd come to Castel Porziano to sunbathe and go swimming right next to Mussolini, even if the estate did belong to her husband's family. Belgian by birth, extremely cultivated, brought up to become the Queen of Italy, Maria José's attitude to her own body was perhaps more Nordic in spirit, less prurient and more relaxed, than Mussolini's Mediterranean and working-class view. Such a contrast is the only explanation for the way Mussolini described the incident to Petacci. Once she got to the beach Maria José put her swimsuit on, a two-piece, daring for the time. "You know, I'm not impotent, but that woman next to me, almost naked, brushing her thighs, her legs against me, who moved about revealing everything... she hadn't the slightest effect on me. I remained completely indifferent, distant, my senses were sleeping. Nothing, I tell you, nothing, my cock didn't even raise its head a little, nothing. On the contrary it hid away. The more she moved and revealed, the further it shrank. [Petacci:] 'It must be republican.' He laughs: Yes, that's right, I just felt it wanted to go to sleep. I couldn't succeed in feeling any physical attraction for her. But at times she was provoking. I even saw her pubic hair, when she crossed her legs. And then it was hot under the sun... It's exciting to have a naked woman so near, who kept touching my legs. On our own in a beach hut, I mean I'm not made of wood. And yet I was wood. I wasn't a man but a politician – nothing, I tell you nothing. Not a hair moved. I wonder what she was thinking? That I'm impotent? [...] Any other woman who arrived and was naked like that, I'd have taken her. But with her I couldn't, I didn't feel a thing, not a thing. How can you explain that? And yet she's not ugly, she's got a nice body, nicely shaped, slim. Her face is a bit plain, and she's got such big feet – you should see them. And that frizzy blond hair, I don't like that. But even with a woman uglier than she was – and she wasn't ugly – I'd have had her. Yet with her I didn't. Why ever not?"[22]

Petacci wrote her entries just after her meetings or telephone conversations with Mussolini, and she wrote them rapidly while her memory of his words was still fresh in her mind. Punctuation is the first casualty of her haste, and errors of grammar and syntax are frequent, but the speed with which she wrote also shows that she was concerned to get down as accurate a transcription as possible. If we look at the gist of the episode just quoted, we find the princess Maria José being subjected to Mussolini's close examination as he watches every move she makes in her swimming costume, quick to notice every portion of flesh she bares, using the reactions of his "cock" to measure the closeness of their bodies. However, the passage taken as a whole also suggests that the princess had decided to check out for herself the truth of Mussolini's reputation. The future "Queen of May" returned to Castel Porziano several times after this visit, bringing a lady in waiting with whom Boratto struck up a friendship: "I was very glad to spend time with the lady in waiting. She often offered me cigarettes with the unusual brand name 'Me ne frego' ['I don't give a damn', a Fascist motto] which were sent especially from Egypt for the princess. After a few months the Duce ordered me to find some pretext to turn her away whenever she next arrived."[23]

A letter by Romano Mussolini, the penultimate son of the Duce, has recently emerged and was published on the weekly gossip magazine *Oggi* at the beginning of September this year, offering a possible new perspective on the ties between Mussolini and Maria José. "At home we have actually often talked about the political and sentimental relationship between Maria José and my father, and I can say in all honesty that Mother was always (even if naturally with some reserve) very explicit about it: between my father and the then Princess of Piedmont there was a short, intimate relationship, which I believe my father later decided to break off." Romano Mussolini's letter, dated 1st July 1971, was addressed to the journalist Antonio Terzi, the deputy editor of *Corriere della Sera*. Terzi decided not to publish the letter at the time (it was discovered by his son in the family archive only this year) and, apparently, never replied to it. Romano Mussolini's claims are an example of *relata refero* – he was reporting what he had heard from his mother during conversations at home. Such conversations dealt with both the political and sentimental relationship, therefore they were not centred around the couple's love affair, but were of a broader nature. Romano Mussolini does not give a date, but we can assume he is talking about the immediate post-war period, when he was old enough to take part in such conversations without his mother being embarrassed to talk about it with him. What Claretta Petacci wrote is also a report of what her lover told her. However, this contradicts the figure of the Duce as it appears throughout her diary: it seems strange that he would not boast about having conquered Her Royal Highness herself. Common sense suggests that Mussolini, rejected or at least rebuffed by such a wilful, learned and intelligent woman, declared her "a bit plain", with "frizzy blond hair" and such "big feet". History cannot be written just using common sense: it requires documents and evidence. Elsewhere in his letter, Romano Mussolini wrote to Terzi: "In all good faith I can confirm that I have read some of Maria José's love letters to my father." These letters are nowhere to be found, but if they were to emerge one day and be authenticated, then they could be used as a primary source from where to reconstruct the events and the relationship between the Duce and the future queen.

If we look at everything Mussolini did (or said he did) during the day – the newspapers and reports he read, the documents he had to write, the women he entertained, the official audiences, the telephone calls, the books he read, his travels – it becomes clear that he couldn't possibly have succeeded in fitting all these activities in. It is extraordinary that he managed to spend so much time at the seaside, even if the beach hut had a study. In the summer he only spent two or three hours a day in his office in Palazzo Venezia. Yet he always seemed to have time to spare and even to waste, such as when he asked Boratto to construct a bowling green where they could play at bowls together (the chauffeur notes that Mussolini was a beginner at the game, but became angry if he started to lose, so Boratto had to let him win every now and then, so Mussolini wouldn't give up). In the winter, as soon as the first snows fell in the mountains, Mussolini would go off to ski at Monte Terminillo (Boratto again adds the comment that despite having one of the best ski instructors available he never became a proficient skier). Later on, Monte Terminillo became one of the places where he took his favourite mistress Claretta Petacci for their trysts. On one occasion, when Petacci was ill, Boratto, who always knew what was going on, saw her sister Miriam enter the private entrance to Mussolini's suite in the hotel where he stayed while skiing and sneak out again the following morning. "Petacci and her sister, Miriam, usually stayed in the Hotel delle Nazioni in Rieti. From there they would arrive at about ten in the morning, join the Duce at Campo Forogna and spend the day skiing, having lunch on the slopes. In the evening, if the Duce was staying in the hotel, Claretta would remain in the presidential suite, but on the evenings when she didn't feel well it was her sister Miriam who stole into Mussolini's bedroom and then – so the owner of the hotel told me – slipped out the following morning before it was light, so acting as a substitute for her sister in the Duce's sexual attentions."[24]

Boratto's story might seem outlandish, like one of those false notes that threaten to undermine an entire piece of evidence, but other external testimonies would seem to confirm its truth. Petacci immediately noticed that her sister was no longer the childlike Mimi who accompanied Mussolini on their strolls through the woods: "We walk along quite fast, until we slow down near a grassy ditch. A nightingale is singing in the middle of a grove of trees and we listen to it entranced. Mimi catches up with us and he stops to talk and looks at her in a different way, like a man, as he's never done before. I am slightly puzzled. In fact, as we continue our walk, he behaves like a man who thinks he's attractive, who wants something, and other things I won't write here. His smile is artful. Then he thinks I've understood and runs away, jumping over ditches."[25]

In his close analysis of Petacci's diary, Giorgio Fabre has discovered that on a couple of pages there are lines written in someone else's handwriting. "A comparison with the only known autograph document in the handwriting of Miriam known as Mimi, Petacci's sister, which I have been able to consult thanks to the staff of the Central State Archive, would seem to confirm that the writing in the diary is indeed Miriam's. At the time she would have been fourteen or fifteen, and she knew about her sister's affair with Mussolini. When her writing stops, another hand takes over, which is undoubtedly Claretta's."[26]

So the two sisters increasingly became accomplices, with Claretta even "lending" her diary to Miriam, and not just to read its intimate descriptions, including some explicit ones of her various sexual activities with Mussolini, but to make her own contribution by writing a few lines in it herself. It is probable that Claretta, like the grand royal mistresses of the past, cynically adapted herself to the new situation: having seen that Mussolini had his eyes on her sister and realizing she could do nothing to stop it, she made Miriam into an ally rather than a rival.

On 16th March 1928, Mussolini presented his new electoral law, which had been approved by the Grand Council, in parliament. Only fifteen deputies voted against it: any space left for political manoeuvre for what remained of the parliamentary opposition had now been definitively removed. The law stipulated that there should be a single list of four hundred candidates to fill four hundred seats in parliament. The list would be approved by the Grand Council and presented to the electorate in its entirety, who, at the ballot box, could only vote "yes" or "no". If there was a majority in favour, even by just a single vote, then the entire list was approved. It was a plebiscite rather than an election, and everything was ready for it to go ahead, but Mussolini put it off for another year. His greatest political success to date had still to be achieved.

There were many forces trying to slow down and, if possible, stop the secret negotiations with the Vatican. Mussolini himself retained his innate anti-clerical convictions but stooped to compromise by getting married with a religious ceremony and having his children baptized, coming out against the use of contraception, ensuring there was a clerical presence in the armed forces and blocking the republication of his early writings. Yet all this was still not enough; with some apprehension, Mussolini realized that he would have to tackle head on the complex and shifting hierarchical politics of the Church. On numerous occasions Catholic clubs, associations and cooperatives had been attacked by Fascist squads. Mussolini's best tactic was once again to wait and appear to be the great mediator. He had to prepare Fascism gradually for what he intended to do, so that the last *ras* could be coaxed into accepting the future concordat, and he had to win over and reassure the King and the House of Savoy. For the Church too there was a great deal at stake, something which was apparent from the very first secret meeting which Mussolini had attended and which, much later, he spoke about in a session of the Grand Council: "The first contact took place one evening in the spring of 1923 in the residence belonging to senator Count Cantucci, a former head of Rome's Catholic organizations, in Piazza della Pigna. My interlocutor on that occasion? [...] No less a personage than the Vatican Secretary of State, Cardinal Pietro Gasparri."[27]

The Vatican needed to protect its vast patrimony of buildings in Rome and throughout the country, but it also wanted to defend its role and room for action in Italian society, the moral patrimony of lay Catholic movements and of the education of new generations now and to come. The Pope was adamant about this: the Church would not be excluded. This was highly contentious terrain; Mussolini too was interested in the younger generations, since, alongside the day-to-day political manoeuvring to maintain and increase the regime's power, he also had a longer-term strategy based on instilling Fascism into the new generations of Italians. These concerns influenced the negotiations. Many Catholics viewed the establishment of relations with the regime with apprehension. A fierce debate broke out in the press about the fundamental issues at stake in seeking to reach an agreement, and all negotiations came to a halt for seven months.

"In the whole of history there has never been a problem which has not been resolved either by force or by patience or by wisdom, and this is true also for the 'Roman Question'. The Fascist Regime, which has the whole of the twentieth century ahead of it, has the capacity to succeed, without renouncing any of the fundamental rights which pertain to the state, where liberal democracy has repeatedly failed. The conclusion is this: the task will be arduous, but it is not impossible." With these words Mussolini ended his text in the official despatch of the Fascist Party on 20th October 1927. They were a signal for the secret negotiations to resume. But the factions opposed to a successful outcome, who were working with equal security as far as their membership was concerned, had no intention of giving up. Father Tacchi Venturi, who could boast he had ministered the Communion to Mussolini during the Easter Mass, was one of the principal negotiators for the Vatican. Venturi was a colourful figure, worthy of some of the other tales of intrigue and espionage associated with the Vatican. An attempt was made on his life on 27th February 1928. He escaped with wounds, and Mussolini ordered a police investigation. The motives for the attack were clear enough, but it was more difficult to identify who had planned and carried it out. The only strong response to the incident was to speed ahead with the negotiations. An agreement was reached on the flat-rate sum the state would pay to the Vatican by way of compensation, and the clauses of the concordat and the financial agreement were duly drawn up.

On 11th February 1929, Cardinal Pietro Gasparri representing the Vatican and Mussolini for the Italian state signed the final version of the agreement in the great hall of the papal palace in the complex of the Basilica of San Giovanni in Laterano. On the same day, in what was a gift for the regime's propaganda, the Pope paid tribute to Mussolini as a "man of destiny". The event sent the press wild with enthusiasm; the myth of the Duce seemed unassailable. The Lateran Pacts – the official name for the concordat – spelt an end to the People's Party, but at the same time reassured Catholics in general. The regime had solved the main outstanding problem left over from the unification of the country, nearly sixty years after Bersaglieri troops had breached the Porta Pia gate into the city and put an end to the Papacy's temporal rule.

Mussolini also had a gift for the Pope: he outlawed Freemasonry, the historical enemy of the Church, removed the archives belonging to the lodges, had their symbols destroyed and burnt. While the secret negotiations with the Vatican were going on, the Obedience of Piazza del Gesù had sought to bring Arnaldo Mussolini over to their side by offering him the highest position in the order, the "33rd". He had turned them down, and it seems curious that the masters of that branch of the Freemasons didn't in their wisdom have the foresight to check before exposing themselves to such a public refusal. Shortly after the signing of the concordat, Mussolini was gratified to read an article by his brother in which Arnaldo had written: "The unreasonable objections coming from a small part of the Freemasons in hock to the interests and conditions of foreign fraternities needed to be overcome. Benito Mussolini, famed as a *condottiere*, statesman and inspiring leader, has brought clarity to the political and spiritual state of affairs in Italy, has gone beyond mere rhetoric, has followed his instinct and his presentiment of what a great achievement such a reconciliation would represent."[28]

Now the Duce was ready to go to the country with his plebiscite. It was held the month after the signing of the concordat, on 24th March 1929, and in the wake of the agreement the Azione Cattolica (Catholic Action) movement, the Catholic press, the parishes and other religious associations urged the faithful to vote and to vote in favour. The regime obtained 98.4 per cent of the votes. The four hundred men on the list that had been the sole object of the vote duly took their seats in a perfectly useless parliament.

But while the signing of the Lateran Pacts had put relations between Church and state on a new footing, it had not put a stop to the polemics over certain issues. The basic problem remained the country's younger generation. Mussolini saw the Fascist movement as a faith of which he was the supreme interpreter, a view which inevitably came into conflict with the faith represented by the vicar of Christ on earth. For the Duce, with the signing of the concordat, Catholicism had been integrated into the Fascist state. "Other regimes," he declared in a long speech to parliament on 13th May 1929, "another regime, not ours, a liberal democratic regime, a regime run by the kind of men we despise, may think it beneficial to ignore the need to educate the younger generations. That is not Fascism's way. On this question we are implacable. Education is ours. These children must be educated in our religious faith." The Pope responded to Mussolini the following day when speaking to the pupils of a Jesuit college. In his speech, which appeared in the press, the Pope called on the state to complete the work begun by the family and by the Church. "The state does not exist to absorb, to swallow up, to annihilate the individual and the family. This would be an absurdity, it would be against nature, since the family exists before society and the state come into being."

The debate dragged on, with occasional sudden moments of tension, but neither side had any wish to exacerbate the crisis. On 7th June, in another solemn ceremony, the two parties to the concordat exchanged their respective ratifications of the agreement they had signed four months previously. On 25th July the Pope came out into St Peter's Square, the first time since 1870 a pontiff had ventured outside the Vatican; on 5th December a solemn procession, preceded by a cameraman and photographers and followed by a long line of noblemen and other dignitaries, went in the opposite direction: the King and Queen of Italy, who for the first time were received by the Pope on an official visit.

In this atmosphere of general triumph, one of Mussolini's mistresses in the past, Angela Curti, got in touch again with the "man of destiny" and started to visit him in Rome. "For my mother it was the beginning of a golden period: taking up again her love story with Benito Mussolini. [...] She started what was to be a long series of visits to Rome, gradually immersing herself each time in the fascinating and complex world which surrounded him and the power he wielded. Our home was always bustling with her comings and goings, and the packing and unpacking of suitcases. The cases used to fascinate me as a little girl, perhaps because I used to see the happy dreamy expression in my mother's eyes as she packed them, as if she'd slipped something else in them more precious than the beautiful dresses she'd sewn herself."[29]

Gaily humming the songs of her youth – "I like the fragrance of Coty / you bring with you" – Angela Curti, with her elegant underwear and fashionable clothes, made her trips to Rome and back across an Italy which had now been transformed into an entirely Fascist country. The emblem of the *fasces* (a bundle of sticks combined with an axe blade, an ancient Roman symbol of power) now appeared everywhere, displayed in every conceivable activity, to the point that Mussolini himself intervened to have it removed from dustmen's lorries and demand that it shouldn't be sported by singers or hunters. He made no objection, however, when a law was passed making it obligatory to write the word DUCE in block capitals. The regime and the dictatorship was his; the Fascist movement belonged to him alone. The "mystique of Fascism" became an obligatory subject of study in schools, with its basic principle that the Duce knew what needed to be done in all spheres of human endeavour and was always in the right. Italian schoolchildren had to meditate on his pronouncements, increasingly found painted in large capital letters on walls in cities, towns and even along country roads. Every pupil spent hours writing compositions on the Duce's sayings such as "The plough cuts the furrow and the sword defends it".

"The mystique is a mistake" someone might have dared to pun while making very sure they were out of earshot. The regime listened everywhere and to everything. In 1927 a reorganization of the police forces took place, and the body known as OVRA was created specifically for this function. What the initials stood for was meant to be slightly mysterious; they gave off an aura of violence and intimidation. OVRA was a development on a grand scale of the Fascist Cheka of which Mussolini had always denied the existence. There existed one sure interpretation of the "R" and the "A", the last two letters: "*repressione*" ("repression") and "*antifascismo*" ("anti-Fascism"). What this meant in practice and in detail was a constant activity of searches, surveillance, arrests, beatings, murders and an obsessive keeping of records on all so-called subversives, whatever their political beliefs. OVRA could track each and every individual suspected of opposing the regime, and its officials knew at any given moment who they needed to keep under observation, how many stonecutters were facing charges of anti-Fascist activity, how many had succeeded in clearing their names, how many had been sent for trial, how many were under special surveillance – and so on for printers, mechanics, station porters, barbers, nurses, tram drivers, chauffeurs, housewives, watchmakers, glaziers, bakers, administrators, clerks, accountants.

Mussolini believed that opposition would stir back into life at the slightest sign he was releasing his grip – but, characteristically, he did not want to use "only" the methods of informers and thugs. To achieve a real security which would allow him the amplest possible margin for manoeuvre he wanted political control over the situation. He thus allowed rumours to circulate of a partial liberalization of the regime, a lessening of pressure on public life, even the repeal of some of the laws which limited personal liberties. Rather like an amateur fisherman throwing out bait round his boat to attract fish, so Mussolini threw out these apparent concessions to see how much of the opposition would be attracted. The possibility of founding a semi-reformist party was held out to some war veterans. The most concrete proposals were made to the socialist trade-union leader Bruno Buozzi, who was living in exile in Paris. The regime invited him to return to work to bridge the economic gaps which still divided Italians and instil new confidence into the workers. The philosopher Benedetto Croce, who had remained an implacable and untouchable opponent of the regime, was tempted with the proposal of a nomination to the prestigious Reale Accademia d'Italia, and other opposition intellectuals were also contacted, always with the utmost discretion. All refused, "and with this refusal democratic anti-Fascism, represented by men like Buozzi and Croce, not only saved its soul and vindicated its right to claim to govern the country after the fall of Fascism, but also demonstrated that its attachment to freedom was sincere and concrete, not open to political bargaining, and so prevented the regime from claiming that communism was its only enemy."[30]

Recent historical accounts of Fascism have begun to bring out how much the left-wing roots of Fascism tried to survive within the later ideology. It is not simply a question of Mussolini's change of allegiance, which has in any case been seen too simplistically as a betrayal: as we have seen, he pursued power for its own sake, without reference to any moral, ethical or ideological principle. Yet he also managed to carry across into Fascism various left-wing ideas. "Fascism starts as a heterodox movement which takes its inspiration from several political radical tendencies. It is often seen as taking the form of a right-wing – even extreme right-wing – dictatorship, but it was in fact a collage of various ideas, with those coming from the left probably more prevalent. [...] Fascism was more concerned with invoking left-wing ideas, often radical ones, cast in a nationalist mould, than attacking the internationalist and pacifist left. We only need to think of the trends which were absorbed into its ideology: revolutionary syndicalism, socialist irredentism, radical republicanism. The reactionary component within Fascism did its best to neutralize these trends, yet they succeeded in persisting, however fluctuatingly, throughout the twenty years the regime was in power."[31]

It is enough to recall that it was Mussolini's regime which introduced the concepts of a national labour contract based on collective bargaining as well as employment tribunals. These were supposed to advance corporatist aims and resolve any conflicts among "producers" – in other words, between owners and workers – as well as preventing strikes and lockouts, and they were kept under strict central control, but nevertheless they represent innovative thinking in the field of labour relations. In the declining days of the Italian Social Republic, under Nazi power, Mussolini once more tried to adjust the – by now useless – political compass of the regime to the left. And the change of political direction was not merely a question of emphasizing the "social" in the regime's new name, or confined to Mussolini's musings on how to "socialize" private enterprise by introducing policies such as so-called "free" elections to the executive boards of firms like Fiat or Marelli, or by getting representatives from the shop floor to work alongside managing directors. Junio Valerio Borghese, the commander of the famous assault troops the Decima Flottiglia Mezzi d'Assalto (Tenth Assault Vehicle Flotilla), known as the Decima Mas, which remained in the north of the country after the Armistice on 8th September 1943, explicitly attempted to distance himself from reactionary Fascism and make independent contact with the Allies. In a television interview with the author of this book, his assistant Paska Piredda, the only woman with officer ranking in the Decima Mas, responsible for the regiment's external relations and its paperwork, has described the progress of contacts with Partisans from the so-called "Matteotti brigade" and the formation of various "mixed" squadrons made up of Partisans and men from the Decima Mas. She has also confirmed that frogmen paratroopers were sent with amphibious vehicles behind the Allied lines to make contact with that part of the Decima Mas which had gone to the south of the country following the orders of the King. Another of Piredda's memories is the surprise attack launched by a squadron of men from the Decima Mas to rescue Borghese, their commander, who'd been arrested by Mussolini on charges of plotting against him.

The celebrated film director, screenwriter and librettist Piero Vivarelli – he wrote, among others, songs made popular by the singer Adriano Celentano, such as '24,000 baci' and 'Il tuo bacio è come un rock' – was at the time of the war a very young – actually under-age – volunteer serving in the Decima Mas in the north of Italy. In another television interview with the author of this book, Vivarelli has described how he was for a time undecided about whether to join the communist partisans active around Florence, who had been in contact with him, or the Decima Mas. After the war Vivarelli became a fervent communist, to the point of asking Fidel Castro if he could join the Cuban Communist Party (he was already a member of the Italian party and had also adhered to the various extreme left-wing movements which sprang up in later years). For a young person like Vivarelli living under the Italian Social Republic, what shape the political future might take was far from clear.

Vivarelli also spoke about coming across a copy, at the end of March 1945, of a socialist newspaper, the *Italia del popolo*, which was being published with Mussolini's consent. Even though the erstwhile Duce now ruled only half the country, which was in any case occupied by the Germans, he had allowed the formation of a new group to go ahead, the Raggruppamento Nazionale Repubblicano Socialista (National Republican Socialist Grouping), which later transformed itself into a fully fledged political party. It is noteworthy that the title of *Italia del popolo* is a deliberate reversal of that of the Fascist newspaper founded by Mussolini years before, *Il Popolo d'Italia*, almost as if to point out that the new paper was in dialectical opposition to its predecessor. The editor-in-chief was Edmondo Cione, a former student of Benedetto Croce's, who joined the newly established Christian Democrat party after the war was over. He worked with a variety of associates on the paper, including Carlo Silvestri, a

Socialist who had stayed close to Mussolini and who supported the idea of coming to a deal with the Partisans, and Concetto Pettinato, one of the proponents of the racial laws in the late 1930s and a Fascist who was profoundly disturbed by the thought of looming defeat. It was far from easy to produce a socialist newspaper in those twilight days of the regime: it was printed in fifty thousand copies, a notable print run in that troubled period, but its circulation was severely limited, given that most of the copies were regularly destroyed by the black brigades made up of diehard Fascists. At the end of his life Mussolini's thinking lacked sharpness and lucidity; the cloudiness of his ideas can be seen, for example, in the remarks made to Georg Zachariae: "The internal politics of Italy will be characterized by the methodical and equal-handed application of the law on socialization with all the social consequences and forms of provision which will follow on from it. No one will be able to stop me putting such laws into practice. I'm aware that I'll be going against the whole social order as presently constituted; I can foresee I'll be attacked on all sides. The whole of world capitalism and its forces will try to stop me putting my plans into practice."[32]

For the past fifty years historians have tried to erase, at least from general historical awareness, the approaches which Mussolini's regime made towards the political left, and as a result it has been difficult to analyse and assess the recent leanings towards the left shown by various political leaders whose careers have emerged within a right-wing tradition which explicitly identifies itself as stemming from Mussolini's Fascism. Having repudiated Fascism and its crimes, these politicians have surprised many commentators by welcoming – albeit still from a right-wing point of view – such developments as, for example, the enrolment of homosexuals in the armed forces, scientific experimentation with stem cells, the commemoration of the holocaust, the freedom of terminally ill individuals to choose assisted suicide. An unexpected flash of insight about what the future might hold can be found in the notes Mussolini jotted down while in prison after the fall of the regime on 25th July 1943. He wondered what effect the "trauma", as he described it, of his fall would have on younger Italians, brought up under the regime: "What will they look to, these youngsters who've experienced this sudden upheaval? Either to the left, towards extremist positions, or else, in their disappointment and loss of faith, to a lack of belief in anything or anyone."[33]

At different times in his twenty-year rule Mussolini had shown himself open to various approaches and realignments, but only in order to widen his scope for political manoeuvre and reduce the number of his potential opponents. When these moves towards the left ended, as they almost always did, in failure, he soon forgot them and fell back into the profound disillusion he felt for his fellow Italians, at least of his own generation. "But how could he love his fellow men? With a kind of ruthless clairvoyance, he sees them as they really are. Because he rules over them he wants to improve them; he has formed an abstract idea of Italy which is so grand and sublime that the rest of us, actual Italians, cannot help falling short of his ideal."[34]

He was surrounded by crowds of adoring Italians, but by now he had given up the belief that he could mould them according to his notions of strength and virility, ideas of which he himself was utterly convinced but which, as Sarfatti implies, were destined to remain abstractions. Now his hopes rested on the coming generations who would grow up enveloped by his legend. The children who belonged to the Fascist youth movements such as the Balilla formed in the 1920s would grow up to become adult Fascists; it was they who would create the powerful and dominant nation of which he dreamt. And in addition to this belief, he put his hope in numbers, huge numbers: power equalled mass, the Italians had to procreate, the target was sixty million and more of them by 1950. Also the Italians who had emigrated overseas should breed plentifully so that eventually, by sheer strength of numbers, they would take over the countries where they lived. Guided by this vision of the future, Mussolini devised prizes for couples who married and went on to have large families. He introduced "mass weddings" and made sure that cameramen, photographers and journalists broadcast the events to the world. Hundreds of couples would enter the church, where a mass marriage would be celebrated. There would always be officiating priests, since the Catholic Church was an integral part of the vision, but the dominant factor was always the Fascist state. Mussolini never released his grip on the country's younger generations. He started to receive official delegations of mothers from the largest families in the country in order to bestow awards on them; on each occasion he would stress the number of special provisions his government had made for large families. He was aware that the Church pursued a similar policy, and was therefore careful never to let up the pressure:

the newly born belonged to the regime before they belonged to the Church. On this point he was insistent. As late as 1937, eight years after the signing of the Lateran Pacts with the Vatican, Mussolini still felt the need to address a crowd of adoring mothers from the balcony of Palazzo Venezia in the following terms: "As Italian women and Fascist women you have special duties to perform: you must look after our homes (*the crowd shouts out with one voice: Yes! Yes!*); with your unceasing care and never-failing love, it is you who are first responsible for shaping the young – may there be many of them, may they be strong! (*The crowd cries out enthusiastically: Yes! Yes!*) It is you who will breed and mould the generations of soldiers and pioneers who will defend our empire. I ask you: the education you give the young – do you promise it will be Roman, do you promise it will be Fascist? (*The crowd screams out: Yes! Yes!*)."[35]

In addition to having to encourage adoring crowds of mothers who were busy breeding a new generation of Italians, Mussolini found time, in his meticulously planned daily routine, for another category of women – his lovers. As soon as the weather started to get warmer, he would take himself off to the beach at Castel Porziano. Angela Curti was one of the women officially allowed through the sentry point at the entrance to the estate. On her return to Milan she would relate her adventures to her daughter. Mussolini had acquired a new motorboat, named "Alcione", and had asked her to go with him on its first trip. They were alone together on the beach at Castel Porziano and boarded the gleaming vessel; some bodyguards had immediately approached them, but Mussolini sent them away with an imperious gesture. He started the motor and steered the boat out to open sea, heading in the direction of Anzio and Nettuno, with one eye on the horizon and the other on the woman beside him, enjoying her amazement at the speed of the boat over the waves.

Chapter 16

The Brand of Fascism

No one could resist his magnetism: he was intransigent, unbending, with a fierce attention to detail; he always demanded the utmost of the men he worked with, he chose them individually and he moulded them into a single team. This was how Mussolini liked to see himself, but it's actually a description of Arturo Toscanini, the greatest conductor of his generation, at the head of what was considered to be the world's finest orchestra. Take away the mutual respect which governs the relationship between a conductor and his players and the music they play with its message of freedom and they could also be the characteristics of a tyrant. Only the practice of art can allow the exercise of such power. Toscanini had stood as a candidate for Mussolini's party in 1919, and his name in the electoral list had won eighty-four votes, but he had subsequently distanced himself in disgust at the violence of the Fascist squads. He ran La Scala in Milan, the most famous opera house in Italy, and had turned it into a temple or fortress where Fascism was powerless to penetrate. His international reputation as a conductor – he was renowned not only for his interpretations of Verdi but also, among the opera-going public, of Wagner – made him one of the most famous Italians in the world, and as such protected him. Unable to oppose him, Mussolini sought to exploit his fame in the interests of the regime: in 1925, on a visit to La Scala, he took Toscanini's arm and made sure he was seen by the audience thronging the foyer. Toscanini was displeased and didn't change his views.

The maestro vs. the Duce, Act One. On reflection, Mussolini decided to leave Toscanini at the head of La Scala – after all, his worldwide fame was useful for the country. On 14th May 1931 Toscanini agreed to conduct a concert in Bologna. The local Fascists had invited party *gerarchi* and other leading figures to the event and demanded that the Fascist anthem 'Giovinezza' ('Youth') be played at the beginning of the evening. Toscanini refused, and said that if they insisted he would cancel his appearance. The local bigwigs rapidly consulted among themselves and were inclined to avoid an outright conflict – better to snub the maestro by refusing to attend the concert. They forgot to take account of the extremists in the party, however: a squad of thugs took up their positions in front of the theatre and, as Toscanini stepped out of his car, four of them – Vannini, Gelati, Remondini, Ghinelli – set upon him, kicking and punching him. Afterwards, they joined a procession of Fascists who were singing the anthem as they marched through the streets. The incident caused a huge scandal in the international press.

Toscanini paid little attention to the attack, merely sending a telegram of protest to Mussolini, who didn't even bother to reply. Many years later, in the interview with Ludwig, he declared that Toscanini had deliberately chosen to "ratchet up the tension. On the same day he was attacked in Bologna – an uncouth act of aggression I find entirely deplorable – he rejected two proposals of mediation I had made to him. Sometimes you just have to find a formula for agreement. Did you notice the other day how I approached the naval negotiations with France? I started off with a threatening speech, but I still reached an agreement."[1]

In Mussolini's view, some kind of political compromise was needed, but Toscanini refused to accept one. The regime issued an official announcement stating that a citizen had slapped Toscanini's face because of his refusal to perform the anthem. The police then withdrew the conductor's passport, triggering another scandal in the world's press, at which point they gave it back. The regime's special police – the OVRA – started to take an interest in the case. They kept Toscanini's house under surveillance; his visitors had to report to them before entering, and were then registered and automatically marked down as enemies of the regime.

The maestro vs. the Duce, Act Two: open conflict. Toscanini took to accepting invitations to conduct wherever he thought liberty needed defending. He went to Tel Aviv to conduct, without payment, the inaugural concert of the Israel Philharmonic, formed by Jewish musicians who had escaped from persecution. The leading radio station in the world, the NBC in the United States, offered him the conductorship of a new orchestra in New York which would broadcast live concerts; the seventy-year-old maestro accepted with the alacrity of a young man. On 25th July 1943 he was in the middle of a concert when some stunning news arrived; his friends decided not to tell him until the concert was over. But during the interval some-one had left a radio on outside one of the dressing rooms and, as he walked by, Toscanini heard; he paused a moment, listened, and then merely uttered: "At last." In the space of a few hours Italy had got rid of Mussolini; the country was filled with mass demonstrations, cathartic, liberating.

The maestro vs. the Duce, Final Act. Toscanini decided to intensify his personal campaign against Fascism by conducting numerous concerts intended to raise funds to support the war effort and to aid the refugees who had to flee the conflict as the military front moved north through the peninsula. The concerts were extraordinarily suc-cessful – on one occasion, in Madison Square Garden, there was the largest audience ever seen for a concert of classical music. Fiorello La Guardia, the Italo-American mayor of New York, put programmes for the evening signed by Toscanini himself on sale, and even succeeded in selling at auction the conductor's baton. The NBC then suggested to Toscanini that he make a high-quality film of one of his concerts, in the same radio studios from which they were regularly broadcast all over the world; Toscanini, with his characteristic enthusiasm for new technologies, accepted immediately. He got the players, the sing-ers and the choir together, took up his baton and started to play, for the first time with cameras filming the event.

As part of the programme he had deliberately chosen two pieces by Verdi: the overture to *La Forza del destino* and the *Inno delle nazioni*, the *Hymn of the Nations* which the composer had created for the London exhibition of 1862. In the latter piece he also changed a verse in the text, replacing with his own pen a line with "*O Italia, o Italia, o patria mia tradita*" ("O Italy, O Italy, O my betrayed country"). He also included in the concert the Internationale, which on the orders of Stalin was no longer sung as the anthem of Soviet Russia; for Toscanini it had always been the anthem of the workers' and peasants' movement, of world socialism from its beginnings. But his inclusion of the piece later caused problems: when it first came out, Toscanini's film, entitled *Hymn of the Nations*, was a huge success in the United States and in the newly liberated cities in Europe, but once the conflict was over and the Cold War had begun, Hollywood insisted that the part containing the Internationale was cut. Only copies without the offending part were sent to the archives with the intention that just the doctored version would survive rather than the actual concert which Toscanini gave – a futile attempt at censorship, given that nowadays a full copy of the original film has been recovered and is freely available for viewing on the internet.

Mussolini regarded the attack on Toscanini as an accidental distraction as he tried to establish his credentials as an intellectual and patron of the arts, a connoisseur of painting and music and literature. En route to this goal of adding yet another facet to his myth, he sought to correspond frequently with various writers and poets and philosophers – such as D'Annunzio, Ada Negri, Giovanni Gentile, Emma Gramatica. Fired by his ambitions to be seen as a writer, Mussolini composed three historical plays between 1929 and 1931 – *Campo di maggio*, *Villafranca* and *Cesare* – though "composed" is exaggerated: he hired the services of a collaborator, who was not exactly a ghostwriter – there was no secrecy about the partnership – but who provided material support with the actual writing of the pieces. Giovacchino Forzano had been suggested to Mussolini by D'Annunzio and proved to be obedient and enthusiastic; he thanked the Duce for having taken him on as his "executant" and was unfailingly grateful to his leader for having given him the opportunity to contribute. Mussolini would send him notes, ideas, settings and plots. The three plays were about, in turn, Napoleon, Camillo Benso, Conte di Cavour and Julius Caesar, each seen at a moment in their careers when they had to face defeat because of betrayal: "The three historical dramas which Mussolini wrote in collaboration with Forzano clearly show his tendency to project his own self-image and deeds onto different historical contexts – the theme of the solitary leader, intent on the great goal he is pursuing but also aware of the lack of understanding and moral failings of the men who surround him and who should be helping him, conscious too of the need to exploit and force every opportunity to his own advantage..."[2]

Mussolini's cultural ambitions also lay behind the interviews he gave to Ludwig between 23rd March and 4th April 1932. But while he was intent on developing new aspects of his image, he also started to play down one which had turned out to be disappointing. The "Duce as musician" had certainly contributed to the aura which surrounded Mussolini, and many admirers had sent him valuable violins as a token of their devotion. Writing long after the fall of the regime, Paolo Monelli sought out some of the now elderly people in the Romagna who had once heard him play the violin; from their accounts he draws up a description of someone who was "an enthusiastic but mediocre amateur who'd taught himself to play, or at most had had a few basic lessons from the men who played the fiddle at village festivals... Mussolini played the violin more to let off steam than interpret the melodies of the piece as the composer had conceived them..."[3] We've seen how Margherita Sarfatti took her revenge on his serial infidelities by maliciously asking him to play in front of Toscanini; now that their relationship was in decline, she was delighted when he chose to play for her, even over the telephone.

Playing the violin had also provided a link between Mussolini and an accomplished French pianist, Magda Brard. She was born in Brittany in 1903 and had an international reputation as a keyboard virtuoso; she lived a secluded and mysterious existence in a villa – more splendid than Sarfatti's in the same area – on the shore of Lake Como. Using her fame as a pianist, she had set herself to seduce Mussolini – not such a hard thing to do – and after their affair came to an end did all she could to hide it for nearly half a century. At the end of the Second World War she found herself in difficulties, from which only the personal intervention of the Communist leader Palmiro Togliatti had managed to rescue her: the then Minister of Justice had promised to repatriate her to France, removing her from the jurisdiction of an Italian court where she'd been accused of collaboration. In this way the double game which Brard had been playing came to light: as one of Mussolini's mistresses and as an activist in the Resistance who by virtue of her network of contacts had succeeded in rescuing various leading Partisans of Christian Democrat sympathies, such as Enrico Mattei, the future president of Ente Nazionale Idrocarburi (the National Hydrocarbon Corporation, known as ENI), as well as industrialists in the north who had given their support to the anti-Fascist forces, such as the steel magnate Enrico Falck. In 1932 Brard had given birth to a daughter, Vanna, whom her husband, Michele Borgo, had at first refused to acknowledge as his offspring, thus giving rise to various rumours that the girl was yet another illegitimate child fathered by Mussolini. Her birth certainly coincided with the most intense period of Mussolini and Magda Brard's affair. During the 1930s Brard used to have several signed photographs of Mussolini on display, as if by chance, around her house; they served to impress any visiting party *gerarchi* and made it easier to obtain the favours she needed from them in playing her double game. The historian and journalist Roberto Festorazzi succeeded in obtaining an interview with Magda Brard towards the end of her life, when she was in a rest home; despite her great age and physical decline, she showed no regret and talked about herself and what she had done with satisfaction: "'Yes, that's right – Mussolini was my lover.' 'Did you love him?' 'I admired him. He was full of energy and a very good musician – he would play the violin while I accompanied him at the piano. I had a photograph of him with a signed dedication, but I destroyed it...' [...] She repeats with emphasis and with undiminished self-confidence: 'I am Magda Brard!' [...] The tales of the old lady in her nineties might now be seen as senile delusions – if only the doctors and nurses and all the others who surrounded her had realized the wizened old woman was just telling the truth."[4] Brard's virtuoso technique at the keyboard certainly served to cover up her lover's amateur efforts on the violin. Mussolini could dare to play in her company, just as he could within the privacy of the Villa Torlonia, but he knew he wasn't up to performing in public in the way that he played tennis or rode a horse or drove his Alfa Romeo. Quietly, without any publicity, he stopped playing the violin, although, addicted as he was to providing "political" explanations for all his actions, he did once give a highfalutin one: "I gave up playing the violin two years ago, for my own sake. Playing the instrument at first used to refresh me, and then it would agitate me. After half an hour of playing the violin I'd feel calm, after an hour, disturbed. All poisons work like that. I've given the beautiful violins which have been presented to me to talented youngsters who don't have the money to buy their own instruments."[5]

Ludwig's interview with Mussolini came out at the end of 1932 in several countries and became a worldwide best-seller. In Italy it was published by Mondadori in a very large print run. But the publication of the interview was not a straightforward matter: Mussolini realized that he had allowed himself to speak too freely in reply to Ludwig's questions, but too late to have the first edition withdrawn, since it sold out so rapidly. He couldn't stop or change the foreign editions, but he insisted that subsequent Italian editions came out in a revised version, with the excuse that Ludwig's use of the Italian language was incorrect, even though the journalist had written the book in his native language, German, and the text had been translated. Mussolini's claim that he was genuinely cultivated contradicted other declarations he had made which showed his real nature, such as his comment in a letter written on 8th January 1928 that he was not cultured in a general sense but "systematically", in other words, culture was a means, not an end, a tool or weapon for his advancement rather than a mere "adornment".

Effectively Mussolini never succeeded in being seen as a man of culture among the other attainments which formed part of his public image; the idea that he was a man of letters, a novelist, a dramatist, had no basis in actual fact. But at least his efforts to appear so were real: as a letter to the philosopher Giovanni Gentile shows, he was assiduous in using his free time for self-improvement: "Dear Gentile, I must tell you that I've spent these solitary days on the beach at Castel Porziano reading your book *La filosofia dell'arte* from beginning to end with great interest."[6]

On 16th September 1929 Mussolini moved the main seat of government from Palazzo Chigi to Palazzo Venezia. By then he had already left the apartment in Via Rasella and moved to take up residence in Villa Torlonia, where, in November 1929, after many years of living separately, he was joined by his wife and children. In the new and spacious setting of Villa Torlonia he had the rooms organized in such a way that he was able to lead his life independently of his family. "Although he was fond of his family, of his wife (who basically remained a good housewife who almost always kept her distance from affairs of state) and his children (especially his two daughters Edda, who was the most intelligent and whose character most closely resembled his own, and Anna Maria, particularly after she was struck down by paralysis at the age of seven and almost died), he spent very little time at home and lived a completely separate life from them when he was there."[7]

The housewifely Rachele didn't know that their new residence had been found thanks to the offices of Margherita Sarfatti, who had spoken to the villa's owner, Prince Torlonia. The rent that the Duce was charged – one lira – was purely symbolic; the Prince also allowed his staff and their families to use various houses and apartments in the grounds of the villa. The buxom and resplendent Romilda Ruspi was one of the young wives who lived in the villa's grounds – almost as if she were served up on a silver platter for Mussolini's pleasure.

His relationship with her showed no sign of ending; to avoid scandal she had to separate from her husband and move to an elegant apartment in the nearby Via Po.

The comings and goings of various women to Mussolini's living quarters once again threatened to get out of hand, as Boratto testifies: "Quite frequently, while 'R.' [Romilda Ruspi] was being entertained in Villa Torlonia, I would see 'S.' [Margherita Sarfatti] arrive unexpectedly at the staff entrance, since she had private access to the villa's grounds. Sudden secret exits and jealous rows would follow. Rumour had it that Ruspi gave birth to a baby boy during her affair with Mussolini, but I cannot confirm this."[8]

The exits and entrances of R. and of S. in the villa were also observed by the twenty-three-year-old Claretta Petacci, whose family in 1935 moved to a villa in Via Spallanzani, which bordered the villa Torlonia. She had caught Mussolini's attention three years earlier when he was driving his sports car; he had driven past her several times to make sure she had noticed him. She began to be invited to Palazzo Venezia. Now, in the new family home, she could keep a watchful eye on her hero's movements. She would get up early in the morning to see him riding his horse among the trees in the park surrounding the villa, and every now and then he would look up at the mischievous face framed by ringlets which was smiling down at him from a high window. When she became his official mistress, she already knew everything about Ruspi and her seductive arts and tormented Mussolini in the effort to get him to drop such a determined rival. Ruspi put up a stout resistance; she had three children and claimed the Duce was the father of the third, so securing an agreement from him to pay financial support for the boy's upbringing. As late as 1938 Petacci managed to surprise Mussolini just after he had had oral sex with Ruspi: "I insist he tells me the truth; I tell him what happened. He's taken aback and looks amazed, he betrays himself. He goes on denying it, but in the end confirms it by confessing: 'She took a handkerchief and placed it between her legs and then showed it to me, covered in blood. Yes, I confess gestures like these are repugnant – she was coarse. It put me off, so in the end nothing happened.' […] [Petacci:] 'No that's not true, she gave you a blow job.' – 'OK, yes, she gave me a blow job, there, now I've told you.'"[9]

A short distance away from Villa Torlonia, on Via Nomentana, was the stylish villa built in art-nouveau style where another of

Mussolini's long-term mistresses lived, Alice De Fonseca Pallottelli. "Twice a month Mussolini would unfailingly pay a visit to the elegant villa on Via Nomentana where the lady of the house, Signora 'P.' would be expecting him. She was blonde and slim, but no longer in her first youth; she had a seven-year-old daughter. She always made sure the gate to the villa was open for him, probably because she'd been telephoned in advance to expect him. She lived alone; I never saw any domestic staff."[10]

With no chambermaids or housekeepers around, poor Boratto had to fill the time while waiting for Mussolini's tryst with Pallottelli to come to an end by playing games with the daughter in the garden. Mussolini himself admitted to Petacci that he'd realized the children born to Ruspi and Pallottelli were his and was moved when he picked them up in his arms. In particular he thought the little Adù resembled Anna, his and Rachele's youngest daughter, and this seemed to him a good enough proof. Despite Petacci's opposition to them, both Ruspi and Pallottelli managed, just, to maintain their positions. Mussolini remarked to his young mistress: "I see Pallottelli once in a blue moon, she's finished like Sarfatti. The ties with her are like family ones. As for Ruspi – well, your psychology is right – I hold on to her out of a sense of possession. [...] But I've had enough of her too, there's nothing to attract me there, she's flabby, faded. [...] It's just keeping possession of something which is mine. Given that I support her financially, I'd rather she didn't sleep with other men. In any case, it's all relative, because it takes a lot of days, a long time to recharge the batteries."[11]

Just two days after she'd joined her husband in the Villa Torlonia, Rachele discovered some photographs of Bianca Ceccato in his pockets. She decided to accept his usual excuses – "My darling, you are the only woman I really love..." – and never suspected that there was another illegitimate child from this relationship. She was busy establishing her presence in her new home, and the first casualty of Rachele's moving in was not one of his mistresses. In her memoirs she wrote that on arrival in Rome she found her husband entrusted to the care of a housekeeper, one Cesira, and – it was Rachele's impression – it was she who seemed to be the head of the household. She then discovered that Cesira had been employed on the recommendation of – of all people – Margherita Sarfatti. Poor Cesira – even if she didn't consider herself in charge of the household, she had grown used to her independence in running the place, in organizing meals and visits, even regulating Mussolini's sleep. In her own way she had become a power to be reckoned with: many impoverished families used to write to her with demands, asking her to intercede on their behalf to obtain some financial support or a job. As time went by, requests started to arrive from firms in financial difficulties; if she was able to, she passed the letters on to Mussolini, and in this way acted as a privileged channel of access to him. Rachele dug in her heels: she asked Mussolini to dismiss the housekeeper. It is true that he tried to oppose the decision – he recalled the nights he'd spent doubled up in bed with the pain of his ulcer with Cesira always at his side, ready to give him a drink of water or his pills, to provide the tin bowl if he needed to vomit and to clean him up afterwards and wipe his fever-ish sweat away. But Rachele was adamant, and Cesira was sent back to Gubbio. Mussolini ensured that she received a monthly income of six hundred lire from the account of his newspaper *Il Popolo d'Italia*, and in 1939, showing he had not forgotten her, increased it to seven hundred lire (a popular song of the time had the refrain "If only I had a thousand lire a month…"). When the war came, the sum wasn't even enough to put food on the table with; after the war, Cesira's regular income stopped completely.

Mussolini soon got over the loss of his housekeeper; even when he was in Rome and not travelling the country, he spent little time in Villa Torlonia. He slept in a separate room, spent his time read-ing and briefly seeing his children. In the mornings he would take a short horse ride in the villa's grounds or play a round of tennis, while in the evenings he and his family would watch films in the small private cinema he'd had installed – Chaplin, Ridolini, Laurel and Hardy and, in advance of their public distribution and ready to order any cuts, the weekly newsreels produced by the Istituto Luce. He was keen on Walt Disney cartoons: "I saw *Snow White and the Seven Dwarves* – it was marvellous. It was unbelievably beautiful – you should see its colours, the different hues, the drawing! And he's so brilliant at imagining strange things – plants, flowers, birds… it was really splendid."[12]

When Disney paid a visit to Italy in the 1930s, Mussolini asked for him to be presented; the American turned up at the official audience with the Duce with a gift for his youngest daughter Anna Maria – an automated and life-size puppet of Mickey Mouse. Disney returned to the United States full of enthusiasm for the myth of Mussolini, but only a few years later, during the war, he nevertheless contributed to the propaganda effort by using his artistry to produce a cartoon against him, *Der Fuehrer's Face*, which is now regarded as one of the best cartoon films ever made. Lasting just five minutes, it shows Donald Duck having a dream in which Mussolini appears alongside Hitler and Hirohito. It's a masterpiece of its kind but despite this the Disney company prefers it not to be shown nowadays.

Mussolini didn't like receiving visitors at Villa Torlonia, apart from close relatives and other very rare exceptions. As the regime increased its hold on power, the number of Mussolini's presumed relatives tended to increase in direct proportion, much to the astonishment of Rachele, who had never suspected their families were so extensive. The situation got to the point when in 1939 Mussolini ordered a circular to be sent out from the Ministry of Popular Culture informing all state offices to reject any letter or request or other communication from people claiming to be related to him. He followed this up with a list of those who were deemed officially to be members of his family: his children, his sister Edvige Mancini Mussolini, his nephews Vito and Alfredo Mussolini and Agostino Augusto Moschi, the son of Rosa Guidi, Rachele's sister. No one else claiming kinship, outside this limited group of names, was to be allowed through.

After the end of the Second World War, the death of Mussolini and the collapse of the regime, Margherita Sarfatti, in her self-justificatory memoir entitled *My Fault*, paints a very different picture of Villa Torlonia and the surrounding neighbourhood along Via Nomentana. She writes that the residential villas of the area were surrounded by poorer areas. While the children of the well-off families in the villas were all privately educated, the poor sent theirs to the state schools, also attended by the Mussolini children. In 1933 a medical inspector was carrying out examinations in the state schools, and in the course of them came across a sickly little boy who suffered from a squint. The inspector asked how the parents of the child could send him to school in such a condition, but the staff soon warned him to tone down his comments: the skinny, frightened little lad was none other than Romano Mussolini... The anecdote testifies to Sarfatti's continuing desire to attack Rachele, who at the time of the memoir, immediately after the end of the war, had withdrawn completely from public life – but it seems hardly believable. In 1933 any school which had among its pupils one of the children of the by now legendary leader of the country would have regarded it as an honour and a privilege, and the idea that a mere provincial medical inspector could have examined Romano Mussolini without knowing who his father was is impossible. Sarfatti's malice against Rachele is seen in other pages of the memoir, for example, in criticizing the latter's ability to write properly (according to Sarfatti at least): "'I do wish she wouldn't keep spelling "*baci*" ["kisses"] as "*bachi*",' Mussolini would complain to me as he held the long elegant envelopes addressed in her ugly scribble, the fine writing paper suitable for a lady's bureau spoilt with the clumsy handwriting of the housewife. On the back of the envelope there was the odd scrawl '*Pedisse Rachele Mussolini*'. She never learnt to spell the word '*spedisce*' ['sends' = 'sender'] correctly, always getting the *s*s wrong, just as Mussolini himself, with his provincial accent, never managed to pronounce the name of the political movement he had invented right, always saying '*fassi*' or '*fassism*' or '*fassista*'."[13]

Journalists were kept away from Villa Torlonia; at most, they were summoned first thing in order to see the Duce at his morning sports activities. Mussolini had early on laid down – and in no uncertain terms – his vision of what journalism was about: on 10th October 1928 he had declared in front of a meeting of seventy of the country's newspaper editors that "the Italian press is Fascist and should feel pride in fulfilling its duty to fight in a united front under the banners of Fascism". He regarded all newspapers as party newspapers – belonging to one party, his own; the idea of a free press was merely part of the baggage of the old order of things, which the new regime had replaced. A new ontological conception of what information was for now ruled, summed up in the formula, to be applied consistently in every area of life: "Avoid what is harmful and do what is useful for the regime". Whenever it was deemed useful, the gates of Villa Torlonia were opened and journalists allowed to enter to exalt the Duce in all his splendour, and when they couldn't do this, they filled their pages with reports of dog shows, competitions for singing canaries, gymnastic tournaments and fashion parades. There was very little actual news to read, especially news of crime, since this would threaten to cloud the sky that, under Mussolini's regime, was supposed to be always bright. When it was seen that some journalists were slow to adhere to the new criteria, displaying an unwarranted attachment to their old professional independence of action and opinion, the Ministry for the Press and Propaganda started to send out personal warnings from the Duce criticizing their work, while their more submissive colleagues received personal commendations. Picture the state of mind of a journalist who received a reprimand from the Duce. Journalists were seen as mere "labourers" at the service of the so-called mass culture by means of which Mussolini hoped to mould his new Italians and modify the old ones; they were there merely to echo and amplify the Duce's extemporized slogans, such as the one he improvised when he emerged onto the balcony of Palazzo Venezia in front of the assembled crowds brandishing a book and a gun in his hands, the new symbols for the education of Fascist youth.

"The book and the gun" came to be seen alongside the *fasces* as one of the leading symbols of the regime, exalted by its propaganda, reviled by its opponents – but the motto was in fact merely the result of chance. "There was a crowd of students in Piazza Venezia who were applauding him and urging him to appear on the balcony. Mussolini had no wish to address them, since he couldn't think of anything he wanted to say. So he went and fetched a gun from off one of the walls and also grabbed a book without looking at it..."[14] As he stepped out onto the balcony holding these objects aloft, a roar went up from the crowd; from that moment onwards "the book and the gun" became the leading slogan for Fascist education, the symbol towards which the perfect Fascist youth (*"Libro e moschetto / Fascista perfetto"*) should aspire. Today the idea seems laughable, but at the time it was an extraordinary phenomenon: the symbols galvanized the younger generation, who transmitted their enthusiasm to their families – peasants, factory and office workers, all sections of society became involved. The maximum levels of public consensus for the regime derived from its penetration of the country's educational system; the endless lessons of Fascist mythologizing had the effect Mussolini had planned. The influence of the regime's blanket propaganda was profound on the generation which grew up after the March on Rome. The new means of communication, radio and cinema (through the Luce production company) were powerful transmitters. Even in an area of the country as remote as the Barbagia in inland Sardinia, about as far from Mussolini's imperial city of Rome as it was possible to get in the Italy of the time, the children played at being "country housewives". Racing around among the cherry and almond trees and the great rocks, the tallest girl would reach the outside stairs of the cottage and run up them to take her place on the small central balcony, her head just appearing above the parapet, and there she would shout out the words she had heard earlier on the radio from one of Mussolini's speeches to the crowds in Piazza Venezia. Below, playing among the great granite boulders shaped by the wind and the rain, the other little girls would wrap pieces of cloth round cushions and stones, turning them into dolls – all the numerous offspring which the regime demanded from Italian women, making the little girls feel like the "housewives" they'd heard the grown-ups speak so much about.

On one occasion Mussolini lifted the rules which protected Villa Torlonia from unwanted visitors to allow a team of American filmmakers in to create a documentary on his domestic life. Making sure at the outset that the distribution of the completed film within Italy would be prohibited, Mussolini gave his consent to being filmed sitting in an armchair and reading the newspaper – wearing thick reading glasses to do so – and for his children to be filmed as they went to school. Only Rachele managed to avoid the camera, although she underestimated a cameraman's skill in keeping one eye fixed on the camera focus and the other on the alert for anything else happening in the background – in this case the American operating the camera noticed that Rachele had come out of the kitchen, quickly panned over to her and succeeded in filming her as she moved.

The family had various domestic pets in their new residence, including three dogs, called Pitini, Charlot and Brock, and an angora cat called Pippo. During the war the very popular singing sisters known as the Lescano Trio, whose records were always hits with the Italian public, recorded a song with the strange line "But Pippo Pippo doesn't know / That when he passes everyone in the city laughs…" Pippo was the name of the Allied Forces' small reconnaissance aeroplane which regularly flew over Italian cities after they had been bombed to assess the effects of the raids. However, some preferred to see an allusion to Mussolini's cat. Despite their phenomenal success (one of their records sold more than 300,000 copies) the three sisters happened to be Jewish and were dragged into the tragic events of the Holocaust. "I knew about the importance of race as early as 1921. How can they think I'm imitating Hitler, who hadn't even been heard of then. The idea is laughable. The race must be defended. […] It's necessary to instil Italians with a sense of the race, so that they don't go on to produce half-castes who will destroy all that's finest in us" – a remark of Mussolini's transcribed by Petacci.[15]

For a long time Mussolini's anti-Semitism appeared as a kind of undertone, as if submerged in the flood of political and promotional activity, the often self-contradictory articles, declarations and speeches he produced every day, and this lack of prominence given to the theme is reflected in the view – widely held even now – that Italian anti-Semitism was a "minor" phenomenon, milder or in any case different from the Nazi version. In the interview he gave to Ludwig, Mussolini declared: "Anti-Semitism doesn't exist in Italy. Italian Jews have always been good citizens and courageous soldiers. They occupy leading positions in universities, in the armed forces, in the banks. Several army generals are Jews – such as Modena, the commander in Sardinia, while another general is head of the artillery regiments."[16] It should be remembered when reading this statement that Ludwig was himself Jewish, that he was writing for a non-Italian public, and that Mussolini immediately came to regret having allowed the publication of the book.

In 1936 several officials from the Fascist Ministry of Internal Affairs visited the concentration camp in Dachau and wrote a report praising the efficiency with which it was run. In the same year, in an article which was published on 31st December in *Il Popolo d'Italia*, Mussolini wrote: "People who don't give much thought to the matter – or pretend not to – ask how anti-Semitism comes about, in what ways and for what reasons a man becomes an anti-Semite even though reality has provided him with some clear evidence? The answer is simple: anti-Semitism is inevitable whenever Jewishness appears excessive, too visible, too intrusive, too dominating. The excessively Jewish gives rise to those who are anti-Jews." Even if Italian Jews were never forced to wear yellow stars, the regime's racial laws against them can by no stretch of the imagination be described as mild. Mussolini kept Italian Jews – the citizens of his state – hanging on as he decided what was best to do about them. They became his hostages. It was the laws he passed which provided the legal basis for their subsequent deportation, and when the round-ups began, it was his state which paid five thousand lire to anyone who denounced or captured a Jew. His real attitude towards the Jews is evident in the numerous remarks found in Petacci's diary: "They look on us as goyim. They exploit us and hate us. They're rootless and godless – one day they're Poles, the next Turkish or French. They settle down wherever it suits them best, and they squeeze you dry. They're a cursed race, they killed God. They think that we took our God from them – I reply that they denied him and killed him because he wasn't one of them – otherwise they would have recognized him. He didn't belong to their race, so they killed him. They've got no excuse."[17]

Hitler, when he was once challenged by a woman over the Jewish question, replied by saying that no one remembered the Armenian massacre, and we find the same reference to the first genocide of the twentieth century in Mussolini's remarks as written down by Petacci in her diary. Despite the grammatical mistakes and the illegible words, the meaning is only too clear: "Ah [?] these filthy Jews, they [word illegible] should all be destroyed just destroyed once and for all [?] not because I was generous but because I was scared by Roosvel [sic] because they're so powerful [I] couldn't touch them, I'll massacre them just like the Turks did I interned seventy thousand Arabs, I could put fifty thousand Jews into internment, all shut up on a big island, or I'll destroy them. [...] They're filthy. I regret [not having?] come down hard on them. But on 7th November [they'll see?] what my iron fist is capable of. I'll destroy [them?]."[18]

It was not only in public life that Mussolini used his iron fist; his private life was far from being untouched by his violence. On the night of 15th July 1935, Ida Irene Dalser committed a fatal error, the last such mistake in her life. She managed to prise open the grating on the window of her cell in the psychiatric hospital in Pergine. Perhaps sheer desperation gave her the strength, as it gave her the ingenuity to soak various sheets and tie them together to form a rope by which she could climb down out of the window. An official visit by Mussolini to Trento was about to take place; the city's police chief gave strict orders that the "mad" woman was to be captured as soon as possible, something which, given the number of spies there were around working for the regime, was easy to do. Dalser was sent to another psychiatric hospital on the island of San Clemente in Venice, where she was kept in isolation and her relatives forbidden from visiting her. The treatment was harsh, and she died on 2nd December 1937. Her son Benito Albino was still alive, although in 1932 the Ministry of Justice had changed his surname from Mussolini to Bernardi – Giulio Bernardi, who'd been brought in by the regime to help to camouflage this embarrassing offspring, was the boy's guardian or foster-father. But since it wasn't possible to stop the boy talking to other young people of his age, it was decided to enrol him in the navy and send him off to Shanghai on a ship. The ship's captain, however, soon realized how disturbed the young man was and did not feel capable of taking responsibility for him; he had him sent back to Italy in 1935 with the order that he be referred to the naval hospital for examination. The medical checks found him to be fit mentally and physically, but despite this, rather than being dismissed, he was sent straight to the asylum in Mombello, near to Milan. His clinical file shows that he had asked voluntarily to be admitted as a patient to a psychiatric hospital so that he could receive appropriate treatment. A doctor declared it was necessary to administer the method of induced coma, an alternative to electroshock therapy; nine separate times he was put into a coma by being injected with insulin. He died on 26th August 1942, given a pauper's funeral and buried in the cemetery at Lambiate. For security reasons his name was not written on his tomb, which was marked only by a small column and a number: 931.

As the effects of the Great Depression spread throughout the world, the women of Milan and Turin took to the streets chanting "Long live the Duce, but give us food!" The sudden fall in industrial output meant that half a million factory workers found themselves jobless and destitute. Mussolini, as usual, was uncertain how to react. He intervened directly in the services set up to distribute food to the neediest, insisting that portions be increased by adding rice or suchlike. He gave orders that whoever wished to emigrate were to be allowed to apply for passports, as long as they had no criminal record and had done their military service. He took measures to save some banks from collapse, such as the Credito Italiano and the Banca Commerciale, and he set up the Istituto Mobiliare Italiano or IMI to oversee reforms to the country's economic and financial system. But it was the secret services – the OVRA – which were given most to do during the crisis. The workers who came out on strike tended to be supportive of the Duce, but among their leaders and organizers Communist agitators had begun to re-emerge; the regime's repression was harsh, and many arrests were made. Remembering perhaps his own past activities as a socialist revolutionary, Mussolini decided to test for himself the mood of the working classes in the north, but was disconcerted by what he found. In Turin, where Fascism had always been less popular than elsewhere, the regime's trade-unionists could hardly manage to control the situation. In the nearby cities of Novara and Vercelli even the *mondine* or rice-weeders had gone on strike, while the workers in the industrial town of Sesto San Giovanni on the outskirts of Milan listened to a speech from the Duce in silence – what applause there was noticeably coming only from the local Fascists gathered round the podium.

In this climate of tension, a new wave of terrorist attacks was unleashed. Explosive devices were sent to the editorial offices of *Il Popolo d'Italia* and *Corriere della Sera*, while a bomb killed two railwaymen at the Tiburtina station in Rome. In 1931 and again in 1932 the police arrested individuals accused of plotting to assassinate Mussolini. Despite the fact they had not carried out their attempts, both Michele Schirru, a migrant, and Angelo Sbardellotto received death sentences which were immediately executed.

In 1931 Gandhi paid a visit to Rome as part of a European tour to win support for the cause of Indian independence. The Pope refused to see him, since Vatican diplomats ruled that his dhoti – the traditional white cotton garment worn by poor peasants in India, which Gandhi had woven with his own hands – was unseemly. Mussolini received him, but decided to avoid an official ceremony in the Palazzo Venezia and organized a reception instead in the cinema room in his private residence in Villa Torlonia. Gandhi's anti-British stance was not unwelcome to Mussolini and, according to his wife, he also admired the methods Gandhi adopted, telling his children that the Indian was a saint who had had the genius to hit on a political weapon no one had used before: goodness. Bruno and Vittorio were entertained by the small half-naked visitor who caused such headaches for the security services on the occasion of his visit. "I can still see the faces of all those guests from the beau monde who had been invited to the reception when Gandhi entered the room, leading a pet goat on a leash: a great silence descended on the crowd, all of whom were taken aback by the sight – his scanty clothing, first of all, and then the goat."[19] Gandhi was pleased with his welcome and gave a speech thanking and praising the Duce.

In dealing with the effects of the Great Depression on the world's economy, Mussolini found that a policy he had devised for other purposes came in useful. On 24th December 1928 he had had a law, bearing his name, approved to set up a project for the reclamation of vast tracts of malaria-infected marshland. The work had begun in July 1929, just before the Wall Street Crash. The aim of the project was the so-called "ruralization" of Italy, to increase the country's agricultural output to the point where large numbers of the urban population would move into the country. From this point of view, the policy turned out to be a complete failure, however the regime's propaganda and Mussolini's rhetoric tried to paint it: "A life spent working in the fields is a healthy life both physically and spiritually. Breathing the fresh air out in the sunshine makes the body strong; country living provides families with the best conditions for their own security and development. In industrial and urban societies women have no time to attend to their homes and families, whereas in the countryside women rule their houses and their families like queens."[20]

But the policy of public works proved useful in confronting the economic crisis: the reclamations and the building of new towns offered jobs and land to cultivate at a time when there were millions of unemployed. Mussolini's demographic policies were a failure, however; despite the tax on unmarried men, the bonuses for large families, the loans to help young couples get married, the creation of associations and centres of assistance for mothers, there was no sudden boom in population growth, something on which Mussolini was relying for the future of the regime, the "true" Fascism of the coming age when a new generation would have grown up now purified of the all too characteristic "Italian" shortcomings of their parents.

Mussolini did not trust the Fascist comrades with whom he had come to power, nor did he respect them – on the contrary he was openly scornful of their abilities. The only one who aroused his fear and envy was the *quadrumviro* from the March on Rome, Italo Balbo, whose exploits as a pilot threatened to overshadow Mussolini's own image as an "expert and daring airman", a key component of his public persona. He may have asserted confidently in his interview with Ludwig that he believed there "could never be a second Duce, and if there were the Italians wouldn't accept him",[21] but all the same he preferred not to risk the possibility. Balbo was the only man who could have become "a second Duce", and as such win the support of the country, a valid substitute in the event that an assassination attempt on Mussolini's life proved successful; so he made sure Balbo was relegated to Libya as the colony's governor, out of harm's way.

Shortly after the beginning of the Second World War, Balbo's plane was shot down at Tobruk by "friendly fire" from an Italian warship; the regime organized a solemn funeral service in Rome for the former *quadrumviro*.

There was an element missing in the image of Mussolini as an accomplished pilot. On 28th May 1935 Mussolini wrote in his diary: "Today Bruno passed his exams to become a pilot. I watched him land the plane, which he did brilliantly. Let it not be said that I've brought up my children to have an easy life."[22] Bruno had been named after the figure of Giordano Bruno; when his third son was born, in 1917, Mussolini was still fervently anti-clerical. When the boy passed the exam for his flying licence, Mussolini was undoubtedly and sincerely pleased, yet the boy's success caused a problem, since he himself had not yet obtained one. The fact that Mussolini already had grandchildren was not mentioned by the regime's propaganda machine; the Duce had to be seen as "eternally" youthful. Bruno's success as a military pilot also threatened to cast a shadow over Mussolini's image, making him seem old and behind the times. And yet he had invented the mythic coupling of Fascism and aviation, the Duce who governs the country like the pilot who controls the plane. There was a mystic element to this too: the Duce as a kind of archangel of Fascism descending from the skies in an act of "divine providence" rather than being born on earth to a "humble" family. And, finally, flying also equalled virility: over the main entrance to the Ministry of the Air Force visitors could read the words "*Chi vola vale, chi non vola non vale, chi vale e non vola è un vile*" ("The man who flies is brave, the man who doesn't fly is not brave, the man who's brave and does not fly is a coward"). The news bulletins started to carry information such as the following: "Today, at 3 p.m., the Duce left the hydroport on the Rome Lido and carried out a training flight on board a three-engine flying boat S.66 / Rome, 19, night. After a reception for the mothers of large families at Palazzo Venezia the Duce left for the Littorio airport, where he boarded an S.81 which he piloted during a training flight lasting nearly two hours."[23]

Finally the time came when Mussolini could take the test to obtain his pilot's licence. It was 13th January 1937. The examining panel was made up of the head of the General Command, the head of the Cabinet and the commander of the airport. The idea that the Duce might fail the test was inconceivable. According to the rules, he had to pilot a plane in solo flight, but no one was prepared to take the responsibility for sending him up on his own without a support pilot, and no one was prepared to tell him that they were planning to do this. The night before the flight, a young but experienced pilot was smuggled into the cockpit of the plane, with some difficulty as there were numerous security patrols. Mussolini took off, leaving the Fascist officials below him gazing skywards anxiously; only the head of General Command, General Valle, knew about the second pilot and could remain serene. After the flight, Mussolini brought the plane down to land to a round of applause. The young pilot stowed away in the cockpit had to wait until darkness fell before he could get out.

Making sure he was the focus of media attention was a recurrent problem for the Duce. Famous figures and *gerarchi* like Balbo were not the only ones who got in the way – the main obstacle was the monarchy and the fascination felt by the Italian masses for it. On 8th January 1930 in the Cappella Paolina in the Quirinale Palace, the heir to the throne Umberto was married to the Princess of Belgium Maria José; the wedding would have had less public impact if the Lateran Pacts had not been signed a few months earlier. The newly wed couple were received by Pius XI. The ceremony was followed by an enraptured crowd of onlookers, and the newspaper reports were full of details of the bride's dress, the wedding cake, the guest list and the delegations sent by the different regions wearing their local costume. A few months later, in October 1930, another royal wedding took place: the Princess Giovanna, the daughter of Victor Emanuel III, married King Boris of Bulgaria. The austere ceremony took place in the Sacro Convento in Assisi; Giovanna was a lay member of the Franciscan order and didn't want any pomp, also because of the economic crisis which was afflicting the country. Once again, the crowds went wild at the sight of the couple. In the procession out of the church, Mussolini, due to ceremonial protocol, found himself almost at the back after crowned heads and royal princes, with an unknown noblewoman on his arm, given that Rachele had refused to attend.

With his feeling that the whole regime depended on him, and his distrust and scepticism about others, Mussolini could not abide the thought that someone else might establish a direct rapport with the masses and be acclaimed by the people he thought of as belonging to him. As we have seen, he only really put his entire trust in one individual, his brother Arnaldo, who not only replaced him as the editor of *Il Popolo d'Italia* and dealt with the family's business affairs, but also acted as his advisor, the man who could be depended upon to do the difficult work in delicate negotiations, bringing together different lobbies and interest groups, his alter ego in all those potentially treacherous situations which it was absolutely necessary to tackle head-on, but where Mussolini himself could not or would not become personally involved.

A good example of the way the relationship between the two brothers worked was the marriage of Edda, Mussolini's favourite daughter. Like her father, Edda was headstrong, capricious and impetuous; she had had various love affairs which risked becoming formal engagements. Mussolini, who kept an eye on his daughter's goings-on, had discouraged the suitors. The first had been a Jewish boy. Writing to his sister Edvige, Mussolini said: "In the letter I wrote to Edda, I've asked her to think seriously before taking a step which would scandalize everyone – not to mention that ninety per cent of mixed marriages turn out badly."[24] The second boyfriend managed to get himself invited to supper at the Villa Torlonia, a rare honour, but put paid to any chances he might have had by asking Mussolini at the end of the evening how much Edda's dowry would be. "There was no dowry, and my brother's startled riposte was the only possible and appropriate one (it's likely that the very word 'dowry' struck him as odd and out-of-place, like something from another world)."[25]

Yet Mussolini was intent on finding a husband for Edda before she settled the matter with one of her headstrong decisions. He asked his brother to find a suitable man, and Arnaldo set to work. Scions of the nobility were ruled out at the outset: the idea of a girl "from a poor background" setting up house with a young aristocrat was unacceptable. Arnaldo in turn asked a friend of his, a Sicilian member of parliament, who was intimately familiar with high society in Rome, to help out; thanks to him, they succeeded in picking out the right candidate, and it was a good choice, since Edda did in fact fall in love with the young count Galeazzo Ciano. It's true he was a nobleman, but his family's ennoblement was very recent, acquired by his father Costanzo Ciano for heroism during the First World War. The father, who was also a prominent Fascist and held the "*medaglia d'oro*", which was one of the country's highest honours, also happened to be close to Mussolini – he had been one of the few people to have supported him during the Matteotti crisis. He had become rich when Mussolini had given him the post of Minister of Communications, and his brother Arturo had founded a company to import coal from Germany, which thus became the "preferred" source of supply for the state railway in Italy, for which Ciano's ministry was responsible. Noble status and wealth made the young Galeazzo a good catch. On 24th April 1930 the regime put out the flags in staging the wedding of Mussolini's daughter to Ciano, and so recaptured the focus of public attention. Among the 512 guests included on the "exclusive" invitation list for the reception held in the gardens of the Villa Torlonia there were the most famous names of Rome's upper middle classes and aristocracy, surrounded by more than fifteen hundred security agents to keep order. The newspapers talked about the bride's elegant wedding dress, made by the Roman designers Montorsi, because the regime wished to support the Italian fashion industry, and also the hats and fur coats and capes worn by the female guests. Amid trays of cakes and chocolates, all of them made in Italy, the wedding party was a fitting continuation to the equally successful church ceremony: "At the top of the steps leading to the church doors, two rows of 'the Duce's musketeers', gloomy and rather sinister-looking in their black shirts and with their fierce expressions, awaited the exit of the bride and bridegroom, with their swords raised to form an arch, while behind them, gaily dressed in traditional costume, peasant women from the Romagna danced as at some country celebration. In later years several middle-class Roman weddings imitated the device of having the happy couple leave church under an arch of raised swords, sometimes held by children dressed in the uniforms of the Fascist youth movement."[26]

Mussolini presided at eight weddings in all: apart from Edda's, there were those of the three daughters of his sister Edvige and of Arnaldo's children, as well as the marriages of his own sons Vittorio and Bruno. All the ceremonies were held in the church of San Giuseppe, on the Via Nomentana, which became a kind of Mussolini family chapel, with the usual display of uniforms and fashionable dresses, and the tunnels of drawn swords – one of the regime's favourite symbols – held aloft to form a kind of arch of honour for the couple to pass through. And it was always Mussolini, as the head male of the clan, who accompanied the bride to give her away.

"I stare at the portrait of Sandrino which Arnaldo sent me with a dedication written on it: 'To Benito, our leader, this branch of the tree broken off at the age of twenty'."[27] In August 1930, barely four months after Edda's wedding, Arnaldo's eldest son, Sandro, died; his father never recovered from the blow and passed away on 21st December 1931. Mussolini thus found himself without the support of his brother, increasingly harassed by the thought of having to deal with things on his own and a lack of trustworthiness among his associates and the party leadership. At the same time, his relationship with Sarfatti, the only other person in whom he could confide, was drawing to an end.

> It is possible to speculate that a psychological connection might exist between the death of his brother, the end, shortly afterwards, of the relationship with Sarfatti (the only really meaningful one in the 1920s and early 1930s) and the increasing frequency of short-lived affairs, involving no emotional commitment, with women who must have flattered his male pride and confirmed to him, even in this private sphere of activity, his prestige and magnetism. [...] Whatever the case, it is certainly true that Arnaldo's death made Mussolini's human solitude almost total and exacerbated his psychological tendency to distrust people, his feeling that the associates who surrounded him were weak and vacillating, and that therefore he alone was the prime mover, the leader who had to do everything and to whom everything referred.[28]

From this time onwards, Mussolini turned in on himself completely, indulging in a series of brief but frequent sexual adventures. When he finally re-emerged from this period, he would come to rely more and more on the cloying, nest-like intimacy constructed for him by his new mistress Claretta Petacci.

Chapter 17

Home Is Where the Heart Is

Mussolini's sexual activities have been described as a whirlwind, but the term can be misleading; though prolific, they were in fact remarkably well organized by the staff in Palazzo Venezia. One only needs to look at the procedures carried out by the relevant secretarial office. Every day saw the arrival of numerous letters as well as telephone calls from female admirers; the women who already had Mussolini's private number could call him direct, while the others were put through a filtering process – in the office responsible for his private affairs – to ascertain whether they were suitable enough candidates for the Duce's consideration. The letters presented a real problem; the so-called experts in the private office examined each letter individually – they acquired in effect a real expertise in recognizing the handwriting on the envelopes. If it belonged to one of the women who was on the "authorized" list, the letter was forwarded to Mussolini unopened; if the hand was an unfamiliar one, then the envelope was opened and its contents examined. Once this had been done, the information contained in the letter was forwarded to a special police unit so that the appropriate security checks could be carried out. After the selection based on these checks was made, the letters which survived the filtering process were delivered to Mussolini, so that he could make a further selection of the women he wished to see; the preparatory procedures meant that he could be sure there were no problems of security with any of them.

He usually saw them in the late afternoon. The social niceties were not observed – no introductory small talk to break the ice, no tea and biscuits were offered (only Claretta Petacci managed to get this). Mussolini's office, in the vast room known as the Sala Mappamondo (World Map Room), contained just three pieces of furniture: a huge desk, his own chair, and an armchair opposite for his visitor. The visits never lasted more than half an hour, and the women were never allowed to leave in a ruffled state – they would emerge with their hair combed and their clothes adjusted and trim. "Mussolini's technique varied according to the category of visitor: with the 'regulars' he would use the huge carpet under the desk, while the 'newcomers' would be taken to one of the long stone seats which formed part of the window bays, covered with a thick mattress-like cushion designed to fit them. I realized this only because I was surprised to see Mussolini and his lady friends always in lively conversation, so I took to carrying out an inspection of the room: after a search I would find that the cushion in the window seat was rumpled, while from time to time I'd come across a dropped hair clip on the carpet."[1]

Mussolini's valet also recalled the different physical types of women who visited Mussolini, in demonstration of the fact that he had no particular preferences as far as this aspect was concerned: Signora B. was tall, dark-haired, plump and attractive, while T. from Rome, though still dark-haired, was skinny and plain; C. from Milan again was dark-haired but tall and well built, not too refined but not common either, whereas the Countess R. from Rovigo was a beauty, blonde and curvaceous.

When Claretta Petacci, the curly-haired brunette whose breasts had caught and held Mussolini's attention, started to make inroads, the bewildering number of lovers started to decline; only a few of the long-term mistresses, what might be called the "historical" ones, managed to survive. At this point the meticulous efforts of the "private office" in the Palazzo Venezia were directed towards making sure Petacci's increasingly frequent visits were kept secret. Only two security guards and the valet Quinto Navarra were informed; the latter has described in his memoirs how the visits to Palazzo Venezia were organized so that no one ever saw her come or go. She would leave her home and take a taxi to a prearranged meeting place, where a motorbike with a closed sidecar would be waiting for her; she got into the sidecar, making sure the windows were covered with thick cloth panels. The motorcyclist was a plain-clothes policeman. They would cross the city, circle round Palazzo Venezia and enter through a rear doorway in Via degli Astalli. Any passer-by who saw the vehicle would assume it was just a courier carrying an urgent delivery. Once inside the inner courtyard, the "delivery" would emerge from the sidecar and take the private lift to the Duce's personal apartments on the first floor. Rachele knew about the visits, and wrote about

them in a tone of understandable defensiveness (though the assertion about her husband's nights away from home is not true): "All
the while this affair was going on, Benito never spent a night away
from home. He never introduced Claretta Petacci to anyone or went
out in public with her. They were forced to have brief rendezvous,
usually in the small sitting room in Palazzo Venezia."[2]

Once in Palazzo Venezia, Petacci frequently had to wait for Mussolini to finish with his round of official visitors – the ministers, *gerarchi*,
bankers and all the others who had been granted an audience with
the Duce. One example of how such meetings were conducted can
be found with Pietro Gazzera, an army general whom Mussolini had
appointed as Minister for War in September 1929. He took up his
post at a time when political and military conflict with France and
Yugoslavia were real possibilities, and he found himself at the head
of armed forces suffering from a lack of both real coordination and
sufficient financial resources. "Once general Gazzera had crossed
the wide space which separated the entrance from Mussolini's desk
he found himself opposite the Duce, who preferred to dress in a
suit rather than in uniform when he was at work. Mussolini would
remove his glasses when his visitor arrived, as he preferred not to
be seen in them and, contrary to the rule that the Fascist salute was
to be used on all occasions, would welcome him with an ordinary
shake of the hand."[3]

Gazzera opened his files and started to take notes, but after a while
Mussolini suggested he stop writing. Gazzera then had to commit
everything to memory; when he left Palazzo Venezia he would sit in
his car writing down everything which Mussolini had said to him,
much of which was improvised and unofficial – insistent urges for
military adventures, sudden surprise attacks, like the time Mussolini
asked him to prepare an operation to invade France. Gazzera was
a professional soldier and considered it his duty to inform Mussolini that the country's armed forces were in no state to undertake
an attack on another country, but the party *gerarchi* despised the
general as yet another mere technician who'd been appointed to the
government instead of a committed Fascist, and they continued to
encourage Mussolini's desires for conflict.

In July 1933 Mussolini took over the running of the Ministry of
War; for the military adventures he had in mind a professional soldier
was of no use. While Gazzera and others came and went in Palazzo

Venezia in the effort to reason with the Duce, in a private sitting room the women who'd been summoned to an appointment had to while away the time they spent waiting. Every so often Mussolini's official valet Navarra – elegant and distinguished-looking – would quietly make an appearance to see if there was anything they needed and to keep their spirits up. He was aware that the higher the rank of the woman – whether it was Angela Curti just arrived from Milan or the restless Marchesa Giulia Brambilla Carminati or the refined Princess Sveva Vittoria Colonna – the more likely she was to be irritated by the fact she was kept waiting. Navarra would treat them kindly, hoping to soothe their impatience. He once found Claretta Petacci reading a book on Madame de Pompadour, and on another occasion leafing through a copy of the popular women's magazine *Vita femminile*, the editor of which, Ester Lombardo, just happened to be yet another of Mussolini's mistresses.

Petacci wanted to bring a halt to the constant stream of women in Palazzo Venezia and so eliminate her competitors. Her campaign was helped by the fact that Mussolini's libido was no longer as powerful as it used to be. "There was a time when I had fourteen women on the go and would see three or four of them every evening, one after the other – at 8 p.m. I'd have Rismondo, then Sarfatti, then Magda [Brard]. On one occasion I rounded off the evening at one in the morning with an insatiable Brazilian woman who'd have finished me off if a huge storm hadn't damaged one of the walls. That was what my sex drive was like. I wasn't in love with any of them, I had them because they attracted me, I enjoyed it [...] But you've put paid to all that, believe me. [...] I've gradually stopped seeing all of them."[4]

Giulia Brambilla Carminati was one of the regular mistresses who attempted to hang on, even writing to Mussolini criticizing Petacci. But the younger woman took her revenge by transcribing in her diary, with obvious relish, the vulgar remarks of her lover which signalled her own victory: "Yes, you're right, Brambilla is like an old slack cow – you could fit several... well, you get my meaning. [...] She's an old whore, a filthy bitch. Women like her or Sarfatti, once they get to a certain age, will go with their drivers, their menservants, the porter – and they'll pay them for the pleasure."[5]

The death of Mussolini's brother Arnaldo was also advantageous for Petacci; Mussolini, plunged in the emptiness he had created round himself, continued to distrust everyone and concentrate work in his own hands. In the *Pensieri Pontini e Sardi*, the notes he jotted down during his first period of imprisonment after his fall from power on 25th July 1943, he wrote: "In the whole of my life I have never had a single friend. I've often wondered if this was an advantage or a disadvantage to me. I now think that it was an advantage, because it means that many people are free from feeling sorry for me – I mean, free from suffering with me."[6]

In the summer of 1932 Mussolini got rid of Augusto Turati, the Fascist Party secretary; his private life was fairly chaotic, and on his dismissal he was the subject of open criticism from other leading members of the party. Mussolini had Giovanni Giurati elected in his stead, but didn't like him, and so had him replaced only a year later with Achille Starace, notorious for his slow-wittedness, something that was the butt of innumerable jokes, such as his having to write "Salute the Duce!" on the palm of his hand so that he wouldn't forget to. Starace became the Duce's faithful mouthpiece, the loyal mastiff who'd set off to carry out Mussolini's slightest wish, docile and ready to submit when told off, an enthusiastic organizer of Fascist ceremonies and parades, down to the most ridiculous details. At one point Starace issued an order that all official communications should end with the phrase "Long live the Duce!", much to the intense irritation of Mussolini, who yelled at Starace, asking him how on earth he imagined a father might feel receiving a letter from the army telling him: "Your son Corporal X has broken his leg. Long live the Duce!"

It was Starace who handled the daily administration of the regime's infiltration into every aspect of social life in Italy. Even new blocks of social housing had to be constructed in such a way that, seen from the air, they formed the word DUX. Huge Ms would be displayed at local fairs and festivals. The myth of Mussolini, now fully synonymous with his politics, spread throughout the country: "I saw distinctly, perhaps more clearly than any other Italian, how serious the situation was in Italy. The dictatorship which ruled over us was not merely political, ideological and military; its power extended over internal combustion engines, borax powder, bicycle tyres, translations from the Latin classics, cameras, refrigerators, electric lamps, fizzy-drinks factories. Mechanically I would open and close the door of Mussolini's office, where he sat alone and isolated, trying desperately, throughout the working day, to stay in touch with a nation whose reality eluded him, with problems he pretended to know about, with men who, most of the time, came to see him either to deceive him or deceive themselves."[7]

The Duce was supposed to be present in the minds and in the houses of each and every Italian – but their homes could also be a place where they could take refuge from the regime and its intrusions, so it was better that these new citizens – or rather subjects of the new state – should be brought out from their houses as often and for as long as possible. Mussolini was intent on organizing the collective life of the nation in such a way that it worked and fought for the priorities set by the regime. His aim was to take children away from their families when they were six, hand them over to the state – in other words, the Duce – and then after six decades of mass existence hand them back, so to speak, for a final period of secluded rest – very secluded in order not to spoil the perennially youthful image of Italy under Fascism. In Mussolini's eyes, this kind of collective life spent under the shadow of gigantic Ms seemed an intrinsically appealing vision.

Yet the vision clearly risked coming into conflict with the Church's youth movement, Azione Cattolica; neither Mussolini nor the Pope had any intention of giving ground on the subject of who was to educate the country's younger generations. What was at stake was the influence and control either side could acquire over the forma-tion of Italy's future political, administrative and managerial classes; whichever side lost in the effort to establish their version of the con-nections between moral and political behaviour risked being left behind as time went by.

On 29th May 1931 – now without the restraining advice of his brother to guide him – Mussolini ordered all the prefectures in the country to close down any youth associations and movements which did not belong to the party. The Vatican, however, was determined to resist: it opened hard-fought negotiations with the regime with the result that it succeeded in keeping many young people away from direct Fascist influence. It was from among this generation that many of the future founders of the Christian Democrats would come after the war, going on to establish its fifty years of political success. The Church's ability to withstand Mussolini's pressure lay in a hierarchy of men who were the beneficiaries of a centuries-old tradition, while Mussolini was surrounded by figures like Starace. (After eight years as party secretary he too was dismissed, to his enduring bewilderment; he was caught and shot – on the spot – by

Partisans who recognized him among the crowds who had gone to see Mussolini's corpse strung up in Piazzale Loreto in Milan on 29th April 1945; he too had not been able to resist going to see one final time his adored leader.) The men who surrounded the Duce normally didn't last long; he would force them to perform almost impossible tasks and then suddenly dump them without ado, stripping them of their office and status. The technique was deliberate and intended to prevent them from gaining time and space in which to construct their private fiefdoms; if he had not constantly kept them in check, they would have turned into new *ras*, like the provincial leaders he had to defeat earlier, but potentially more dangerous, since they had grown up in the shadow of his power. Mussolini's treatment of Dino Grandi is an example: he appointed him Minister for Foreign Affairs in 1929, only to remove him from the post three years later to take over the running of the ministry himself.

It was in these years that Hitler had started to woo Mussolini, declaring that he regarded the Italian dictator as one of his models, and that Nazism took its inspiration from what he had done. He had even tried to obtain a signed photograph of the Duce, without success. After he came to power, on 5th March 1933, he stubbornly continued to seek out Mussolini as a potential and obvious ally, given the ideological similarities between the two regimes.

On 25th March 1934, on the orders of Mussolini, a second plebiscite was held in the country, in a parody of the free elections which had previously taken place. As in the earlier one, "voters" were only able to respond with a "yes" or "no" to a list of four hundred candidates proposed by the regime. The 1934 plebiscite is accorded hardly any attention in the history books, and yet it was a significant episode, since the result represented the high-water mark of consensus achieved by the regime, even after the pressure to conform, the lack of free choice and the threat of violence have been taken into account: there were fewer than fifteen thousand "no" votes, just 0.15 per cent of all those cast.

Following the plebiscite, Mussolini once again showed a renewed interest in opening towards the left wing. A group of Socialists led by a former mayor of Milan, Emilio Caldara, got in touch with him, and Mussolini agreed to meet them on 18th April, just three weeks after his overwhelming victory in the plebiscite. As usual, he made no firm commitments or undertakings and seemed to remain open to any suggestion. In this particular case the proposal was that a number of Socialist trade-unionists should join the Fascist trade unions declaring their loyalty not to Fascism but to the corporative state. Caldara set about finding supporters for the scheme, but he had failed to understand Mussolini's position – or rather, his lack of one: the proposal came to nothing, although it caused widespread dismay and outrage throughout the anti-Fascists exiles abroad.

Tensions in Europe were high as Nazi Germany moved towards the annexation of Austria; Hitler once more made an attempt to bring Mussolini over to his side. After a series of delays and postponements, a meeting between the two men was finally arranged on 14th June 1934, in a country estate in Stra, near Venice. It was designed to be a strictly private encounter; as such, it was decided that no minutes would be taken of their discussion. Their conversation was in German; Hitler spoke only German, and given the almost informal nature of the meeting no interpreter was present. In the historian Renzo De Felice's opinion, Mussolini knew German fairly well, although he could only speak it hesitatingly; Quinto Navarra's judgement might not have the scholarly authority of De Felice's, but since as Mussolini's valet he must have heard his master speaking in German, his remarks deserve to be taken into account: "Mussolini always suffered from a certain inferiority complex as regards Hitler. During their diplomatic encounters, he never had the courage to admit to his famous interlocutor that he often failed to understand what the Führer said to him in German. The Duce's knowledge of the language was fairly superficial, and he was frequently confronted by words he was unfamiliar with."[8]

Hitler had in any case brought two interpreters along with him, just in case they were needed. One was Eugenio Dollmann, an officer in the SS and a secret agent, who was a philosophy graduate and a specialist in Italian history and art; the other was the polyglot Paul Schmidt, who worked as an official translator for the German Ministry of Foreign Affairs. Silvio Bertoldi interviewed Dollmann, who told him that "Mussolini spoke German, but never really mastered the language despite studying it. My impression was that he spoke it well enough for a casual social conversation or to travel round German without difficulty. But he certainly didn't know the language well enough to have a conversation with Hitler on serious issues of international politics without an interpreter being present."[9]

However, De Felice's assessment that Mussolini had a good enough knowledge of German remains a possibility. Yet we should remember that he was conversing with Hitler, a man who, from as early as the end of the First World War, had been identified and cultivated in right-wing circles as having the right oratorical gifts to fight against the threat of Bolshevik propaganda spreading among defeated German troops. The meeting of the two dictators was a kind of rhetorical duel between two versions of extreme and violent oratory, between two figures who trained themselves (and in the case of Hitler was trained by others) to produce the maximum effect on crowds. Mussolini was attempting to fight these rhetorical duels in a language which wasn't his own, and which he understood and spoke with some difficulty.

From their very first encounters, first at Stra and then at Venice, Mussolini was crushed by the torrent of words which poured out of Hitler. In German Mussolini would have been unable to contradict him, let alone win an argument; only when the conversation was more informal and relaxed – and less significant – might he have been able to assert himself a little. The presence of an interpreter would certainly have made the two dictators' discussion, largely dedicated to the Third Reich's claims on Austria, easier. In order to understand what happened subsequently, it is important to bear in mind the exact sequence of events. Barely two weeks after Mussolini and Hitler met, the so-called "Night of the Long Knives" took place. It is probable that by the time of their talks Hitler had already planned to carry out this massacre. In her memoir *My Fault* – written, it will be remembered, only after the end of the Second World War – Margherita Sarfatti claims that she played a role in the events owing to her friendship with Hermann Göring and uses this to lend credence to her version of what was happening behind the scenes. "When Hitler returned to Germany [from Italy] he told Röhm that the *Anschluss* should be temporarily postponed until a better time and opportunity presented itself. This angered Röhm, who accused Hitler of cowardice in backing down before the Italians, whom he hated and opposed. On the other hand, Göring had a love for Italy as well as an intense admiration for Mussolini, with whom he had been in contact many years earlier. I too had got to know Göring well in the same period. Thus Göring took advantage of the turn of events to oppose Röhm's position and to paint Röhm as the treacherous villain of the piece."[10]

With the murder of Röhm and his entire staff on 30th June 1934 the SA, or *Sturmabteilung*, were eliminated. Less than a month later, the Austrian Chancellor Engelbert Dollfuss was assassinated. His wife and children were on holiday at the time in Italy, at Riccione on the Adriatic coast, staying in a rented villa which Rachele Mussolini had found for them. Dollfuss had been due to join them on the very day he was murdered. "We went immediately to the villa. Signora Dollfuss was resting while the children were playing on the beach. Benito did not immediately tell her the truth about what had happened, but as soon as he began to speak the poor woman seemed completely overcome."[11]

Mussolini responded to the assassination of Dollfuss by moving four army regiments to the border with Austria and declaring he would defend its independence. He also published a series of unsigned articles in *Il Popolo d'Italia* criticizing and often mocking the racism of the Third Reich. On 6th September, in a speech delivered in Bari, he asserted that: "Thirty centuries of history enable us to regard with disdain and pity such doctrines believed in north of the Alps by people who are the descendants of a race which was still illiterate and unable to transmit written records of its past when at the same time in Rome Caesar, Virgil and Augustus were living." Such an assertion was a mere smokescreen for his own increasing anti-Semitism; on the subject of racism he was prepared to say or deny anything so long as it served his political ends. Hitler must have known about what Mussolini was writing and saying, but didn't change course; of the two men, it was he who recognized without a shadow of doubt how close the ties were between their two regimes. He continued to regard Mussolini as a model, especially for the way he used violence as a political tactic. He knew that Mussolini's words were so much hot air; incontestable events and facts would eventually bring the Duce over to his side.

It was hard for Mussolini to conceal what lay at the dark heart of his grip on power: violence, assassination, contempt for democracy, denial of basic freedoms, racism and anti-Semitism. Another significant date in the chain of events around this time was 9th October 1934, when Alexander I of Yugoslavia was assassinated in Marseille. His killers belonged to an Ustashe gang, the extremist Croatian nationalist movement led by Ante Pavelić, who had been trained and financed by Italy. These were the harsh and violent facts of the

Fascist regime, however much Mussolini succeeded in covering them up with his rhetoric, however successfully he managed to fabricate a flattering international image of his rule. "When people compared the two regimes [Germany and Italy], Mussolini's immediately appeared as more humane, 'liberal', peace-loving, and protective of the European balance of power than Hitler's (at the end of 1933 the Jewish press in the United States carried out an opinion poll to find out who were considered to be the doughtiest defenders of the civil and political rights of Jews: Mussolini was among the twelve names chosen). [...] Mussolini's anti-German stance, and in particular his reaction to the Nazi putsch in Vienna, won many plaudits and led many to put their hopes in Italy..."[12]

The European democracies wanted to believe that Mussolini's dictatorship would serve to moderate and restrain the excesses of the Nazi regime in Germany. Such a misplaced hope is already indicative of the intrinsic weaknesses of democratic governments. It became fashionable to talk reasonably about dictatorships, just as in a certain sense the phenomenon itself of dictatorship became popular. There were those who maintained that dictatorship, even in the modern age, was useful as a solution to the problems of democracy. The world seemed to be full of dictators: Mussolini, Lenin, Stalin, Atatürk, Piłsudsky and Hitler (Franco was soon to join the group). And for a certain time Mussolini was skilful in presenting himself as "a man of peace" and a wise mediator who could ward off the storm which was gathering over the continent.

The role brought him a huge amount of attention from the world's press. Requests for interviews with him poured in: the Duce was a "hot topic" that attracted an increased readership. But the editors often had to put up with brief written answers rather than a live interview. One journalist in Egypt asked if Mussolini had Egyptian ancestors, since he bore a striking resemblance to a statue of one of the pharaoh Cheops's court officials. Dino Grandi, when he was the Italian Ambassador to London, under pressure from British press interest pleaded with Mussolini to provide replies to certain questions on his personal life: what sports did he practise, what did he like to eat, how much did he eat and what did he think about women? Every editor was interested in publishing details of his private life, since this was guaranteed to sell more copies. Many journalists who managed to get an interview with him came away fascinated by the charisma he managed to convey. In Cole Porter's 1934 song 'You're the Top', the Duce's name comes in the refrain: "You're the top! You're the Colosseum. You're the top! [...] You're Mussolini!"

Mussolini told Webb Miller, a journalist from the *United Press*, in an interview: "Don't be amazed if I tell I have nothing against jazz. As dance music I enjoy it." His youngest son, Romano, became a professional jazz musician after the war. Webb Miller had first met Mussolini in 1922, in Cannes; he interviewed him in 1931 and again in 1937. On the occasion of the second interview he wrote: "He greeted me warmly and explained to me, with a smile, that he had just got back from a three-hour skiing trip to the mountains. We then had a friendly conversation in English lasting a quarter of an hour. He asked me my opinion of the current European situation. Since our last interview five years before Mussolini's facial expression appeared to have softened. He seemed altogether more genial and the air of authority he conveyed more natural."[13] Mussolini told Miller that he arranged his days to avoid any waste of time and energy. His meals were frugal; he didn't drink or smoke, because they were damaging; he ate a lot of fruit, didn't drink coffee or even tea, except on occasion a herbal tea like lime blossom, and every day for at least half an hour he did some physical exercise. Webb Miller explained to his readers that the Duce was an enthusiast for every kind of "mechanical" sport, from cycling to flying an aeroplane; he also mentioned that he slept on average seven or eight hours a night, never took a daytime nap, was a voracious reader of newspapers and magazines, got through an average of seventy books a year, both new and old publications, and liked to listen to Verdi, Wagner and Rossini.

A more prosaic – and realistic – view of Mussolini's lifestyle can be found in the memoirs of his personal valet, Quinto Navarra, who saw him every day. Navarra relates, for example, how the Duce took Magnesia San Pellegrino in an attempt to cure his constipation, hated perfumes and used toothpicks after meals, though only when he wasn't eating in company. From his wife's memoirs we learn that when he liked a pair of shoes he would wear them all the time (to the point of getting them resoled four times in succession), he liked to wear gloves of deerskin or some other kind of soft leather, preferred to take a shower rather than a bath, had regular check-ups with his dentist (who was, at least until the introduction of the racial laws, a Jew named Piperno), had a manicure and pedicure once a week and every morning rubbed himself down with eau de cologne. He had taken the decision to shave his head – in what was then called *alla romana* ("in the Roman style") – when he realized that no treatment was going to prevent the onset of baldness.

In the early 1930s many events and individual success stories served to enhance, either directly or indirectly, Mussolini's growing fame and prestige. The legendary boxer Primo Carnera won a match, and the victory redounded to Mussolini's advantage; the national football team under the management of Vittorio Pozzo won the World Cup, and Mussolini was able to bask in its success; Italo Balbo completed the first transatlantic flight as leader of a formation – his victory parade down Fifth Avenue in New York, repeated in Rome on his return to Italy, became an opportunity to pay homage to the Duce. Every successful Italian – even Nobel prizewinners like Luigi Pirandello or Guglielmo Marconi – made Mussolini more famous.

At the height of his international acclaim, Mussolini made his riskiest and, as it turned out, luckiest move. At the time he was not merely the formal head of government, but had also taken over the interim running of various ministries – for home and foreign affairs, for the Corporations, for the army, the navy and the airforce, and for the colonies. This last – the colonies – was the new field for Mussolini's activities. He wanted to turn the regime into a colonial power to match Britain and France. A massacre of Italians at Wal-Wal and a series of increasingly bloody clashes on the border between Ethiopia and Somalia finally gave him the opportunity, which he'd been seeking for a long time, to initiate a war.

At the beginning of 1935 he started to mass Italian troops in East Africa, from where, on 3rd October, at five in the morning, the invasion of Ethiopia was launched. The reaction of Britain and France was immediate and uncompromising. The Ethiopian military arsenal was inadequate and antiquated, so they resorted to the only tactic possible in the circumstances: guerrilla warfare. Their emperor Tafari Makonnen, who had come to the throne after a *coup d'état* with the name of Haile Selassie, the 224th representative of a dynasty that traced its origins to the union of the legendary Queen of Sheba (which was another name for Ethiopia) and King Solomon, went to address the League of Nations, the forerunner to the United Nations. The League voted for the harshest possible reprisals against Italy in the form of what today would be called an embargo. Mussolini reacted with the cynicism and unscrupulousness which had always characterized him as a politician: he gave the order for fierce propaganda attacks on Britain, during which he himself wrote some unsigned newspaper articles. He managed to transform his problems in foreign relations into a notable success on the domestic front. The League of Nations had failed to persuade the United States and Brazil to take part in the sanctions against Italy – a decision which was partly due to the very large numbers of Italian migrants in the two countries. Moreover, the sanctions didn't include the most vital import, from a strategic point of view: oil. If the imports of oil to Italy had been blocked, Mussolini would have been forced to beat a hasty retreat from Ethiopia, as he later admitted to Hitler. The world oil market follows a different political logic – often large companies work together in alliances which do not reflect the foreign policy of their respective countries. On this occasion, once again, the interests of American capital invested in oil companies made sure the profitable Italian market was protected, and this had a strong influence on the country's international politics.

The other great source of profit in world business, the arms trade, took more time to catch up with the developments in Ethiopia, although right at the outset various consignments of armaments reached the country from Germany. It was easy for Mussolini to mobilize Italian troops; he appealed to "his" people to volunteer with pride in the defence of Italy's "place in the sun" – as if a country's right to colonies, to the possession of an empire, was some kind of natural right. If perfidious Albion and the haughty French had one, why shouldn't Italy be an imperial power as well? Beguiled by Mussolini's oratory and the regime's propaganda, Italians saw the acquisition of an empire as the road to riches – and not only the poorest classes, those who for several decades had been emigrating en masse to the New World, but the well-off, who greedily envisaged new commercial possibilities and new lands for exploitation. Even intellectual circles were swept up in the wave of popular enthusiasm. The poorest Italians signed up for military service in Ethiopia, setting off with supplies of seeds from their fields in the certainty that victory in the war would see them rewarded with land, while intellectuals supported the campaign in their writings (though in many cases they also enrolled in order to fight).

A large number of Fascist *gerarchi* and ministers – Bottai, Farinacci, Starace, even Galeazzo Ciano – were required by Mussolini to go on active service in the conflict; he wanted to avoid the credit of an eventual victory going only to professional soldiers. In Italy itself the British and French opposition to the invasion provoked a wave of patriotism, while the difficulties the League of Nations had in taking firm action only served to underline the Duce's decisiveness and boldness; meanwhile the Italian military victories in the campaign caused popular enthusiasm to mount. Between the end of 1935 and the beginning of 1936 Mussolini managed to create round himself and the regime a popular consensus, the quality and extent of which had never been seen before. When he appealed, in the face of the sanctions imposed by the League of Nations, to the Italian population to donate precious family items for the sake of the motherland, the result was 37,000 kilos of gold and 115,000 kilos of silver. Even one of the regime's most celebrated critics, the philosopher Benedetto Croce, gave up his gold medal as a senator. Mussolini had played a high-risk game; now all he could do was to raise the stakes even further. He couldn't be seen to settle on a compromise solution; he had to hold out for total victory. But the war threatened to grind on and wear him down. For three months the full force of the Fascist troops in the country produced no appreciable results, until it was decided to resolve the situation by massacring Ethiopian civilians and bombing the hospitals. There are archive photographs of Italian soldiers posing with the heads of Ethiopian guerrilla fighters, a tragic testimony of this phase of the conflict. When cannon, bombs and gunfire didn't work, orders were given to launch gas attacks. Fascist Italy committed numerous war crimes in the pursuit of its empire, although the regime's propaganda machine skilfully concealed all reference to these atrocities and deflected attention instead onto Ethiopian reprisals against Italian soldiers.

Britain attracted world attention with its decision to send a fleet from the Royal Navy to the Mediterranean. Even those closest to Mussolini grew anxious: an escalation of the conflict involving the British was unthinkable. Many Fascist *gerarchi* wavered in their support; even Balbo did not deny rumours that he was opposed to the war; but Mussolini, with his usual arrogant self-confidence, refused to change course. In part he was bluffing, because he knew he had to: he knew perfectly well how dependent the Italian economy had become on the war, with many industries relying wholly on the demand for military hardware, while the state's coffers were overstretched and struggling to support the commitment. But in part his calculations were accurate: his own intelligence services had informed him that the British Navy would not be capable of launching an attack. He realized that the British were giving him a warning: they were prepared to defend the Mediterranean as a vital communication link for their own trade with their Empire and the Middle East.

Mussolini knew that the crisis could not be sustained for a long time: he ordered a decisive attack in Ethiopia while at the same time he tried to introduce a note of calm into the confrontation with Britain by making public statements that Italy had no strategic interests in the Middle East or in Sudan, nor any plans to affect, even indirectly, British interests in the area. On 5th May 1936 Pietro Badoglio, the head of the Italian armed forces, occupied Addis Ababa, bringing the war to an end. On the evening of the same day, from the balcony overlooking Piazza Venezia, Mussolini announced to a vast crowd that "Ethiopia belongs to Italy! It belongs by deed, since our victorious troops have occupied it, and by right, since the Roman sword has brought civilization to triumph over barbarity..."

Struggling to make her way through the roaring crowd, a thirty-six-year-old woman by the name of Madeleine Coraboeuf was trying to reach the building on the opposite side of the piazza which faced Palazzo Venezia and the balcony from which Mussolini was speaking, where a press conference was being held for journalists from the world press. She was attractive – a radiant face, large eyes, her sensual mouth emphasized with red lipstick – and knew how to use her attractiveness to get what she wanted: "She is of medium height, with chestnut-brown hair styled in a wave, and a typically vivacious Parisian face with lively eyes. Her mouth is finely shaped, her lips parted to let you see her regular teeth, slightly stained by nicotine. Her make-up was soberly and carefully applied, obviously with a good deal of thought; her skin had just one wrinkle, a straight one which formed in the middle of her brow whenever she smiled, and the end of her nose, which was somewhat long but regular, turned up oddly."[14]

Madeleine Coraboeuf used a pseudonym that was appropriate enough for her purposes: Magda Fontanges. Madame de Fontanges had been one of Louis XIV's mistresses. She had started off as an actress and ended up as a spy, but at the time she was in Italy – when the Ethiopian war was being waged – she was working as a journalist. Her account of her meeting with Mussolini in the course of her visit to Italy is interesting because it reveals the four-stage progress of one of his typical "flings", both from his point of view and the woman's. Magda Fontanges had come to Italy determined to interview the Duce whatever it took. Her professional standing as a journalist was not significant (when the English-language magazine *Liberty* published her piece, it described her as only a "moderately successful" journalist, but also – what was obviously more to the point – as "a woman of exceptional charm").

In March 1936 Fontanges was forced to wait a fortnight in Sestri Levante on the Ligurian coast before being cleared to proceed to Rome. Once there, she came to the attention of Dino Alfieri, the regime's Undersecretary for Press and Communication who, besotted, took to following her round the city (under the impression that he was leading her). The first step was to enter Mussolini's circle, so that she could get to meet the man himself, a goal she succeeded in achieving on 20th April 1936. "Since morning I have been occupied with preparations. At two o'clock I started to dress. I have decided on a Jenny ensemble – a black dress in cloqué tissue with white trimmings at neck and sleeves; the coat is black also, with gathers at the shoulders and trimming of silver fox; the hat is a small Rose Valois panama with white trimming. The handbag and shoes are of black buckskin with patent-leather trimmings. The gloves, from Alexandrine's, are buckskin and black kid. [...] Very few photographs give an exact image of his face. His eyes have an incomparable radiance, which is fascinating, and I defy anyone to meet him for the first time without feeling somewhat disturbed!"[15]

The second step consisted in overcoming the distance between the "head of government" and "the journalist interviewer", so that the barriers and formalities separating the two roles – and the two bodies – could be done away with. The first physical contact between the two took place on 25th April. Possibly it was Mussolini who initiated it, but there are two players in every process of seduction. "He has walked with me to the desk. 'I have only a few moments. I am very busy today. But I am going to ask you to come again tomorrow... just like that... to chat!' He comes nearer to me. His voice has become very soft, even effeminate. His face, so gay at Littoria, has assumed a grave expression. I judge that it is prudent to keep a wise reserve and to wait. So, feigning a formal attitude and trying to make my voice sound as natural as possible, I assure him that I am at his disposal and very flattered by the honour he shows me. Mussolini observes me in silence for a moment, then walks about for a few paces. Again he comes to a stop, this time very close to me, keeping his eyes half closed. Suddenly he places both his hands on my shoulders."[16]

Now that this mutual confidence had been established, the next step consisted in transforming what was a friendly physical contact between them into a more intimate one – a kiss. In order to achieve this, when they next met, on 27th April, Mussolini started from the point at which they had concluded their previous encounter, the territory he had already conquered.

> Mussolini is seated at the desk, writing. He springs to his feet and rushes to greet me. Without preamble, he rests both his hands on my shoulders, and in that same gentle voice which so intrigued me at our meeting yesterday, he asks, in French: "Have you thought of me a little?" From then on, the conversation between us is familiar, intimate. I reply quickly: "Not for one minute did your memory leave me!" We walk a few steps, then he stops again, grips my shoulders, leans towards me and says deliberately: "I think you are beautiful. You please me!" In response, I place my arms round his neck. My mouth brushes against his and I say: "And you, Benito – do you know I love you?" The expression of his face softens then, and, holding me tightly, he gives me his first kiss. I feel the sensation of intoxication so strong that everything vanishes about me. As soon as I am able, I question him: "Since when did you desire to see me not officially?"[17]

At this point, after further kisses, Fontanges decided it was a good moment to obtain some political news she could put in her article. She enthusiastically praised his handling of the crisis with the League of Nations and his bold risk-taking on the international political scene, and then asked him point-blank: "What is the news concerning Addis Ababa?" The Italian troops had launched brutal gas attacks to crush the last remnants of Ethiopian resistance. Mussolini replied to her question with a fervent "Good!" – and with this immediately started the fourth stage in the process of seduction, aware that she might think she was merely the latest in a line of conquests. Convinced that women were attracted by male brutality, he said: "But Ethiopia does not exist! The most beautiful thing in the world is what is happening to the two of us! [...] Then I'll take you to a secret chamber... but you must not tell anyone you know the private apartments... You know, I have no time to see you long today – at least, not as long as I would wish!' We are still clasped together. Suddenly his face contorts and in a hoarse voice he murmurs: 'You know... I am brutal. You are not afraid? You feel how much I desire you!'"[18]

The following day, 28th April, with a sudden burst of energy, the prize at the end of the fourth and final stage in what was, for Mussolini, a very familiar script, was carried off. Once more Mussolini started from where they had left off at the previous meeting, with Fontanges now installed in the "private apartments".

Catlike, as if about to grasp a prey, Benito has returned, and he comes towards me. "It is a great privilege to come here. No one has the right to disturb me here; I come when I wish to be alone, when I need to think – or to rest." I think that he comes here for other reasons also... and, suddenly jealous, I imagine in pale visions the faces of women he must have known before me. I tell him that. A bit scornful, he smiles. "Perhaps. But I don't remember anything about it! No one has left a trace, I swear to you!" He has embraced me again, growing very tender. "As a rule, my mind is not involved! I am not in the habit of wasting my time! Didn't I give you a different impression? I believe you haven't much to complain of." Then a sort of frenzy sweeps him, he becomes brutal and he says: "You have known Il Duce – now you shall know the man!" He has taken off his coat, and in his sports shirt he appears astonishingly young. Heeding nothing but his instinct, he leaps at me. Before I have time to utter so much as an exclamation, I am caught up in strong arms.[19]

As Fascist troops advanced over Ethiopian territory with gas attacks, their intense affair continued. On 5th May, when the troops finally entered and took Addis Ababa, Mussolini received Fontanges in an atmosphere of wild enthusiasm: "And he laughs as he struts around. Then, removing the scarf, he flings it around my neck and pretends to strangle me... and that make-believe struggle ends in kisses."[20]

After this meeting, Fontanges went back to her hotel to write up her article, until, in the afternoon, the concierge of the hotel suddenly started to shout: "Roll up, roll up!" With sirens wailing and bells chiming, a vast crowd from all over the city was gathering in Piazza Venezia. The Duce appeared on the balcony to announce the conquest of Ethiopia, while Fontanges made her way through the mass of people to join the other journalists in the building which faced Palazzo Venezia, where, only a few hours before, she'd been locked in intimate contact with the founder of the Italian empire. None of the journalists gathered that day knew anything about the brutal costs of the victory; the barbarity of the campaign was not talked about for many years, and the silence endured even after the end of the Second World War, when defeated Italians tried to lick their wounds by taking refuge in the myth of their fundamental decency – "Italians are good folk".

Yet it is hard to understand why a debate continued throughout the second half of the twentieth century on the use of gas attacks in Ethiopia when documentary evidence had been available from the 1950s onwards in the complete edition of Mussolini's writings and speeches edited by Edoardo and Duilio Susmel. The two historians were Fascist sympathizers, but declared the thirty-five volume work to be "free of any verbal intervention or tendentiousness in such a way that the *Opera Omnia* [*Complete Works*] present, in exact chronological sequence, an authentic representation of Mussolini's attitudes and activities".[21] They took the Latin motto *historia fit documentis* ("history is made of evidence") as their guide, and in the process their work has become a primary reference source for all subsequent biographers, historians and scholars of the period. The documentary compilation is complete to the point of including the telegrams Mussolini sent to the army generals in command of the campaign in Ethiopia.

20th February 1936 (Top secret) 2053: In agreement with Your Excellency's observations on the use of bacteriological warfare. Mussolini.

29th March 1936 (Top Secret) 3652: In view of enemy tactics, authorization to use gas of all kinds and on any scale renewed. Mussolini.

2nd June 1936 (Top Secret) 4696: To Field-Marshal Rodolfo Graziani. All rebel natives taken prisoner must be executed.

8th June 1936 (Top Secret) 6595: To Field-Marshal Rodolfo Graziani. Gas to be used to finish off rebel natives, as in Ankober.

8th July 1936 (Top Secret) 8103: To Field-Marshal Rodolfo Graziani: authorization renewed to carry out systematic campaign of terror and extermination against rebel natives and those supporting them. Maximum retaliation only way to bring situation under control in short time. Confirmation awaited. Mussolini.[22]

As she made her way through the hurrahing crowds gathered to celebrate Italy's new empire, Magda Fontanges could feel sure of herself. She had become the Duce's latest mistress; she was allowed access to his private apartments; and she – she alone – had the biggest journalistic scoop of the time waiting to be published. The French ambassador in Rome, the Comte Charles de Chambrun, approached her with the intention of persuading her to become a secret agent for the French military intelligence services, the Deuxième Bureau. Thus Coraboeuf-Fontanges's career as a spy began. However, she had the fault of speaking rather too freely. Even Rachele came to know about her relationship with Mussolini, and when he himself learnt that his new conquest was a mere spy he immediately paid her off with 15,000 lire and had her expelled from Italy.

In the meantime, the Comte de Chambrun had fallen under the spell of this "exceptional charming woman" and, breaking the fundamental rule in intelligence that all personal involvement should be avoided, tried to become her (supplementary) lover. The matter started to go badly: at the Quai d'Orsay station in Paris, Fontanges tried to shoot the ambassador, but failed to kill him. The crisis continued, and shortly afterwards she attempted suicide by taking twelve tablets of Nembutal – the same sleeping pills which Marilyn Monroe used to kill herself thirty years later – but she was taken to hospital and her stomach pumped. She published, in French and in English, the story of her sexual encounter with the Duce, to huge success. She became a spy for the Nazis, and during the German occupation the mistress of the head of the Gestapo in France; after the war she was arrested as a collaborator. In 1960 she took another overdose of sleeping tablets, and this time succeeded in taking her own life. One of Mussolini's closest associates, the diplomat Giuseppe Bastianini, commented on the affair shortly after it had finished: "Fontanges was simply another instalment of the usual story – more exciting – and more annoying – than the others because she was a foreigner and capable of kicking up a fuss to attract attention. Nowadays, alongside – and above – all the one-night stands and brief escapades, the favourite dominates – Claretta Petacci. To my mind there's nothing remarkable about her, but she knows very well what she's doing and she's also got the backing and encouragement of her family, who are on the make and don't mind how. A nice state of affairs, no? The Duce can do whatever he wants to, let him sow his wild oats till he's got no more left, but then he should face the music, by God, and pay up the debts in love he's incurred."[23]

The pattern of Mussolini's relationships with women only rarely followed the rhythms of his political career. A long time might pass before the beginning of a new affair or the development of an older one would have an impact on his public life. But the reverse is also true: times of intense political activity can be mirrored by small events and recurrent situations occurring in his private life – one example would be what now appears as the long uniform phase of furious sexual activity in Palazzo Venezia, organized by his staff, against the backdrop of the decline of his relationship with Sarfatti and the final removal, in an all too physical sense, of Dalser. Important events in his public life could coincide with significant developments in his sexual career – a case in point would be the victorious Ethiopian campaign and his concurrent affair with Fontanges and Petacci's arrival on the scene. And it was a sudden intensification of the relationship with Petacci which marked the end of one phase and the beginning of another. On 6th May 1936 Mussolini announced the new Italian Empire from the balcony of Palazzo Venezia; on 31st May Petacci recorded in her diary that she had had sex with the Duce. She was married, and while this naturally presented no problem from Mussolini's point of view, it was an insurmountable obstacle for her. It is difficult to say whether she was prompted by her own instincts or by someone else's advice, but she knew that in such cases the woman's will was paramount, and she showed what she wanted in terms that left no room for compromise: in June she declared that she regarded her husband with physical loathing and could not even bear to be near him. In July they were legally separated: the road was clear for her to become Mussolini's official mistress.

"Allow me to love your daughter," Mussolini is supposed to have said to Petacci's mother, Giuseppina Persichetti, in the belief that such a quasi-official – and quasi-gallant – declaration of interest in the young brunette who had cast a spell over him showed he was in control of the situation, whereas in actual fact it was she who was taking the initiative. Her rapacious family, headed by her father, the medical doctor Francesco Saverio Petacci, had devised a plan in which the key element was their daughter giving birth to a child by Mussolini. Petacci manoeuvred – or was manoeuvred – skilfully. She wisely never asked Mussolini to separate from his wife Rachele. She identified the other women he frequented and began to get rid of them one by one. In 1937, one year after his escapade with Fontanges, Mussolini was practically in Petacci's hands. She began to transcribe the confidential talk she would have with him during their sessions together. "I don't know how many women have really been in love with me. A handful, none of them perhaps. Now that I come to look back, in hindsight, I can see that no one – or very few – really loved me. Take Countess Magda de Fontanges, for example. She asked me 'When will you let me go to bed with you?' 'You're not ready yet, we need to wait a bit.' I lost some important papers because of this woman. I trusted her, but she turned out to be a spy. She took notes – my opinions of the King, of the House of Savoy, on certain leading politicians. And she published them. Nothing to be done about that now. [...] She used to talk about things with no shame at all, typically French. She once said her pants made a curious ripping sound when I threw her on the bed."[24]

At the same time as he was seeing Fontanges, ordering gas attacks and arranging a final extermination of the remaining Ethiopian troops, Mussolini continued to pursue the utopia of ruralization which, even though by now an evident failure in Italy itself, he hoped to export to the newly occupied Ethiopia: "The Italians are a race of brave pioneers and clever farmers who in the very first year of the empire have started to transform the agricultural fortunes of Ethiopia. Few other peoples would have the energy to confront the immensely laborious tasks of building thousands of kilometres of roads under the tropical sun or tilling barbarian lands nearly 5,000 kilometres away from their homeland."[25]

While Mussolini was at the height of his popularity in the triumphal spring days of 1936, his ambassador in London, Dino Grandi, had an audience with the new king, Edward VIII, to provide reassurances in the wake of the recent crisis between the two countries. Grandi was in direct contact with Mussolini; his instructions were to put Italy's relations with the British Empire on the best possible footing.

Among British politicians he admired Churchill above all – the man who later led the resistance to Hitler and who, in planning with the backing of the United States the landings in north Africa and southern Europe, dealt a death blow to Mussolini's regime. "Churchill has the best brain in Britain. He's the embodiment of the country's three-hundred-year-old – yes three centuries! – sense of its imperial destiny." [...] His judgement of Lloyd George varied according to the Welsh politician's own changing attitudes towards Italy. He feared his cunning and quick-wittedness and admired him for his humble social origins. His confidence in MacDonald was limited. He used to say: "It'll be a hard job to get people like this to appreciate the new Italy under the Fascists."[26]

The celebrations for the victory in Ethiopia reached a climax in Mussolini's speech to the nation on 9th May 1936, which was broadcast to the nation. When, to wild enthusiasm, he announced the birth – or rather the rebirth – of the Italian Empire, it seemed only logical that the King, Victor Emmanuel III, should assume the title of Emperor, but Rachele, who'd been caught in a taxi in the midst of the crowds, later told her husband how surprised and disappointed people had been at his announcement that the King was now emperor. For once, Petacci was in agreement with her lover's wife: "He puts his hand over my mouth and smiles as I say again that he's the emperor. 'Let's leave it, I detest courtiers. Let's not talk any more about it, the subject's over and done with.'"[27]

Mussolini's personal valet, Quinto Navarra, was skilful at handling the simultaneous and unexpected arrivals, as occasionally occurred, of Petacci and Sarfatti in Palazzo Venezia; he would send them up and down different staircases within the vast building, and the merit was his if their paths never crossed and unseemly cat fights were avoided in what was the seat of government. He even managed to organize two different waiting rooms. But one day the Duce gave him an abrupt and deeply disagreeable command: Navarra was to tell Margherita Sarfatti, after she had already been kept waiting for over two hours, that she would not be allowed to see him. Sarfatti had also been forbidden to come to Villa Torlonia, Mussolini's private residence, which – as we have seen – she herself had originally procured for him through her contacts with Prince Torlonia; the arrival of his wife and children to live with him had provided him with the justification. "As his wife, Rachele was protected by the laws of common morality, while Sarfatti had enjoyed the typical unauthorized power of a mistress. She was seen as despotic and had acquired many enemies who longed to see her fall from favour. Her aura of fascination, which had once won so much praise, had been replaced by a peremptory air of command; she had been spoilt by the adulation of those around her and had lost her supreme poise as an accomplished woman of the world."[28]

The marriage of Mussolini's favourite daughter to Galeazzo Ciano had brought Sarfatti another implacable enemy. Edda had emerged from an irresponsible and troubled adolescence to become an elegant and unconventional young woman; she loved sport and driving fast cars, and often wore trousers. She wanted to exercise influence over her father and came to detest his former mistress as her rival. Mussolini was not overly concerned with the age of the women he slept with, but Sarfatti, now nearly sixty, must have seemed to him truly old, a vestige from an earlier period in his life, now definitively over, and in the way. Besides, seeing her reminded him that he too was no longer young. Speaking of her to Petacci, he punned on her name calling her "*rifatti*" ("redone", "done over") instead of Sarfatti – "that old witch Rifatti". His brother Arnaldo had protected her, but after he died Mussolini had removed her from the editorial board of *Il Popolo d'Italia*. By now he had appropriated the ideas she had produced, without deigning to acknowledge his debt. He couldn't even be bothered to tell her in person their relationship was over; he got his valet to slam the door in her face instead.

Sarfatti played her hand, such as it was, as best she could. She organized the wedding of her daughter Fiammetta in the same church, San Giuseppe on the Via Nomentana, where all the members of the Mussolini clan had been married. The ceremony was Catholic – Fiammetta had recently been converted – and splendid – like Edda, she was marrying a count, Livio Gaetani dell'Aquila d'Aragona, a Fascist parliamentary deputy and, as a member of the Consiglio Nazionale delle Corporazioni (National Council of Corporations), a rising figure in the regime. The wedding took place on 15th October 1933, and the reception which followed it was one of the last of the great events Sarfatti stage-managed. She did her utmost to ensure it was an important political gathering with the presence of Fascist *gerarchi* and foreign diplomats, including the German ambassador Ulrich von Hassell. She still hoped there might be a space for her and a role she might play in the increasingly rigid organization of the regime. In reality although her old friends and allies – such as Dino Alfieri, who started his career as a young lawyer in her husband's legal practice and was now a member of the Grand Council and Undersecretary to the Corporations, where her new son-in-law also worked – were happy to accept her invitations to her daughter's wedding, they were already distancing themselves from her. Edda saw the wedding as a vulgar invasion of the territory she now regarded as her own and prepared a trap for her rival. She paid a strapping young man to make approaches to Sarfatti; he succeeded in getting the older woman to accompany him to a club with a shady reputation. The police, duly tipped off, raided the place and found Sarfatti without identity documents and took her to the police station where she was held overnight. The next morning Edda made sure her father heard the news.

There came a moment when Margherita Sarfatti realized that she was no longer involved in any committee or occupied any formal position in the regime. She had been the editor of the journal *Gerarchia*, but there was no longer any role for her in the actual hierarchy of power. Under Fascism women were considered appropriate only for the lower grades. The country's artists and their production had now been absorbed into the Fascist Corporations, part of Mussolini's totalitarian system of power which Sarfatti alone obstinately refused to understand. The art movement she had founded – Novecento – had broken up; some of the artists who had belonged to it denied publicly that it had originated as Sarfatti's idea. The painter Mario Sironi accused her of creating Jewish art. One of the few remaining artists who still defended her was Pietro Maria Bardi, but more perhaps because of his personal circumstances than out of conviction. He ran an art gallery on the Via Veneto in Rome together with yet another of Mussolini's mistresses, Anna Normandia. In order to stay open their gallery needed the protection of the Sindacato Nazionale Fascista delle Belle Arti, the Fascist organization dealing with the fine arts. For Anna Normandia, Sarfatti was merely a defeated rival mistress; when her turn arrived to make way for the entry of Petacci onto the scene, she asked Mussolini for money, got what she wanted, and promptly disappeared from his life.

But Sarfatti didn't need money, and she was not prepared to disappear so ignominiously. She decided to travel to the United States. On 15th April 1934 she was received with ceremony at the White

House, almost as if she were Italy's "First Lady" (there was no other woman in Italy capable of occupying such a role at international diplomatic meetings). She had a long conversation over tea with President Roosevelt, along with his wife Eleanor, son James and daughter-in-law, and was fascinated by the Roosevelts' personalities. As her journey across the US continued, she became convinced that America would have an important future role to play in world affairs. However, no news of the enthusiastic reception which greeted her on her travels in North America ever reached Italy; the newspapers avoided all mention of the visit. All her efforts to reacquire some of the prestige she had once enjoyed in Italy seemed destined to fail.

She made an attempt to vindicate herself by reminding people that she had been a Fascist from the very beginning, supporting the regime with her cultural activity. She once more played the role of the grieving mother of a war hero killed in action. She commissioned one of the leading Italian architects of the day, Giuseppe Terragni, to design a monument for his tomb; Terragni came up with a striking piece of work, situated at the top of a hill in the high plateaus near the town of Asiago. But the gesture came too late. The monument was unveiled in 1935; it was raining heavily. Mussolini – whose political fortunes had begun with the ex-Arditi who had flocked to the ceremonies he and his mistress had organized in commemoration of her fallen son – refused to attend. The times were changing: it was no longer advisable to be seen paying homage to a Jew. But Sarfatti refused to face the truth of the situation. She believed that art and culture could serve the cause of Fascist education and couldn't see that systematic propaganda had replaced them. She still believed in the myth she had created, but the regime had transformed it into a cult.

Now even so recent a time as 1933, when Sarfatti was one of the hidden movers behind the negotiations which led to the formation of the "Pact of Four" between Italy, France, Great Britain and Germany, seemed suddenly remote. The very fact that a woman could claim her right to a leading role in the regime was a source of irritation, and Sarfatti's pretensions that she and the Duce had shared a heroic past became intolerable. Last – but certainly not least – was the most serious problem, her Jewishness: "Long before the racial laws were introduced [in 1938], anti-Semitism was rife in Italy; Sarfatti, despite her conversion to Catholicism (and baptism) and her exalted vision of the Catholic Church as some kind of sacred manifestation of 'Romanness', an exclusive emanation of the Italian 'race', became once more, in the eyes of the regime, merely a Jew, just as she had always feared."[29]

By the time the so-called *Manifesto degli scienziati razzisti* (*Manifesto of Racial Scientists*) was published in 1938, representing a toxic injection of anti-Semitism into Italian society and culture, Sarfatti had already made her plans to leave the country. Until the day of her departure she tried to behave as normal: "In October 1938, just before going abroad, I went to take my leave of the Queen, in a private and informal audience. I inwardly knew that I was leaving for a long and possibly permanent exile from Italy, the country which had changed so much from the Italy I had loved."[30]

On 4th November 1938 she attended the usual public ceremony for the anniversary of the victory in the First World War. Petacci noted in her diary: "I went to the ceremony in Piazza Venezia. Sarfatti was there. I didn't care, but the thought troubled me that that old ruin had once been his lover."[31] Ten days later Sarfatti crossed the border into Switzerland; her idea was to start a new life somewhere else, in one of the Americas. But she didn't prosper; many were suspicious of this Fascist Jew. Her sister Nella stayed in Italy and, together with her husband, was deported and died while in one of the cattle trucks travelling to Auschwitz.

Sarfatti came back to Italy after the war, in 1947, to live in her villa at Cavallasca on Lake Como. She died on 30th October 1961 at the age of eighty-one. She wrote nothing more on Mussolini and Fascism, and refused to be interviewed on the subject. The historian and biographer of Mussolini Renzo De Felice did manage to meet her, but gained no new historical information from the visit:

I had the good fortune – in terms of ordinary curiosity, more than anything else – to have a long conversation – lasting an entire winter afternoon – with Margherita Sarfatti, shortly before she died, in a hotel suite on the Via Veneto in Rome. Our conversation revealed no new facts or evidence but, on the other hand, it helped me considerably to understand who she was, to understand – and here we're touching on the psychological complexities of human beings, as well as on the psychological insight historians need if they're going to understand what really occurred – the type of influence she must have had over several years. After my conversation with her, for example, I started to wonder how much the myth of 'Romanità' came from Mussolini and how much was instead more the result of Sarfatti's influence over him. Certainly I have never known anyone like her so pathologically obsessed with the myth of Rome.[32]

By the time the Fascist cult of Rome had reached its apotheosis with the conquest of Ethiopia and the revival of the "new" Roman Empire, Margherita Sarfatti had already been marginalized and excluded. The Ethiopian campaign was a period of crisis for the anti-Fascists too. Italian Communists, already weakened by the harsh repression carried out by the regime's secret police, had a radical change of tactics: judging the Italian masses who were cheering Mussolini on to be now completely under the sway of Fascist ideology, they decided to make this appeal to them, published abroad in the newspaper *Lo stato operaio*: "We stretch our hands out to the Fascists, our brothers in labour and in suffering, since we want to wage alongside them the sacred battle for food, for work, for peace. [...] We declare that we are ready to fight alongside you and the whole of the Italian people to carry out the aims stated in the Fascist manifesto of 1919 and for all causes which involve the specific or general interests of the workers and the Italian people."

The change of tactics had been decided by the International Communist Organization, the Comintern; Italian Communists, who were working in exile and in isolation, remote from what was actually happening inside Italy, knew that the appeal would create an uproar in the anti-Fascist camp. The Fascist regime did not enjoy solid support among the industrial workers in Turin and Milan; Mussolini was well aware of the fact, but limited himself to keeping the situation under tight control. A challenge which did, however, take him unawares came from within the Fascist ranks themselves when intellectuals and the younger generation more generally started to demand a more active participation in political life. At first Mussolini bided his time as he considered how to respond to this new and unexpected phenomenon, but after the war in Ethiopia began he decided to impose his authority and rally the party to the old cry of "Believe, obey, fight". Once the war had been won and the new empire proclaimed, however, he re-examined, in a swing to the left, the demands being raised by the young in an effort to work out how much room for manoeuvre they gave him. They represented a feeble wind of change which hoped to push the regime towards a degree of liberalization; Mussolini responded by modifying certain restraints and making limited concessions and waited to see what reactions this would produce.

His position as far as international politics was concerned was also strong; the rest of the world now accepted that Ethiopia was Italian and once again began to look to Mussolini as the sole European leader who could restrain Hitler. The regime was more firmly established than ever before; it authorized various publications, including a journal edited by the former leader of the Italian Communist Party Nicola Bombacci, who had become a Fascist supporter and would be a follower of Mussolini until the capture and death of both in 1945. As for the discontents on the extreme right wing of the Fascist Party, Mussolini chose to ignore them. It is also the case that he was preoccupied at the same time with a family tragedy: his youngest daughter, Anna Maria, fell seriously ill with polio and was in danger of dying. The event shook Mussolini, who had never been able to deal with the prospect of illness either in himself or in his children. His worried wife thought, with her usual down-to-earth common sense, that this might be a good moment to appeal to her husband to stand down; plucking up her courage, she told him he had reached the pinnacle of his political career, the moment of his greatest success; the time had arrived to retire in order to be with his family. Mussolini's reply was brusque: "So you think I should hand in my resignation? So we can go and raise chickens in Romagna? Be serious, Rachele!"[33]

His success intoxicated him. Rachele could go on looking after the house, he would forge ahead in the mission only he could accomplish. In this period he was convinced he would die in his bed only after he had achieved his life's work and transformed Italy into a great nation. He began to see himself as an invincible and invulnerable hero, trailing a cloud of glory: weren't the bombs and bullets that had been thrown at him and missed him proof? He told journalists he liked living dangerously, whereas in reality he was bald, short-sighted, stout despite his rigid diet, preoccupied with his various ailments, from his stomach ulcer to his constipation, isolated and without a single close friend. The newly dubbed "Founder of the Empire" was undergoing a profound transformation in 1936. The continual psychological tension was a source of stress, but he couldn't operate without it – he needed it to hold the regime in his grasp. On 11th

June he reshuffled the government, abolishing various ministries and introducing new ones. The change that attracted most attention was the appointment of his young and ambitious son-in-law Galeazzo Ciano as Minister for Foreign Affairs. It was widely thought that at the zenith of his career Mussolini had with this choice elected his successor, the new Duce-in-waiting who would ensure the future glory of the regime.

And what if Mussolini had gone into retirement in 1936?... Counterfactual history can be fascinating, even entertaining, and many have asked themselves this question. The truth is that in this period Mussolini began, so to speak, a second life which followed on wearily from the first. "I am Mussolini, not some kind of fool who can spend time talking about matters outside his work. If people saw me they'd think I'd gone crazy or soft. I've got a whole world to take care of, a people to govern, it all comes down to me. I'm not just any person – I give you too much of my time as it is. Sometimes I think I'm stupid."[34]

Despite his complaints at the direction their relationship was taking, Petacci's transcription of these remarks serve as a sign of her own victory: Mussolini had conquered the Empire, but she had conquered him. Her diary is filled with sentimental passages like this one from 4th November 1937: "With amazement we watch the sun set in a blaze of gold and red. There are rays of light striking through the clouds, while on the left of the sky it's like something out of the Bible: across a backdrop of lead there are grey, weird, stormy-looking tangles of cloud formations coloured cyclamen-pink. The sea on that side glints steely-grey while on the right it is blue. The sun sets behind the horizon, a marvellous golden disk. Every now and then he gives me a small kiss and hugs me. Now the sun has gone down completely, we feel moved, we're almost shaking. 'I've never done this with a woman, kissing her as the sun goes down. I love you. [...] You would make an enchanting imperial *Marschallin.*'"[35]

It is not hard to imagine the expressions on the faces of Hitler, Goebbels, Göring, Himmler as they read the transcripts of such remarks, made in telephone calls from Mussolini to his mistress that were regularly intercepted.

Sarfatti's view of Mussolini at this period, as described in her memoir *My Fault*, is rather different from Petacci's sugary tones. She writes that he could no longer brook the slightest remark which might be intended as a criticism of him. His former mistress attributes a notable courage to herself for not hiding from Mussolini her disapproval of the false empire he was building in Ethiopia or her horror at the alliance with Germany into which he was leading Italy. There is no trace of what she had earlier emphasized – her friendship with Göring and her own contribution to the complex diplomatic relations between the two regimes – in her final judgement on Fascism: "I distanced myself from Fascism, much to my grief, when it started to degenerate, when it began to imitate what itself had started out as an imitation of Fascism, or rather a sadistic and grotesque parody of it: Nazism."[36]

During an official visit to the Third Reich in 1937 Mussolini spoke these words in the toast at an official banquet in honour of Hitler: "From my arrival on German soil, I have been surrounded by the spirit of a great nation, allied in friendship to us: the Germany of the Brownshirts, Hitler's Germany."[37] In the evening he would telephone Petacci and their sentimental conversations would no doubt once again have been listened to with surprise by the German official who had the job of tapping the calls. Just one year after they had first slept together, Mussolini's relationship with Petacci was firmly established, and the couple called each other on average twelve times a day. Hitler and other prominent Nazis must have been privy to these conversations through the transcriptions provided by the German intelligence services, but were nevertheless still capable of listening, with the appropriate demeanour, to such expressions as the following from Mussolini's speech in German at the banquet: "We both have an exalted idea of work in all its manifestations as a sign of men's nobility; we both rely on our country's youth, to whom we hold up the virtues of discipline, courage, tenacity, patriotism and a stoic refusal of an easy life. The new Roman Empire has been the creation of this new spirit at work within Italy, and German renewal is likewise the creation of the spirit..."[38]

After 8th September 1943 Mussolini would deliver up Italian Jews to the concentration camps in the culminating gesture of his alliance with Germany. On returning to Italy after his official visit in 1937 he declared in a public speech: "Blackshirts! I have brought back from Germany and from my conversations with the Führer a lasting impression. The friendship between our two countries, which we have consecrated in the formal political alliance of the Rome-Berlin Axis, is now implanted in our hearts for ever."[39]

He thought that he had opened a new phase in the development of the Fascist regime. It hardly mattered that he was contradicting the consistently anti-German stance he had maintained up till then. As he approached sixty he was ageing rapidly; he was entering a political tunnel in the conviction that this new development would be accompanied by new life. He was aware of physical decline, but thought he could control it and that his new and much younger mistress would help him to continue exercising and preserving his sexual vigour. Petacci would clasp him to those breasts which filled him with ecstasy.

His new mistress was seeing off one by one Mussolini's other lovers, but she was also busy advancing the fortunes of her own widespread clan around her own privileged access to the Duce. First and foremost among the beneficiaries were her brother and her father. She was given a hidden account for the ostensible purpose of charitable works. The money was supplied, in secret, far from the possibility of any public accountability, by the undersecretary at the Ministry for Internal Affairs, Guido Buffarini Guidi, who was directly answerable to Mussolini and to him alone. Her sister profited from the connection too, being taken on as an actress – under the name Miriam di San Servolo – in the Rome film studios at Cinecittà. When her first film, *Le vie del cuore* (*The Ways of the Heart*) was shown at the annual Venice Film Festival, the audience was made up of leading members of the regime – ministers, businessmen, academics, senior civil servants – who flocked to pay homage to the new star. The *gerarchi* who sensed they could take advantage of the connection were soon buzzing round the Petacci clan, while those who found themselves excluded started to plot against them. But whatever their attitude, all the men around the Duce were aware that with the political alliance with Hitler and the relationship with Petacci Mussolini had opened a new chapter in his career. "Darling, please don't keep on asking me – especially when you call me – what work I'm doing, who I'm seeing, and especially what my meetings are about. It's risky doing that, do you understand? I don't want to tell you about what I'm doing, especially over the telephone. I don't know if my calls are tapped. They might be. So just remember this when you start asking questions... I'm working my guts out and you treat me badly. I've become a real idiot, a fool. It's just not on, you've got to show some respect for the work I'm doing."[40]

Nevertheless, with a smile and undeterred, she went on transcribing their conversations. She would reread them to herself and smile again: the powerful Duce came across as touchingly uncertain of himself. But she felt sure of herself and of the new and inspiring direction her life was taking. The stage was set: herself and the new empire, linked by a single man, the man who was her lover.

In July 1936, the year of his greatest triumph, barely a month after the crowds had gathered to celebrate the conquest of Ethiopia, Mussolini, together with Hitler, sent arms and airplanes and troops to fight in the civil war which had broken out in Spain. Like many of us when we feel we're starting a new chapter in our lives, Mussolini decided to reorganize some of the small details of his daily life, including his desk, the vast table in his huge office in the so-called World Map Room in Palazzo Venezia. Many an awestruck journalist or *gerarca* or general had sat on the far side of the desk; now Mussolini placed a trinket on it, a small model of a little cottage and a heart with the words "Home is where the heart is". With this knick-knack in front of him Mussolini would draw up his plans for his country's participation in what would become the greatest tragedy ever to befall humanity, the Second World War. And like a talisman, the trinket protected the Petacci clan as it went about its business. As things turned out, it was Petacci herself who showed the most integrity: unlike her family, she never sought to make money out of the relationship and she ended up paying for her loyalty with her life. But no one cared about how she had lived when she was killed alongside Mussolini, after she had made a final desperate attempt to prevent the execution. Her body was put onto a lorry and displayed in Piazzale Loreto, where she was strung up by the feet. People took pity on the nakedness of the upside-down corpse and pinned up her skirt to conceal it, but when the body was taken to the mortuary no autopsy was thought necessary. No one cared how she had been killed. Her own end became a mere appendix to the mystery surrounding Mussolini's death. But a detailed historical account of the period between the high point of Mussolini's myth in 1936 and its end in his death and that of his mistress will only emerge when all the relevant documents have finally been released; when that happens, there will be another – and a different – story to tell.

21. Mussolini in 1918, when he was editor of *Il Popolo d'Italia* (top left).
22. The memorial plaque affixed in 1923 above the door of the offices in which *Il Popolo d'Italia* was first set up in November 1914 (top right). 23. The Duce's office at *Il Popolo d'Italia* up to February 1922 (below).

24. Arnaldo Mussolini, the Duce's brother (described in Mussolini's *My Life* as the "super journalist of Italy"), who took over the editorship of *Il Popolo d'Italia* in 1922 (top left). 25. Margherita Sarfatti, Benito Mussolini's lover and first biographer, who was instrumental in the creation of the Mussolini myth (top right). 26. A stylized, classical-looking bust of Mussolini by Adolfo Wildt, used as a frontispiece for Sarfatti's *Dux* (bottom left). 27. The 1932 paperback reprint of the Italian edition of *Dux* (bottom right).

The building of the Mussolini myth: four pictures from Margherita Sarfatti's *Dux*.
28. Mussolini the "aviator", 1920 (top left).
29. Mussolini horse-riding in the Campagna Romana, 1923 (top right).
30. Mussolini playing with his pet lion Italia in her cage, 1923 (bottom left).
31. Mussolini holidaying on a boat in Nettuno, 1925 (bottom right).

32. Mussolini just before the March on Rome, 1922 (above).
33. The March on Rome: the main railway station in Milan patrolled by Blackshirts (below).

34. The March on Rome: Blackshirts patrolling outside the Fascist
headquarters in Milan (above). 35. Fascist leaders with Mussolini (below).

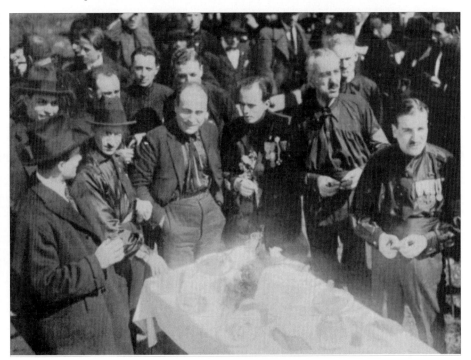

The consolidation of power. 36. Prime Minister Mussolini in 1922 (top left).
37. Mussolini as Minister of the Navy, inspecting the naval officers in Ostia in 1925 (top right).
38. Mussolini as Minister of the Air Force, presiding over an aircraft competition
in 1923 (bottom left). 39. Mussolini with the Prince of Piedmont (Umberto) and his
undersecretary Giacomo Acerbo at a Balilla parade (bottom right).

40. The inauguration of the Casa del Fascio at Signa, near Florence, in 1928, with Fascists wearing Roman costumes grouped at the entrance.

41. Mussolini addressing a Fascist rally.

21. Mussolini in 1918, when he was editor of *Il Popolo d'Italia* (top left).
22. The memorial plaque affixed in 1923 above the door of the offices in which *Il Popolo d'Italia* was first set up in November 1914 (top right). 23. The Duce's office at *Il Popolo d'Italia* up to February 1922 (below).

24. Arnaldo Mussolini, the Duce's brother (described in Mussolini's *My Life* as the "super journalist of Italy"), who took over the editorship of *Il Popolo d'Italia* in 1922 (top left). 25. Margherita Sarfatti, Benito Mussolini's lover and first biographer, who was instrumental in the creation of the Mussolini myth (top right). 26. A stylized, classical-looking bust of Mussolini by Adolfo Wildt, used as a frontispiece for Sarfatti's *Dux* (bottom left). 27. The 1932 paperback reprint of the Italian edition of *Dux* (bottom right).

The building of the Mussolini myth: four pictures from Margherita Sarfatti's *Dux*.
28. Mussolini the "aviator", 1920 (top left).
29. Mussolini horse-riding in the Campagna Romana, 1923 (top right).
30. Mussolini playing with his pet lion Italia in her cage, 1923 (bottom left).
31. Mussolini holidaying on a boat in Nettuno, 1925 (bottom right).

32. Mussolini just before the March on Rome, 1922 (above).
33. The March on Rome: the main railway station in Milan patrolled by Blackshirts (below).

34. The March on Rome: Blackshirts patrolling outside the Fascist headquarters in Milan (above). 35. Fascist leaders with Mussolini (below).

The consolidation of power. 36. Prime Minister Mussolini in 1922 (top left).
37. Mussolini as Minister of the Navy, inspecting the naval officers in Ostia in 1925 (top right).
38. Mussolini as Minister of the Air Force, presiding over an aircraft competition
in 1923 (bottom left). 39. Mussolini with the Prince of Piedmont (Umberto) and his
undersecretary Giacomo Acerbo at a Balilla parade (bottom right).

40. The inauguration of the Casa del Fascio at Signa, near Florence, in 1928, with Fascists wearing Roman costumes grouped at the entrance.

41. Mussolini addressing a Fascist rally.

APPENDICES

Appendix 1

Mussolini and the Crowd

Nothing could stop the crowd. They tried driving them back by letting off the water cannons, forming a cordon to resist the pushing and shoving, pointing rifles against them and then firing into the air. There were so many people blocking all the roads around it that it was difficult to get into the square. Those on the edges of the throng tried to push their way forward or stand on tiptoe to get a better view over the sea of heads and hats; a few young lads climbed up the lamp-posts. There were many women, soldiers in uniform, firemen and several photographers. A soldier with a film camera had jumped onto an open lorry which was slowly trying to make its way through, while another cameraman in a white raincoat was shouting at people to clear the view as his right hand rewound the machine's spring mechanism. At the centre of the crowd was a circle of corpses thrown on the ground any old how, just as they'd been unloaded from a lorry some hours earlier, at dawn. Those who'd got near them had spat and urinated on them; others, armed with pistols, had shot randomly at the bodies, while others preferred to throw rotten vegetables on them as a sign of their contempt. "Come on, make one of your speeches!" jeered some of those who'd been forced to listen too often to the Duce's rallies. Kicks were aimed at Mussolini's head and Petacci's body. The crowds wanted to see them and wanted to strike them; their day of revolution had arrived.

It was the vast crowd pressing around those corpses that was in control. Whoever the individuals were who made it up – couples holding hands, housewives who'd left their household chores behind for the morning, elderly teachers who'd never handled a gun in their lives, even at a funfair – they had all been transformed into a single mass of people. The ridiculous and despised Achille Starace, the former secretary of the Fascist Party, had been identified as he stood among them, wearing of all things a tracksuit, just as if he was on his way to compete in the stadium of the National Olympic Committee, of which he had once been the chief. The crowd made way for one brief frozen minute as the Partisans took aim and shot him then surged forward again, their bloodthirsty frenzy unassuaged. Those who had just arrived tried to push forward to that circle of dead bodies that marked the end of a long story. Someone had the sensible idea of hanging the bodies up so that everyone would be able to see them. He hung them by the feet from the roof of the petrol station, an act which has been described as one of "Mexican butchery" transposed to the psychopolitical drama of contemporary Italian history, but one doesn't need to know much about human anatomy to realize that if they'd been strung up the other way round their bodies would have dropped off leaving only their heads hanging.

At the sight of the bodies the crowd went wild. A priest who seemed unaffected by their rage calmly approached Petacci's corpse and concealed what perhaps struck him as especially obscene by tying up her skirt round her legs with a safety pin and a bit of string. The Partisans forced a nearby printing firm to reopen so that a poster showing a photograph of the fifteen Resistance fighters whose bodies had been put on display in the very same square less than a year before could urgently be produced and distributed. A woman started to collect contributions from the crowd for the families of the men who'd been killed. But the bystanders only had eyes for the bodies dangling from the roof. Anyone approaching the square from one of the surrounding avenues was inevitably sucked in and became part of the audience witnessing this final act. That morning in Piazzale Loreto is the subject of a poem by Salvatore Quasimodo. Entitled 'Laude 29 aprile 1945' ('Laud for 29th April 1945'), it describes a mother who in the crowd talks to her dead son who has been killed earlier by the Fascists:

(*Son*): Mother, why do you spit on a corpse hanging head down, with its feet tied to a beam?
Don't the other bodies hanging alongside disgust you?
That woman, with her stockinged legs in a macabre cancan
And her throat and mouth like flowers which have been trodden on!
Stop, mother, shout to the crowd to go away.
They're not weeping, they're leering,
They're happy. Already the veins heave with flies.
You've shot at that face now: oh mother, mother, mother!

(*Mother*): We've always spat on corpses, my son:
On bodies hung from window gratings,
From ships' masts, burnt to ashes in the name of the Cross,
Torn apart by dogs for a handful of grass at the edge of the master's
estate.
After two thousand years of Communion,
Whether alone or amid the crowd, it's an eye for an eye,
And a tooth for a tooth.
Our heart wants to rip open the heart which ripped open yours, my
son.
They gouged out your eyes, they crushed your hands to bits so you
would betray a name.
Show me your eyes, stretch out your hands: you are dead, my son!
And it's because you are dead you can forgive: my son, my son, my
son!

(*Son*): This oppressive heat, these smoking ruins,
The fat green flies clustered round the hooks:
Anger and blood rightly flow. But not for you and not for me, mother,
Tomorrow they'll pierce my eyes and hands again.
Pity is the centuries-old cry of the murdered man.

Mussolini knew he might one day fall into an abyss as deep as the
crowd which gathered round his corpse in Piazzale Loreto. While it
is difficult to know for certain how much Nietzsche or Marx he had
actually read, whether he really attended Pareto's university courses
while he was in Switzerland or to what extent he was influenced by
the books of Georges Sorel during his time in prison, his knowledge
of the work of Gustave Le Bon is not in doubt – of one text in particular, which he kept with him as an inseparable companion, a kind
of *livre de chevet*, *La Psychologie des foules* (published in English as
The Crowd: A Study of the Popular Mind): "One of the books that
interested me most was Gustave Le Bon's work on the psychology
of the crowd."[1]

    Gustave Le Bon was known for his intellectual eclecticism: he dab-
bled in archaeology, anthropology, physics, sociology and psychology and was capable of writing perceptively on all of these different
subjects. He was famed for his eccentric behaviour and his extravagant way of dressing, while dinners at his house had a reputation
for turning into theatrical performances. He was excluded from the
world of academia, but his writings were keenly followed by men who

worked in the nascent advertising industry – and by aspiring dictators. Theorists of mass communication have studied his insights into
crowd psychology, while the propaganda machines of various kinds
of political regimes have also drawn on them. "Is it possible to love
a dictator?" Emil Ludwig asked Mussolini in one of his interviews.
Mussolini's reply was unhesitating: "Yes it is. When the masses fear
him. The masses love strong men. The masses are female." (In the
proofs Mussolini corrected the last phrase and substituted "like a
woman" instead.)[2]

But Le Bon's analysis has been useful in democracies too – take this
passage for example (and remember it was written in 1895): "The
candidate who hits upon a new verbal formula which has no precise
meaning and can be adapted to any number of different sets of aspirations is bound to succeed."[3] These words are still true today, over
a hundred years after Le Bon wrote them, for all election candidates
everywhere, including those running for the presidency of the United
States. Le Bon's book *La Psychologie des foules* – so full of telling
insights it could be said to border on prophecy and written in a fluent,
unacademic style – could easily be used as a manual – to be read and
reread – by the man who wanted to learn how to dominate a crowd.

Mussolini must have known the following passage from Le Bon's
book, written fifty years before the events in Piazzale Loreto: "All
crowds, therefore, are female, but this aspect is characteristic above
all of crowds in Mediterranean countries. The man who depends on
their support for his career will have a speedy and vertiginous rise
to power, but he risks falling over the Tarpeian precipice at every
moment, and the day will certainly come when he plunges into
the abyss."[4] The crowds who gathered in Piazzale Loreto were the
same as those who lynched a man in Louisiana merely because they
thought he had committed a crime or those who enjoyed watching
the blood flow from the guillotines in the Place de la Bastille or
who stormed the Winter Palace in St Petersburg despite the soldiers
armed with bayonets directed at them. On 29th April 1945, crowded
round the petrol station, there were poets and artists, doctors and
intellectuals, journalists and men who worked in the film industry,
clergy and housewives – a vast range of people from different social
backgrounds and of differing levels of attainment, not all of them
speaking the same language and certainly drawn to the spectacle
for a variety of reasons – but whatever they thought and wanted

as individuals had, in those circumstances, no possibility at all of making itself felt.

Over the course of the morning many drifted away to be replaced by others. It was a textbook example of a shifting crowd formed of very different kinds of people, yet capable of infecting or cancelling out each single individual who came to form part of it.

> Just by joining a crowd, men abase themselves, they drop down the scale of civilized behaviour. Taken by himself, an individual may be a person of cultivation; as part of the crowd, he's led by his instincts, he becomes a barbarian. He acquires the spontaneity, the violence, the ferocity – as well as the capacity for enthusiastic acts of daring and heroism – which characterize primitive peoples. He also becomes like them in his tendency, as part of a crowd, to let himself be swept along in doing things which quite clearly undermine his own self-interest as an individual. In a crowd individuals become like mere grains of sand driven on by the wind just as it pleases.[5]

The influence of Le Bon can already be found in the early Mussolini who embraced a fideistic vision of socialism, in the political agitator who was more concerned to give the masses something to believe in than helping them to reason, whose impassioned diatribes from the dais at political meetings would incite workers and labourers to go and face the soldiers' platoons sent to suppress their protests. The idea is already implicit in Le Bon's *La Psychologie des foules*, and the agitator can profit from the lesson: "The crowds of men who go on strike do so much more in obedient response to a command than out of any wish to obtain an increase in their pay packets."[6]

Yet it is improbable that Mussolini's reading of Le Bon played a direct part in his transition from socialism to Fascism. Le Bon's formulas are too simple to have effected such a complex process, made up as it was of numerous intermediate shifts in position as Mussolini acted and reacted to the changing political circumstances and the emergence of new personalities. But Mussolini's familiarity with the book and his reflections on its message may well have served to undermine his idea of socialism – Anna Kuliscioff had already had her doubts about how firm Mussolini's commitment was and had communicated her misgivings to other members of the Socialist Party. "The obvious weakness of socialist beliefs will not prevent them taking root among the masses. The real drawback of the socialist credo in comparison with the religious faiths lies only in this: that whereas they place the prospect of future happiness entirely in the afterlife, with the result that no one's in a position to complain if it's not achieved, the promise of happiness which socialism holds out is intended for the here-and-now, so when it's revealed as empty people abandon their faith in it."[7]

Le Bon's judgement here turned out to be over-hasty and simplistic, although his insight into the consequences of the conflict between socialist and religious credos is striking. Mussolini's unexpected enthusiasm for military service when he was called up in 1905 has puzzled many of his biographers: some just record it, while others, like Sarfatti, try to explain it by seeing it as the key event in the transformation of the "new man" into the "Duce"; another approach is Cesare Rossi's, who views it as an act of characteristic political cynicism, of the need to adapt to one's circumstances in order to come out on top. It is not known if Mussolini had already come across Le Bon's book when he was first called up for military service, but if he had, the following passage might well have struck him and given him pause for thought, even more so because it quotes Napoleon:

> The great statesmen of every age and in every country, including absolutist despots, have always regarded their popular image as the basis of their power. They have never sought to govern without it. "I brought the war of the Vendée to a close by making myself a Catholic," Napoleon declared to the Council of State. "I made myself a Muslim to conquer Egypt and by becoming an Ultramontanist I brought the Italian clergy over to my side. If I were to rule over the Jews, I'd offer to rebuild the Temple of Solomon."[8]

By the time Mussolini had achieved power, he knew Le Bon's "manual" by heart; he had worked with it, and now its lessons were second nature to him; he could follow the instinct developed over decades of political activity. It is pointless – and was so even at the time – to criticize the content of his speeches, since this had almost no relevance to the goals of his political actions; what counted was the sense of ritual and of theatre, the ability continually to sense and "play" the audience whatever the circumstances were. Gestures were important – they needed to be visible even from a great distance – as well as the power of the voice, its tones, its pauses, its sudden accelerations. "A logical sequence of reasoning would be completely incomprehensible to a crowd; it is in this sense we can say a crowd is incapable of reasoning or using reason with a purpose and similarly of being influenced by reasoned argument. [...] In the intimacy of his connection with the crowd, the orator is able to evoke the images which bring it under his spell."[9]

Establishing an intimate rapport with the crowds who came to listen to him became second nature for Mussolini, like an experienced and consummate actor who, as soon as he enters on stage, is capable of holding the audience's attention. Mussolini's techniques can be identified in all his most famous speeches, such as the one proclaiming the Italian victory in Ethiopia or the declaration of war in 1940, but they are perhaps most easily seen in what we might call his "routine" appearances during his visits to small towns and villages throughout Italy, when there was no "great event" to enthuse the crowds who turned out to hear him and with whom he needed to make contact. In these cases, of course, the "great event" was the man himself, his presence in flesh and blood: Mussolini enacted and embodied – literally – absolute power. Sarfatti described his technique as an orator in an article published in *Il Popolo d'Italia* on 22nd February 1923:

> Benito Mussolini's speeches should not be regarded as merely calls for revolution; they are themselves acts of revolution. When he speaks, Mussolini takes no pleasure in forming rotund phrases just as he doesn't gesture pompously with his arms; he shuns all such obviousness. With a warrior's masculine sobriety and succinctness, Mussolini sums up a situation, issues a command, evokes an emotion. His style of eloquence is *sui generis*: it is simple and direct and adheres to the facts. It consists in a series of prosaic expressions, which seem unpoetical to the point of brutality, but on occasion attain a kind of lyricism in the way he can move from the essential to the non-essential, without any ornamentation, "strangling the neck of rhetoric", as a great lyric poet once urged us to do.

A good example of Mussolini's oratorical style can be seen in the speech he gave during a visit to Cremona on 7th October 1934. He had been in power for twelve years, and was now the supremely popular Duce; he'd seen off all his opponents, both the once democratically elected parties and the internal opposition to him among the Fascists. Cremona had in fact been home to his most dangerous enemy within the party, Roberto Farinacci, who had been the city's local *ras*. Rumours had reached Mussolini that Farinacci might have been involved in the assassination attempt in Bologna some years previously. In 1929 Mussolini had succeeded in getting Farinacci removed from the Grand Council and in stripping him of all his power. But now, once more in Farinacci's home town, he had no need to go on the attack: for the Cremonese who gathered to listen to him the Duce was a legendary figure and as such untouchable. The dictatorship he had established was strong and firm. In that same year he had sent troops to the Austrian border in an attempt to curb Hitler's ambitions for annexation. The United States press had just included him in a list of the twelve leading Christian defenders of the Jewish race. Thus Mussolini arrived in Cremona sure of himself and unconcerned about having to prepare what he was going to say; he knew that it would be sufficient to put himself on display and follow a tried-and-tested rhetorical routine he could now perform by heart. It was enough to be himself. "In human crowds, the leader has an important role to play. It is the sheer force of his will which provides the focus round which all the rest form their opinions and from which they take their lead. The crowd is like a flock of sheep; they need a master to guide them."[10]

Mussolini's arrival in the town had been trumpeted for months: the life of the entire community – its schools, barracks, farms, factories, local associations – had been involved in planning the success of the great day. The purpose of the visit was to inaugurate the town's "Sacrario" or memorial to those who had given their lives in the Fascist revolution; after the ceremony, he was driven through the streets lined with festive crowds waving pennants and banners and then watched the long parade which had been organized in his honour – soldiers, Fascist militia, Blackshirts, labourers carrying hoes and rural housewives with wooden rakes passed by at a running march under his balcony, while the Fascist anthem 'Giovinezza', played by one of the local bands, blared out from the loudspeakers all over the town. At last Mussolini climbed onto the "Arengo", the pulpit-like balcony at the front of the "Arengario", the medieval town hall, from which for centuries speakers had harangued the local populace. The speech was regarded as so much a routine formality that *Il Popolo d'Italia* published only a short summary of what Mussolini said in its issue on the following day; a similar brief résumé can be found in the *Opera Omnia*. But the speech can be heard and also seen as part of the multimedia work *Combat Film*: the film of the event was shot by an amateur cameraman, and as a result has some technical shortcomings, but it is precisely because it is not the regime's customary propaganda footage "touched up" by the Istituto Luce that we can observe Mussolini together with the behaviour and reactions of the crowds more closely.[11]

"Hail Duce! Hail Duce! Hail Duce!" – an impassive Mussolini, seen in half-length, waits as the crowd acclaims him. He is mentally preparing himself to launch his speech. The preliminaries are never a mere formulaic ritual for repetition on each and every occasion; they are an essential part of the process of making contact with the particular audience he's addressing. "The laws of reason and logic have no effect on crowds. In order to conquer a crowd, one must first become aware of the emotions they are feeling, pretend to share them, and then attempt to shape them, by evoking powerful images based on simple associations of ideas."[12] The crowd in the Cremona piazza finally quietens down into an expectant hush; right from the outset, it seems that Mussolini wants to shape this silence; when he begins to speak, he stops for numerous pauses between words, making the adjectives and verbs stand out in isolation.

> Blackshirts of Cremona [*pause*], when [*pause*] gathered together [*pause*] you were present [*pause*] in Piazza Venezia in Rome [*pause*] I promised you [*pause*] that I would come to your city [*pause*] for the opening [*pause*] of the Memorial [*pause*] for your fellow citizens who gave their lives for the Fascist cause [*pause*]. Today [*pause*] I am fulfilling [*pause*] my promise [*a longer pause and an attentive silence*] and it is not without deep emotion [*pause*] that I crossed the threshold [*pause*] of the monument [*pause*] which will stand [*pause – and now Mussolini stirs himself, raising his voice and tone, waving his right arm in the air as if to beat time*] for ever and for every generation to come [*pause*] as a remembrance of the voluntary sacrifice [*pause*] offered up [*pause*] by the Blackshirts of Cremona [*ovation and new chants of "Duce, Duce, Duce…"*].

The sequence of sentences and concepts no longer has any importance; it is single words which convey an image to the listening crowds, who are not called upon to follow a line of reasoning or an analysis, but only to receive passively the speaker's evocations. "Sacrifice", "monument", "remembrance", "promise", "inauguration", even "today" – all are intended to carry a significance which is quite separate from the part they play in the sentence. The pauses Mussolini introduces are frequently so long and the emphatic intonation he places on certain words so marked that all sense of the overall syntactic structure of the sentences is lost and each word seems to stand alone.

> The pennants of the squadrons [*pause*] which were worn [*pause*] by the bands [*pause*] of valiant [*pause*] and pioneering young men [*pause*] will be placed on the monument [*pause – and then he suddenly unleashes a torrent of words without taking breath*]. They will keep watch over the fallen, just as the fallen will keep watch over the glorious deeds which represent the heart of our passionate endeavours and the culmination of our ardent faith [*"heart" and "faith" stand out in the sudden cascade of words; there are shouts of approval from the crowd; a pause while Mussolini looks round with an air of satisfaction*]. This is the fifth time [*pause*] I have had the fortune [*pause*] to be able to speak to you [*pause – he places his hands on his hips and puffs out his chest*] in this magnificent piazza [*pause*]. Remembering [*at this point the camera moves away from Mussolini and begins slowly to pan over the assembled crowds*] my previous visits [*pause*] means reliving [*said with great emphasis*] fifteen glorious years in the life of Cremona and in the life of Italy.

The camera's panning shot over the crowd reveals that they look like the audience in a cinema; we see all their faces, since all of them have taken up positions from which they have a direct sight of Mussolini. They're not just listening to him, they want to see him, and so, as the camera moves over them, from Mussolini's perspective on the balcony, we see all their upturned individual faces gazing on the Duce. The Duce's body was, after all, the main communicative element in a speech which otherwise consisted of nothing more than a rudimentary association of a few simple ideas. Four minutes have passed since Mussolini began to speak, but in terms of content he's said only that he's kept his promise to come back on a fifth visit to the town to inaugurate its new monument for the Fascist martyrs. The four minutes have had more pauses in them than ideas, and yet they have been vital in establishing a rapport with the crowd. Like an actor having to improvise a monologue in some makeshift open space rather than in the usual confines of a theatre, Mussolini waits for the crowd to settle itself, for each person to move to get the best sightlines so their vision is not obstructed. Anyone watching the film today will find his posturing ridiculous – the way he juts his chin out, puffs out his chest with hands on hips, the caricature-like expressions of anger and satisfaction which play over his face – but that is because we are used to a televisual representation of reality, seen on our small screens every day. We might add that Mussolini himself was aware of the absurd effect of some of his expressions when they were projected onto a cinema screen and ordered them to be cut. But the spectators in the crowds which filled the piazzas of Fascist Italy were "mere grains of sand", in Le Bon's expression; the visual message communicated by the body of the Duce had to reach them even if they were standing at a great distance.

Mussolini is now sure he has caught the attention of the crowd packing the square and continues:

> "It was a hard time [*pause*] when [*pause*] our fertile and productive land [*pause*] was racked by disturbances [*said with theatrical effect, the Rs explosively rolled*] from extremists [*pause*], from Bolsheviks [*pause*]. It was hard to tell which were more dangerous and more harmful [*applause and acclamation*] like the difference between white and black..."

He's made a mistake, and someone in the crowd shouts it out: Fascists wear black but Mussolini has inadvertently used the image of white and black to describe his opponents. His puffed-out chest collapses and he laughs, turning towards the area of the crowd where the shout came from. He replies as though in a normal conversation among friends, bringing the situation under control without the least sign of embarrassment. "You should know how to retrieve your steps, if necessary, and above all to stay alert at every moment to the emotions which can suddenly arise."[13]

Mussolini waits for silence to settle again before resuming his stance as actor-orator.

> On the first occasion I came [*pause*], there were the early groups of Fascists [*pause*] formed around an energetic leader who has been with you for twenty years [*a reference to Farinacci: Mussolini can now afford to pay this benevolent tribute to a former rival – and his followers who are in the audience – he has now been definitively marginalized*], who [*pause – he gesticulates and strikes the air with his right fist*] undertook the first fighting [*pause*] and inflicted the first defeats on our enemies [*pause*]. The second time I came was just before the March on

Rome [*pause*]. I announced it in this very piazza [*pause*]. Since [*pause*] the time was ripe [*here he raises his right hand as if plucking a fruit which is hanging from the branch of a tree*]. A new and powerful political class was emerging [*pause*], which grew out of the radiant victory of Italian arms in the world war [*ovation*] and was inspired [*pause*] by a new political credo [*pause*] which summed up all the best hopes of the Italian people.

Fifteen years had passed since the end of the First World War and Mussolini in his speeches continues to repeat that Fascism – and Fascism alone – was the rightful inheritor of the honours of victory, the only political movement which had proved capable of understanding the feelings of the returning soldiers. We know that this is untrue, that the Fasci attracted only a minority of veterans after the war and that Mussolini himself had attempted to join the left-wing interventionist movement but had been rejected. But now it is enough to say something in order to make it true; whether it is or not no longer matters. "Assertion, pure and simple, untouched by reasoning and evidence, is a foolproof method of instilling an idea into a crowd. [...] Yet assertion only acquires real influence if it is repeated continuously, as much as possible, and always in the same terms. [...] Thanks to repetition, assertion can penetrate people's minds and stay there with all the force of demonstrable truth."[14]

Every advertising agency knows that you need to repeat the same message innumerable times to get it to stick in the public's mind; it's a fundamental rule in publicity for any product – a drink, a gadget, a perfume or soap – including a political idea. Mussolini can now allow himself a sudden flourish and bring the crowd to a new pitch of excitement by calmly telling them how he deprived them of their freedom, abolished democracy and eliminated his democratic opponents:

You [*here he lifts a pointing finger to the sky as if about to warn the entire piazza*] sensed [*pause*] that the die was cast [*pause*], that we had reached the Rubicon [*and now he begins to shout out an unstoppable stream of words while his fist punches the air*], that we had to take the old class of politicians who had proved inadequate during the war and inadequate during the peace which followed it and eliminate them [*he slices the air with his hand*], forcing them [*pause*] decisively [*pause*], courageously [*pause*], to sacrifice themselves [*pause*] so that the way could be cleared for the new and enthusiastic forces which were springing from the eternal and inexhaustible and unfailingly youthful spirit of the Italian people [*a wild ovation which turns into the usual chant of "Duce, Duce..."*].

Mussolini continues his sally against his enemies by attacking the last form of democratic opposition he faced – or what he calls the "attempt" to oppose him – the so-called "Aventine Secession" when, following the murder of the Socialist leader Matteotti, the democratic parties formally withdrew from parliament in 1925. By now whatever Mussolini says triggers a wave of enthusiasm in the crowd: no one gives a thought to the concepts of liberty or equality or fraternity, because the communicative technique quite simply ensures that such thoughts become impossible. "Individuals in a crowd lose their individual wills and turn, instinctively, to the one man who is in control of his."[15]

Once again for the purposes of self-aggrandisement, Mussolini then compares Italy's situation to that of other countries afflicted by "political disorder" and "economic travails". He boasts that the programme of public works – such as the draining of marshland – initiated under his rule has to some extent alleviated the effects of the global economic depression; indeed its success has been imitated by Roosevelt and his "New Deal" in democratic America. Before he reaches his conclusion, he turns his attention specifically to Cremona:

And since [*pause, and again he slows down*] I am speaking [*pause*] to a gathering [*pause*] largely made up of rural workers [*he places his hands on his hips, a long pause*], I wish [*pause*] to praise [*pause*] the steadiness [*pause*], the tenacity [*pause*], the courage [*pause*], the patience of these rural labourers [*pause*]. I want to add that there are already signs of a new dawn on the horizon [*pause*]. Yet there remain two questions [*he points his index and middle fingers at the crowd*], two problems [*pause, still pointing the two fingers*], two very serious issues [*pause, still holding the gesture*] which are of particular concern to you [*pause*], which are [*pause*], land for grazing and milk production [*applause; pause*]. Two fundamental aspects of farming production [*pause*], two problems [*pause*] that can and will be swiftly resolved by means of discussion in the relevant corporation.

Just as Le Bon's "manual" describes, the two local problems of agriculture and stock-farming are not discussed or analysed in any way; Mussolini simply repeats – four times – that there are two issues and that they must be dealt with. Talking about how he might try to resolve them was certainly not the right way to keep the crowd's enthusiasm alight. In Le Bon's view, in a crowd which has become a single entity, whose constituent individuals have lost their identities, this can only be achieved by invoking such things as glory, honour, religion, fatherland, and indeed Mussolini launches the conclusion of his speech with a verbal fireworks display woven around such matters:

> Comrades of Cremona [*long pause*], I won't let another ten years pass before I return to visit you [*huge applause, he swells up, with jutting jaw and hands on hips, but someone in the crowd shouts out a comment which makes him laugh, and he returns to normal. He laughs in a relaxed manner, but then gathers himself up and with swelling chest starts again*]. Blackshirts of Cremona [*pause*], at the head of us, as we march along [*pause*], we see our fallen martyrs [*pause*], just as their memory [*pause*] is preserved religiously in our hearts [*pause, and then the final uninterrupted flourish*]. Led by such a glorious advance company of men, Blackshirts of Cremona, we will march on towards all the goals we have set ourselves, and we will achieve them! [*Ovation followed by a chant: "Duce, Duce, Duce..."*]

When Mussolini seized power in 1922, he had a small group of thirty-five parliamentary deputies – the "new men" he refers to in his speech – but precisely because they were "new" they were also inexperienced politicians. Despite the smallness of their numbers, in the parliamentary chamber Mussolini behaved as if he had the immemorial right to run the place. He was supported by a personal army of individuals who with their violent and sadistic behaviour resembled a gang of brigands rather than professional soldiers – and professional troops of soldiers could easily have broken them up. Yet it was not only the Fascists who used strong-arm tactics in the country's streets and squares; the political left and the right-wing nationalists also had their own semi-militarized squads. Mussolini was also the sole owner and editor of a newspaper, and a number of associated periodicals, which were bankrolled by industrialists and landowners (the funding was highly irregular and obscure, of the kind likely to dry up at the first sign of any problem or difficulty). When Mussolini was appointed by the King as the head of the national government and proceeded to transform the position into a personal dictatorship, he was in effect fundamentally a journalist, a practised communicator. He realized the potential of the new radio technology as soon as it appeared on the scene and he poured money into the film industry with the aim of making it a highly effective propaganda tool – Italian cinema audiences were convinced the documentaries and newsreels they watched every week were true. And he was also interested in encouraging the development of television, with its possibility of live relays of the public ceremonies organized by the regime.

In short, in today's language, Mussolini was a mass-media expert, perhaps one of the leading experts of his time. And his interest in the new possibilities of communication presented by the mass media stemmed from his understanding that they could be exploited to his own advantage: in this field he was working for himself, so to speak – he wrote the script, played the leading role, directed and produced. But it was the display of his own body which was fundamental to his public appearances: with his torso stripped naked as he harvested the wheat, wearing a white suit at country dances or swimming trunks as he strolled along the beach, sporting a cocked hat as he greeted the King on official occasions – the primary consideration was always to draw attention to his physical presence, his shaven head *alla romana*, his swelling chest, his determined jaw, his deliberately menacing – or in the regime's propaganda-speak, "magnetic" – gaze.

One of the regime's leading *gerarchi*, Giuseppe Bottai, asks in his memoirs how it was that Mussolini's physical presence became so important for Fascism, in a sense quite literally embodying it. He freely admits that Mussolini was not tall, yet managed to give the impression he was. He also writes that Mussolini's eyes were quite normal in size but as he gazed at you they seemed huge – in reality Mussolini practised this effect of staring eyes in the belief that it helped to communicate his single-minded strength of purpose. (Later research into advertising techniques has shown that in publicity images consumers are always instinctively attracted to models with large eyes, just as cartoon characters – from Disney to Japanese anime – are drawn with wide eyes to make them more appealing.)

The possessed eyes of the syphilitic subject (both inherited as well as acquired on his own initiative), the jaws – like an illiterate navvy's – of the acromegalic rachitic were already adorning the pages of the *Italia illustrata* weekly magazine; already, still dewy from the priestly unction bestowed in their confirmations, little Marias all over Italy were beginning to gaze longingly on his features; already, as Magdas, Milenas and Filomenas all over the country stepped down from their wedding altars, their vulvas were beginning to throb at the thought of him; in their white veils crowned with garlands of orange blossom, posing before the photographers for photographs as they passed out of the narthex, they were dreaming of the splendid and audacious whirl of his edifying truncheon.[16]

Clearly there were Italian women who had no interest in Mussolini's body or any wish to submit themselves to his normal – abrupt to brutal – sexual tactics, but they did not and could not make their refusal explicit. Those who had a different view of the matter were all too visible – the women who would willingly have offered their bodies up to Mussolini in dance halls and on beaches, the middle-aged ladies and the young girls who wrote to him enthusiastically offering to bear his children.

"I'm not a professional lecher,"[17] Mussolini once remarked to his last mistress, Claretta Petacci, who, as was her wont, duly recorded the remark in her diary. "I'm not an old lecher," he repeated, as he tried to convince her that casual penetrative sex with this or that woman meant nothing to him, it was nothing more than a habit, just a way of relieving himself. But there were many young Fascist women at the time who would have been content to give themselves to him even for that. People still remember how the Fascist *gerarchi* took to shaving their heads *alla romana*, tried to make their jaws look prominent, stood with their hands on their hips – attempting to imitate Mussolini's postures when he spoke to the crowds. But they could never succeed – and it wasn't because he was better-looking. He wasn't good-looking, nor was he tall. It wasn't a question of appearances but of "aura" – similar to what happens between lovers, that beguiling attraction made up of looks and returned glances between the one who observes and the one who is observed, which perhaps depends more on the person desiring rather than on the object of desire.

The endless number of Mussolini's metamorphoses – orator and journalist, horseman and peasant, motorcyclist and aviator, family man and libertine – were not merely the product of the dictator's own self-presentation and the regime's propaganda machine. They came into being also because the wish to create these mythopoeic constructions was instinct in the Italians themselves. As in Stendhal's psychology of love, Italian men and women who lived under Fascism first imagined the object of their desire and then ensured that the actual Duce corresponded to the ideal they had constructed for themselves.[18]

"Travel light to reach your destination" was one of Mussolini's mottos, but when he finally achieved power he had acquired a lot of baggage – he was at the head of a government made up of various political tendencies, he had rivals within the party, he was faced by a democratically elected opposition which, while demoralized, was still numerous: the Church was keeping a close and wary eye on him, and the country's aristocracy could barely stomach him. But if he didn't travel light on his path to power he certainly travelled alone, and remained so throughout the long years of his dictatorship. He trusted no one apart from his brother Arnaldo, and was incapable of delegating jobs, apart from the editorship of the newspaper *Il Popolo d'Italia* – which, again, he handed over to his brother. "I cannot have friends, and in fact I've got no friends – partly because of my temperament and partly because of my view of others and the way they are. So I don't feel the lack of intimacy or of friendly discussion. If an old friend comes to see me after a long time, any mutual embarrassment we might feel just dissolves away. I follow the careers of my former comrades from a distance."[19]

But Mussolini travelled light on his way to power in another sense: he discarded all sense of principle, every ideal, any concept of the primacy of moral or ethical claims. By the time he took power he had become (what is rare in history) a purely political politician, so to speak, one who wanted power for power's sake. The motto he lived by was at once simple and arduous: "Survive". Mussolini's reign lasted for twenty years, nine months and three days, to which can be added the one year, seven months and two weeks represented by Fascism's dark finale, the Italian Social Republic, which Hitler had wanted Mussolini to create.

Writing on the death of his brother Arnaldo, Mussolini reflected on what would happen to himself after his own death: "I've only one wish: to be buried in the family tomb in the San Cassiano cemetery. I'd be a fool if I asked to be left alone after my death. Round the tombs of those who've led the huge transformations we call revolutions there can never be any peace. But all that's been done can never be cancelled; my spirit, immaterial at last after this brief earthly interlude, will go on living the immortal and universal life of God."[20] This was written at a time when his sexual activities were still frenetic and the sheer physicality of his public image had enabled him to cast his rival in Italy's duopoly of power, the puny King Victor Emmanuel, into the shade. Bleaker thoughts on his death were jotted down by Mussolini in the notes he wrote while in captivity after he had fallen from power on 25th July 1943. It is worth looking more closely at this episode in his career, when as a prisoner he was moved from the *carabinieri* barracks in Rome at first to the island of Ponza and then to the island of La Maddalena off the north-east coast of Sardinia.

Getting Mussolini out of Rome in secrecy was complicated. He wasn't allowed to go home to the Villa Torlonia and had to leave for Ponza without even a change of underwear. It was only on 30th July that a lobster fisherman on the island, Antonio Feola, was permitted to bring over, on board his motorboat, two suitcases sent by Rachele containing underwear, clothes, ten thousand lire and a few photographs of their children. In that August of 1943 it was bakingly hot under a blazing sun on La Maddalena, and the place was full of sullen Italian officers and suspicious German navy crew; isolated from the main theatres of war on the mainland, it was also crawling with spies. Hitler had set up a special SS group commanded by captain Otto Skorzeny; made up of some of the best German intelligence agents, it was given a single task to carry out: to find Mussolini and free him, with the help of the Luftwaffe parachute division under their commanding general Kurt Student. An agent from Skorzeny's team, Lieutenant Warger, arrived on La Maddalena disguised as an interpreter; thanks to his knowledge of Italian he was able to get first-hand information from the island's inhabitants. It was not hard for Warger to come across traces of the island's special "guest". Badoglio, who had taken over from Mussolini as the head of government when the latter was deposed, had sent the head of the military police General Saverio Polito to accompany Mussolini to the island. Polito had reported back that La Maddalena was swarming with German marines, and despite all the precautions that had been taken to maintain the utmost secrecy news of Mussolini's presence on the island was already circulating. The former Duce was being held in the Villa Weber, a short distance outside the island's small main town. On 14th August Polito called at the villa, together with the Admiral Bruno Brivonesi, the chief naval commander in Sardinia, to talk to Mussolini. The two men told him about the anti-Fascist demonstrations which had taken place throughout Italian towns and cities, with statues of the Duce being smashed to pieces in towns and cities and his portraits being taken down and burned. After their conversation had ended, Mussolini wrote in his notebook: "It would be naive of me to be surprised at the reaction of the masses. Leaving aside my enemies who've been waiting in the wings for twenty years, and the people I've punished or disappointed, etc., the ordinary mass of people has always been ready to pull down the idols they worshipped yesterday, even at the cost of repenting their actions the following day. Yet in my case this won't happen – I feel in my blood – that infallible voice – that my star has set for ever."[21]

Obviously Mussolini knew that his notes were being read by the military guards who had been put in charge of him. His lines were also intended to send them a reassuring message: they needn't fear, the founder of Fascism now considered himself finished and done with "for ever". Mussolini's political instincts had not entirely abandoned him, however: true to form, he kept various options open for as long as he could. He had listened attentively to the depressing accounts told him by Polito and Brivonesi during their two-hour encounter, but he was also keeping one ear cocked for more hopeful sounds which were coming from those who remained loyal to his legend. When he had been transferred from Ponza to La Maddalena, the soldiers guarding him had got the daughter of the caretaker of the Villa Weber, Maria Pedoli, to do Mussolini's laundry for him regularly. It was she who smuggled in a report, written on two sheets of foolscap, of the events which had taken place after 25th July, the day of Mussolini's arrest, written by the former *podestà*, or Fascist mayor, of La Maddalena, Aldo Chirico. Chirico was a committed Mussolini loyalist and happened to have access to inside information, since a cousin of his, Colonel Ettore Chirico, had been responsible for guarding Mussolini as a prisoner during his first days of captivity in Rome. It was very soon an open secret that the Duce was on the island. Chirico and other local Fascists started to organize plans to liberate him. Mussolini himself mentions – in *Pensieri Pontini e Sardi* – one clumsy attempt, their first, which the *carabinieri* managed to stop a short distance away from the Villa Weber. Maria Pedoli continued to smuggle messages in and out of the house; Mussolini's notes were usually signed "Mussolini (defunct)". His moods must have been variable – depression and discouragement, detachment, the wish to leave public life altogether and a nostalgic longing to be back in his house in the Romagna. On the other hand this was the man who had founded OVRA, the regime's extremely efficient secret police: the amateurishness of hiding notes in Pedoli's laundry basket cannot have escaped his notice. It was obvious any messages would be discovered, so signing himself "defunct" could have been merely a decoy. Rachele Mussolini in her memoirs mentions the precautions she had to take at this time when she wrote to her husband: "I was allowed to write to him, but I didn't know where he was. I had to give my letters to the *carabinieri*, who forwarded them. I knew all correspondence with him was being checked; in one letter I wanted to tell him that many people in the Romagna were waiting for his return, so I wrote, 'Here everyone is waiting for the river to start flowing again.' Benito replied: 'I'm very sorry to hear, Rachele, that Romagna is suffering from drought...'"[22]

A small piece of paper – the authenticity of which has been proved, but which is written in a very different style, and with different contents, and is not signed "Mussolini (defunct)" – has recently come to light thanks to the painstaking researches of Enrico Manieri. The paper has been roughly cut to measure about twelve by ten centimetres; it was folded very small and tucked into the back of a book. The note on it reads: "Count the number of guards round the villa. Dr Chirico is willing to help you – he will give you details of the plan. I am grateful for all you are doing. Destroy this note when you've read it. 16th August. Mussolini." We do not know who the intended recipient was, but the note makes it clear that Mussolini was himself attempting to devise an alternative plan for his escape – where he intended to go and what he purposed to do there is impossible to tell.

As long as he was alive, even at moments of despair, he went on looking for possibilities of political manoeuvre, even at the last when there was nowhere to go, but he could not have foreseen that the manoeuvres would continue after his death, around his dead body. In a letter written while he was on La Maddalena – one of those he knew would be opened and read by the military police – he wrote that the last ten months had reduced him to the state of being three-quarters dead while the rest was a mere heap of skin and bones. During the period of his imprisonment on the Gran Sasso in the Apennines, still alternating between bouts of depression and efforts to find a way out of his impasse, he attempted suicide; the end of his regime was bloody and violent, and he would have been unable to foresee how his legend would persist, how the cult of his body – that "heap of skin and bones" – would live on. It is possible to establish when the cult started to be constructed: the wounds he received as a soldier during the First World War, which were widely reported in the national press. The wounds were a vital element in his campaign to win over the support – and the votes – of the veterans as they returned from the front. It is far more difficult to pinpoint the end of the myth. According to the official version, which, however, does not stand up to detailed historical examination, Mussolini is said to have been shot on 28th April in Giulino di Mezzegra, a small village on the shores of Lake Como; what is certain is that Colonel Valerio, the code name for Walter Audisio, the Partisan who executed him – again according to the official version of events – was the man who took the body to Milan. He probably realized that a straightforward announcement of the execution might not be enough to convince people the dictator was dead; it was necessary to put the corpse on public display in order to humiliate it and put an end to the myth. The local Partisans round Dongo didn't have the authority to oppose Audisio's decision; they let the lorry carrying its cargo of corpses leave for Milan while they went round showing – like a relic – the Luftwaffe overcoat which Mussolini had worn in his final attempt to disguise himself and evade capture.

In the early afternoon on 29th April, the US High Command, the Vatican represented by Cardinal Alfredo Ildefonso Schuster and the various heads of the alliance of Partisan troops in northern Italy, the Comitato di Liberazione Nazionale dell'Alta Italia (National Liberation Committee of Northern Italy), or CLNAI, combined forces to get the corpses removed from Piazzale Loreto, but they couldn't stop people flocking to the site. On the canopy of the petrol station from which the bodies had been hung, the name of each had been painted with an arrow pointing down for easier identification. Over the next few days normal activity resumed at the petrol station (as far as that was possible given the fuel shortage), and the few cars which were still in circulation started to call at what had become the most famous petrol pumps in the country, just so they could fill their tanks where drops of blood and other matter had fallen from the corpse of Mussolini the myth. Small crowds gathered to read out the names painted on the edge of the canopy, and every demonstration and protest march in the city would include Piazzale Loreto as part of their route, as if the petrol station had turned into a symbol of the new Italy. During the regime tourists had flocked to Piazza Venezia hoping to catch a glimpse of Mussolini and, according to Fascist propaganda, Italians could never have enough of gazing at him. There was a lugubrious aftermath to this touristic interest as people started to visit the mortuary where the bodies had been brought from Piazzale Loreto on 29th April. One of the cameramen who was working with the Fifth Army, Morris Berman, admitted in a later interview that he had arranged the corpses of Mussolini and Petacci so they were linked arm-in-arm: "I thought theirs was the kind of love story which would interest the public, and so I put them in that position."[23]

When these images were released by the United States National Archives in Washington fifty years ago, there was a worldwide interest in them. On that April day in 1945, the mortuary where the bodies had been taken was full of Partisans, soldiers, journalists, spies, photographers and cameramen as well as ordinary people who were curious to see the corpses; when they found those of Mussolini and his mistress they wanted to be photographed smiling alongside them. Even the room where they were taken the following morning at 7.30 for autopsies to be carried out was full of spectators milling about. Everyone wanted to take photographs of Mussolini's penis, the activities of which had for so long engaged the Italian public's imagination (a similarly prurient interest was aroused by the discovery in the Russian autopsy of Hitler's corpse that the German dictator had had a single testicle). For a long time it was widely believed that Mussolini had syphilis. On the day of the autopsy, American intelligence agents managed to obtain a part of Mussolini's brain in order to take it back to the United States for laboratory analysis. Over twenty years later, in March 1966, an official from the US Embassy in Rome knocked on the door of Rachele Mussolini's house and handed her a yellow envelope containing a small box with six glass slides wrapped in cotton wool and cellophane: the remains of her husband's brains which the American authorities had now decided to return to her.

The sheer confusion in the autopsy room on the morning on 30th April probably meant that the surgeon who carried out the examination was unable to do it properly and made some mistakes; Mussolini's corpse was the first one he examined, but he forgot to look at the state of the clothing found on him, which might have provided important evidence for future historians.

The body was finally laid to rest – if we can call it that – in the Musocco cemetery in Milan. The tomb was numbered but, in the naive hope it would remain undiscovered, no name was placed on it. Neither the military nor civil authorities took any measures to protect the site, despite the fact that many people knew where it was located. There are reports in the newspapers of the time of people going there at night to dance or even urinate over the tomb. On the night of 22nd April 1946, a young Fascist supporter called Domenico Leccisi – he'd been born in 1920, just after Mussolini started his ascent to power – decided to show the country that the Duce, a year after he had been shot and buried, could still have a political impact. Leccisi, along with two other Fascist companions, easily circumvented the wardens who were supposed to protect the cemetery, dug up the tomb and retrieved the coffin, from which they removed the by now disintegrating corpse – two finger bones dropped off while they were carrying it – and took it away with them. The seizure of the Duce's dead body had the planned effect – in its own way it was a brilliant political *coup de théâtre* – and caused a sensation. The news broke on the eve of the first anniversary of the general Partisan uprising on 25th April, although this coincidence may not have been in Leccisi's mind when he planned it: it is more likely it was a decision taken on the spur of the moment, to benefit from the fact that the police in Milan were fully occupied in dealing with disturbances which had broken out in the city's main prison. Photographs and film footage of the empty grave went round the world, while in Italy the newspaper reports of the event, often replete with gruesome details, had an influence on the course of the electoral campaigns which were then underway in the country – the most significant in the nation's history – for the referendum to decide whether Italy should remain a monarchy or become a republic, and for the election of members to the newly created Assemblea Costituente della Repubblica Italiana (Constituent Assembly of the Italian Republic), who would draw up the new constitution.

The theft of Mussolini's corpse was the first sign that the Fascist movement still existed and still claimed a political role. On 26th December 1946 a group of veterans who had been part of the Italian Social Republic after 1943 founded the Movimento Sociale Italiano

(Italian Social Movement). The new party chose as its symbol a flame in the three colours of the Italian flag burning above a stylized representation of Mussolini's coffin, the same coffin which Leccisi had prised open in his attempt to effect a political resurrection using the dictator's body. A police investigation into the theft of the corpse was carried out, and on 31st July 1946 Leccisi was arrested. His arrest turned out to be the making of him: he became a popular figure on the extreme right wing and won election as a parliamentary deputy, gaining more votes than the top name in the list of the Italian Social Movement (MSI) candidates, Pino Romualdi, born in Predappio in 1913 and reputed to be one of Mussolini's illegitimate offspring (his jaw in particular resembled the Duce's). Leccisi the gravedigger remained in parliament until 1963, when his view of himself as a "left-wing Fascist" led him into conflict with the party's leadership, which eventually excluded him from running at the elections. Before then, in 1957, his vote had been crucial in saving the government headed by Adone Zoli, a friend of the Mussolini family and from the same region as they were, in a parliamentary vote of confidence. Until that year, Mussolini's body had remained in hiding in the chapel of the Capuchin monastery at Cerro Maggiore near Legnano; it was in 1957 that the Zoli government decided it should be restored to the family. It was buried in a tomb in Predappio, where it has remained, attracting an average of over one hundred thousand visitors each year. On various significant anniversaries – of his birth, of his death, etc. – various neo-Fascist ceremonies are held there, the object of much criticism and condemnation, yet the local council finds it difficult to prevent them, since this rather particular business brings a lot of money into the small town.

The crowds in Piazzale Loreto in 1945 were huge, but nevertheless only a tiny minority of the Italian population saw with their own eyes the corpses hanging upside down. Later accounts of the episode – in history books and in newspapers, and occasionally on television – attempted to reconstruct what happened there using only a few blurred images, but in April 1994 a programme was broadcast which succeeded in opening up the wounds of this national psychodrama to the extent that it became front-page news in all the national papers and was also reported abroad. It was due to a series of coincidences. The author of the present book had discovered in the film collections of various archives around the world – the United States National

Archives in Washington, the Imperial War Museum in London, the State Archives in New Zealand and in other countries which had supported the Allied forces during the war – some of the original film footage shot by the cameramen who accompanied the troops throughout the Italian campaign. After a close examination of the content of the reels, I proposed making a television series based on this material to be called *Combat Film*. The idea was to show in each episode the films exactly as they had been shot at the time, without making any cuts or editing them in any way, even leaving the original clapperboard shots in as a kind of proof of their authenticity. The transmission triggered a storm of criticism in the newspapers, much of it based on the belief that the date of the broadcast was a deliberate provocation: shortly before the programmes were shown, on 27th March 1994, a new and untested coalition formed by Silvio Berlusconi together with Gianfranco Fini's Alleanza Nazionale (National Alliance), the successor party to the Fascist Italian Social Movement founded in 1946, had won the general election. In actual fact the footage and the proposal had been sitting in the offices of the Italian state television corporation for over a year waiting for the directors of RAI 1 to give it the go-ahead. The decision to proceed with the making of the film was accompanied by what are in large media companies the usual moves and countermoves of institutional politics, with the result that I was at first assigned a co-author and then, together with him, relegated to a merely supporting role in the final phase of production when the film footage was shown in the studio. The channel's main executives then took over direct control of the post-production editing and direction. For the programme, which was recorded only a few hours before being broadcast, three politicians were invited as the main studio guests: a young – born in the 1950s – and prominent politician from the left, a leading representative of the Christian Democrats who'd been a dispatch rider in the war for the Partisans and a leader from the political right who'd fought on the side of the Italian Social Republic. All three behaved exactly as politicians invited to a television debate on some current issue behave. Yet in this particular programme the guests invited to comment needed a considerable knowledge of the particular historical background if they were to interpret the films correctly, especially as there was no commentary – the films were shown exactly as they were originally shot, i.e. without sound. The three politicians in the studio had not even had the opportunity to see the films before the programme began recording. The transmission was watched by a record thirty-five per cent of the Italian population, including youngsters who'd never seen black-and-white films of such excellent quality before on Italian television and thought they were recent reconstructions rather than fifty years old. No one in Italy – apart from the crowds which gathered on that April morning in 1945 in Piazzale Loreto – had ever seen so clearly and so vividly the event which took place there; the entire ten-minute sequence shot by the military cameraman was shown in the first episode, and no one was prepared for the impact such a scene would make or for the thought that such "Mexican butchery" had occurred in the most advanced and well-administered city in northern Italy.

It was thought that any potential impact could be dealt with by making sure the choice of studio guests reflected a political balance. The necessary background to the film was not explained – the fact that, on 10th August 1944, nine months before the display of Mussolini's corpse in Piazzale Loreto, and in exactly the same location, fifteen men had been shot by the Fascists as a reprisal for attacking Nazi troops and their bodies left on the ground for days on end. Milanese workers would stop in silence to gaze at the dead bodies and secretly vow to take revenge; some women ran the risk of placing flowers near them. The entire city was stunned by the massacre. At one point in the film, among the crowds who have come to see Mussolini's strung-up corpse one sees an individual holding up a photograph of a relative who had been one of the men shot in the previous year – but there was no one in the studio when the programme was broadcast to explain this detail, and the people who could have explained were never asked.

And so it went on – no one explained why the firemen let off the water cannons, why the bodies had been hung upside down, why the Partisans reacted in the way they did and what Allied soldiers were doing in the middle of the crowd. Left to speak for itself, the footage made its impact on public and critics alike. But even the way the film was presented was wrong. The editors of the programme were aware of the violent nature of the scenes shown, with the frenzied crowd spitting and kicking at Mussolini's head as his body lay on the ground, and none of the guests was able to give an adequate analysis or explanation of what was seen. A few hours before the recorded programme went out, the people responsible for the transmission decided to try to soften its emotional impact by literally distancing it from the viewers, in other words, replacing some full-screen close-up shots of Piazzale Loreto with others where the cameraman, still in the square, was filming from farther away. In addition they decided to show the film on the screen in the studio behind the row of seated guests. The effect was reminiscent of the famous scene in Stanley Kubrick's *Spartacus*, when the gladiator slave, played by Kirk Douglas, is locked in desperate combat with his towering black opponent, Draba, played by Woody Strode. At a certain point Kubrick shifts the camera position to behind the patrician Crassus, sitting with his friend Gabro, as they watch the fight from their VIP seats; in this way the actual cinema audience in front of the screen is forced to "stretch forward", so to speak, to try to see what's going on behind the two spectators. The gladiators' fight is taking place in the background and is made that much more dramatic and involving by being framed by Kubrick within the shot of the two Roman aristocrats and their trivial chatter. In the same way the audience watching the Piazzale Loreto film on the television screen at home had to "stretch forward" to see what was actually happening in the square.

Appendix 2

Key Figures

GIACOMO ACERBO (1888–1969)
Born to a noble family, Acerbo was a volunteer during the First World War. Affiliated with the Freemasons, he became undersecretary to Mussolini during the latter's first government and subsequently Vice President of the Chamber of Deputies and a minister. A member of the Grand Council of Fascism, he voted for the motion to strip Mussolini of his powers at the meeting of 25th July 1943. He managed to escape from the Fascists of the Italian Social Republic and was in hiding until he was captured by the Allies in 1945. After the war he was sentenced to death, although this was then commuted to forty-eight years' imprisonment, subsequently reduced to thirty. The sentence was finally annulled by the court of appeal in 1951, and Acerbo was reinstated as a university professor. His name is still remembered for the "Acerbo law", passed in 1923, which created a majoritarian electoral system designed to guarantee the Fascist Party two thirds of all parliamentary seats.

LUIGI ALBERTINI (1871–1941)
Albertini was the editor of *Corriere della Sera* from 1900 to 1925. Under his editorship the *Corriere* grew and became the most important and widely read newspaper in Italy. In 1921 he appointed his brother Alberto as co-editor, entrusting him with an executive role in the management of the newspaper, although retaining the title of editor for himself. Albertini was a senator from 1914 and was outspoken in his opposition to Fascism. He was ousted from the *Corriere* in 1925.

RINO ALESSI (1885–1970)
Alessi was a journalist and contributor to *Avanti!* and other socialist newspapers. A volunteer during the First World War and a friend of

417

Mussolini since their youth in Romagna, he followed the Duce when he moved from socialism to Fascism. Alessi wrote a number of plays and novels and was the editor of the Trieste newspaper *Il piccolo*.

GIOVANNI AMENDOLA (1882–1926)
Amendola was Professor of Theoretical Philosophy at the University of Pisa, a journalist for *Il Resto del Carlino* and *Corriere della Sera* and one of the founding members of *Il mondo*. An artillery officer during the First World War and a deputy who sided with the liberal faction in the Chamber, he became Minister for the Colonies and one of the major figures of anti-Fascism. In 1926 he was attacked by Blackshirts, later dying from his injuries.

GIORGIO ASSUMMA (1935–)
Assumma, a former president of the Italian Society of Authors and Publishers, is a professor of copyright law at the Università Statale di Roma III and the president of the Fondazione Internazionale Perseus.

WALTER AUDISIO (1909–73)
An accountant by profession, Audisio was an active member of the clandestine Italian Communist Party during the Fascist period. He was arrested and confined to the island of Ponza in 1934, later joining the Resistance following Italy's surrender to the Allies on 8th September 1943 and adopting the code name "Colonel Valerio". According to his testimony, it was he who killed Mussolini and Claretta Petacci at Giulino di Mezzegra. After the war he became a deputy and later a senator.

MIKHAIL BAKUNIN (1814–76)
A revolutionary Russian philosopher and one of the major proponents of anarchism, Bakunin was born to a noble family of landowners. Condemned to death in Russia, he was pardoned by the Tsar and his sentence was commuted to life imprisonment in Siberia. He managed to escape and in 1865 he moved to Italy.

ANGELICA BALABANOFF (1869–1965)
Balabanoff was born to a noble Ukrainian family. After receiving a degree in literature in Brussels, she became a socialist activist and relocated to Rome in 1900. She joined the Italian Socialist Party, and

met Lenin in Switzerland. In 1917 she joined the Bolshevik Communist Party and became secretary of the Third International. After a disagreement with Lenin and other Bolshevik leaders, she moved back to Italy in 1922 and took shelter in Switzerland and the United States during the Fascist period. After the Second World War, she joined the Partito Socialista Democratico Italiano (Italian Democratic Socialist Party) under the leadership of Giuseppe Saragat.

ITALO BALBO (1896–1940)
Early in his life Balbo was a member of the Mazzinian republican faction and fought in the First World War, receiving many decorations and various promotions up to the rank of captain. He joined the Fascists and became the party's secretary in Ferrara. He was one of the *quadrumviri* during the March on Rome and the leader of many Fascist terror squads. He became Minister of the Air Force and piloted two transatlantic flights in formation. He was the Viceroy of Libya and died when his plane was hit by what the Italian government insisted was "friendly fire" from Italian anti-aircraft artillery in Tobruk.

NICOLA BARBATO (1856–1923)
Barbato was a psychiatrist and one of the major Sicilian socialist leaders. During the uprising of the Sicilian Workers' Leagues, he was arrested and condemned to twelve years in prison. He was elected as a deputy and became a member of the executive of the Socialist Party. He came into conflict with the Mafia and was seriously wounded by one of their hit men. He spent the last years of his life in Milan.

SALVATORE BARZILAI (1860–1939)
A lawyer by profession, Barzilai was elected to the Chamber of Deputies in 1890 and was among the founding members of the Italian Republican Party in 1895. During the First World War he became a minister, responsible for the Austro-Hungarian territories annexed by Italian forces after 1915, and in 1920 was made a senator. He was a high-ranking member of the Masonic organization Grande Oriente d'Italia (Grand Orient of Italy).

GIUSEPPE BASTIANINI (1899–1961)
Bastianini was a second lieutenant in the Arditi during the First World War and became Vice Secretary of the Fascist Party in 1921.

A member of the Grand Council until 1927, he later embarked on a diplomatic career, becoming ambassador in Warsaw in 1932 and in London at the beginning of the Second World War (ending when Italy joined the war in 1940). In 1943 he became Undersecretary for Foreign Affairs. During the Grand Council meeting of 25th July 1943 he voted against Mussolini. Sentenced to death by the Italian Social Republic, he managed to escape to Switzerland.

CESARE BATTISTI (1875–1916)
Battisti was a journalist and a socialist leader of the Trentino region during Austrian rule. Founder and editor of the Socialist newspaper *Il popolo*, during the First World War he fought as a volunteer in a battalion of the Alpini, the division of the Italian army specializing in mountain warfare. Captured by the Austrians, he was hanged as a traitor. In Italy he is regarded as a national hero.

FIORENZO BAVA BECCARIS (1831–1924)
Bava Beccaris was a general during the Crimean War. When, in 1898, there were violent riots in Milan, he ordered the use of cannon on the crowd, causing a massacre. He was honoured by King Umberto I with a Great Cross of the Savoy Military Order and was appointed senator. Gaetano Bresci, the man who killed King Umberto I on 29th July 1900, claimed that his act was meant to avenge the massacre caused by Bava Beccaris.

LEONIDA BISSOLATI (1857–1920)
A lawyer by training, Bissolati was among the most important Socialist leaders between the end of the nineteenth and the beginning of the twentieth centuries. He became the editor of the official Socialist Party newspaper *Avanti!* in 1896 and was elected to the Chamber of Deputies in 1897. Having failed to oppose the colonial war in Libya, he was dismissed from the Socialist Party in 1912. He founded the Partito Socialista Riformista Italiano (Italian Socialist-Reformist Party). He retired from politics in 1918.

BORIS III OF SAXE-COBURG-GOTHA (1894–1943)
Boris III, tsar of the Kingdom of Bulgaria, married Princess Giovanna of Savoy, the daughter of Victor Emmanuel III, the King of Italy, in Assisi in 1930. A reluctant ally of Nazi Germany, Boris was

nonetheless opposed to the deportation of Bulgaria's Jews to Nazi-occupied Poland. He died, possibly poisoned by the Nazis, on his return from a stormy meeting with Hitler.

GIUSEPPE BOTTAI (1895–1959)
Bottai was a lawyer, a journalist and among the leaders of the Fascist Party in Rome. Between 1926 and 1932 he was Undersecretary and then Minister of the Corporations, going on to become Governor of Addis Ababa for a brief period in May 1936 and subsequently Minister for National Education. He was among the subscribers to the Racial Manifesto and voted against Mussolini in the July 1943 meeting of the Grand Council. Sentenced to death by the Italian Socialist Republic, he managed to escape and joined the Foreign Legion, remaining engaged in battles against the Germans. After being amnestied, he returned to Italy, founded the current-affairs magazine *ABC* and became the editor of the newspaper *Il popolo di Roma* (*The People of Rome*).

GAETANO BRESCI (1869–1901)
Bresci, an anarchist, emigrated to the United States, where he was employed as a textile-factory worker. He returned to Italy with a plan to avenge the 1898 massacre of striking workers in Milan. He shot and killed King Umberto I on 29th July 1900. He died in prison under mysterious circumstances, perhaps following an attack by the prison warders.

BRUNO BRIVONESI (1886–1970)
Brivonesi was a commander of the Italian Navy and headed the 5th Naval Division at the beginning of the Second World War. He was tried (and later exonerated) for the loss of seven vessels and two warships from the Duisberg convoy, attacked by the British on 8th November 1941. He was responsible for keeping Mussolini under surveillance during the latter's imprisonment on the island of La Maddalena from 7th to 28th August 1943.

GUIDO BUFFARINI GUIDI (1895–1945)
A lawyer by profession and a volunteer during the First World War, Buffarini Guidi went on to become a Fascist leader in Pisa. He was Mayor of Pisa in 1923, later becoming undersecretary at the Ministry

of Internal Affairs, a post he held from 1933 to 1943. He was one of the subscribers to the Racial Manifesto in 1938 and voted against the motion to depose Mussolini in July 1943, for which he was rewarded by being made Minister for Internal Affairs for the Italian Social Republic. Captured by the Partisans, he was executed in Milan soon after the end of the war, on 10th July 1945.

FILIPPO BUONARROTI (1761–1837)
Buonarroti was an Italian revolutionary who became a French citizen and an active supporter of the Revolution. One of the organizers, with Gracchus Babeuf, of the planned armed uprising known as the "Conspiracy of the Equals" in 1796, he was arrested and banished when the plot was uncovered. Napoleon subsequently pardoned him, and Buonarroti became the leader of a secret society called Adelfia, which then became the Società dei Sublimi Maestri Perfetti (Society of Sublime and Perfect Masters).

BRUNO BUOZZI (1881–1944)
Buozzi was a syndicalist, a reformist socialist and a Socialist Party deputy from 1920 to 1926. In 1926 he escaped to France, where he re-established the General Confederation of Labour, which had been banned by Mussolini. He was captured by the Germans and handed over to the Italian Fascist regime. Freed after the Armistice on 8th September 1943, he joined the Resistance. Captured once again, he was executed by the retreating Nazis, together with thirteen other prisoners, on the Via Cassia in Rome.

GELASIO CAETANI (1877–1934)
Caetani was a mining engineer and became the first Fascist ambassador to Washington in 1922.

CARLO CAFIERO (1846–92)
Born to a wealthy landowning family, Cafiero became one of the foremost figures of revolutionary anarchism. He was influenced by Marx's theories and wrote the *Digest of the First Volume of Das Kapital*. He was arrested several times and, while in prison, attempted suicide. Because of a nervous disorder, in 1891 he was sent to an asylum, where he later died.

EMILIO CALDARA (1868–1942)
Caldara was the Socialist Mayor of Milan between 1914 and 1920.

GIOSUÈ CARDUCCI (1835–1907)
One of the leading Italian poets, writers and critics of the twentieth century, Giosuè Carducci took an active role among the Masonic organizations and was elevated to the 33rd rank of the Rito Scozzese Antico e Accettato (Ancient and Accepted Scottish Rite of Freemasonry). He became a senator in 1890 and won the Nobel Prize for Literature in 1906.

PRIMO CARNERA (1906–67)
A famous boxer and the world heavyweight champion from June 1933 to June 1934. Renowned for his powerful physique (he was six feet eight inches tall and weighed twenty stone) and for his strength, he ended his career as a wrestling champion.

FELICE CAVALLOTTI (1842–68)
One of Garibaldi's "redshirts", as well as a poet and playwright, Cavallotti was elected as a far-left radical deputy in 1873. He fought thirty-three duels, before the fatal one with Count Ferruccio Macola.

ADRIANO CELENTANO (1938–)
One of the most famous Italian songwriters of the twentieth century. Celentano has also enjoyed a successful career as an actor, film director and TV presenter.

COSTANZO CIANO (1876–1939)
A war hero, Ciano was awarded a Gold Medal during the First World War and promoted to the rank of commander. During the Fascist period he became Minister of Communications and President of the Chamber of Deputies.

GALEAZZO CIANO (1903–44)
Galeazzo Ciano was the son of Commander Costanzo Ciano. In 1930 he married Edda Mussolini. In 1935 he was appointed Minister of Press and Propaganda and, the following year, Minister for Foreign Affairs. He voted in favour of the motion to strip Mussolini of his

powers in July 1943, and was later tried and executed for treason by the forces of the Italian Social Republic.

AMILCARE CIPRIANI (1843–1918)

Cipriani was one of Garibaldi's "redshirts" and took part in the Expedition of the Thousand in Sicily. An anarchist and revolutionary, he was forced to flee to London to escape imprisonment. There, he worked as a photographer and even produced a portrait of Queen Victoria.

ORSO MARIO CORBINO (1876–1937)

Corbino was a professor of experimental physics, first in Messina and then in Rome, where he directed the famous Via Panisperna Institute. He became a senator in 1920, Minister for Public Education in 1921 and Minister for the National Economy during the first Mussolini government. In 1935 he became president of the International Centre for Television in Nice.

FILIPPO CORRIDONI (1887–1915)

Corridoni was a syndicalist, a revolutionary socialist and a journalist. He became an interventionist and, though he suffered from tuberculosis, managed to enlist during the First World War and was sent to the front. He died during an attack on an Austrian trench.

ANDREA COSTA (1851–1910)

Costa was the founder of the Italian Revolutionary Socialist Party, one of the forerunners of the Italian Socialist Party. He had a relationship with the Russian socialist Anna Kuliscioff, which resulted in the birth of a daughter, Andreina, in 1881. The following year he became the first Socialist deputy in the Italian parliament. He became Gran Maestro Aggiunto of the Grand Orient of Italy. From 1908 to 1910 he was Vice President of the Chamber of Deputies.

BENEDETTO CROCE (1866–1952)

An internationally renowned philosopher and one of the main proponents of Italian liberalism, Croce became a senator in 1910 and Minister for Public Education in 1920. In 1925 he published the *Manifesto degli intellettuali antifascisti* (*Manifesto of the Anti-Fascist Intellectuals*). In 1938, when the Fascist regime was adopting the racial laws, Croce refused to fill in the racial-classification questionnaire sent to all university professors, and declared that he would rather be forbidden from teaching as a "supposed Jew". After Mussolini's removal from office in July 1943, he became Minister without Portfolio in the governments led by Pietro Badoglio and Ivanoe Bonomi. In 1946 he was elected to the Assemblea Costituente della Repubblica Italiana (Constituent Assembly of the Italian Republic), the institution created to draw up a constitution for the newly formed Republic of Italy.

GABRIELE D'ANNUNZIO (1863–1938)

A poet, novelist, playwright and political and military leader, D'Annunzio was given the sobriquet of "the Bard". Among his numerous relationships, the most famous was with the celebrated actress Eleonora Duse. He was a volunteer during the First World War and took an active part in many daring missions. He led the seizure by Italian irredentists of the port of Fiume in September 1919, later declaring it an independent state when it became clear that he did not have the support of the Italian government. After the failure of this enterprise with the surrender of Fiume to the Italian authorities in December 1920, D'Annunzio retired to his villa in Gardone on Lake Garda.

GUIDO DA VERONA (1881–1939)

Da Verona was a poet and a commercially successful novelist. Jewish by birth, he was marginalized after the promulgation of the racial laws and later committed suicide.

ALCESTE DE AMBRIS (1874–1934)

De Ambris was a journalist and a major figure of revolutionary syndicalism. In 1913 he became a Socialist Party deputy. After enlisting as a volunteer during the First World War, he joined D'Annunzio in his Fiume expedition. He initially supported Mussolini, but later became an anti-Fascist and escaped to France, refusing Mussolini's various offers to return and cooperate with the Fascist regime.

EMILIO DE BONO (1886–1944)

De Bono became a general at the end of the First World War. He joined the Fascists and was the most senior of the *quadrumviri* during the March on Rome. Mussolini appointed him General Director of Public Security. He was Governor of Tripolitania from 1925 to 1928 and became Minister of the Colonies in 1929. He was at the head of the Italian army during the first stage of the invasion of Ethiopia. He voted against Mussolini during the Grand Council meeting on 25th July 1943. During the Italian Social Republic he was captured and, along with others accused of betraying the Duce, tried for treason and sentenced to death, in what became known as the "Verona trial".

RENZO DE FELICE (1929–96)
De Felice was one of the leading Italian historians and is regarded as the greatest expert in Fascist studies. Having studied under Federico Chabod, he joined the Communist Party and, after the Soviet invasion of Hungary in 1956, moved to the Socialist Party. He taught at the universities of Salerno and, later, Rome, where he specialized in contemporary history and the history of political parties.

GIUSEPPE DE FELICE-GIUFFRIDA (1859–1920)
A Socialist and a supporter of the Sicilian Workers' League, he was elected to the Chamber of Deputies in 1892. He became Mayor of Catania in 1902 and took on an interventionist stance during the First World War.

ALCIDE DE GASPERI (1881–1954)
A political leader and journalist, De Gasperi became a deputy representing the Trentino region in the Austrian parliament in 1911, and was elected to the Italian Chamber of Deputies ten years later, after Italy's annexation of Trentino in 1919 as part of the post-war settlement. He founded, along with Don Luigi Sturzo, the staunchly Catholic People's Party (later reorganized as the Christian Democrats). A fierce anti-Fascist, De Gasperi was arrested and imprisoned in 1927. After Mussolini's removal from office in July 1943, he became Minister without Portfolio, later Minister for Foreign Affairs, finally becoming Prime Minister in December 1945, a post he held during the period of constitutional transition that followed the end of the war, making him the first head of government of the Italian Republic. He is considered one of the fathers of post-war Italy and of the European Union.

ENRICO DE NICOLA (1877–1959)
A lawyer and a political leader, De Nicola was President of the Chamber of Deputies from 1920 to 1924 and President of the Senate from 1951 to 1952. Following the fall of the monarchy the Constituent Assembly elected him interim Head of State in 1946. He was President of the Constitutional Court from 1956 to 1957.

ARDITO DESIO (1897–2001)
A geologist and explorer, Desio was a volunteer during the First World War. A professor of geology at the University of Milan, he took part in various expeditions, including, in 1954, the Italian-led mission to the top of K2.

ENGELBERT DOLLFUSS (1892–1934)
Dollfuss was Austrian Chancellor from 1932 to 1934. He had close ties with Mussolini and was the founder of Vaterländische Front, a Fascist-inspired party. He strove to avoid Austria's becoming part of Hitler's Germany, and was assassinated by Nazi agents.

EUGENIO DOLLMANN (1900–85)
Dollmann was a colonel in the SS, directly appointed by the Führer. He was Hitler's interpreter and a Third Reich secret agent, as well as an expert on Italian art. After the war he received support and protection from the American and Italian secret services.

AMERIGO DUMINI (1894–1967)
An American citizen born to an Italian father, Dumini was a volunteer in the Italian army during the First World War. According to the Sardinian writer Emilio Lussu, he loved to present himself as "Amerigo Dumini, eight homicides". He led the Cheka squad that killed the socialist leader Giacomo Matteotti in 1924, a crime for which he initially received a five-year prison sentence – although he was amnestied by Mussolini after only eleven months. After the war he was tried again, this time receiving a life sentence (although he was released from prison in 1953).

LUIGI FACTA (1861–1930)
Facta was the last prime minister of Italy before the advent of Mussolini. He served as a deputy from 1892, becoming prime minister

in 1922. He did not oppose Fascism and was appointed senator in 1924.

ENRICO FALCK (1899–1953)
An industrialist close to the lay Roman Catholic association Azione Cattolica (Catholic Action), Falck was involved in anti-Fascist activities and was one of the founding members of the Christian Democrat party, becoming a senator in 1948.

ROBERTO FARINACCI (1892–1945)
A journalist by profession, Farinacci worked on the railways for a long time, following the same path from socialism to Fascism trod by Benito Mussolini. He was elected as a deputy in 1921. He was known as the Cremona *ras*, and embodied the most violent side of Fascism, which routinely employed beatings and force-feedings of castor oil. After obtaining (through a purchased thesis) a degree in jurisprudence, he acted as the defence lawyer for Amerigo Dumini during the latter's first trial for the killing of Giacomo Matteotti. Captured by the Partisans, he was executed on 28th April 1945.

LUIGI FEDERZONI (1878–1967)
A journalist, lawyer and intellectual, Federzoni was one of the founders of the Italian Nationalist Association. From 1923 to 1928, he was a minister in the Mussolini government, later becoming President of the Senate (1929–39). He was among those who signed against Mussolini during the Grand Council session on 25th July 1943. He was condemned to life in prison in 1945, but was amnestied two years later.

FILIPPO FILIPPELLI (1889–1961)
A lawyer and journalist, Filippelli was the founder of the newspaper *Corriere italiano*. He provided the car used in the killing of Giacomo Matteotti and wrote a memoir in which he criticized Mussolini.

ALDO FINZI (1891–1944)
The son of a wealthy Jewish family, Finzi was baptized and given a Catholic education. A volunteer during the First World War, he took part, together with Gabriele D'Annunzio, in a flying mission over Vienna for the distribution of propaganda leaflets. He joined the

Combatants' Leagues in 1920 and accompanied D'Annunzio on his Fiume expedition. He opposed the racial laws and was expelled from the Fascist Party. He later joined the Partisan movement in Rome. He was captured and executed by the Nazis in the massacre at the Fosse Ardeatine in March 1944.

GIOVACCHINO FORZANO (1883–1970)
A lawyer, journalist, playwright and film director, he was a friend of Mussolini and wrote libretti for Mascagni, Puccini and Leoncavallo.

GIOVANNI FRIGNANI (1897–1944)
Frignani was Lieutenant Colonel of the *carabinieri* and was post-humously awarded a Gold Medal for heroism after his death in the Fosse Ardeatine massacre. He arrested Mussolini after the Duce had been ousted on 25th July 1943. He organized a clandestine resistance group of those Roman *carabinieri* who had escaped the deportation order issued by the Germans on 7th October 1943.

GIUSEPPE GARIBALDI (1807–82)
The famous patriot, soldier and *condottiere*, known as the Hero of the Two Worlds – the most important figure of the Italian Risorgimento.

PIETRO GASPARRI (1852–1934)
Gasparri was the Secretary of State for the Vatican. Having taken his religious orders in 1877, he taught ecclesiastical history and theology and was ordained as a cardinal by Pius X in 1907. Together with Mussolini, he was a signatory of the Lateran Pacts on 11th February 1929.

PIETRO GAZZERA (1879–1953)
As a general, Gazzera took part in the war between Italy and Turkey and the First World War. He was the Minister of War from 1929 to 1934, when he became a senator. He commanded the Italian army in Ethiopia and Somalia during the Second World War and was a commissar for the prisoners of war after the Armistice on 8th September 1943.

VITO GENOVESE (1897–1969)
Vito Genovese was the head of one of the most important Mafia families of the American branch of Cosa Nostra. After emigrating

to the United States with his parents in 1913, he was arrested for the first time in 1915 and later became a close friend of Lucky Luciano, the *"capo di tutti i capi"* ("boss of all bosses"). Wanted by the New York police, he escaped to Italy in 1937. After Mussolini's removal from power in 1943, Genovese became the official interpreter for Colonel Charles Poletti, a former Governor of New York who had been sent to Italy by the Allies to facilitate a return to civil government.

GIOVANNI GENTILE (1875–1944)
A famous philosopher and the Professor of Theoretical Philosophy and History of Philosophy at Palermo and subsequently Pisa and Rome, Gentile was responsible for attempting to codify Fascist ideology in the *Manifesto degli intellettuali del Fascismo* (*Manifesto of the Fascist Intellectuals*), written in 1925. He was Minister for Public Education during the first Mussolini government, instituting a programme of reforms that had a profound influence on the Italian educational system. He became more and more detached from Fascism following a series of disagreements, especially on the question of the Lateran Pacts. However, he decided to join the Italian Social Republic after 8th September 1943, and was killed by a Partisan commando on 15th April 1944.

GIOVANNI GIOLITTI (1842–1928)
A liberal politician, Giolitti obtained a degree in jurisprudence when he was only nineteen years old. He was first elected as a deputy in 1882 and became Minister of the Treasury in 1889 and Prime Minister in 1892. He subsequently took on several other ministerial roles and was five times prime minister, the last time in 1920.

MARIA GIUDICE (1880–1953)
A Socialist and primary-school teacher, Giudice became secretary of the Voghera Workers' Association in 1903. She lived in exile in Switzerland for fifteen months, and on her return to Italy the following year she became provincial secretary for the Socialist Party in Turin. She was arrested several times for her anti-Fascist activities and retired from politics in 1941.

RAMÓN GÓMEZ DE LA SERNA (1888–1963)
A Spanish writer and the figurehead of Spanish Futurism, the prolific Gómez de la Serna wrote his first book when he was ten and published his first work at the age of sixteen.

EMMA GRAMATICA (1874–1965)
A famous theatre actress, Gramatica was involved in numerous radio programmes for EIAR (later RAI). She also had a successful career in cinema and television.

RODOLFO GRAZIANI (1882–1955)
During his career General Rodolfo Graziani was Governor of Libya, Viceroy of Ethiopia and, during the Italian Social Republic, Minister of War. He became infamous for cruel and bloody repressions in Libya and Ethiopia. He was one of the subscribers to the Fascist Racial Manifesto. After the war he was sentenced to nineteen years in prison, of which he only served two. He was appointed honorary president of the neo-Fascist Movimento Sociale Italiano (Italian Social Movement) in 1954.

GIOVANNI GRONCHI (1887–1978)
Gronchi, one of the founders of the People's Party, was elected as a deputy in 1919 and became Undersecretary of Industry for the first Mussolini government. In 1923 he resigned and withdrew his support from the Fascist administration. He returned to politics after 8th September 1943 and was a minister in the Bonomi and De Gasperi governments. He was President of the Chamber of Deputies from 1948 to 1955 and President of the Republic from 1955 to 1962.

HAILE SELASSIE (1892–1975)
Born Tafari Makonnen, Haile Selassie was Negus of Ethiopia from 1930 to 1974. His assumed name means "Power of the Trinity". Selassie was the founder of the University of Addis Ababa and carried out a programme of modernization in his country. He is considered the messiah of the Rastafarian religion.

ERNEST HEMINGWAY (1899–1961)
A journalist and novelist, Hemingway attained early commercial success with his work and won the Pulitzer Prize in 1953 for *The Old*

Man and the Sea and, in 1954, the Nobel Prize for Literature. He took part in the First World War in Italy as a driver for the American Red Cross and later assisted the troops on the front line (having been exempted from battle because of his impaired sight). He was seriously wounded in July 1918.

RÉMI HESS (1947–)
A French author and sociologist, Hess was born in Reims in 1947 and is currently Professor of Educational Sciences at the University of Paris VIII.

BENITO JUÁREZ (1806–72)
A Mexican national hero, Juárez was President of Mexico from 1861 to 1864 and from 1867 to 1872. With the support of the United States, he led a guerrilla-warfare campaign until the capture of Maximilian of Habsburg, who had been appointed Emperor of Mexico by Napoleon III. The date of his birth, 21st March, is a national holiday in Mexico.

ALEXANDER KARAĐORĐEVIĆ (ALEXANDER I OF YUGOSLAVIA, 1888–1934)
Educated in Geneva and later at the St Petersburg Page Corps military school, Alexander Karađorđević was at the head of an army during the Balkan Wars (1912–13) and led the Serbian forces against the Austro-Hungarian Empire during the First World War. After being routed and forced to retreat towards Albania, his army was rescued by the Italian navy and moved to Corfu to regroup. He was crowned King of Serbs, Croats and Slovenes in 1921, and King of Yugoslavia in 1929, and was assassinated in 1934 in Marseille by a far-right Serbian group led by Ante Pavelić.

KARL KAUTSKY (1854–1938)
A German Marxist theorist, Kautsky was secretary to Friedrich Engels. He was an opponent of Leninism and a fierce critic of the Russian Revolution.

ANNA MIKHAILOVNA KULISCIOFF (1855–1925)
Born Anja Rosenstein to a Jewish family, Kuliscioff was a Russian revolutionary, a physician specializing in gynaecology and among the founding members of the Italian Socialist Party. She

changed her name to Kuliscioff (meaning "labourer" in Russian) to avoid being identified by the agents of the Tsar during her exile. She was arrested many times in Italy and had a daughter (Andreina) from a relationship with the Italian Socialist Andrea Costa.

ARTURO LABRIOLA (1873–1959)
A lawyer, journalist and socialist, Labriola was elected as a deputy in 1913. He became Minister of Work in 1920, during the fifth Giolitti government, and Gran Maestro of the Grand Orient of Italy in 1930. Exiled to France, he resumed contact with the Fascist regime at the time of Italy's invasion of Ethiopia, a campaign that he supported. He was elected to the Constituent Assembly in 1946 and became a senator in 1948.

FIORELLO LA GUARDIA (1882–1945)
La Guardia was an American political leader and the Mayor of New York for three consecutive terms from 1933 to 1945. His mother, a Jewish woman from Trieste, was Irene Coen Luzzato. La Guardia moved to Trieste with his family in 1898. On his return to the United States he became a lawyer, and in 1916 he became the first Italian-American congressman. During the First World War he fought on the Italian front, where he rose to the rank of major and commanded a unit of American bombers. He was a fierce opponent of American Fascism and Nazism and waged an intense war against illegal gambling rings linked to the Mafia. New York City named its second airport after him.

COSTANTINO LAZZARI (1857–1927)
Lazzari was the founder of the Italian Labour Party in 1882, and among the founding members of the Italian Socialist Party ten years later. He was secretary of the Socialist Party from 1912 to 1919 and was persecuted by the Fascists until his death in 1927.

GUSTAVE LE BON (1841–1931)
A renowned French sociologist and psychologist, Le Bon had a strong influence in various political spheres, especially with his most famous work, *The Crowd: A Study of the Popular Mind*.

DOMENICO LECCISI (1920–2008)
A journalist and politician, Leccisi was the founder of a neo-Fascist organization after the Second World War. He is mainly remembered today for stealing Mussolini's body, and he exploited the resulting notoriety in his bid to be elected as a deputy representing the neo-Fascist party the Italian Social Movement, a post that he held from 1953 to 1963. He was a proponent of the so-called "left-wing Fascism". In 1958 he was one of the main supporters of the "Milazzo Operation" in Sicily for the election of the Christian Democrat Silvio Milazzo against the official candidate chosen by the Christian Democrat party. Milazzo's election was made possible thanks to the combined votes of the Italian Communist Party and of the Italian Social Movement.

GINO LUCETTI (1900–43)
An anarchist, Lucetti was one of the Arditi during the First World War. He was opposed to Fascism from a very early stage. Taking refuge in France, he returned to Italy in 1926 to carry out an assassination attempt on Mussolini at Porta Pia in Rome. He was sentenced to thirty years in prison. Freed by the Allies in 1943, he died on a vessel struck by German bombing.

EMIL LUDWIG (1881–1948)
Born Emil Cohn, Ludwig was a German journalist and author of Jewish origin. He became a Swiss citizen in 1932 and emigrated to the United States in 1940. He became famous after penning several successful biographies and interviews with Stalin (1931) and Mussolini (1932).

EMILIO LUSSU (1890–1975)
A lawyer, journalist, writer and anti-Fascist political leader, Lussu was a democratic interventionist during the First World War and wrote one of the most famous books on the conflict, *Un anno sull'altipiano* (*A Year on the High Plateau*). He was the founder of the Partito Sardo d'Azione (Sardinian Action Party), advocating autonomy and federalism. He was the victim of several Fascist attacks and was exiled to Lipari, where he organized a remarkable escape together with fellow anti-Fascists Carlo Rosselli and Francesco Fausto Nitti. During his exile in Paris he was among the founding members of the Giustizia e Libertà (Justice and Liberty) movement. He took part in the Spanish

Civil War, returning to Italy in 1943 and joining the Resistance. He became a minister in the government formed by the Partisan Ferruccio Parri in 1945 and subsequently served in the De Gasperi government. He later transferred his allegiances from the Sardinian Action Party to the Socialist Party, although he split from the latter in 1964 and set up the Partito Socialista Italiano di Unità Proletaria (Italian Socialist Party of Proletarian Unity). He later distanced himself from PSIUP when it became closer to the Communist Party.

CARLO EMANUELE MADRUZZO (1599–1658)
Madruzzo was ordained in 1626 and was Prince Bishop of Trento from 1629 to 1658. He tried, unsuccessfully, to obtain a papal dispensation to marry his lover Claudia Particella.

OLINDO MALAGODI (1870–1934)
A journalist, liberal politician and senator, Malagodi took a stance of firm opposition against Fascism. He was the editor of *La tribuna*.

IVAN MANASEVICH-MANUILOV
A secret agent and a head of department of the Okhrana (the security services or, rather, secret police of Tsarist Russia, established by Nicholas II in 1881), Manasevich-Manuilov was active predominantly in Paris and in Belgium. He made use of ruthless methods, from bribery to torture to the enrolment of agents provocateurs. The fraudulent *Protocols of the Elders of Zion* is thought to be the creation of the Okhrana.

GUGLIELMO MARCONI (1874–1937)
Marconi, the famous physicist and inventor of the wireless telegraph, founded the Wireless Telegraph & Signal Company in London in 1897. The following year he established radio communication between Queen Victoria's summer residence and the royal yacht with the Prince of Wales on board. In 1907 he launched the first radio-telegraphy service across the Atlantic. He was awarded the Nobel Prize for Physics in 1909. He openly displayed his sympathy for Fascism. He was honoured with the title of Marchese by King Victor Emmanuel III. In 1929 he supervised the launch of Radio Vaticana (Vatican Radio).

FILIPPO TOMMASO MARINETTI (1876–1944)
A poet, playwright and the founder of the Futurist movement, Marinetti was a strong advocate and theorist of war. He took part in the conflict in Libya in 1911 as a correspondent, and volunteered during the First World War. He founded the Partito Politico Futurista Italiano (Italian Futurist Party) in 1919, which was soon merged with Mussolini's Combatants' Leagues. He took part as a volunteer in the invasion of Ethiopia and, at the age of sixty-six, in that of Russia. He joined the Italian Social Republic after 8th September 1943.

ENRICO MATTEI (1906–62)
An entrepreneur and businessman before the Second World War, Mattei became involved in anti-Fascism in 1943 when he joined a group of Christian Democrat Partisans, going on to play a key part in the Christian Democrat Party's Comitato di Liberazione Nazionale dell'Alta Italia (National Liberation Committee of Northern Italy). He was among those who demanded Mussolini's execution after his capture. After the war he was put in charge of the national oil company created by the Fascists, AGIP, which under his leadership discovered large oil and gas deposits in Italy itself. He then led AGIP's replacement, Ente Nazionale Idrocarburi (ENI), through which he negotiated a number of significant oil concessions in the Middle East, thereby limiting the power of the world's large oil companies (the "seven sisters", as he called them).

GIUSEPPE MAZZINI (1805–72)
A lawyer, journalist, campaigner for unification and republican political leader, Mazzini is considered one of modern Italy's founding fathers. Because of his revolutionary activities, he was forced to seek refuge abroad for long periods, with frequent stays in London. In 1866 he was elected deputy in the Messina district. The elections were repeated three times, having twice been declared invalid because there were two death sentences on Mazzini's head. However, Mazzini was elected again at the third run, and his death sentences were amnestied in 1870.

GIACINTO MENOTTI SERRATI (1876–1926)
A maximalist socialist leader, Menotti Serrati took on the editorship of *Avanti!* when Mussolini was ousted from the Socialist Party

following his switch to interventionism during the First World War. He was a leader of the Socialist Party's maximalist faction, although he stayed with the party when it split and the Italian Communist Party was formed in 1921. He led the revolutionary wing of the Socialist Party into a merger with the Communist Party in 1924.

WEBB MILLER (1891–1940)
An American journalist and war correspondent, Miller reported on General Pershing's expedition against Pancho Villa in Mexico, the First World War, the Spanish Civil War, the Italian mission in Ethiopia and the Russian invasion of Finland. He won the Pulitzer Prize in 1922.

DON GIOVANNI MINZONI (1885–1923)
Minzoni was ordained as a priest in 1909 and served as a chaplain on the front during the First World War. He joined the People's Party and came into conflict with Fascism, especially on the subject of the education of young people. He was bludgeoned to death on 23rd August 1923 by a terror squad led by Italo Balbo.

MARIO MISSIROLI (1886–1974)
Missiroli began his career as a journalist when he was only fifteen years old and was editor of several newspapers during his life: *Il Tempo* (co-editor in 1918), *Il Resto del Carlino* (1919–21), *Il secolo* (from 1921), *Il Messaggero* (from 1946) and *Corriere della Sera* (1952–61). In 1962 he was elected president of the Italian journalists' union.

ARNOLDO MONDADORI (1889–1971)
Mondadori was the founder of the eponymous publishing house, now the largest in Italy. While working as a typographer in a stationer's office, he issued his first publication, the socialist-anarchist magazine *Luce!*, in 1907. In 1919 he moved the publishing house from Ostiglia, near Mantova, to Milan.

MANLIO MORGAGNI (1879–1943)
A journalist and a socialist, Morgagni was the first managing director of *Il Popolo d'Italia*, Mussolini's newspaper, and took an interventionist position during the First World War. He became president

and managing director of the Fascist regime's press agency Stefani. He committed suicide when he heard the news of Mussolini's arrest.

ODDINO MORGARI (1865–1944)
A journalist, socialist and the secretary of the Turin branch of the Socialist Party, Morgari became editor of *Avanti!* in 1908. He looked after the international relations of the Socialist Party.

CESARE MORI (1871–1942)
Mori was a prefect and later a senator. Remembered for his "energetic" methods and the use of violence in his repression of the Mafia in Sicily, he is still called "the Iron Prefect". During his time in Bologna he was one of the few police commanders to oppose the violence of the Fascist terror squads. He retired from active service in 1922 because of his conflicts with the Fascists. Two years later Mussolini called him back to service with the task of eradicating the Sicilian Mafia, and in 1925 he was appointed Prefect of Palermo. He was made a senator in 1929, possibly because Mussolini felt that he was becoming too prominent.

FILIPPO NALDI (1886–1972)
A journalist and entrepreneur, Naldi became editor of *Il Resto del Carlino* in 1914 and three years later founded *Il Tempo*. He was instrumental in obtaining the necessary capital to support the publication of Mussolini's *Il Popolo d'Italia*. One of his contributors, Filippo Filippelli, was involved in the killing of the Socialist leader Giacomo Matteotti. He acted as an intermediary in the oil deals between the Fascist regime and the American oil companies. After 25th July 1943 he sided with Pietro Badoglio and Victor Emmanuel III against Mussolini.

ADA NEGRI (1870–1945)
Ada Negri was a leading Italian poet and drew inspiration for her poetry from her job as a primary-school teacher and her working-class background. She became a Socialist and came into contact with Filippo Turati and Benito Mussolini. She considered herself Anna Kuliscioff's spiritual twin. She joined the Fascist regime and was appointed a member of the Reale Accademia d'Italia by Mussolini.

PIETRO NENNI (1891–1980)

A journalist and political leader, Nenni began his career in the ranks of the Republican Party. As the founder of Bologna's Combatants' League, he is numbered among the first Fascists. He later joined the Socialist Party and was appointed editor of *Avanti!* in 1923. He lived in exile in France from 1926 and took part in the Spanish Civil War, later becoming one of the leaders of the Italian Resistance. His daughter Vittoria died in Auschwitz. He was elected to the Constituent Assembly in 1946 and was Minister for Foreign Affairs from 1946 to 1947. In 1952 he was awarded the Stalin Prize for Peace, which he returned after the harsh Soviet repression of Hungary in 1956. He was elected as a deputy in later governments, rising to the rank of Deputy Prime Minister twice. In 1970 he became a senator for life. He was one of the founders of the Italian centre-left.

FRANCESCO SAVERIO NITTI (1868–1953)

A journalist, economist and radical thinker, Nitti was Professor of Financial Law at the University of Naples. An avowed anti-Fascist, he was elected as a deputy in 1904, became a minister several times and served as prime minister from 1919 to 1920. He opposed the rise of Fascism and was forced into exile in 1924. He returned to Italy in 1944 and was elected as a member of the Constituent Assembly and later as a senator.

MAX NORDAU (1849–1923)

Born Simon Maximilian Südfeld in Hungary, Nordau was a sociologist, physician and journalist. In 1897 he founded, with Theodor Herzl, the World Zionist Organization, devoted to the establishment of a Jewish homeland in Palestine.

GUGLIELMO OBERDAN (1858–82)

Born in Trieste to an Italian father and a Slovene mother, Oberdan became a proponent of Italian irredentism, Italianizing his real name, Wilhelm Oberdank. He refused to fight wearing the Austrian uniform, deserted and escaped to Rome, where he continued his engineering studies. He organized a failed assassination attempt against the Emperor Franz Josef in Trieste, and was hanged on 20th December 1882.

SERGIO PANUNZIO (1886–1944)
A journalist, jurist, socialist and a major figure of revolutionary syndicalism, Panunzio had close political links with Mussolini. An interventionist during the First World War, he was given indefinite leave because of his haemophilia. He joined the Fascists and supported Mussolini's subsequent drift to the right. He was the main theorist of Fascist corporatism and took an active role in the reformation of the Italian Civil Code.

VILFREDO PARETO (1848–1923)
An economist and sociologist, Pareto gained a degree in engineering studies from the Turin Polytechnic in 1870. He became managing director of the Società delle Ferriere Italiane (Association of Italian Steel Factories). He later returned to his research on economy and sociology, and became Professor of Political Economy at the University of Lausanne in Switzerland. He had good relations with Georges Sorel and many other foreign politicians and economists.

GIORGIO PINI (1899–1987)
Having fought in the First World War as a private, Pini joined the Bolognese ranks of Fascists in 1920. He later became a journalist and in 1930 took on the editorship of *Giornale di Genova* and later the *Gazzettino di Venezia*. In 1936 he was appointed editor-in-chief of *Il Popolo d'Italia*. After the Second World War, he joined the neo-Fascist Italian Social Movement, becoming one of the major figures of the so-called "left wing" of the party.

LUIGI PIRANDELLO (1867–1936)
A prolific novelist, short-story writer and playwright, Pirandello was awarded the Nobel Prize for Literature in 1934. His first great commercial success was with the novel *Il fu Mattia Pascal* (*The Late Mattia Pascal*), published in 1904. He is perhaps best known for experimental dramatic works such as *Sei personaggi in cerca d'autore* (*Six Characters in Search of an Author*), first performed in 1921. He was among the subscribers to the *Manifesto of the Fascist Intellectuals* in 1925.

PASKA PIREDDA (1917–2009)
Piredda was the only female officer of the assault-troops unit known as the Decima Mas. After gaining a degree in colonial studies in Rome, she became assistant to the unit's commander, Junio Valerio Borghese, and later the press officer. The niece of Nobel Prize-winning novelist Grazia Deledda, she was the female face of Fascism in the propaganda of the Decima Mas, appearing also in a famous poster of the time. After 8th September 1943 she gathered a wealth of documents relating to the history of the Decima Mas.

PIUS XI (AMBROGIO DAMIANO ACHILLE RATTI, 1857–1939)
Having taken Franciscan orders in 1874 and been ordained as a priest in 1879, Ratti pursued an academic career within the Church and obtained three degrees (philosophy, canonical law and theology). He was an expert mountaineer and reached the top of Monte Rosa in 1889 (the first to do so on the eastern side), Mount Cervino in the same year and Mont Blanc in 1890. He wrote several articles for the Italian Alpine Club magazine. He was appointed Archbishop of Milan and Cardinal in 1921. The following year, on 6th February, he was elected Pope. In 1929 he signed with Mussolini the Lateran Pacts, which recognized the Vatican as an independent city state, thereby ending the so-called "Roman Question".

VÁŠA PŘÍHODA (1900–60)
A virtuoso violinist, Příhoda is regarded as one of the best interpreters of Paganini's music. When he was nineteen, Toscanini discovered him playing at the Caffè Grand'Italia in Milan and helped him launch his career. In 1930 he married the violinist Alma Rosè. He was accused of collaborating with the Nazis, having played in Nazi Germany and in the Third Reich-occupied territories of Czechoslovakia.

GAVRILO PRINCIP (1894–1918)
A revolutionary from the nationalist group known as Young Bosnia, at the age of nineteen he organized, with five other subversives, the assassination of the Archduke Franz Ferdinand, the heir to the throne of the Austro-Hungarian Empire, on 18th June 1914 in Sarajevo. Only he and Nedeljko Čabrinović were arrested. He died in prison in Terezín from tuberculosis and repeated beatings.

MASSIMO ROCCA (AKA LIBERO TANCREDI, 1884–1973)
A journalist, politician and contributor to *Avanti!*, where he met
Mussolini, Rocca (who used the pen name Libero Tancredi) was
an interventionist during the First World War. He contributed to
Il Popolo d'Italia and founded, together with Giuseppe Bottai, the
magazine *Critica fascista* (*Journal of Fascist Criticism*), where he
condemned the more extreme forms of Fascism and the activities of
terror squads. For his radical stance following the assassination of
Giacomo Matteotti, he was expelled from the Fascist Party and was
forced to flee to France. He restored his links with Fascism during
the period of the Italian Social Republic.

ALFREDO ROCCO (1875–1935)
A jurist and politician, Rocco taught at the universities of Urbino,
Parma and finally Rome. Elected as a deputy in 1921, he became
President of the Chamber of Deputies in 1924. He was Minister
for Justice between 1925 and 1932 and the author of the new penal
code commissioned by the Fascist regime. He was appointed as a
senator in 1934.

PINO ROMUALDI (1913–88)
A journalist and politician, Romualdi was among the founding
members of the neo-Fascist Italian Social Movement. He was born
in Predappio, the same town as Mussolini. This contributed to the
legend that Romualdi was one of the Duce's illegitimate sons. After
enlisting as a volunteer during the Second World War, he joined the
Italian Social Republic. During this period he openly boasted about
the anti-Semitic activities and deportations of Jews carried out by
the Fascist regime. Sentenced to death after the end of the war, he
was pardoned following the general amnesty decreed by the Justice
Minister Palmiro Togliatti in 1946.

CESARE ROSSI (1887–1967)
A journalist who contributed to many socialist newspapers including
Il Popolo d'Italia, Rossi was one of Mussolini's closest associates.
After the March on Rome he became chief press officer to the new
regime. However, he became estranged from the Fascist movement
after he was one of the people on whom Mussolini tried to lay responsibility for the killing of the Socialist leader Giacomo Matteotti.

The Duce ordered his arrest in June 1924, but he was released in December 1925, after which Rossi escaped to France. He was arrested again by the Fascist police in 1928. In 1947, during the second Matteotti trial, he was arrested but later released without charge due to lack of evidence.

MARIA RYGIER (1885–1953)
A writer for many socialist newspapers, Rygier was an interventionist during the First World War and contributed to *Il Popolo d'Italia*. Having become opposed to Fascism, she sought refuge in France in 1926.

ANTONIO SALANDRA (1853–1931)
Salandra was Professor of Administrative Law at the University of Rome, a conservative politician, a deputy, a member of several executives and Prime Minister from March 1914 to June 1916. In later life he became a senator.

GAETANO SALVEMINI (1873–1957)
A famous historian, politician, socialist and anti-Fascist. He lost his wife and his five children in the Messina earthquake in 1908. During the First World War his position was one of democratic interventionism. Elected as a deputy in 1919, he took a strong anti-Mussolini stance. After being arrested and tried, he escaped to Paris and subsequently Great Britain and the United States, where he taught at Harvard. He continued his activities in the USA, Great Britain and France over the course of the Second World War, at the end of which he returned to Italy. In 1955 he was the recipient of an honorary degree from the University of Oxford.

PRINCE AIMONE OF SAVOY-AOSTA, DUKE OF AOSTA (1900–48)
Prince Aimone was the Duke of Spoleto and a commander in the Italian navy. He became Duke of Aosta in 1942 when his elder brother Amedeo died in a British prison camp in Kenya. The same year, he was crowned King of Croatia with the name Tomislav II. He abdicated in 1943 without ever having set foot in his kingdom. He married Irene, Princess of Greece, who bore him only one son, Amedeo, born during the war. After the end of the war he went into exile, as did the rest of the male offspring of the House of Savoy, and died suddenly in Argentina aged forty-eight.

ELENA OF MONTENEGRO, PRINCESS OF SAVOY (1873–1952)

Born in Montenegro, Elena became Queen of Italy when she married Victor Emmanuel III, with whom she had five children: Umberto, Yolanda, Giovanna, Mafalda and Maria Francesca. Very popular with the Italian people, she followed her husband into exile after the referendum on the abolition of the monarchy in 1946.

GIOVANNA OF SAVOY (1907–2000)

The third daughter of Victor Emmanuel III and Elena of Savoy, Giovanna became Queen of Bulgaria when she married King Boris III, who died in 1943, possibly the victim of a Nazi poison plot. Giovanna was forced into exile together with her children. The heir to the throne, Simeon, a child at the time, returned to Bulgaria after the fall of the Communist regime and was elected prime minister.

MARIA JOSÉ OF SAVOY (1906–2011)

Princess of Belgium, in 1930 Maria José married Umberto, the heir to the throne of Italy. The couple had little in common, and their marriage was not a happy one, although they had four children together. The Princess had received a cosmopolitan education, was an art lover and was openly anti-Fascist. The relationship between her and Mussolini was marked by a mutual diffidence and coldness. In particular, she supported the Partisan movement during the Second World War. Although she was in effect separated from her husband, she also went into exile after the referendum on the abolition of the monarchy. She was allowed to return to Italy only after the death of Umberto.

UMBERTO II OF SAVOY (1904–83)

The only son of Victor Emmanuel III and Elena of Savoy, Umberto was the Prince of Piedmont, the heir to the throne, and married Maria José, Princess of Belgium, with whom he had four children. He became king on 9th May 1946, after the abdication of his father, Victor Emmanuel III. On 2nd June of the same year, a referendum transformed Italy into a republic. Although the monarchy lost by a very narrow margin and there are still suspicions of vote-rigging, the "King of May" – as Umberto was nicknamed – accepted the result, wishing to avoid a further split in an already divided and war-ravaged country. He died alone, in exile at Cascais in Portugal, having long since been abandoned by his wife, Maria José.

VICTOR EMMANUEL III OF SAVOY (1869–1947)
The son of Umberto I and Margherita of Savoy (Umberto's cousin), Victor Emmanuel was King of Italy from 1900 to 1946, Emperor of Ethiopia from 1936 to 1943 and King of Albania from 1939 to 1943. His reign spanned two world conflicts and the twenty years of Fascist rule. He remains a controversial figure to this day, having abandoned Italy after the Armistice on 8th September 1943. In an attempt to save the monarchy, on 9th May 1946 he abdicated in favour of his son Umberto. He went into exile in Alexandria with his wife Elena.

ANGELO SBARDELLOTTO (1907–32)
An Italian anarchist with a criminal record, Sbardellotto was arrested in 1932 and found in possession of a fake passport and a gun. Sentenced to death for having planned the assassination of the Duce, he was executed at the age of twenty-five after a forced confession and a brief trial.

EDOARDO SCARFOGLIO (1860–1917)
A poet, author and journalist, Scarfoglio married the writer Matilde Serao in 1885. Together, they founded *Il Mattino di Napoli* (still the most widely read newspaper in southern Italy). He was a friend of Gabriele D'Annunzio and a major figure in cultural and social circles in Italy towards the end of the nineteenth century and the beginning of the twentieth.

MIKE (MICHELE) SCHIRRU (1899–1931)
Born in Sardinia, Schirru emigrated at a very young age to the United States, where he became a naturalized American. He was linked to the anarchist movement and took part in the struggle to support Ferdinando Nicola Sacco and Bartolomeo Vanzetti, anarchists accused of murdering two people during a robbery in Massachusetts in 1920. In 1931 he travelled to Rome with a plan to kill Mussolini, but he was arrested, probably after being betrayed. Condemned to death, he was executed the day after his arrest.

ALFREDO ILDEFONSO SCHUSTER (1880–1954)
A Benedictine monk, Schuster was ordained as a priest in 1904. In 1918 he became Abbot of St Paul Outside the Walls in Rome. He was a member of the Amici Israel association, an organization established

by the Catholic Church to fight anti-Semitism and racism. He became Archbishop of Milan in June 1929 and cardinal the following month. On 13th November 1938 he preached a sermon against the recently approved Fascist racial laws in the Duomo of Milan. After the demise of the Italian Social Republic, in a climate of general insurrection, he organized a meeting between Mussolini and the leaders of the Resistance in his archbishopric. When the bodies of Mussolini and other Fascists were hung by their feet at Piazzale Loreto, Schuster demanded respect for all corpses, as he had done the previous year when he had asked the Germans to remove the Partisans' bodies from that same square. In 1952 he was appointed the first president of the Conferenza Episcopale Italiana (Italian Episcopal Conference).

MARIO SIRONI (1885–1961)
A painter, scenographer and architect, Sironi studied at the Accademia di Belle Arti di Roma and then moved to Milan, where he joined the Futurist movement. He contributed to *Il Popolo d'Italia*, Mussolini's newspaper, as an illustrator, and there befriended Margherita Sarfatti and became a member of the Novecento group. He was the major contributor to the 1932 Exhibition of the Fascist Revolution in Rome.

OTTO SKORZENY (1908–75)
An Austrian-born SS officer, in July 1943 Skorzeny was ordered to form a special commando unit to execute Operation Eiche, a rescue mission to liberate Mussolini, then imprisoned in a hotel at the top of the Gran Sasso mountains. After the successful completion of the mission, he was placed at the head of the Special Operations department of the Reich's security service. He was one of the organizers of the harsh reprisals following the failed assassination attempt on Hitler on 20th July 1944. Captured in May 1945, he was tried and fully acquitted of all charges. According to some theories, Skorzeny organized the escape of many SS officers from Germany at the end of the war.

GEORGES EUGÈNE SOREL (1847–1922)
A civil engineer by training, Sorel moved to the fields of philosophy and sociology, becoming a theorist of revolutionary syndicalism. His most famous book is *Reflections on Violence*, published in 1905 in a

trade-union journal, and three years later in book form. Sorel was a fierce opponent of the First World War and later a supporter of the Russian Revolution and Bolshevism.

ACHILLE STARACE (1889–1945)
An ordinary soldier, Starace was promoted to the rank of officer of the Bersaglieri corps during the First World War and received several decorations. He was one of Mussolini's most trusted men, described by the Duce as "the mastiff of the Fascist revolution". He was the founder of the Combatants' League in Trento and, in 1923, was entrusted with the task of creating the Voluntary National Security Militia. He was elected as a deputy in 1924, and Mussolini appointed him Secretary of the Fascist Party in 1931. When, in 1939, support for the Fascist regime began to wane, Mussolini dismissed him. After the 8th September 1943 he joined the Italian Social Republic, but Mussolini gave him no active role. He was captured by the Partisans on 28th April 1945 and executed by firing squad the following day in Piazzale Loreto, where the bodies of Mussolini, Claretta Petacci and other Fascists had been amassed.

MAX STIRNER (1806–56)
Born Johann Kaspar Schmidt, the German philosopher Max Stirner was one of the first theorists of anarchist individualism. He studied at the University of Berlin under, among others, Hegel. He belonged to a group of young followers of Hegel, which included Bruno Bauer, Ludwig Feuerbach, Engels and Marx. His most famous work is *Der Einzige und sein Eigentum* (*The Ego and Its Own*), first published in 1845.

KURT STUDENT (1890–1978)
A Luftwaffe general and the commander of the German paratroopers during the Second World War, Student was responsible for planning Operation Eiche, the mission to liberate the imprisoned Mussolini in 1943. He was involved in the defence of Normandy in 1944, and later captured and held in custody by the British until 1948.

DON LUIGI STURZO (1871–1959)
Of noble birth, Sturzo was a priest and a political leader. Having been ordained in 1894, he gained a degree in theology at the Pontifical

Gregorian University in Rome two years later. He became involved in politics and in 1905 was elected as a councillor for the province of Catania. In 1919 he founded the Italian People's Party. He opposed Fascism and achieved the withdrawal of Catholic members of parliament from the first Mussolini government. He lost the support of the Vatican (which was involved in secret negotiations in connection with the Lateran Pacts) and was forced into exile in London, Paris and finally New York. At the end of the war he returned to Italy, and seven years later he was appointed a senator for life.

DON PIETRO TACCHI VENTURI (1861–1956)

A Jesuit priest and historian, Tacchi Venturi was the intermediary and main point of contact between Mussolini and Pius XI during the negotiations leading up to the Lateran Pacts. He also mediated in the dispute between the Duce and the Pope over the question of the education of young people.

ENRICO TELLINI (1871–1923)

Tellini was a general in the Italian army who took part in the war between Italy and Turkey in 1911 and later in the First World War. In 1923 he was dispatched by the League of Nations as the head of a mission to patrol the border between Greece and Albania, and was killed in an ambush near the city of Ioannina.

REGINA TERRUZZI (1862–1951)

A teacher and socialist writer, Terruzzi was a member of the Lega per la Tutela dei Diritti delle Donne (League for the Protection of Women's Rights) as well as the founder of the Socialist Women's Union. During the First World War she was an interventionist and warmed to Mussolini's ideas, later taking a critical stance against the violence of the Fascist terror squads.

PALMIRO TOGLIATTI (1893–1964)

Togliatti was one of the founders of the Communist Party and its secretary from 1927 until his death. He was also one of the most powerful members of the Comintern. In 1944 he became Deputy Prime Minister and the following year the Minister for Justice. In June 1946 he issued a general amnesty, resulting in the release of thousands of

Fascist prisoners. He was elected to the Constituent Assembly in 1946 and remained a member of parliament throughout his life.

ARTURO TOSCANINI (1867–1957)

After studying the cello and composition at the conservatoire, in 1886 Toscanini, who was then nineteen, was offered the opportunity to direct an orchestra. He became the greatest conductor of his time. In 1898 he was invited to conduct at La Scala in Milan. He also conducted at the Met in New York and at Bayreuth, and he directed the inaugural concert of the Palestine Symphony Orchestra (later the Israel Philharmonic Orchestra). He joined the Fascist movement in 1919, but subsequently became a fierce opponent of the regime and sought refuge in the United States, where the NBC Symphony Orchestra was founded for him. He returned to Italy after the war to conduct again at La Scala, restored after the bombings. In 1949 he was appointed a senator for life.

CLAUDIO TREVES (1869–1933)

A journalist, socialist and anti-Fascist leader, Treves took on the editorship of *Avanti!* in 1910. During the First World War he was an anti-interventionist. Only after the Battle of Caporetto in October-November 1917 did he change his position in favour of a pact of national unity as a reaction to the humiliating defeat suffered by the Italians. In 1906 he was elected to the Chamber of Deputies. In 1926 he went into exile, first in Switzerland and later in France.

FILIPPO TURATI (1857–1932)

A lawyer, journalist and socialist leader, Turati was among the founding members of the Socialist Party in 1892. He was elected as a deputy in 1896. He was an anti-interventionist during the First World War, but moved to an interventionist position after the defeat at Caporetto in 1917. In 1926 he fled to France to escape from the Fascist regime.

GIUSEPPE VERDI (1813–1901)

The great Italian composer had his first opera performed at La Scala in Milan in 1839. After a disastrous reception of his second work, *Un giorno di regno* (*King for a Day*) in 1840, his *Nabucco* was performed at La Scala in 1842 and was a roaring success. From then on he wrote a new opera almost every year, with increasing success, coming to be perceived as the greatest living opera composer. Verdi was a patriot and a supporter of the Risorgimento movement. He was elected as a deputy in the first parliament of unified Italy in 1861 and became a senator for life in 1874.

OLINDO VERNOCCHI (1888–1954)
Vernocchi was one of the major figures of the Socialist Party and co-edited *Avanti!*, the party's official newspaper, with Pietro Nenni and Riccardo Somigliano. He was the last secretary of the Socialist Party before the advent of the Fascist dictatorship. He tried, unsuccessfully, to escape to France in 1927. Mussolini did not place him in forced internment, probably for reasons of political propaganda, wanting to show that he could afford to leave such a prominent Socialist at liberty. He was elected as a member of the Constituent Assembly in 1946.

PIERO VIVARELLI (1927–2010)
A composer, scriptwriter and film director, Vivarelli was among the young volunteers in the assault-troops unit commanded by Junio Valerio Borghese, the Decima Mas. After the war he joined the Italian Communist Party, and was the only Italian to be allowed by Fidel Castro to join the Cuban Communist Party. He directed a great number of films, many under the pseudonym Donald Murray. He was also active as a songwriter (among his most famous works are Celentano's '24,000 baci' and 'Il tuo bacio è come un rock').

EDITH WHARTON (1862–1937)
Born to a rich New York family, Edith Newbold Jones married the banker Edward Wharton in 1885. She moved to France in 1907, divorcing her husband six years later. She published her first novel (set in Italy) in 1902 and won the Pulitzer Prize in 1921 for *The Age of Innocence*.

GEORG ZACHARIAE (1888–1965)
Zachariae was a German physician sent by Hitler to treat Mussolini. He looked after the Duce during the last nineteen months of his life.

ANTEO ZAMBONI (1911–26)
An Italian anarchist, Zamboni was only fifteen years old when he shot Mussolini in Bologna on 31st October 1926. He was lynched on the spot by the Fascists. The circumstances surrounding this assassination attempt are unclear; Mussolini himself described Zamboni as "the *supposed* would-be assassin".

TITO ZANIBONI (1883–1960)
A reformist socialist, Zaniboni was against Italy's intervention in the First World War, but was conscripted and gained two medals. He was elected as a deputy for the reformist Socialists in 1921. He organized a failed assassination attempt against Mussolini on 4th November 1925. He was sentenced to thirty years in prison, later commuted to exile on Ponza. He was freed on 8th September 1943. The following year he was appointed High Commissioner for the liberation of Italy from Fascism, and in 1945 he became High Commissioner for refugees and displaced persons.

Notes and References

CUE TITLES

ADC   De Felice, Renzo, *Mussolini il duce*, I. *Gli anni del consenso. 1929– 1936* (Turin: Einaudi, 1974)

CAL   Calipso, *Vita segreta di Mussolini* (Rome: IEDC, 1944)

CAM   Navarra, Quinto, *Memorie del cameriere di Mussolini* (Naples: L'ancora del Mediterraneo, 2004)

CES   Rossi, Gianni Scipione, *Cesira e Benito* (Soveria Mannelli: Rubbettino, 2007)

CHI   Curti, Elena, *Il chiodo a tre punte* (Pavia: Iuculano, 2003)

CM   Ludwig, Emil, *Colloqui con Mussolini* (Milan: Arnoldo Mondadori, 1950)

COM   Buttignon, Ivan, *Compagno Duce* (Bresso: Hobby & Work, 2010)

DAN   Guerri, Giordano Bruno, *D'Annunzio. L'amante guerriero.* (Milan: Mondadori, 2008)

DD   Boratto, Ercole, *Diario sul Duce* (file JZX-6220, National Archives, Washington, sent by Agent CB 55 (X-2, Oss, Roma), 1946

DEL   Canali, Mauro, *Il delitto Matteotti*, (Bologna: Il Mulino, 1997)

DM   Rafanelli, Leda, *Una donna e Mussolini* (Milan: Rizzoli, 1946)

DMVP   *I diari di Mussolini (veri o presunti) 1939* (Milan: Bompiani, 2010)

DUX   Sarfatti, Margherita, *Dux* (Milan: Mondadori, 1982)

FAU   Sarfatti, Margherita, *My Fault*, in Festorazzi, Roberto, *Margherita Sarfatti. La donna che inventò Mussolini* (Costabissara: Angelo Colla Editore, 2010)

FSD   Pieroni, Alfredo, *Il figlio segreto del duce* (Milan: Garzanti, 2006)

LOV   Fontanges, Magda (Coraboeuf, Madeleine), *Love Affair with Mussolini*, Liberty, 1940

MAR   Lussu, Emilio, *Marcia su Roma e dintorni* (Turin: Einaudi, 1945)

MAS   D'Aurora, Giorgio, *La maschera e il volto di Magda Fontanges* (Milan: Cebes, 1946)

MCE   Rossi, Cesare, *Mussolini com'era* (Rome: Ruffolo, 1946)

MF   De Felice, Renzo, *Mussolini il fascista* (Turin: Einaudi, 1966)

MFB   Mussolini, Edvige, *Mio fratello Benito* (Florence: La Fenice, 1957)

MP   Mussolini, Rachele, *Mussolini privato* (Milan: Mondadori, 1980)

MPB   Monelli, Paolo, *Mussolini piccolo borghese* (Milan: Garzanti, 1983)

MR   De Felice, Renzo, *Mussolini il rivoluzionario* (Turin: Einaudi, 1965)

MS   Petacci, Claretta, *Mussolini segreto*, ed. Mario Suttora (Milan: Rizzoli, 2009)

MSA   Urso, Simona, *Margherita Sarfatti* (Venice: Marsilio, 2003)

MSAD   Wieland, Karin, *Margherita Sarfatti. L'amante del Duce* (Turin: Utet, 2006)

MSC   Zachariae, Georg, *Mussolini si confessa*, (Milan: Garzanti, 1966)

MTQ   Bertoldi, Silvio, *Mussolini tale e quale* (Milan: Longanesi, 1973)

PF   Le Bon, Gustave, *La psicologia delle folle* (Milan: Longanesi, 1980)

RAZ   Fabre, Giorgio, 'Mussolini, Claretta e la questione della razza. 1937–38', in *Annali della Fondazione Ugo La Malfa – Storia e Politica*, XXIV, 2009

RN   De Felice, Renzo, *Il Rosso e il Nero*, ed. Pasquale Chessa (Milan: Baldini e Castoldi, 1995)

SAGC   Nenni, Pietro, *Sei anni di guerra civile* (Milan: Rizzoli, 1945)

ST   De Felice, Renzo, *Mussolini il duce*, II. *Lo Stato totalitario. 1936–1940* (Turin: Einaudi, 1981)

TM   Balabanoff, Angelica, *Il traditore Mussolini* (Rome, Milan: Avanti, 1945)

WORKS BY BENITO MUSSOLINI

AC   *L'amante del Cardinale*, (Trento: Reverdito, 1986)

DG   *Il mio diario di guerra, 1915–1917* (Milan: FPE, 1966)

MAY   *La tragedia di Mayerling*, (Trento: La Finestra Editrice, 2005)

OMN   *Opera Omnia*, ed. Susmel, Edoardo and Susmel, Duilio (Florence, La Fenice, 1951–63)

PNF   *Partito Nazionale Fascista. Il Gran Consiglio nei primi cinque anni dell'Era Fascista* (Rome: Libreria del Littorio, 1927)

INTRODUCTION

1. *MS*, p. 222.
2. Ib. p. 376.
3. *RAZ*, p. 349.
4. *MS*, p. 225.
5. Pasolini, Pier Paolo, *Petrolio* (Milan: Mondadori, 2005), Appunto 67, p. 278.
6. Mosse, George L., *Il Sole 24 Ore*, 14th May 2006.
7. *RN*, p. 146.
8. Chessa, Pasquale and Raggi, Barbara, *L'ultima lettera di Benito*, (Milan: Bompiani, 2010), p. 31 (Archivio Centrale dello Stato, fascicolo 98, foglio 112.1.f)
9. Ib. pp. 61–2 (Archivio Centrale dello Stato fascicolo 51, foglio 8).
10. Ib. p. 82 (Archivio Centrale dello Stato, fascicolo 29, foglio 64).
11. 'Signor Mussolini's personal affairs'. The National Archives of UK, Kew (Fo 371/22444).
12. *RN*, p. 153.
13. Ib. p. 158.
14. Mack Smith, Denis, *La Stampa*, 27th May 1996.
15. Renzo De Felice interviewed by Giorgio Fabre, Panorama, 18th November 1990.
16. Bobbio, Norberto, *La Stampa*, 26th May 1996.
17. Giorgio Amendola interviewed by Piero Melograni, in Amendola, Giorgio, *Intervista sull'antifascismo* (Bari: Laterza, 2008) pp. 12–14.
18. Colletti, Lucio, *Il Corriere della Sera*, 27th May 1996.
19. Sabbatucci, Giovanni, *Il Sole 24 Ore*, 14th May 2006.
20. *Corriere della Sera*, 28th May 2010.
21. Sullivan, Brian, *Il Corriere della Sera*, 27th June 1994.
22. *RN*, pp. 140–42.
23. *DMVP*, Introduzione.
24. Ib. p. 236.

CHAPTER I

1. *MFB*, p. 24.
2. *CM*, p. 39.
3. Mussolini, Benito, *My Life. Youth*, The Saturday Evening Post, 5th May 1928, p. 4.
4. *MFB*, p. 14.
5. *MR*, p. 6.
6. *My Life. Youth*, op. cit., p. 4.
7. *MSC*, p. 139.
8. *TM*, p. 25.
9. *Vita di Arnaldo* (1932), OMN, XXXIV, p. 141.

CHAPTER 2

1. *La mia vita dal 29 luglio 1883 al 23 novembre 1911*, OMN, XXXIII, p. 248.
2. Ib. p. 231.
3. Ib. p. 245.
4. Fest, Joachim, *Hitler, una biografia*, (Milan: Garzanti, 1999), p. 25.
5. *MFB*, p. 12.
6. *Vita di Arnaldo*, OMN, XXXIV, p. 145.

7. *La mia vita*, OMN, XXXIII, p. 224.
8. *CM*, p. 194.
9. *La mia vita*, OMN, XXXIII, p. 226.
10. Ib. p. 230.
11. Ib. p. 235.
12. *MS*, p. 263.
13. *TM*, p. 49.

CHAPTER 3

1. *MCE*, pp. 279–80.
2. *Gehes Codex*, Dresden, 1939.
3. Bertoldi, Silvio, *Gli arricchiti all'ombra di Palazzo Venezia* (Milan: Ugo Mursia Editore, 2009), pp. 34–5.
4. *MF*, p. 381.
5. Tonelli, Anna, *E ballando ballando – La storia d'Italia a passi di danza* (Milan: Franco Angeli, 1998), pp. 68–70.
6. Ib. p. 85.
7. Hess, Rémi, *Il valzer, rivoluzione della coppia in Europa* (Turin: Einaudi, 1993), p. 271.
8. Ib. p. 267.
9. *La mia vita*, OMN, XXXIII, p. 238.
10. Ib. p. 239.
11. Ib. p. 246–47.
12. Ib. p. 247.
13. *MS*, p. 99.

CHAPTER 4

1. *MP*, p. 78.
2. Ib. p. 80.
3. *DUX*, p. 85.
4. *La mia vita*, OMN, XXXIII, p. 251.
5. *MR*, p. 35.
6. *CAL*, p. X.
7. *CM*, p. 149.
8. *MSC*, p. 140.
9. *TM*, p. 16–7.
10. *MP*, p. 80.
11. *TM*, p. 19.
12. *MFB*, p. 32.
13. *La mia vita*, OMN, XXXIII, p. 258.
14. *CM*, p. 41.
15. Cordova, Ferdinando, *Il 'consenso' imperfetto* (Soveria Mannelli: Rubbettino, 2010), p. 301.

CHAPTER 5

1. *MP*, p. 22.
2. *My Life. Youth*, op. cit., p. 5, p. 117.

3.   *Vita di Arnaldo* (1932), OMN, XXXIV, p. 147.
4.   *La mia vita*, OMN, XXXIII, p. 261.
5.   *MFB*, p. 159.
6.   Ib. p. 158.
7.   *MS*, p. 236.
8.   *My Life. Youth*, op. cit., p. 117.
9.   *TM*, p. 110–11.
10. *La mia vita*, OMN, XXXIII, p. 261.
11. Ib. p. 262.
12. *MS*, p. 179.
13. *DUX*, p. 102.
14. Ib. p. 102.
15. Ib. p. 102.
16. Ib. p. 103.
17. Ib. p. 103.
18. *TM*, p. 44–5.
19. *La mia vita*, OMN, XXXIII, p. 262.
20. Ib. p. 262.
21. Ib. p. 264.
22. *MCE*, p. 34.
23. *MFB*, p. 38.
24. *La mia vita*, OMN, XXXIII, p. 265.
25. *CAL*, p. 9.
26. *La mia vita*, OMN, XXXIII, p. 265.
27. *MP*, p. 23.
28. Ib. 24–5.
29. *MS*, p. 81.
30. *MP*, p. 25.
31. *La mia vita*, OMN, XXXIII, p. 266.
32. *MR*, p. 67–8.
33. *MP*, p. 26.
34. Ib. p. 27.
35. Ib. p. 28.
36. Ib. p. 29.
37. *La mia vita*, OMN, XXXIII, p. 266.
38. *MTQ*, p. 43.
39. *CM*, p. 186.

CHAPTER 6

1.   *AC*, p. 44.
2.   Ib. p. 45.
3.   Ib. p. 45.
4.   Ib. p. 57.
5.   Ib. p. 76–7.
6.   *La mia vita*, OMN, XXXIII, p. 239.
7.   *MFB*, p. 32.
8.   *DUX*, p. 117.
9.   *MS*, p. 153.
10. *Tg1Storia No. 268* (1st March 2010), Rai Uno. Interview by Giorgio Assumma.

11. *MAY*, p. 233.
12. Ib. p. 242.
13. *MR*, p. 88.
14. *OMN*, IV, p. 104–6.

CHAPTER 7

1. *MCE*, p. 48.
2. *La lotta di classe, 14th December 1912*, in OMN, V, p. 380.
3. Siragusa, Mario, 'Stragi e stragismo nell'età dei Fasci siciliani', in *La Sicilia delle stragi*, ed. Marino, Giuseppe Carlo (Rome: Newton Compton, 2007), p. 122.
4. *La lotta di classe, 23rd March 1912*, in OMN, IV, pp. 118–19.
5. *MSAD*, p. 108.
6. *DUX*, p. 135.
7. *MCE*, p. 239.
8. *MSAD*, p. 57.
9. *MS*, p. 405.

CHAPTER 8

1. *DM*, p. 21.
2. Ib. p. 23.
3. Ib. p. 48–51.
4. *TM*, p. 118.
5. *DM*, p. 109.
6. *MR*, p. 139.
7. *MFB*, pp. 160–1.
8. *DM*, p. 168–9.
9. *TM*, p. 75–6.
10. *MS*, p. 208.
11. *MR*, p. 160–1.
12. *DM*, p. 122.
13. Ib., p. 123.
14. Ib. p. 124.
15. Ib. p. 131–32.
16. *MP*, p. 39.
17. *DM*, p. 160.
18. *MTQ*, p. 83.
19. *TM*, p. 115.
20. *Pensieri Pontini e Sardi*, OMN, XXXIV, p. 286.
21. *DUX*, pp. 152–53.
22. *CM*, p. 149.
23. *DM*, p. 253.
24. *DUX*, p. 163.
25. *DM*, p. 282.
26. *MR*, p. xxiii.
27. *MFB*, p. 50.
28. *MCE*, p. 71.
29. *OMN*, VI, pp. 404–8.
30. *CM*, p. 58.

CHAPTER 9

1. *OMN*, VII, pp. 473–4.
2. Ib. p. 486 (from *L'Avanti!*, 27th March 1915)
3. Ib. p. 489.
4. *MP*, p. 44.
5. Ib. p. 42–3.
6. *Il Popolo d'Italia*, No. 259, 29th October 1921.
7. *CM*, p. 46.
8. *MR*, pp. 307–8.
9. *MP*, p. 42.
10. *DG*, p. 14.
11. Ib. p. 25.
12. Ib. p. 13.
13. Ib. p. 46.
14. Ib. p. 72.
15. Ib. p. 41.
16. *OMN*, VII, p. 381.
17. *MS*, p. 94.
18. *DG*, p. 155–57.
19. *DUX*, p. 177.
20. *MFB*, p. 161.
21. *MP*, p. 81.
22. Ib. p. 82.
23. Ib. p. 83.
24. *FSD*, p. 30.
25. *MS*, pp. 273–74.
26. Ib. p. 437.
27. Ib. pp. 451–52.
28. *MFB*, p. 65.

CHAPTER 10

1. *MCE*, p. 203.
2. Ib. p. 206.
3. *DUX*, p. 203.
4. *FAU*, p. 409.
5. *MFB*, p. 85.
6. *MSAD*, p. 145.
7. *MSA*, p. 128.
8. *MR*, pp. 391–92.
9. *Il Popolo d'Italia*, No 53, 3rd March 1921.
10. *MP*, p. 84.
11. 'Rapporto Gasti, 4th June 1919', in *MR*, p. 736.
12. *ADC*, p. 166.
13. *OMN*, XI, p. 509 (from the *Caffaro* of Genoa, 2nd August 1918).
14. *MFB*, p. 99.
15. Vicini, Sergio, *Fasciste* (Bresso: Hobby & Work, 2009), p. 181.
16. *MR*, p. 498.
17. *DUX*, p. 221.

18. Ib. p. 217.
19. *MCE*, pp. 83–4.
20. *OMN*, XIV, pp. 486–87.
21. *MCE*, p. 93.
22. *MP*, p. 49.
23. Ib. p. 49.
24. *MSAD*, p. 110.

CHAPTER 11

1. *MSAD*, p. 177.
2. 'Rapporto Gasti, 4th June 1919', in *MR*, p. 733.
3. *MP*, p. 55.
4. *MR*, p. 567.
5. *FSD*, p. 48.
6. *MS*, pp. 121–22.
7. *CM*, p. 143.
8. *MR*, p. 627.
9. Melli, Giorgio, *Le donne di Mussolini* (Milan: Astoria, 1960), p. 76.
10. *CHI*, pp. 20–21.
11. Ib. p. 14.
12. Rossi, Gianni Scipione, 'Alice, la donna segreta di Mussolini' (2009), www.storiainrete.com
13. *MFB*, p. 108.
14. Ib. p. 100.
15. *MCE*, p. 108.
16. Arendt, Hannah, *Le Origini del totalitarismo* (Milan: Edizioni di Comunità, 1967), pp. 234–35.
17. *MCE*, p. 104.
18. *CM*, p. 112.
19. *MSAD*, p. 175.
20. *SAGC*, pp. 13–15.
21. *MS*, p. 282.
22. *MF*, p. 234.
23. Ib. pp. 264–65.
24. *MCE*, p. 229.
25. *DAN*, pp. 274–75.
26. *MF*, p. 282.
27. *MCE*, p. 230.
28. *DAN*, p. 277.
29. 'Rapporto Gasti, 4th June 1919', in *MR*, p. 736.
30. Susmel, Duilio, *Nenni e Mussolini* (Milan: Rizzoli, 1969), p. 153.
31. *MP*, p. 64.
32. *FAU*, p. 69.
33. *SAGC*, pp. 135–136.
34. *MCE*, pp. 119–20.
35. *MP*, p. 65.
36. Mussolini, Benito, *Il tempo del bastone e della carota. Storia di un anno: ottobre 1942–settembre 1943* (Milan: Mondadori, 1944), p. 167–68.
37. *MAR*, p. 72.

38. *DUX*, pp. 276–77.
39. *MAR*, p. 121.
40. Ib. p. 123.
41. Ib. p. 123.
42. Ib. p. 124.
43. *CM*, p. 94.

CHAPTER 12

1. *DD*, p. 17.
2. Ib. p. 17.
3. *CM*, p. 217.
4. *DD*, p. 18.
5. Ib. p. 18.
6. *Il Popolo d'Italia*, No. 297, 12th December 1922.
7. *DD*, p. 19.
8. Ib. p. 20.
9. Ib. p. 20.
10. *MS*, p. 101.
11. Ib. p. 126.
12. Ib. p. 225.
13. Ib. p. 100.
14. Ib. p. 405.
15. *MFB*, p. 164.
16. *DUX*, p. 241.
17. *MSA*, pp. 13–14.
18. Ib. p. 165.
19. *DUX*, p. 240.
20. *CM*, p. 166.
21. *MCE*, p. 144.
22. *PNF*, p. 4.
23. Ib. p. xi.
24. Ib. p. xii.
25. *MCE*, p. 251.
26. *DUX*, p. 294.
27. *PNF*, p. x.
28. *DUX*, p. 246.
29. *MAR*, pp. 152–53.
30. *MCE*, p. 137.
31. *MP*, p. 75.
32. Reichardt, Sven, *Camicie nere, camicie brune* (Milan: Il Mulino, 2009), pp. 66–67.
33. *MF*, p. 390.

CHAPTER 13

1. *MAR*, p. 191.
2. *MCE*, p. 184.
3. *MSA*, pp. 172–73.
4. Ib. p. 159.
5. *MCE*, pp. 142–43.

6.   *CES*, p. 36.
7.   Ib. p. 34.
8.   *DUX*, p. 295.
9.   Ib. p. 295.
10. Ib. p. 294.
11. Ib. p. 294.
12. *CHI*, p. 17.
13. *CES*, p. 51.
14. *Il Popolo d'Italia*, No. 234, 30th September 1923.
15. *DUX*, p. 253.
16. *MS*, p. 397.
17. *MCE*, p. 207.
18. Maurano, Silvio, 'Mussolini e il re mio padre', interview with Umberto II of Savoy, *Settimana INCOM*, 1959.
19. *CM*, p. 96.
20. *MSC*, p. 65.

CHAPTER 14

1.   *FAU*, pp. 95–6.
2.   Rossi, Gianni Scipione, 'Alice, la donna segreta di Mussolini' (2009), www.storiainrete.com
3.   *MSC*, p. 9.
4.   *MS*, p. 394.
5.   *DD*, pp. 40–1.
6.   *MS*, pp. 104–5.
7.   *DEL*, p. 100.
8.   Ib. p. 112.
9.   Ib. p. 275.
10. Ib. p. 253.
11. Tompkins, Peter, *Dalle carte segrete del duce* (Milan: Il Saggiatore, 2004), p. 115.
12. *MF*, p. 645.
13. Maurano, Silvio, 'Mussolini e il re mio padre', interview with Umberto II of Savoy, *Settimana INCOM*, 1959.
14. *OMN*, XXI, p. 235.
15. *FAU*, pp. 90–1.
16. *MCE*, p. 209.
17. *MP*, p. 84.
18. *MS*, p. 406.
19. *MSA*, p. 161.
20. Ib. p. 163.
21. De Begnac, Yvon, *Palazzo Venezia: storia di un regime* (Rome: La Rocca, 1950), p. 353.
22. *CAM*, p. 22.
23. *DD*, p. 24.
24. *MP*, p. 110.
25. *CAM*, pp. 150–51.
26. *DD*, p. 25.
27. *DUX*, pp. 299–300.

CHAPTER 15

1. *DD*, p. 27.
2. Ib. p. 27.
3. *MSAD*, pp. 266–67.
4. *RAZ*, p. 357.
5. *DD*, p. 38.
6. *MS*, p. 67.
7. Ib. pp. 78–79.
8. *MPB*, p. 139.
9. *Il Popolo d'Italia*, No. 264, 6th November 1925.
10. *DD*, p. 39.
11. *Vita di Arnaldo* (1932), OMN, XXXIV, p. 175.
12. *FSD*, p. 56.
13. Ib. p. 60.
14. *MF*, p. 210.
15. Ib. p. 381.
16. Mussolini, Benito, *Storia di un anno* (Milan: Mondadori, 1944), p. 176.
17. *COM*, p. 47.
18. *OMN*, XXII, p. 82.
19. *DD*, p. 29.
20. Ib. p. 30.
21. Ib. pp. 31–2.
22. *MS*, pp. 285–86.
23. *DD*, p. 44.
24. Ib. p. 34.
25. *MS*, p. 333.
26. *RAZ*, p. 349.
27. *MCE*, p. 176.
28. *Vita di Arnaldo* (1932), OMN, XXXIV, p. 163.
29. *CHI*, pp. 18–19.
30. *MF*, p. 482.
31. *COM*, pp. 18–19.
32. *MSC*, p. 174.
33. *Pensieri Pontini e Sardi*, OMN, XXXIV, p. 296.
34. *DUX*, p. 308.
35. *OMN*, XXVIII, pp. 204–5.

CHAPTER 16

1. *CM*, p. xlvii.
2. *MF*, p. 32.
3. *MPB*, p. 152.
4. Festorazzi, Roberto, *La pianista del duce* (Milan: Simonelli, 2000), pp. 10–14.
5. *CM*, p. 208.
6. *ADC*, p. 28.
7. Ib. p. 19.
8. *DD*, p. 28.
9. *MS*, pp. 375–76.
10. *DD*, p. 48.

11. *MS*, p. 466.
12. Ib. p. 442.
13. *FAU*, p. 81.
14. *CAM*, p. 85.
15. *RAZ*, p. 355.
16. *CM*, p. 72.
17. *RAZ*, p. 359.
18. Ib. pp. 363–64.
19. *MP*, p. 123.
20. *OMN*, XXVIII, p. 87.
21. *CM*, p. 131.
22. *Parlo con Bruno*, OMN, XXXIV, p. 209.
23. *OMN*, XXVIII, pp. 297–98.
24. *MFB*, p. 122.
25. Ib. p. 123.
26. Guerri, Giordano Bruno, *Un amore fascista. Benito, Edda e Galeazzo.* (Milan: Mondadori, 2005), p. 66.
27. *Vita di Arnaldo* (1932), OMN, XXXIV, p. 169.
28. *ADC*, p. 303.

CHAPTER 17

1. *CAM*, p. 143.
2. *MP*, p. 87.
3. Novero, Giuseppe, *Mussolini e il generale* (Soveria Mannelli: Rubbettino, 2009), p. 100.
4. *MS*, p. 319.
5. *MS*, p. 268.
6. *Pensieri Pontini e Sardi*, OMN, XXXIV, p. 294.
7. *CAM*, p. 95.
8. Ib. p. 125.
9. *MTQ*, p. 130.
10. *FAU*, p. 321.
11. *MP*, p. 141.
12. *ST*, p. 540.
13. *OMN*, XXVIII, p. 137.
14. *MAS*, p. 12.
15. *LOV*.
16. Ib.
17. Ib.
18. Ib.
19. Ib.
20. Ib.
21. *OMN*, I, Introduzione.
22. *OMN*, XXVIII, pp. 265–66 and 312–21.
23. *MAS*, p. 43–44.
24. *MS*, p. 102.
25. *OMN*, XXVIII, p. 88.
26. *MCE*, p. 236.
27. *MS*, p. 352.

28. *MSAD*, p. 275.
29. *MSA*, p. 206.
30. *FAU*, p. 369.
31. *MS*, p. 443.
32. De Felice, Renzo, *Intervista sul fascismo*, (Bari: Laterza, 1975), p. 12.
33. *MP*, p. 5.
34. *MS*, p. 249.
35. Ib. p. 80.
36. *FAU*, p. 361.
37. *OMN*, XXVIII, p. 245.
38. Ib. p. 251.
39. Ib. p. 253.
40. *MS*, p. 331.

APPENDIX I

1. *My Life. Youth*, op. cit., p. 118.
2. *CM*, p. 64.
3. *PF*, p. 219.
4. Ib. p. 63.
5. Ib. p. 55.
6. Ib. p. 83.
7. Ib. p. 183.
8. Ib. p. 96.
9. Ib. p. 93.
10. Ib. p. 152.
11. *Combat Film. Inediti Italiani*, home video (Rome: Rai Eri and Bramante, 1995).
12. *PF*, pp. 146–47.
13. Ib. p. 147.
14. Ib. pp. 146–47.
15. Ib. p. 83.
16. Gadda, Carlo Emilio, *Quer pasticciaccio brutto de via Merulana* (Milan: Garzanti, 2005), p. 44.
17. *MS*, p. 172.
18. Luzzato, Sergio, *Il corpo del Duce* (Turin: Einaudi, 1998), p. 17.
19. *CM*, p. 213.
20. *Vita di Arnaldo* (1932), *OMN*, XXXIV, p. 190.
21. *Pensieri Pontini e Sardi*, *OMN*, XXXIV, p. 285.
22. *MP*, p. 246.
23. *Alleati* (docufilm), Rai Tre, Rome, 1999.

Index

PAGE NUMBERS IN BOLD REFER TO RELEVANT
ENTRIES IN APPENDIX 2, KEY FIGURES

Mussolini, Rachele (Mussolini's wife): 57–58, 63, 65, 71–72, 85–88, 91, 93–100, 103, 109, 112–13, 126, 133–34, 143–44, 152, 155–56, 163–65, 170–71, 173, 177, 180, 189, 196–97, 199, 219, 221–22, 235, 245, 266, 286–87, 296, 300–1, 335, 337–340, 342, 346, 349, 354, 362, 373, 375–76, 382, 406, 408, 410

Mussolini, Romano (Mussolini's son): 95, 314–15, 339–40, 364

Mussolini, Sandro (or Sandrino, Arnaldo Mussolini's eldest son): 352

Mussolini, Tancredi (brother of Mussolini's grandfather): 25

Mussolini, Vito (son of Arnaldo Mussolini): 339

Mussolini, Vittorio (Mussolini's son): 95, 164, 252, 346, 351

Mussolini's Secret Life, see *Vita segreta di Mussolini*: 6, 85

Naldi, Filippo (journalist and politician): 139–42, 144, 195, **438**

Nanni, Eugenio (schoolmate of Mussolini): 52

National Alliance, see Alleanza Nazionale

National Confederation of Fascist Unions of Professionals and Artists, see Confederazione Nazionale dei Sindacati Fascisti dei Professionisti e degli Artisti

National Fascist Federation of Rural Housewives, see Federazione Nazionale Fascista delle Massaie Rurali

National Fascist Party (political party): 129, 175, 211, 214, 241–43, 249–50, 267–68, 282–83, 290, 296, 318, 357, 382, 389, 417, 419, 429, 442, 447

National Federation of Agricultural Workers, see Federazione Nazionale dei Lavoratori della Terra

National Institute of Fascist Culture, see Istituto Nazionale di Cultura Fascista

National Liberation Committee of Northern Italy, see Comitato di Liberazione Nazionale dell'Alta Italia

National Republican Socialist Grouping, see Raggruppamento Nazionale Repubblicano Socialista

National Socialist Congress, (political organization): 87, 106, 113, 116, 122, 135–36, 250

Navarra, Quinto (Mussolini's valet and factotum): 291–92, 354, 356, 360, 364, 376

Negri, Ada (poet): 193, 332, **438**

Nenni, Carmen (wife of Pietro Nenni): 109

Nenni, Eva (daughter of Pietro Nenni): 109

Nenni, Giuliana (daughter of Pietro Nenni): 109

Nenni, Pietro (republican leader): 106–9, 116, 135, 155–57, 184–85, 194, 207, 212, 221, **439**, 450

Nenni, Vittoria (daughter of Pietro Nenni): 109, 439

Newbold Jones, Edith, see Wharton, Edith: 450

Nicholas II, Tsar of Russia: 435

Nietzsche, Friedrich (philosopher): 23, 391

Nigris, Candido (son born in 1907 from the affair between Mussolini and Luigia Pajetta Nigris): 79, 81

Nitti, Francesco Fausto (anti-Fascist activist): 434

Nitti, Francesco Saverio (economist and politician): 180, 190, 197, 217, **439**

Nordau, Max (sociologist): 85, **439**

Normandia, Anna (Mussolini's mistress): 378

Novecento (art movement): 253–54, 258, 378, 446

Oberdan, Guglielmo (Italian irredentist): 21, 27, **439**

Oberdank, Wilhelm, see Oberdan, Guglielmo